OUR RIGHTS

ARTICLE the FIFTH.

A well regulated militia, composed of the body of the People, being the best security of a free State, the right of the People to keep and bear arms, shall not be infringed, but no one religiously scrupulous of bearing arms, shall be compelled to render military service in person.

ARTICLE the SIXTH.

No soldier shall, in time of peace, be quartered in any house without the consent of the owner, nor in time of war, but in a manner to be prescribed by law.

ARTICLE the SEVENTH.

The right of the People to be secure in their persons, houses, papers and effects, against unreasonable searches and seizures, shall not be violated, and no warrants shall issue, but upon probable cause supported by oath or affirmation, and particularly describing the place to be searched, and the persons or things to be seized.

ARTICLE the EIGHTH.

No person shall be subject, except in case of impeachment, to more than one trial, or one punishment for the same offense, nor shall be compelled in any criminal case, to be a witness against himself, nor be deprived of life, liberty or property, without due process of law; nor shall private property be taken for public use without just compensation.

ARTICLE the NINTH.

In all criminal prosecutions, the accused shall enjoy the right to a speedy and public trial, to be informed of the nature and cause of the accusation, to be confronted with the witnesses against him, to have compulsory process for obtaining witnesses in his favor, and to have the assistance of counsel for his defence.

ARTICLE the TENTH.

The trial of all crimes (except in cases of impeachment, and in cases arising in the land or naval forces, or in the militia when in actual service in time of War or public danger) shall be by an Impartial Jury of the Vicinage, with the requisite of unanimity for conviction, the right of challenge, and other accustomed requisites; and no person shall be held to answer for a capital, or otherways infamous crime, unless on a presentment or indictment by a Grand Jury; but if a crime be committed in a place in the possession of an enemy, or in which an insurrection may prevail, the indictment and trial may by law be authorised in some other place within the same state.

OUR RIGHTS

David J. Bodenhamer

THE ANNENBERG
PUBLIC POLICY CENTER
OF THE UNIVERSITY OF PENNSYLVANIA

OXFORD
UNIVERSITY PRESS

To Penny, my lovely and delightful companion
in the pursuit of happiness

Oxford University Press, Inc., publishes works that further
Oxford University's objective of excellence
in research, scholarship, and education.

Oxford New York
Auckland   Cape Town   Dar es Salaam   Hong Kong   Karachi
Kuala Lumpur   Madrid   Melbourne   Mexico City   Nairobi
New Delhi   Shanghai   Taipei   Toronto

With offices in
Argentina   Austria   Brazil   Chile   Czech Republic   France   Greece
Guatemala   Hungary   Italy   Japan Poland   Portugal   Singapore
South Korea   Switzerland   Thailand   Turkey   Ukraine   Vietnam

Published by Oxford University Press, Inc.
198 Madison Avenue, New York, New York 10016
www.oup.com

Oxford is a registered trademark of Oxford University Press

Library of Congress Cataloging-in-Publication Data

Bodenhamer, David J.
Our rights / David J. Bodenhamer. — 1st ed.
    p. cm.
Includes bibliographical references and index.
ISBN-13: 978-0-19-531340-6 (cloth)   ISBN-13: 978-0-19-532567-6 (paperback)
ISBN-10: 0-19-531340-2 (cloth)   ISBN-10: 0-19-532567-2 (paperback)
1. Civil rights—United States. I. Title.
  KF4749.B546 2006
  342.7308'5—dc22

                                                          2006030136

Printing number: 9 8 7 6 5 4 3 2 1

Printed in the United States of America
on acid-free paper

Frontispiece: Using this copy of constitutional amendments that was drafted by the House of Representatives in 1789, the Senate reduced and modified the amendments that later became the Bill of Rights.

Contents

Introduction

On August 23, 1984, the *New York Times* carried a brief story on its inside pages about a disorderly march in Dallas, Texas, the host city for the Republican National Convention. The incident had begun as a protest against the renomination of President Ronald Reagan for a second term. About one hundred people were arrested for disorderly conduct; among them was Gregory Lee Johnson, who was charged under a Texas law outlawing the desecration of "venerated objects." He had burned the American flag.

Tried and convicted in a Dallas court, Johnson received the maximum penalty of a year in jail and a $2,000 fine. No doubt many people believed he deserved the sentence. Few things stir the emotions of Americans as strongly as an assault on our patriotic symbols. In this instance, the attack was especially troublesome because Johnson had appeared to be such an all-American male. He was born in the nation's heartland, Indiana, and had grown up on military bases as the son of a soldier. But Johnson was not a sympathetic figure. He had joined the Revolutionary Communist Party, an anti-American group. While the flag burned, he and other members of the demonstration had shouted, "America, the red, white, and blue, we spit on you."

Johnson appealed his conviction, and the case ended up in the U.S. Supreme Court. The justices ruled, 5 to 4, that the First Amendment's guarantee of free speech protected Johnson's act. He was expressing a political opinion, which clearly fell within the protections of the Bill of Rights. "If there is a bedrock principle underlying the First Amendment," Justice William Brennan wrote for the majority, "it is that the government may not prohibit the expression of an idea simply because society finds the idea itself offensive or disagreeable." The minority, citing the value of the flag as a historical symbol of national unity, saw Johnson's actions as an incitement to violence, not the protected expression of an idea. "Flag burning is the equivalent of an inarticulate grunt or roar that...is most likely to be indulged in not to express any particular idea, but to antagonize others," Chief Justice William Rehnquist argued.

"I came here from Czechoslovakia, a country with a deep and humane tradition of democratic values, crushed first by the Nazis and then by the Soviets and their disgusting little puppets.... So America, its traditions and values and its flag are important to me. Foremost among those values is the principle that no one shall be punished for his political expressions—no matter how offensive or bizarre."

—Professor Charles Fried, Harvard University, testimony before the House Judiciary Committee (1989)

Texas v. *Johnson* revealed a deeply divided nation. The decision brought a storm of criticism, as well as voices in strong support of the decision. Congress immediately enacted the Flag Protection Act in response, and when a bare majority of the Court narrowly ruled that it, too, was unconstitutional, a movement began to amend the Constitution. The House of Representatives passed a flag-protection amendment on six occasions from 1995 to 2005, but each time it failed to obtain the required two-thirds majority vote in the Senate. In mid-2006, the controversy still was alive, with the amendment failing by one vote in the Senate from passing to the states for ratification. The American public remains split over what is most important—upholding a symbol of national unity and order or protecting free speech.

The flag-burning case featured a clash between two legitimate ends of democratic government— the protection of individual rights and the promotion of public order and security. This conflict is nothing new in our history. We have often fought over how far we can extend our rights without threatening our unity and our security. The controversy over the Iraq War at the beginning of the twenty-first century made this issue real for new generations of Americans, but in fact war only heightens the tension between these two goals.

What we may not recognize is how old this debate is. It was present during the American Revolution, the period that defined much of how we think about liberty and about the role of government. But even by 1776, the debate surrounding rights and order was already centuries in the making. It stretched to a time "when the memory of man runneth not," as one English medieval law book put it. This contest between individual rights and public order has resulted in what we view today as our rich heritage of freedom, a hard-won prize of Anglo-American history.

In many popular versions of our national past, the framers of the Bill of Rights captured our essential liberties in the first ten amendments to the Constitution. Many people assume these rights had self-evident meanings, which judges today simply apply to new circumstances. The truth is far messier. Our rights have never been free of controversy, and they have never been the responsibility of courts alone. Throughout American history, rights have been invented and repudiated, fought over and striven for, expanded and violated. Scarcely was the ink dry on the Bill of Rights when debates began about what the words meant.

Led by Senate minority leader Robert Dole of Kansas, in 1990 several prominent senators announced a proposal to enact a constitutional amendment against flag burning. For decades, Americans have been divided over whether flag burning should be banned as desecration of a national symbol or protected as free speech. In 2006, an amendment prohibiting flag burning failed to pass the Senate by one vote.

"The word 'security' is a broad, vague generality whose contours should not be invoked to abrogate [abolish] the fundamental law embodied in the First Amendment. The guarding of military and diplomatic secrets at the expense of informed representative government provides no real security for our Republic."

—Justice Hugo L. Black, concurring opinion,
New York Times Co. v. *United States* (1971)

Still, it would be misleading to feature these conflicts too prominently in the story of American rights. As consistent as the debate has been, so too has been the expansion of our rights in number, scope, and practice. Freedom of speech, for example, is more extensive today than at any time in the nation's past. Freedom of religion once meant the right to embrace Christianity; today, it protects citizens of any faith—or of none. What is meant by due process of law, our fundamental guarantee of fairness, differs widely from its definition a few decades ago.

It also would be inaccurate to attribute the expansion of rights to the judiciary alone. We have added new rights to the Constitution by amendment, for example, creating the right of eighteen-year-olds to vote. Statutes have also added new expressions of individual liberty, as when civil rights laws of the 1960s gave new force to the Fourteenth Amendment's promise of equal protection. Some states have recognized rights for their residents beyond what is listed in the U.S. Constitution, such as the right to an education.

Many advances in our rights have resulted from the claims of political, ethnic, or religious minorities, as well as social misfits; often, they believe things or live in ways that are far outside the mainstream. In a democracy, we wonder, why should the rights of these few trump the will of a majority? Why should we extend constitutional protections to people accused of heinous crimes, for instance, or to anyone who has opinions or a lifestyle unacceptable to the vast majority of citizens? These are fair questions, but they ignore the role of rights in our society. We understand liberty to belong to individuals, not simply to society generally, so we have chosen to safeguard personal liberty as much as possible within the need for public order. The best ways to guarantee this liberty, we have decided, are to limit the power of government to act arbitrarily or without rules and to recognize that majorities can themselves be unfair or even tyrannical.

Rights are essential both to our conception of liberty and to what we have defined as the proper role of government. They have alternately expanded and contracted throughout our history and have been the subject of some of the most divisive fights we have experienced as a nation. But this statement begs several important questions: What are rights? Where did they come from? How have they changed? How do we understand our rights today? We can discover answers to these questions from the history of our constitutional development and from the specific history of some of our most significant rights. But first we must understand what we mean by rights.

In their simplest form, individual rights are legally enforceable claims to personal freedom or liberty. A right allows a person to do something—or to avoid doing it—and that action can be enforced by an order from a court of law. The claim of a right may be made either against government—for example, forbidding government to interfere with freedom of press—or may be enforced through government, as when courts forbid a hotel from racially discriminating against guests. An assertion of individual freedom, if it is truly a right, cannot be denied; it has to be granted; it is based on a duty to respect the right.

Consider this example: John Doe is deeply opposed to the reelection of his mayor, whom he mistakenly considers corrupt and inept; he refers to her in public as "lower than pond scum." He decides to voice his opinion every afternoon from the gazebo in a park near city hall. The place he chooses is one traditionally open to political candidates, but his fellow townspeople are so appalled by his extreme statements—he once said he would vote for a Nazi rather than the current mayor—that they seek to prevent him from disgracing the community. But John Doe has a legal claim, one guaranteed by the First Amendment, to free speech. He can go to court, if required, and get an order that prevents any interference with his ability to exercise (or enjoy) this freedom. Even if the judge is the mayor's closet political ally and best friend, the law requires her to support John Doe's claim to free speech.

The language of rights can be confusing. We use the word itself—*right* or *rights*—in many different ways: a right to life, a right to vote, a right to choose, a right to counsel, a right to believe one's own eyes, a right to declare a couple married, a right to do what we please. Of course, not all of these uses of the word mean the same thing. The founding generation believed certain rights—

Italian immigrants in New York City take free classes in citizenship and English at their local public library in 1943, in preparation for citizenship tests and ultimately naturalization as U.S. citizens.

life, liberty, and the pursuit of happiness—were inalienable; they were natural, or universal, rights and could never be surrendered. At other times, the word refers to fundamental rights found in the U.S. Constitution; they cannot be changed unless two-thirds of both houses of Congress and three-fourths of the states agree to the change. The right to vote for citizens aged eighteen and older is a fundamental right; so is the right to assemble peacefully and to enjoy freedom of press or religion. Other rights are entitlements granted by the legislature and may be changed by a simple majority vote: the right to drive a car, for example, is available to anyone who meets the minimum age and performance criteria set by the state, which can change the eligibility requirements at any time. Other common uses of the word *right* do not address a legal claim at all. "Children have the right to have a doctor close to home," as a recent ad announced, expresses a personal opinion and a moral judgment, not a legal claim; you cannot ask the legal system to act on it or make other people accept it.

When we talk about individual rights, we usually mean guarantees of liberty contained in federal and state constitutions or in laws made to enforce these guarantees. We sometimes divide these rights into the two categories of civil rights and civil liberties. The term *civil rights* refers to the legal protection we have against injury, discrimination, and denial of rights by private individuals, groups, or government because of a categorical bias, such as a denial of service based on race or gender. Civil rights may be contained in the Constitution or they may be defined by laws made under constitutional authority. Civil liberties are the legal guarantees, especially under the First Amendment, that protect us from government interference with our political actions, such as freedom of speech, press, assembly, and the like. These categories, civil rights and civil liberties, reflect contemporary usage. Earlier generations used the terms *privileges, franchises,* and *immunities,* as well as *rights,* and these terms still have special meaning for lawyers.

Regardless of the language we use, rights are not self-interpreting, self-enforcing, or absolute. The definition of a right not only has changed over time, but its modern meaning may differ from one situation to another. The First Amendment protects freedom of the press, but what does this phrase mean? At one point in the late 1790s, a person could be punished for printing criticisms of the government. Today, you have a right to publish your political views, no matter how extreme or how critical, although you still do not have the right to publish obscenity. Clearly, this claim of individual freedom has had different meanings throughout our history. Also, rights do not enforce themselves. They must be demanded, usually through a court order. Finally, rights are not absolute. People have a right to speak freely without fear of punishment, but they do not have a right to yell "fire!" falsely in a crowded theater. Under this circumstance, the public has a stronger claim to safety than an individual has to freedom of speech. We recognize the limits on our rights in common language when we say that our right to swing our arms ends where another person's nose begins.

Individual rights are creations of our history. In almost every instance, they have arisen out of a struggle against the abuse of power by government and oppressive majorities. In our democracy, written constitutions and access to open courts make it possible for claims of rights to come from any citizen, and throughout American history cases have arisen from every quarter by all sorts of individuals. At times, courts have chosen to follow precedent, or previous interpretations, even in the face of apparent injustice; at other times, these challenges have led to an expansion of rights, often by fitting old meanings to new conditions. No single answer exists to the question of where our rights come from, but in a democracy, there ultimately is one answer to how we maintain rights—through our own understanding of and attention to them. For this reason, we must first know the history that gave birth to our individual liberties.

Chapter 1

Our Rights in American History

Rights are expressions of individual liberty. The history of America is, on the whole, a story of individual liberty and rights. In 1776, the signers of the Declaration of Independence boldly proclaimed their belief in the right of equality—"all men are created equal"—and in the inalienable rights of life, liberty, and the pursuit of happiness. The founding generation considered individual rights so critical to freedom that only a promise to add them to the new Constitution ensured ratification of the nation's fundamental law. Almost ninety years later, as the Civil War threatened the nation's existence, President Abraham Lincoln used the same language of rights and liberty to remind his fellow citizens about the importance of their campaign to save the Union. So has every President in every war called upon Americans to defend what we all identify as our heritage of freedom and the rights that protect it. Even when we disagree most with each other about what course the nation should take, we often express our choices in the language of rights.

We usually associate our rights with the Bill of Rights, the first ten amendments to the Constitution. It is our touchstone to what the revolutionary generation defined as a "great experiment in liberty." But its guarantees were, in many ways, a listing of rights the framers considered to be their own inheritance from countless generations that preceded them. Now, we judge the Bill of Rights to be our gift from the past. Only when we look carefully do we recognize how this legacy of rights has changed in response to new conditions. Our rights, like our understanding of liberty, are not static. They are dynamic expressions of freedom. What is most constant in the history of individual rights is how each successive generation has contributed to defining the liberties we claim today.

When English settlers migrated to the New World, they came with a royal guarantee that they would continue to have the "rights and privileges of Englishmen." The pledge was important. It promised continued ownership of a

---

"There is something back of the [Constitution and the Union], entwining itself . . . closely about the human heart. That something, is the principle of 'Liberty to all'—the principle that clears the path *for all—gives* hope *to all—and, by consequence,* enterprise, *and* industry *to all."*

—President Abraham Lincoln, "Fragment on the Constitution and the Union" (1861)

---

long tradition of English liberty that was thought to stretch at least to the Magna Carta (or Great Charter) in 1215, when English noblemen forced King John to abide by the "law of the land," or as it was known later, "due process of law." Embodied in these phrases were two core contributions to the English understanding of rights: the idea of fairness and the concept that no one, not even the king, was above the law. Although the document applied only to the king and barons, the most powerful class in English society, over time its guarantee of rights became understood as a commitment to all English citizens.

Much of the early history of rights centered on protections for property and for individuals accused of crimes, because in these areas the state most often exercised arbitrary power. Rights of the accused offer the clearest example of what Englishmen understood to be their heritage. By the time the earliest North American colonies were established, numerous guarantees already existed to ensure a fair criminal trial for Englishmen. The Massachusetts Puritans included many of these protections in their first law code, the Body of Liberties, in 1641: the promise of speedy trial and equal justice, protection against being tried twice for the same crime (double jeopardy), and the prohibition of torture, among others. The long seventeenth-century struggle between king and Parliament for supremacy further limited the power of government and added to the rights of Englishmen, including the right of petition, a limited form of freedom of speech, a right to release the accused from detention upon a guarantee to appear at trial (bail), and prohibition against excessive fines. The Bill of Rights of 1689, which Parliament adopted after ousting King James II in the Glorious Revolution, put these rights in written form. Unlike the Magna Carta, it extended them to the English population as a whole, including the colonists.

Much of what the English settlers to the New World considered to be rights was found in the common law, the case law of English courts, not in statutes or state documents. Common law contained what had become customary practice in English society. As with the Magna Carta, it emphasized rights of the accused: the promise of a speedy and public trial by jury; prohibition of ex post facto laws, or laws that criminalized behavior after it had occurred; and the guarantee of habeas corpus, a procedure that required government to bring a person under detention before a court to determine if legal reason existed to hold him. Common law also offered some protection for the rights of widows and children, the right of compensation for the taking of private property, and the openness of courts to all citizens. Not only did colonial assemblies and courts adopt common law, but colonists looked as well to English law books for further instruction on their rights and privileges.

The colonists were not satisfied with reliance on their charters alone because they could be changed too easily. Early on, they put their liberties into writing as a way to prevent imperial encroachment. The Massachusetts Body of Liberties in 1641 summarized these rights and added a few additional safeguards; it was, in effect, the first bill of rights in American history. The Pennsylvania Charter of Liberties and Frame of Government, both written in 1682, also protected the rights of colonists from government interference, as did the New York Charter of Liberties and Privileges enacted the following year. Most colonies adopted this practice of converting customary rights and privileges into written protections, and they often extended these liberties beyond those claimed by their cousins in the mother country.

By the eve of the Revolution, these safeguards had become part of a shared language about liberty that guided colonial resistance to British attempts to tighten control over the empire. But it would be a mistake to draw a direct line of descent from the colonial understanding of rights to our understanding today. The words are similar but not their substance. Due process of law, for example, held a sharply different meaning in the seventeenth and eighteenth centuries than it does in the twenty-first. Then, it referred to a fair process only; now it also means a fair result. Personal rights were important, but the good order of society took precedence over individual liberty. Still, the colonial contribution to modern ideas about rights was significant, not as much as a list of rights but as a set of attitudes about individual liberty. The colonists by necessity had adapted English laws and customs to a new world and, in the process, claimed full ownership in the great tradition of English liberty. But they went further than mere imitation. They had simplified the law and made it accessible in written form to all settlers. They had been willing to reform the law and had added rights not recognized in the British Isles. Their biggest contribution, however, was an acceptance of legal change and a willingness to mold law to social needs and circumstances. This flexibility became a trait that defined American society and allowed the ancient maxim of due process to become as expansive as the continent itself.

Colonists entered the struggle for independence with a view that individual rights restrained the exercise of arbitrary power, especially by the central government; by restraining power, rights protected liberty. Three rights were especially important to the colonial understanding of liberty: trial by jury, the right to property, and due process of law. Representative government also was significant. These rights and this form of government above all protected local communities from tyranny exercised by a government far removed from them. The colonial view of liberty, after all, centered on the community first. The belief that rights belonged to individuals was the product of a later age.

In seeking greater control over the colonies, Great Britain threatened the local autonomy that all English colonists had come to consider their birthright. The list of grievances that poured from colonial pens from 1763 to 1776—and captured in a long litany in the Declaration of Independence—reveals how valuable the colonists considered self-government and how closely it was tied to their notion of rights. Taxation without representation was an interference with their right to property. Trials of alleged smugglers, such as Boston merchant John Hancock, by a judge alone violated the right to a public jury trial by members of the local community. Suspension of local courts denied due process of law.

Grievances are rights in reverse—they identify rights under threat—and by this measure the Declaration of Independence is an important gauge of what the colonists believed was at stake. British actions, the document charged, robbed Englishmen of their heritage. Each action of the imperial government mocked an essential ingredient of English liberty; collectively, they proved an intention to deprive the colonists of their freedom. "We are obliged," the people of Newburyport, Rhode Island, petitioned Parliament, "to submit to a Jurisdiction…where the Common Law, the collected wisdom of the British Nation for Ages, is not admitted." Other revolutionaries were more blunt. In *A Summary View of the Rights of British America* (1774), Thomas Jefferson alleged that the British were pursuing nothing less, than a "deliberate, systematic plan of reducing us to slavery," a condition that left individuals with no rights and no freedom.

The colonists declared independence to save their liberty and the rights that made it possible, but in the process they became revolutionaries intent on creating what they called "a new order for the ages." The founding generation set out not only to build a new frame of government, but also to identify what rights were necessary to protect liberty. Their search led them to a different understanding of the nature of government itself. They focused on republicanism, a form of government that rested clearly on the consent of the governed and thus, by definition, exercised limited power. They discovered rights not in English history alone but in the laws of nature, or natural law. These rights went beyond the common law, and because they existed before societies were formed, they belonged to individuals, not communities.

Signed by Peter Stuyvesant, governor of New Netherland, and written in Dutch with formal secretarial calligraphy, this 1662 document granted Christian Pietersen two lots with a garden and farmhouse. Legal rights to land ownership were established early in colonial America.

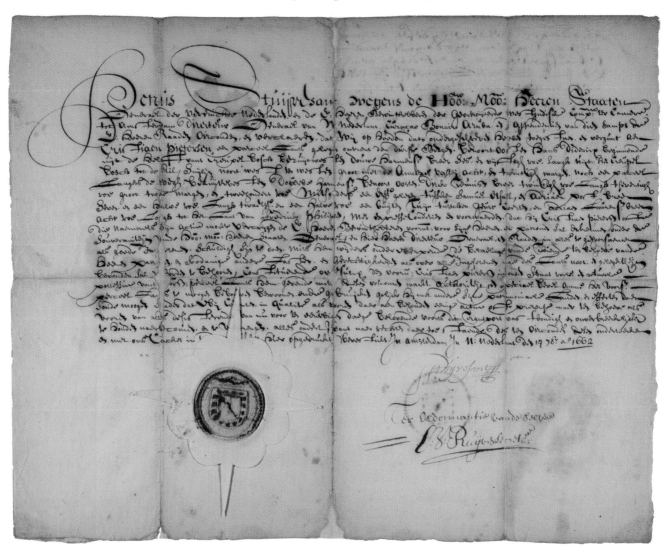

New state constitutions and later, the federal Bill of Rights, contained more expansive safeguards of liberty than had been listed in colonial protests. The founding generation also put these rights in writing and gave them the force of fundamental law, protections that could not be changed easily. The most important model was the Virginia Declaration of Rights in 1776. Written by George Mason, the declaration contained sixteen articles, with seven enumerating the rights of citizens, including the right of religious belief. Other states followed suit, usually listing the rights as part of the state constitutions. At first, revolutionary legislatures did not seek popular ratification of their actions, which raised questions about whether or not the constitutions restrained the legislatures themselves. In 1780, however, Massachusetts submitted its new constitution for voter approval, thus placing rights beyond the reach of legislative majorities. All other states soon adopted this innovation, as did the new federal constitution in 1787. Rights now existed as fundamental law.

The importance of this development became clear during and after the Constitutional Convention, which met in Philadelphia in 1787 to replace the inadequate Articles of Confederation, the nation's first constitution. The fifty-five delegates faced a critical problem: how to grant government enough power to do its job without also giving it the power to threaten liberty? Their answer revealed how far the revolutionaries had advanced in their understanding of the relationship between power and liberty. First, they based all power or sovereignty (the right to rule) in the people, not the government, an idea known as popular sovereignty. Government had only the authority granted to it in a written constitution ratified by the people. To restrain government even more, the framers divided power in two fundamental ways. They created three separate and coequal branches of government—legislative, executive, and judicial—and required the cooperation of each to exercise power fully. Then they divided power further between the states and the national government. This principle, federalism, entrusted the central government, the one they feared most, with only the power necessary to serve truly national functions, such as defense and regulation of commerce between the states. The powers not granted to the central government, including the critical authority to define and prosecute crimes, would remain with the states, which by definition were closer to the people.

The delegates believed that these restrictions on government—popular sovereignty, a written constitution, separation and balance of powers, and federalism—would be sufficient protection for the rights of individuals. The Constitution contained no bill of rights, but it did not need one, its advocates reasoned, because the new government could not exercise any power not granted to it explicitly. But when the Federalists, or supporters of the Constitution, submitted it to state conventions for ratification, they learned that a large number of voters were not convinced by this argument. Thomas Jefferson, for example, believed the absence of a bill of rights was a serious defect. A listing of rights, he explained, "is what the people are entitled to against every government on earth." The absence of a declaration of rights, Anti-Federalists protested, made the Constitution unacceptable because it was in the nature of government, especially central government, to infringe on the rights of the people. It soon became apparent that ratification would not occur without a promise to address this deficiency. Led by James Madison, the Federalists pledged to amend the Constitution to include clear safeguards for individual liberty.

As a newly elected member of the House of Representatives, Madison submitted nine amendments to the first Congress in 1788. The proposals borrowed heavily from the Virginia Declaration of Rights and the various state bills of rights. Madison listed two types of guarantees: rights necessary for representative government, such as freedom of speech, press, and peaceable assembly, and rights of the accused, including protections against double jeopardy and self-incrimination as well as the right to trial by jury. In all, his proposals covered twenty-six paragraphs. Over the next month, these safeguards were molded into twelve amendments; by 1791, the states had ratified ten of them. These ten became known as the Bill of Rights.

During the debates over the ratification of the Constitution, Madison at first had resisted a declaration of rights because he feared it would be only a "parchment barrier," a mere paper incapable of protecting liberty. He came to believe instead that written constitutional guarantees were necessary because they would remind people of "the fundamental maxims of free government," especially the close link between individual rights and personal liberty. They would serve as "good ground for an appeal to the sense of community," he concluded, if states or oppressive majorities threatened liberty. He worried much about majorities running roughshod over the rights of minorities, especially in matters of conscience, and he feared states would not be able to resist this kind of tyranny. In fact, Madison initially had proposed that the Bill of Rights apply to the states as well as the central government, a result not achieved, even in part, until the twentieth century. Who would enforce the Bill of Rights on behalf of individuals whose rights were threatened? Here, Madison believed the answer was more certain. An independent judiciary, operating through courts open to all citizens, would come to consider themselves "the guardian of these rights," he argued. They would "resist every encroachment on rights expressly stipulated for in the constitution," forming an "impenetrable bulwark against every assumption of power in the legislative or executive."

Madison's views are instructive for understanding our rights under the Constitution. Although most of his contemporaries viewed the Bill of Rights as a standard that enabled people to judge their government, Madison believed it promoted self-government by enabling citizens to resist any impulse—fear, selfishness, and prejudice, among others—that threatened America's great experiment in liberty. Enforcement of rights by an independent judiciary, he argued, provided a means to correct injustices that were sure to occur in any human society but which could not be allowed to exist in a society dedicated to liberty.

The federal Bill of Rights resulted from a rich mix of English history, colonial experience, and revolutionary ideas. It was the product of a society far different from our own, and no one at the time seriously believed that its protections benefited American Indians, African Americans, or even white women. But for all the flaws of its creators, the list of rights was far advanced for its time. The legacy of liberty the Bill of Rights gave to the new nation became the envy of the rest of the world. Since 1791 we have been debating exactly what this legacy means.

Almost from the moment of their passage, the rights promised in the new constitutional amendments came under dispute. The desire to safeguard individual liberty did not disappear—if anything, it became stronger—but when faced with practical problems, people disagreed about what government could and could not do. The 1790s, for example, witnessed a ferocious debate between Secretary of the Treasury Alexander Hamilton and Secretary of State Thomas Jefferson about the power of the central government. The debate became intensely partisan, and when it appeared to threaten national security, Congress passed a law, the Sedition Act of 1798, forbidding anyone to criticize the government or government officials. Although the law expired three years later, it was clear that the founding generation had sharp differences of opinion about what freedom of speech or freedom of the press meant in practice.

On the whole, however, the concern for rights became more intense in the decades following the Revolution, although the focus shifted from the federal to the state governments. The United States was becoming more democratic, with most states removing property qualifications for voting and officeholding by the 1820s to allow all adult white males to participate in government. The nation had also embraced capitalism, which emphasized individual risk and reward. Both developments reinforced the notion of individual rights, especially property rights, and they strengthened as well a demand for fair procedure, or due process, to ensure equal opportunity in the political arena and the marketplace.

Ensuring these protections of liberty was primarily the responsibility of the states. In 1833, the U.S. Supreme Court ruled, in *Barron* v. *Baltimore,* that the Bill of Rights restrained the federal government alone. Most individual rights, then, were protected by state constitutions and state judiciaries. In some ways, this decision had a limited effect because almost every state constitution included the set of rights contained in the federal amendments, and some exceeded the federal safeguards. But the decision also meant that the interpretation and enforcement of rights could vary widely from state to state.

Rights of the accused occupied much of the nineteenth-century attention to individual liberty. No other part of the law had a more intimate relationship to everyday life than did criminal justice. Judges at first interpreted their state constitutions to offer significant protections to anyone accused of crimes. They insisted on following procedure strictly, such as requiring that indictments, or formal accusations of crime, use precisely the words required by law. The goal of such precision was twofold: the defendant needed to have exact knowledge to prepare his defense, and the indictment's precise language ensured that the state could not use the alleged facts to support a second trial for the same offense. Judges resisted any pressure to loosen these safeguards. "The harmless decision of today becomes the dangerous precedent for tomorrow," an Indiana court warned. The regard for proper procedure was no "idle technicality"; "the people have no better security than in holding officers of the state to a reasonable degree of care, precision, and certainty in prosecuting the citizen for a violation of the law."

An insistence on strict adherence to procedure diminished by the mid-nineteenth century, as fear of crime increased in tandem with the growth of cities. Public demands for order and security had profound implications for

Local officials gather in front of the Mariposa County Courthouse in the San Joaquin Valley of California in the 1880s. Courthouses were among the first civic structures erected as new communities emerged throughout the United States. Nineteenth-century courthouses often housed all the functions of local government, not simply its courts. Courthouses still play a central role in many counties today, especially in rural areas.

rights of the accused. By the end of the century, states were, in effect, running as many as three different criminal systems, each with its own standard of due process, as illustrated by Alameda County, California, home to Oakland. At the bottom was assembly-line justice. It was a highly bureaucratic process that used plea bargains—negotiated sentences in exchange for a plea of guilty—to move people accused of minor crimes swiftly from arrest to imprisonment. The handling of ordinary but serious property crimes was only marginally less routine, with fewer than half the cases going to trial and the vast majority of defendants being found guilty. Only for the most serious crimes—murder and robbery chief among them—did rights of the accused play any part in the criminal process. These cases grabbed public attention, and the duel of lawyers acted to educate citizens on an idealized version of American justice and the rights of defendants. Of course, for immigrants and blacks even the most routine administration of due process was often a mirage, a constitutional pledge they could not redeem.

Still, the promise of individual rights maintained a powerful hold on Americans. The nineteenth century witnessed numerous reform movements designed to extend the Bill of Rights and other democratic safeguards of liberty, some of them newly invented, to excluded groups. Women made one of the strongest demands, and at the Seneca Falls Convention in New York State in 1848, they put their case for voting rights and property rights in a Declaration of Sentiments, Grievances, and Resolutions that borrowed language from the Declaration of Independence. Workingmen used Jefferson's term, "inalienable rights," to lobby for fair wages and the ability to use their free time as they saw fit, which they wanted to include in the list of individual rights. Both of these movements succeeded after decades of struggle, but it was another nineteenth-century campaign that had the most profound effect on our rights as we know them today. This movement sought the abolition of slavery.

Union victory in the Civil War effectively ended slavery and led to three new amendments, each adding new rights, and one, the Fourteenth Amendment, containing within it the seeds of a veritable revolution in our conception of rights. The fruit of the Thirteenth Amendment was the right to freedom through the abolition of slavery; the Fifteenth Amendment guaranteed the right to vote to the freedmen. But it was the Fourteenth Amendment that changed the traditional relationship of national and state governments. Previously, Americans were citizens of their states; they looked primarily to their state constitutions for protection of their rights. The Fourteenth Amendment established national standards for citizenship and made every person born in the United States both a citizen of his state and a citizen of the nation. Equally important, it declared that "equal protection of the laws" and "due process of law" were guarantees for all citizens.

For the first time, the federal government had the responsibility to protect the rights of citizens—at least in theory. On the whole, however, federal courts did not interpret the amendment in this fashion during the last half of the nineteenth century, in part because the framers of the amendments did not define what they meant by such general phrases as "due process of law." Contrary to the expectations of the framers, the Supreme Court held that the amendment did not require states and local governments to respect the guarantees of the Bill of Rights. The justices instead followed traditional practice and allowed states wide discretion to protect individual liberty as they saw fit. For example, in *Plessy* v. *Ferguson* (1896), the Court held that state-mandated racial segregation of railroad cars did not violate the equal protection clause of the Fourteenth Amendment. The doctrine, known as "separate but equal," justified

The suffrage movement advocated women's full and equal participation in civic affairs, including not only the right to vote but also the right to serve on juries. Jurors were selected from voting rolls, so it was only after the passage of the Nineteenth Amendment to the Constitution in 1920 that women could sit on juries. This all-woman panel in San Diego, California, selected shortly thereafter, was surely quite unusual.

the widespread racial segregation and discrimination that finally ended as a matter of law in the 1960s. The *Plessy* decision, although repugnant to us today, reflected a much different view of rights and the role of states than we hold in modern America. It implied that the right to associate was a social right, subject to regulation by democratic majorities though legislative acts. Separating the races by law did not deny individuals their political rights, or so many people believed. Now we understand that racial discrimination prevents the enjoyment of other rights, such as equal protection of the laws. This view, however, became accepted only in the twentieth century.

The Fourteenth Amendment initially became a bulwark not for the civil rights of individuals but for the property rights of monopolistic corporations. From the late nineteenth century through the first three decades of the twentieth, big business dominated the American economy as never before. The U.S. Supreme Court proved to be its strong ally, first by declaring in 1886 that a corporation was a person for purposes of the Fourteenth Amendment and then by reading the amendment as protecting freedom of contract, but not other individual rights, such as freedom of speech, from government interference. In effect, this stance prevented most state and federal regulation of economic activity in the name of protecting individual liberty.

The late nineteenth and early twentieth centuries witnessed reform movements to reconcile the promise of American life with its harsher realities. The rapid growth of industry, emergence of a national market, the closing of the frontier, and rise of big cities following the Civil War had changed forever the earlier vision of a republic of small farmers and independent shopkeepers. These developments created great national wealth and moved the United States from a third-class nation to a world power, but they also brought many social ills, from child labor to massive urban poverty. In response, reformers lobbied against the prevailing notion that property rights limited the government's power to regulate the marketplace; they argued instead for an expanded view of governmental power sufficient to ensure fair competition and equal justice.

Educated citizens are necessary to the effective functioning of a democracy, but even after the passage of the Reconstruction amendments to the Constitution in the 1860s, African American children often were denied the same quality of education provided to white students. That right was not guaranteed until the Supreme Court's decision in Brown v. Board of Education *(1954), which cleared the way for the integration of American public schools.*

They were aided in these efforts by a new way of thinking about law and the role of judges. In a series of lectures in 1881, Justice Oliver Wendell Holmes, Jr., suggested that "the life of the law is not logic but experience." By this, he meant that social and economic change influenced the way we interpret the law; reaching the right decision in a case was not simply a matter of reasoning from abstract principles but also recognizing how to apply the law to changing circumstances. Advocates of "legal realism" argued that judges had to look beyond legal rules, including precedent (how previous judges had interpreted the law), to understand how the law would work in the world outside the courtroom. Legal realism also assumed that courts had a responsibility to keep law abreast of the times. This new understanding of law and courts was instrumental in the move to strengthen protection for individual rights in the twentieth century.

The first step was to challenge the traditional view that individual property rights were sacred. The Supreme Court had adopted an exalted view of the marketplace, seeing it as the ideal arrangement for securing the utmost economic liberty. The prevailing notion was that, without any interference or aid from government, individuals freely bargained with each other in an unregulated, open market. They sold their labor to the highest bidder, accumulated and exchanged their property as they wished, and used their talents and energies to create wealth for themselves and their families. The result of this unrestrained competition benefited the nation, as when railroad builders risked bankruptcy to develop a transportation network that was the envy of the world. This view, of course, was fantasy. Ordinary shop owners in no way competed equally with millionaire industrialists; common laborers had no ability to set their own wages; poor people had no money to invest in a business. It was an idealized picture of an economy that, in fact, valued monopoly over competition and in which government routinely devoted public assets to private gain, as when it gave land to railroad magnates. But the Court based its ideas of economic liberty on theory more than reality, so its decisions were hostile to any attempt to regulate the outcome of private economic arrangements. One decision, since discredited, even discovered in the due process clause a "liberty of contract" that protected corporations from state laws, even though the Constitution never mentions such a right.

What had happened was a change in the meaning of due process. Initially, the term meant only that government had to follow its own laws or procedures when making decisions or taking actions. If it did, then the result was thought to be fair. The new interpretation of due process looked instead to the result of the decision-making process: was it fair, and if not, who decided the right result—legislatures or judges? The answer under the new view was that government could follow all its established procedures and still deprive citizens (or corporations) of their rights because the result of the decision-making process was unfair. Judges would decide when this occurred. The idea that due process meant an acceptable result and not simply a fair process was called substantive due process. It represented a shift in interpretation that came to a head when states sought to regulate the monopolistic practices of corporations, for example, by establishing the rates railroads could charge. The Supreme Court usually struck down these laws because, even if the state followed its procedures to the letter, the result of the regulation was an infringement on the corporation's property rights. Regulation had resulted in a loss of freedom by the corporation to set its rates at whatever price the market would bear. Significantly, the Court did not apply this same logic to individual rights, which remained under state protection—or, too often, as in the case of racial minorities, were not protected at all.

Ultimately, this stance disappeared when monopolistic practices and market excesses resulted in the economic collapse known as the Great Depression of the 1930s. After initial resistance to economic reforms, the Court retreated from its belief in the supremacy of economic rights and accepted government regulation of property as a reasonable exercise of congressional power to regulate interstate commerce. But the justices' attempt to shield property rights from state regulation under the due process clause of the Fourteenth Amendment suggested that individual rights might be protected in similar fashion. Were the guarantees of free speech, fair trial, rights to counsel, and other safeguards of the Bill of Rights included in the meaning of the Fourteenth Amendment's due process and equal protection clauses?

The aftermath of World War I presented an opportunity to test this idea. Free speech was at issue. After the United States entered the war, the federal government sought to suppress dissent as harmful to the war effort. Much of the concern focused on attempts by union organizers, many of them self-proclaimed communists, to use wartime labor shortages to force concessions from business, even if it harmed military production. State courts had long refused to protect radical or offensive speech, and they also suppressed speech if it was accompanied by action that threatened public order, such as might occur at a union rally. At first, the Supreme Court followed this line of reasoning: it upheld convictions under state laws of antiwar protestors, including a candidate for U.S. President (*Debs* v. *United States,* 1919), because their speech presented "a clear and present danger" to the war effort. The First Amendment right of free speech did not protect individuals from state laws designed to ensure public order. By 1925, however, the Court had changed its mind, not about the meaning of free speech but about the role of the First Amendment. It ruled for the first time, in *Gitlow* v. *New York* (1925), that the freedoms of speech and press "are among the fundamental personal rights protected by the due process clause of the Fourteenth Amendment from impairment by the states." It would be several years before the full impact of this decision became apparent, but it marked the beginning of a new era for individual rights.

By the late 1930s, the Court was marching under the banner of incorporation for First Amendment freedoms. In 1937, the justices rejected an argument that the Fourteenth Amendment's due process clause incorporated, or included, the Fifth Amendment's ban on double jeopardy, but Justice Benjamin Cardozo, writing for the majority, ruled that it did incorporate all the provisions of the First Amendment. These rights—speech, press, religion, and assembly—were freedoms of expression, which Cardozo called "the matrix, the indispensable condition" for nearly all other freedoms. Other rights, however, were subject to selective incorporation, or inclusion one by one in the meaning of due process: the Court would apply only those rights that are, in Cardozo's words, "of the very essence of a scheme of ordered liberty" and could be considered fundamental because they were so deeply rooted in American traditions. This standard meant the Court would consider individual rights on a case-by-case basis. It was a position that divided the justices; some argued that all of the Bill of Rights applied to the states under the Fourteenth Amendment, a view known as total incorporation.

The debate over selective versus total incorporation had barely begun when successive international crises, World War II and the Cold War, plunged the Court once more into a debate about how to reconcile liberty and security. It was a problem as old as the Constitution itself, and it centered on how far individual rights extended in times of threat. The first cases to test the limits came from an unlikely source, Jehovah's Witnesses, a religious group that claimed First Amendment protection for their children's refusal to salute the flag in school, as required by state laws. The law infringed upon their right to the free exercise of their religious beliefs, they argued, since they owed allegiance only to God. Initially, the justices deferred to legislative judgments: the need to encourage patriotism, they concluded, was sufficiently important to justify a minor infringement of religious belief. But when accounts of public attacks on the Witnesses reached Court chambers, several justices reversed course and held in 1943 that the First Amendment protected freedom of religion from state interference.

Generally, the fascist assault on liberty during World War II, as seen in Nazi Germany, renewed American belief in the necessity of individual rights. President Franklin Roosevelt used his fireside radio chats to remind the nation of the need to protect "essential human freedoms." He called for a "second Bill of Rights" to include new guarantees, such as the right to a home, adequate medical care, and old age insurance, among others. But this expansive talk was not always consistent with rights in action. With the Japanese attack on Pearl Harbor, the federal government ordered the relocation of Japanese Americans into internment camps. Scholars today agree that the executive order violated the equal protection clause of the Fourteenth Amendment; it treated one group of citizens differently based solely on their ethnicity. But in 1943, the U.S. Supreme Court decided otherwise. It was not willing to challenge the President's order that internment was necessary in time of war, even when the government could produce no evidence of a real threat. In times of crisis, concerns about national security trumped individual rights, at least for certain groups of Americans.

The Cold War, the struggle between democracy and communism, as embodied by the United States and the Soviet Union, also raised challenges to individual rights, especially First Amendment freedoms of speech and association. The exposure of domestic spy rings and the communist takeover of Eastern Europe and China persuaded national and state governments to launch massive loyalty programs to purge communist sympathizers. At first, the Supreme Court supported convictions under laws designed to punish anyone who belonged to an organization that merely advocated the overthrow of the government. These decisions represented a setback in protection for individual rights because they punished beliefs, not actions, which departed from the Court's movement toward a broader view of First Amendment freedoms. Once public hysteria subsided in the mid-1950s, however, the justices reverted

A public defender represents his client before a jury in Oakland, California, in the mid-1950s. This rare courtroom image was shot by the renowned documentary photographer Dorothea Lange.

once again to a more liberal interpretation of these safeguards. They operated under the increasingly accepted view that the due process and equal protection clauses of the Fourteenth Amendment applied to the states as well as the federal government. What remained to be decided were what liberties these clauses included under their protection.

In the 1950s, the Court began a dramatic expansion of individual rights that lasted through the 1960s, and its decisions created a rights consciousness that remains strong today. In some ways, the new attention to rights was simply a continuation of a prominent theme in American history. Each decade since the nation's founding had brought some new assertion of rights—a right to freedom, a woman's right to vote, a right to organize. Some of the claims resulted in fundamental law: both the right to freedom and woman suffrage were products of constitutional amendments. Other rights, such as the right to organize, were recognized by statute. What was different in mid-century was the leadership of the Supreme Court in applying the Bill of Rights creatively to new situations.

One explanation for the Court's newfound aggressiveness was the appointment of Earl Warren as chief justice. Warren was a former California district prosecutor, attorney general, and governor who became chief justice in 1953. His tenure signaled a shift in judicial style from restraint to activism. He rejected the belief that judges should make decisions based on narrow case facts rather than broad constitutional principles. He specifically dismissed as "fantasy" the notion that justices should be impartial. "As a defender of the Constitution," he wrote in his memoirs, "the Court cannot be neutral." He sought a broad and active role for the high bench: the "Court sits to decide cases, not to avoid decision." More important, Warren believed the Constitution contained moral truths that were essential to enlightened government. It was the Court's duty to apply these principles, even if it overturned laws favored by a large majority of citizens. The Court's role, he believed, was to champion individual liberty, especially for people without a meaningful political voice.

Nowhere was this judicial philosophy more evident than in his attitude toward the Bill of Rights. It codified the "sense of justice" humans were born with and provided the basis for bringing American law "more and more into harmony with moral principles." These views required the "constant and creative application" of the Bill of Rights to new situations. "The pursuit of justice," Warren said in a *Fortune* magazine article in 1955, "is not the vain pursuit of remote abstraction." It was an active search for a fundamental moral guide to the problems of daily life, led by an independent judiciary. This process suggested continual revision of the catalog of rights, leaving "a document that will not have exactly the same meaning it had when we received it from our fathers" but one that would be better because it was "burnished by growing use."

Other justices were ready to embrace Warren's judicial philosophy, and the emerging civil rights movement provided a ripe test bed for their new activist stance. African Americans protested the nation's continuing segregation and its failure to live up to the promise of equality contained in the Thirteenth, Fourteenth, and Fifteenth Amendments. The Court had taken hesitant steps toward enforcing equal protection of the laws against actions of state governments in the 1930s and 1940s, especially in cases of extreme and overt use of government power in support of racial discrimination, but it was the Warren Court's willingness to address segregation in public schools that advanced the cause of equal rights most dramatically. In *Brown* v. *Board of Education* (1954), the Court rejected the *Plessy* doctrine of "separate but equal" and mandated an end to educational segregation "with all deliberate speed." The *Brown* decision marked a victory for legal realism—the Court considered sociological evidence of the harmful effects of segregation on black children—and it effectively ended the Court's tendency to accept legislative judgments on such issues. Over the next decade, the justices gave new life to the equal protection clause as a means of protecting the rights of African Americans and, later, the rights of women. Despite strong resistance from southern states, the nation was ready to follow the Court's lead, as evidenced by congressional passage of new civil rights acts in 1964, 1965, and 1968, all designed to erase racial discrimination from American life.

Acting with unprecedented boldness, the majority of justices on the Warren Court promoted a new understanding of individual rights, one that restrained the abuse of governmental power and, in their view, promoted a just society. The reforms came so swiftly that many commentators labeled them as revolutionary—and in a sense, they were. What had changed was the willingness to broaden individual rights aggressively in areas where traditionally legislatures had set standards. There were sweeping reforms of the electoral process, political representation, school desegregation, government support of religion, obscenity, and free speech, among others, all based on new interpretations of constitutional rights. New rights were inferred—invented, critics complained—from the Constitution's language, and chief among these implied rights was the right to privacy.

Rights of the accused were also fertile ground for the expansion of individual liberties, and they were by far the most controversial actions of the Warren Court. Between 1961 and 1969, the Court accomplished what previous courts had stoutly resisted: it applied virtually all the procedural guarantees of the Bill of Rights to the states' administration of criminal justice. Adopting the strategy of selective incorporation, the justices explicitly defined the Fourteenth Amendment phrase "due process of law" to include most of the rights outlined in the Fourth, Fifth, and Sixth Amendments. The result was a national standard that governed all criminal proceedings at both federal and state levels. The justices even extended these rights beyond the courtroom to the nation's police stations and jailhouses, places previously thought to be subject to local control only. The Court claimed not to diminish states' rights but instead to elevate inadequate state practices to a higher national standard. In the process, however, it ignited a firestorm of criticism that the expansion of these rights favored criminals at the expense of public safety.

By the late 1960s, the remarkable expansion of individual rights was nearing an end. Americans were increasingly uneasy about the course of reform charted by the Warren Court. Critics complained that the rights of individuals had taken precedence over the order and security of society. The decade's turbulent history appeared to support this conclusion: urban riots, political violence, and increased crime were cited as evidence. Conservatives also charged that judges had upset the constitutional balance by making law, which was a legislative function, and that, in turn, subverted democracy. The Warren Court record became a major issue in the 1968 Presidential election. The winning candidate, Richard Nixon, promised to appoint law-and-order judges who would interpret the Constitution strictly, as he believed the founders intended, and halt, if not reverse, the trend toward greater liberalization of individual rights. Subsequent elections also featured this theme, with Ronald Reagan making a similar pledge to stop the creation of "judge-made rights."

Two successive chief justices, Warren Burger and William Rehnquist, both appointees of conservative Republican Presidents, held similar views, but the Courts they led during the last three decades of the twentieth century left much of the Warren Court's legacy in place. The justices did not abandon the newfound catalog of individual rights but focused instead on what these rights meant in practice. On occasion, their decisions brought the same public opposition that had greeted the more controversial cases from the 1960s, as in *Texas* v. *Johnson* (1989), when the justices upheld flag burning as protected speech under the First Amendment. In some instances, the Court reaffirmed explicitly what had once been viewed as a radical decision. In 2000, for example, the justices upheld the Miranda warning—"you have the right to remain silent"—in an opinion written by Chief Justice Rehnquist, once a vocal critic of the Warren Court case that mandated this rule. In other areas, the justices went beyond the 1960s decisions to expand or affirm individual liberties, especially the rights of women and affirmative action programs designed to remedy past racial discrimination.

Concern about whether the Supreme Court had overstepped its proper role by its aggressive expansion of Bill of Rights protections was not new in American history. It was the same criticism levied by progressive reformers early in the twentieth century against judges who cited a right to economic liberty as a shield against regulatory laws passed by democratic majorities. What made this challenge especially contentious in the late twentieth century, however, was a resurgence of what came to be known as "rights consciousness," or a widespread willingness on the part of individuals and groups to push for the recognition of new rights. The awareness of rights to be asserted against government and others has long been a hallmark of our national culture. It is in fact a legacy of our revolutionary beginnings, but rights consciousness has rarely been stronger in our past than it has been since the 1960s. Not only has it led to claims of new rights to fit the needs of a modern age, but it has raised again questions about the role of rights in American democracy.

It is difficult to know whether decisions of the Warren Court led to the growth of rights consciousness or whether the justices simply were responding to a renewed awareness of rights. The demand for individual freedom came from many quarters. The American Civil Liberties Union, founded in 1920 to protect constitutional rights, led many of the fights for greater individual liberty. So, too, did the National Association for the Advancement of Colored People (NAACP), a significant number of national labor unions, the National

Rifle Association, and a host of other interest groups. Courts can act only when someone presents a claim for a legal decision, so in some sense, the growing culture of rights arose from the demands of countless litigants. But it is also true that Supreme Court decisions during the 1960s spurred the growth of rights consciousness, if for no other reason than they influenced lower courts, which settle most cases, to be more receptive to rights claims.

When a citizen asks the courts to enforce a right, the lawsuit often results in an application that goes far beyond what he or she sought. In the early 1960s, for instance, a poor defendant, Clarence Earl Gideon, believed he had been denied his right to an attorney in his criminal trial, so he appealed his conviction. The Supreme Court agreed with him in 1963, but its decision went further and announced a right for all indigent defendants to be represented at state expense in felony trials. Later this right was extended to all criminal cases where the potential loss of liberty was at stake, even for minor crimes. The same result was true of the right to privacy, a right not found by name in the Constitution but legitimately inferred from other rights. In 1965, the Warren Court supported the argument that this right prevented a state from prohibiting the use of birth control by a married couple, but later decisions led to its application in new areas, including the right of a woman to have an abortion and protection of consenting gay adults from arrest under state laws.

As a society, we have often debated how far to extend individual rights, but some of the decisions of the 1960s and later, especially those involving civil rights, introduced a new concept, group rights, into American constitutional law. After the Supreme Court's landmark rulings mandating equal treatment regardless of race in schools and public facilities, questions arose about how to remedy or correct racially discriminatory practices. One answer was affirmative action, which focused attention on an individual's membership in a racial or ethnic group and allowed race to be used as a positive factor in decisions about employment and admission to higher education. These programs, which the Court has accepted as constitutional under the equal protection clause, reflected a shift from rights as a protection against government to rights as a way to change social relations. What began as an effort to correct long-standing discrimination against blacks soon moved into new rights claims for other groups that have suffered discrimination—women, gays and lesbians, ethnic minorities, and the disabled, among others.

Significantly, some of these claims are pursued in the political arena and through the legislative process, both at state and federal levels, and not through the courts alone. The Americans with Disabilities Act of 1990, for example, established legal rights for physically and mentally handicapped citizens. Not all claims are accepted by courts, legislatures, or voters, however. In the 1970s, women's rights advocates pushed hard for an Equal Rights Amendment—which says that equality under the law shall not be denied on the basis of one's sex—but fell heartbreakingly short in the ratification process.

We may be more rights conscious today than at other time in our history, but we remain divided over how far our rights extend. The eruption of new claims to rights and organizations dedicated to promoting them historically has been met with resistance and angry backlash. In many ways, this conflict

> *"[The Constitution] is an enabling (and a constraining) document. It sets forth a mechanism for making and applying law, and it creates a framework for representative government. It protects our basic freedoms, such as our rights to speak and to worship freely. It protects the basic fairness of our system, so that majorities cannot unfairly and systematically oppress minorities. It gives us the freedom to choose. But it does not tell us what to choose. It forces us, as a community, to choose democratically how we will solve our Nation's problems."*
>
> —Justice Stephen Breyer, commencement address, New School University, New York City, May 20, 2005

has made rights talk even more contagious. Rights claims, after all, are made by someone who alleges a denial of liberty against the government or someone else. It is hard to think in terms of common values or community when engaged in rights talk; too much focus on individual liberties can skew our sense of the interests we hold in common. Still, what is most striking about the conflict over rights has been its democratic character. Rights are now a matter of public debate. When we confront each other over our individual rights, we are doing the work of democracy. Like the founding generation, we are trying to figure out what rights and liberties are required for a just and free society.

It is up to each of us to claim our rights and to engage in the work of a free people. Fortunately, our history is full of individuals who have demanded their constitutional protections and, in the process, advanced liberty for us all. In the twenty-three cases discussed in this book, it is ordinary citizens, for the most part, who have sought rights they believed were lawfully theirs. The claimants represent a cross section of Americans—young, old, well known, obscure, middle class, poor, respectable, and disreputable. One of the best ways we can protect our rights and our liberty is to understand what they demanded as their right—and why. They made history when they received an answer to their claim of individual liberty, but in these instances, as the novelist William Faulkner reminded us, the past is not dead, it is not even past. The rights these individuals sought remain vital, changing expressions of freedom. As members of a democratic society, we must always decide whether they moved the nation closer to the ideals established by the founding generation and whether they still represent the values the Constitution should protect today.

"All Men Are by Nature Equally Free"

The Virginia Declaration of Rights was the first written listing of the rights of citizens in the newly independent United States. Drafted by George Mason, a wealthy planter and political leader, the declaration set forth principles of government and individual rights of citizens. Adopted unanimously by the Virginia Convention of Delegates on June 12, 1776, it served as the model for other state declarations of rights as well as the federal Bill of Rights.

I That all men are by nature equally free and independent, and have certain inherent rights, of which, when they enter into a state of society, they cannot, by any compact, deprive or divest their posterity; namely, the enjoyment of life and liberty, with the means of acquiring and possessing property, and pursuing and obtaining happiness and safety.

II That all power is vested in, and consequently derived from, the people; that magistrates are their trustees and servants, and at all times amenable to them.

III That government is, or ought to be, instituted for the common benefit, protection, and security of the people, nation or community; of all the various modes and forms of government that is best, which is capable of producing the greatest degree of happiness and safety and is most effectually secured against the danger of maladministration; and that, whenever any government shall be found inadequate or contrary to these purposes, a majority of the community hath an indubitable, unalienable, and indefeasible right to reform, alter or abolish it, in such manner as shall be judged most conducive to the public weal.

IV That no man, or set of men, are entitled to exclusive or separate emoluments or privileges from the community, but in consideration of public services; which, not being descendible, neither ought the offices of magistrate, legislator, or judge be hereditary.

V That the legislative and executive powers of the state should be separate and distinct from the judicative; and, that the members of the two first may be restrained from oppression by feeling and participating the burthens of the people, they should, at fixed periods, be reduced to a private station, return into that body from which they were originally taken, and the vacancies be supplied by frequent, certain, and regular elections in which all, or any part of the former members, to be again eligible, or ineligible, as the laws shall direct.

VI That elections of members to serve as representatives of the people in assembly ought to be free; and that all men, having sufficient evidence of permanent common interest with, and attachment to, the community have the right of suffrage and cannot be taxed or deprived of their property for public uses without their own consent or that of their representatives so elected, nor bound by any law to which they have not, in like manner, assented, for the public good.

VII That all power of suspending laws, or the execution of laws, by any authority without consent of the representatives of the people is injurious to their rights and ought not to be exercised.

VIII That in all capital or criminal prosecutions a man hath a right to demand the cause and nature of his accusation to be confronted with the accusers and witnesses, to call for evidence in his favor, and to a speedy trial by an impartial jury of his vicinage, without whose unanimous consent he cannot be found guilty, nor can he be compelled to give evidence against himself; that no man be deprived of his liberty except by the law of the land or the judgement of his peers.

IX That excessive bail ought not to be required, nor excessive fines imposed; nor cruel and unusual punishments inflicted.

X That general warrants, whereby any officer or messenger may be commanded to search suspected places without evidence of a fact committed, or to seize any person or persons not named, or whose offense is not particularly described and supported by evidence, are grievous and oppressive and ought not to be granted.

XI That in controversies respecting property and in suits between man and man, the ancient trial by jury is preferable to any other and ought to be held sacred.

XII That the freedom of the press is one of the greatest bulwarks of liberty and can never be restrained but by despotic governments.

XIII That a well regulated militia, composed of the body of the people, trained to arms, is the proper, natural, and safe defense of a free state; that standing armies, in time of peace, should be avoided as dangerous to liberty; and that, in all cases, the military should be under strict subordination to, and be governed by, the civil power.

XIV That the people have a right to uniform government; and therefore, that no government separate from, or independent of, the government of Virginia, ought to be erected or established within the limits thereof.

XV That no free government, or the blessings of liberty, can be preserved to any people but by a firm adherence to justice, moderation, temperance, frugality, and virtue and by frequent recurrence to fundamental principles.

XVI That religion, or the duty which we owe to our Creator and the manner of discharging it, can be directed by reason and conviction, not by force or violence; and therefore, all men are equally entitled to the free exercise of religion, according to the dictates of conscience; and that it is the mutual duty of all to practice Christian forbearance, love, and charity towards each other.

Private Property and Public Use

In 1822, a wharf owner in Baltimore sued the city for economic loss caused when the city diverted several streams and lowered the water level around his dock. He claimed a taking of his property without just compensation, in violation of the Fifth Amendment. Chief Justice John Marshall, writing for a unanimous Supreme Court in Barron v. Baltimore *(1833), concluded that the Bill of Rights restrained only the federal government, not the states. This view no longer prevails. Today, almost all of the guarantees of the Bill of Rights have been incorporated by the Fourteenth Amendment as restraints on the states.*

The plaintiff in error contends that it comes within that clause of the fifth amendment to the constitution, which inhibits the taking of private property for public use, without just compensation, He insists that this amendment, being in favour of the liberty of the citizen, ought to be so construed as to restrain legislative power of a state, as well as that of the United States. If this proposition be untrue, the court can take no jurisdiction of the cause....

The constitution was ordained and established by the people of the United States for themselves, for their own government, and not for the government of the individual states. Each state established a constitution for itself, and, in that constitution, provided such limitations and restrictions on the powers of its particular government as its judgment dictated....

In their several constitutions they have imposed such restrictions on their representative governments as their own wisdom suggested; such as they deemed most proper for themselves. It is a subject on which they judge exclusively, and with which others interfere no farther than they are supposed to have a common interest....

We are of opinion that the provision of the fifth amendment to the constitution, declaring that private property shall not be taken for public use without just compensation, is intended solely as a limitation on the exercise of power by the government of the United States, and is not applicable to the legislation of the states.

CHAPTER 2

The Right to Freedom

The U.S. Constitution and its Bill of Rights contain the rights of a free people, but they do not guarantee freedom explicitly. The Thirteenth Amendment does. Designed to fulfill the promise of the Emancipation Proclamation of 1863, it outlawed slavery—"Neither slavery nor involuntary servitude…shall exist within the United States, or any place subject to their jurisdiction"—and, by implication, it also established freedom as a fundamental American right. Freedom has had many meanings for Americans, but at its core, the definition has always been set against slavery, the opposite of what freedom promised, which was the liberty to choose and act without coercion or restraints.

In 1863, President Abraham Lincoln issued his proclamation abolishing slavery in regions not under Union control, but in fact the document did not free a single slave. Americans at the time recognized its limited effect: the Emancipation Proclamation had no legal status. The Thirteenth Amendment, ratified in December 1865, remedied this problem by making emancipation part of the nation's fundamental law. Debated then and now was the question of whether the amendment went beyond merely freeing the slaves. Did it promise, in addition, a full measure of freedom for all Americans?

Efforts to define freedom began with the European settlement of North America, but the struggle was most fierce during the Civil War and its aftermath of Reconstruction. Until then, Americans usually defined freedom in relationship to the African slavery they knew—slaves were not free, and free men were not slaves. By abolishing slavery, the war destroyed this assumption. It also changed the way Americans thought about the Constitution. In the decades leading to the Civil War, the Constitution had become an increasingly sacred text. Americans rarely considered changing it; after the Bill of Rights, it had been amended only twice, the last time in 1804. They especially avoided changing the founding generation's language on slavery, but the debate over abolition forced Americans to view the framers' work as imperfect and incomplete. It also provided them an opportunity to build on the founders' commitment to liberty. In this sense, the adoption of the Thirteenth Amendment represented a transforming moment when the nation redefined freedom and made it part of its fundamental law. Americans were reconstructing the nation to create a more perfect Union and to extend its promise of liberty to all people.

Adoption of the Thirteenth Amendment came after a long political struggle as first Congress and then the state ratification conventions debated what its words meant. Its champions believed the amendment proclaimed not only the end of slavery and its vestiges, or traces, but also guaranteed former slaves all the rights that defined freedom. "Mere exemption from servitude is a miserable idea of freedom," a legislator from Massachusetts argued. Others did not favor extending a full complement of rights to African Americans but recognized

A black man reads a newspaper report of the 1863 Emancipation Proclamation, by which President Abraham Lincoln freed all African Americans residing in slave states. That document granted those African Americans the most basic liberty: personal freedom.

> *"If our free society is to endure, and I know it will, those who govern must recognize that the Framers of the Constitution limited their power in order to preserve human dignity and the air of freedom which is our proudest heritage. The task of protecting these principles does not rest solely with nine Supreme Court justices, or even with the cadre of state and federal judges. We all share the burden."*
>
> —Justice William J. Brennan, Jr., "My Life on the Court" (1997)

that slavery was incompatible with the nation's claims of liberty. Opponents objected to the broad enforcement power granted to the federal government in Section 2, arguing that it undermined federalism, the division of power between state and central governments. In this view, opponents were correct. The amendment altered the American constitutional order. For the first time, a national law significantly limited the power of the states to define the status of its residents.

The amendment quickly spawned two statutes under its enforcement authority—the Civil Rights Act of 1866 and the Freedmen's Bureau Act. The bureau bill extended equal rights to state laws and enforced them through military courts when states failed to do so. Readmission of states into the Union would end the military courts, however, so the civil rights law declared that blacks were citizens and guaranteed them legal equality throughout the nation. They were entitled to the "full and equal benefit of all laws and proceedings for the security of persons and property" as whites enjoyed. Both measures asserted broad national authority to define rights essential to freedom and provided for enforcement of these rights, if necessary, in federal courts. These acts, and others that followed, depended in part on the enforcement power given to Congress under the Thirteenth Amendment. Tolerating discrimination, one senator explained, "would be perpetuating that lingering prejudice growing out of a race having been slaves which it is as much our duty to remove as it was to abolish slavery." It was necessary to remove these vestiges for the guarantee of freedom to have any meaning.

This view failed to receive support from the Supreme Court, which tended to ignore the Thirteenth Amendment. The justices conceded that the amendment guaranteed freedom from slavery, and not simply for blacks. Although "[N]egro slavery alone was in the mind of the Congress," the Court noted in its 1873 decision in the *Slaughterhouse Cases*, "if Mexican peonage or the Chinese coolie labor system shall develop slavery of the Mexican or Chinese race . . . this amendment may safely be trusted to make it void." The Court's decision in the *Civil Rights Cases* (1883) also suggested that the enforcement section gave Congress the authority to outlaw "badges and incidents" of slavery. But the justices defined these badges and incidents narrowly. They ruled, for example, that the amendment did not give Congress the power to enact laws against private discrimination or to prohibit racial discrimination in public accommodations, such as railroads. Finally, in 1906, the Court struck its strongest blow against the amendment when it declared that state courts alone could decide when violations of the amendment had occurred.

With this history, it is not surprising that much of the twentieth century's civil rights legislation relied not on the Thirteenth Amendment but on the Fourteenth Amendment, adopted in 1868. The latter amendment forbade states from abridging the rights of citizenship or denying citizens due process and equal protection of the laws. In the late 1960s, however, the Thirteenth Amendment did emerge suddenly and dramatically as a constitutional guarantee of freedom. This outcome was not on the minds of a mixed-race couple from St. Louis in 1965, however. They simply wanted to buy a nice house in a quiet suburb, but discovered they could not.

Joseph Lee Jones and his wife, Barbara, both federal employees in Missouri, read an advertisement in 1965 for the Paddock Woods subdivision then being developed in St. Louis County. The new suburb sounded ideal. It would house around one thousand people and boasted all the amenities needed for a comfortable lifestyle, including a country club. But when they made an offer on a home, they were told they could not buy it. Joseph Jones was an African American, and the agent explained that the developer, the Alfred H. Mayer Company, did not sell to blacks as a matter of policy. It believed whites would not buy lots if blacks were their neighbors. The fear was based in an unfortunate reality: the vast majority of Americans in the 1960s lived in residentially segregated neighborhoods.

In 1948, the Supreme Court had ruled in *Shelley* v. *Kraemer* that state enforcement of such restrictive covenants, or legal restrictions forbidding blacks to purchase property, was unconstitutional under the equal protection clause of the Fourteenth Amendment. The Joneses could have used this decision to challenge the Mayer Company's policy. But the company, in anticipation, claimed that it was operating solely as a private company; it had developed the subdivision solely on its own, without any state involvement. So the Joneses relied instead on the Civil Rights Act of 1866, which Congress had passed to enforce the Thirteenth Amendment. The company's actions, they argued, violated a surviving remnant of this act that promised "all citizens of the United States shall have the same right, in every State and Territory, as is enjoyed by white citizens thereof, to purchase real property." Joseph and Barbara Jones were asking the justices to do something the Court had refused to do ever since the Thirteenth Amendment passed—declare that the amendment outlawed private discrimination as a violation of the rights of free citizens.

The Supreme Court agreed with the Joneses, by a vote of 7 to 2, that the Thirteenth Amendment abolished the "incidents and badges of slavery" as well

Members of the House of Representatives celebrate its passage of the Thirteenth Amendment to the Constitution on January 31, 1865. Ratified in December of that year, the amendment banned "slavery and involuntary servitude," thus guaranteeing freedom as a condition of American citizenship.

as slavery itself. This concept was not new to the Court; it had used the language in its 1883 decision in the *Civil Rights Cases,* but with a different result. Then, it interpreted the incidents and badges of slavery narrowly to exclude private acts of discrimination; now, it viewed these acts as impermissible. "Just as the Black Codes, enacted after the Civil War . . . were substitutes for the slave system, so the exclusion of Negroes from white communities became a substitute for the Black Codes. And when racial discrimination herds men into ghettos and makes their ability to buy property turn on the color of their skin, then it too is a relic of slavery," the Court determined.

The real issue at stake was the meaning of freedom itself. During the debate over the Civil Rights Act of 1866, Senator Lyman Trumbull from Illinois, who led the fight to adopt the Thirteenth Amendment, warned that measures such as the Black Codes threatened the freedom won for all Americans on the battlefields of the Civil War: "The trumpet of freedom that we have been blowing throughout the land has given an 'uncertain sound,' and the promised freedom is a delusion," he claimed. In *Jones* v. *Alfred Mayer Co.,* the justices answered his concern. "At the very least," the majority opinion stated, "the freedom that Congress is empowered to secure under the Thirteenth Amendment includes the freedom to buy whatever a white man can buy, the right to live wherever a white man can live. If Congress cannot say that being a free man means at least this much, then the Thirteenth Amendment made a promise the Nation cannot keep."

With the ratification of the Thirteenth Amendment, Americans had reimagined their Constitution. This first Reconstruction amendment established freedom as a condition of U.S. citizenship, but its meaning was uncertain. As the nation's attention turned away from the conditions of ex-slaves in the 1870s, the Thirteenth Amendment faded into relative obscurity—until the decision in *Jones* v. *Alfred Mayer Co.*

Although dormant for many decades, the amendment was never entirely forgotten. On numerous occasions, especially in the nineteenth century, the Supreme Court struck down various laws on peonage (forced labor for payment of debts) as violations of the ban on involuntary servitude. But memory of the amendment's promise rested largely with African Americans, who viewed it in both a negative and positive light. For many blacks in segregated America, freedom still was more hope than reality, though the amendment was also a symbol of how far they had come. Many

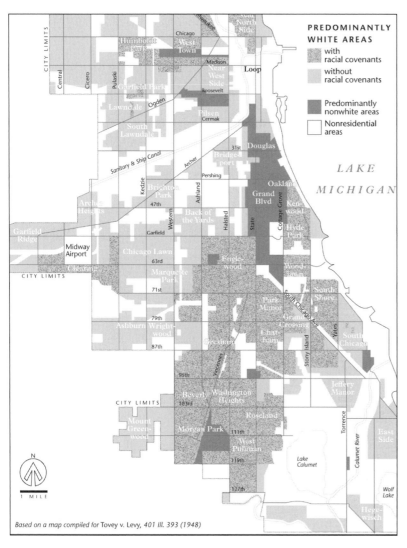

Between 1916 and 1948, faced with the Great Migration of rural blacks to the industrial cities of the North, the Chicago Real Estate Board helped property owners establish restrictive covenants that prevented blacks from buying or even living in houses in many neighborhoods of the city. This map—which was used in a 1948 lawsuit brought to enforce the covenants—shows those areas with such restrictions.

PREDOMINANTLY WHITE AREAS

with racial covenants

without racial covenants

Predominantly nonwhite areas

Nonresidential areas

Based on a map compiled for Tovey v. Levy, 401 Ill. 393 (1948)

African-American communities, for example, celebrated February 1, the date in 1865 when Abraham Lincoln signed the Thirteenth Amendment, as Freedom Day. When Congress in 1947 established the date as an annual celebration, the man who lobbied most for the new National Freedom Day, an ex-slave from Georgia, said the amendment "not only freed the black man legally, but laid the groundwork for the white man's [freedom] as well."

What this freedom entailed was open to debate, but increasingly in the twentieth century a variety of causes invoked the amendment's promise. Since the 1960s, legal scholars have argued that the Thirteenth Amendment should protect exploited workers, abused women, neglected children, and all other victims of relationships that bore the vestiges of slavery or involuntary servitude. In a 1969 case concerning major league baseball, a star player, Curt Flood, challenged league rules against free agency, or the ability to negotiate his own contract, as a violation of the amendment's guarantee of freedom. He lost his case (although baseball owners later abandoned their restrictive rules), but what was important was a renewed debate about what defines freedom.

The struggle over the amendment's meaning is far from over. In this sense, the first part of the Constitution to establish freedom as a right of all Americans is not unlike the more well-known amendment, the Fourteenth, that followed it. With the Fourteenth Amendment, the questions that begged answers centered on the rights included in its elusive phrases of "due process" and "equal protection." The Court over time has interpreted the Fourteenth Amendment to include many of the rights outlined in the Bill of Rights. The Thirteenth Amendment cannot claim this constitutional legacy, but it does not need to. Its contribution is different but complementary. With its passage, Americans understood that the Constitution was not written on tablets of stone, with their rights engraved for all times and incapable of change. Each generation has the ability to challenge and enlarge on the work of previous generations. Rights can be expanded and created, not simply accepted. Freedom can be evaluated and redefined, not simply celebrated. Both freedom and the Constitution that protects the rights that accompany freedom are living achievements, not relics of a dead past. The Thirteenth Amendment made freedom part of our constitutional birthright; it also invited us all to continue the debate over what freedom means.

"We tend to think the case has been made that a free society is a stable society, that a free society is the birthright of all people. We do not know why we must make the case all over again when judgment has been given in our favor. . . . History teaches that freedom must make its case, again and again, from one generation to the next. The work of freedom is never done."

—Justice Anthony M. Kennedy, speech at the annual meeting of the American Bar Association, August 9, 2003

Civil Rights for Former Slaves

After the Civil War, Congress passed two civil rights acts (1866 and 1875) that sought to secure the rights of freed slaves and to enforce the provisions of the Thirteenth and Fourteenth Amendments. The 1875 act especially sought to prohibit private discrimination against blacks in such matters as access to inns and public transportation. One of the central issues that emerged was whether the Thirteenth Amendment allowed Congress to outlaw "vestiges of slavery," or the discrimination that resulted from African Americans' previous status as noncitizens.

In the Civil Rights Cases *of 1883, Justice Joseph P. Bradley wrote for an 8-to-1 majority of the Supreme Court, which interpreted the Thirteenth Amendment narrowly and ruled that it did not authorize Congress to outlaw discrimination.*

It is true that slavery cannot exist without law any more than property in lands and goods can exist without law, and therefore the thirteenth amendment may be regarded as nullifying all state laws which establish or uphold slavery....

We must not forget that the province and scope of the thirteenth and fourteenth amendments are different: the former simply abolished slavery: the latter prohibited the states from abridging the privileges or immunities of citizens of the United States, from depriving them of life, liberty, or property without due process of law, and from denying to any the equal protection of the laws. The amendments are different, and the powers of congress under them are different.... Under the thirteenth amendment, it has only to do with slavery and its incidents.... Under the thirteenth amendment the legislation, so far as necessary or proper to eradicate all forms and incidents of slavery and involuntary servitude, may be direct and primary, operating upon the acts of individuals, whether sanctioned by state legislation or not....

When a man has emerged from slavery, ... there must be some stage in the progress of his elevation when he takes the rank of a mere citizen, and ceases to be the special favorite of the laws, and when his rights as a citizen, or a man, are to be protected in the ordinary modes by which other men's rights are protected.... Mere discriminations on account of race or color were not regarded as badges of slavery.

Justice John Marshall Harlan registered a strong dissent in the Civil Rights Cases. *His view was later adopted by the court in* Jones v. Alfred Mayer Co. *(1968).*

The thirteenth amendment...did something more than to prohibit slavery as an institution, resting upon distinctions of race, and upheld by positive law. ...[I]t established and decreed universal civil freedom throughout the United States. But did the freedom thus established involve nothing more than exemption from actual slavery?...Was it the purpose of the nation simply to destroy the institution, and then remit the race...to the several states for such protection, in their civil rights, necessarily growing out of freedom, as those states, in their discretion, choose to provide? Were the states, against whose solemn protest the institution was destroyed, to be left perfectly free...to make or allow discriminations against that race, as such, in the enjoyment of those fundamental rights that inhere in a state of freedom?...

That there are burdens and disabilities which constitute badges of slavery and servitude, and that the express power delegated to congress to enforce, by appropriate legislation, the thirteenth amendment, may be exerted by legislation of a direct and primary character, for the eradication, not simply of the institution, but of its badges and incidents, are propositions which ought to be deemed indisputable.

I do hold that since slavery...was the moving or principal cause of the adoption of that [thirteenth] amendment, and since that institution rested wholly upon the inferiority, as a race, of those held in bondage, their freedom necessarily involved immunity from, and protection against, all discrimination against them, because of their race, in respect of such civil rights as belong to freemen of other races.

"A New Birth of Freedom"

Military historians agree that the Battle of Gettysburg was the turning point of the Civil War. It also marked the time when the abolition of slavery, rather than preservation of the Union, began to emerge as a goal of the war. On November 19, 1863, President Abraham Lincoln delivered the Gettysburg Address, to dedicate the battlefield. The short speech signaled this new goal when he spoke about "a new birth of freedom." The Thirteenth Amendment, which abolished slavery when it was ratified after the war, guaranteed freedom to all Americans.

Fourscore and seven years ago our fathers brought forth on this continent a new nation, conceived in liberty and dedicated to the proposition that all men are created equal. Now we are engaged in a great civil war, testing whether that nation or any nation so conceived and so dedicated can long endure. We are met on a great battlefield of that war. We have come to dedicate a portion of that field as a final resting-place for those who here gave their lives that that nation might live. It is altogether fitting and proper that we should do this. But in a larger sense, we cannot dedicate, we cannot consecrate, we cannot hallow this ground. The brave men, living and dead who struggled here have consecrated it far above our poor power to add or detract. The world will little note nor long remember what we say here, but it can never forget what they did here. It is for us the living rather to be dedicated here to the unfinished work which they who fought here have thus far so nobly advanced. It is rather for us to be here dedicated to the great task remaining before us—that from these honored dead we take increased devotion to that cause for which they gave the last full measure of devotion—that we here highly resolve that these dead shall not have died in vain, that this nation under God shall have a new birth of freedom, and that government of the people, by the people, for the people shall not perish from the earth.

The Right to Equal Protection of the Laws

"All, too, will bear in mind this sacred principle, that though the will of the majority is in all cases to prevail, that will to be rightful must be reasonable; that the minority possess their equal rights, which equal law must protect, and to violate would be oppression."

—President Thomas Jefferson, First Inaugural Address, March 4, 1801

"All men are created equal." This phrase has stirred hearts around the world for more than 200 years. It is one of the values most associated with the United States, but nowhere is the language of equality among individuals found in the Constitution. It comes instead from the Declaration of Independence, the document that signaled the intentions of the founding generation. Not until after the Civil War did the nation's governing charter include equality before the law as a constitutional guarantee, when the Fourteenth Amendment promised, "Nor shall any State...deny to any person within its jurisdiction the equal protection of the laws."

When Thomas Jefferson wrote the Declaration of Independence, few people believed in social or economic equality. The document's language did not mean the founders intended to level society. Like others of their day, they accepted upper and lower classes, or social hierarchy, as natural. What they desired was an equal opportunity for people to make the most of their abilities and to stand equal before the law. This idea was quite radical in the late eighteenth century, even though it is common today. It departed sharply from the world of privilege enjoyed by the men who led the Revolution. The declaration also pledged more than these men were willing to grant in fact; equal opportunity did not apply to women, slaves, the poor, native Americans, and many immigrants. Yet as limited as the ideal was in practice, all Americans ultimately were heirs to its promise.

The notion of equality as an essential part of democracy became deeply embedded in American society during the first half of the nineteenth century. Alexis de Tocqueville, the French visitor whose classic work, *Democracy in America* (1835), remains the best guide to the young nation's character, noted the popular insistence that "rights must be given to each citizen or to no one." The Civil War tested this principle, but the Union victory reaffirmed not only the nation's unity but also its commitment to equality before the law. When it became apparent that the defeated Confederate states were intent on severely restricting the legal and economic rights of former slaves, Congress passed the Fourteenth Amendment, which the states ratified in 1868. It made all persons born in the United States citizens of the nation and of the state where they lived. It also prohibited any state from "abridging the privileges and immunities of citizens of the United States," or denying its citizens "due process of law" or "equal protection of the laws." For the first time, the concept of equality became part of the Constitution.

The framers of the Fourteenth Amendment used open-ended phrases— "due process of law" and "equal protection of the laws"—that had no clear or settled definition. Most scholars believe that they intended, at a minimum, to apply the protections of the Bill of Rights to the states, but this is not what happened. In a series of cases during the late nineteenth century, the Supreme Court ruled that Americans had to turn to their states, rather than the federal government, for protection of their rights. The justices also voided most federal laws designed to protect blacks and decided that Congress did not have the power under the amendment to prohibit private acts of discrimination. The Court in fact supported state laws requiring discrimination, most famously in *Plessy* v. *Ferguson* (1896), when it interpreted the equal protection clause to allow racial segregation as long as separate facilities were equal. The Fourteenth Amendment, the Court decided, "could not have been intended to abolish distinctions based upon color." This "separate but equal" standard used to justify legal discrimination made the equal protection clause, in effect, a dead letter.

African Americans did not accept segregation willingly, however. Throughout the first half of the twentieth century, they resorted increasingly to the courts to win recognition of their rights. Led by the National Association for the Advancement of Colored People's (NAACP) Legal Defense Fund, blacks won significant victories on issues related to voting, police brutality, and rights of the accused. World War II played a big role in changing American attitudes. Segregation and the violence against blacks that accompanied it reminded many Americans of Nazi Germany's efforts to breed a pure race and to exterminate entire groups of people who failed to satisfy Adolf Hitler's notion of desirable human traits. After black soldiers demonstrated their courage on the battlefields, President Harry Truman acknowledged their contribution in 1947 by ending segregation in the U.S. Army. In 1950, the Supreme Court held in two cases that segregated law schools and graduate programs could never be equal to ones provided for whites. Four years later, in *Brown* v. *Board of Education,* the standard of "separate but equal" was discredited completely when the justices unanimously decided that segregated education was inherently unequal; it violated the Fourteenth Amendment's promise of equal protection of the law.

"*I think that democratic peoples have a natural taste for liberty. Left to themselves, they seek it out, love it, and suffer if deprived of it. For equality, however, they feel an ardent, insatiable, eternal, invincible passion. They want equality in liberty.*"

—Alexis de Tocqueville, *Democracy in America* (1835)

A black soldier from the U.S. Army's 12th Armored Division stands guard over Nazi prisoners in the German forest in 1945. The dedicated service of black soldiers, who served primarily in segregated units until President Harry Truman integrated the armed forces by executive order in 1948, was influential in the elimination of Jim Crow policies in the military and American society in general.

> *"[I]n view of the constitution, in the eye of the law, there is in this country no superior, dominant, ruling class of citizens. There is no caste here. Our constitution is color-blind, and neither knows nor tolerates classes among citizens. In respect of civil rights, all citizens are equal before the law. The humblest is the peer of the most powerful. The law regards man as man, and takes no account of his surroundings or of his color when his civil rights as guarantied by the supreme law of the land are involved."*
>
> —Justice John Marshall Harlan, dissenting opinion,
> *Plessy* v. *Ferguson* (1896)

Separate facilities for whites and blacks—whether theater seating, schools, water fountains, restrooms, even Coke machines—were the rule in the American South well into the 1960s.

The *Brown* decision was one of the most momentous in Supreme Court history. It stimulated a revolution in civil rights and revitalized the Fourteenth Amendment's equal protection clause. The unavoidable logic of *Brown* was that if separating people in school on the basis of race violated the equal protection clause, then so did racial segregation in other parts of public life. In case after case, litigants used the *Brown* doctrine successfully to challenge statutory segregation, while the civil rights movement pushed the nation to open all of American public life to equality before the law.

Soon the Court was faced with questions about laws that regulated private conduct on the basis of race. One of the most volatile of these issues concerned interracial marriage. Southern states prohibited it, but how could law regulate matters of the heart? Were these laws a violation of the equal protection guarantee of the Fourteenth Amendment? In the 1960s, a young Virginia couple was determined to find out.

Newlyweds Richard and Mildred Loving were asleep in their home in Caroline County, Virginia, in July 1958, when they were awakened by flashlights shining in their faces. The intruders demanded to know why they were in bed together, and the Lovings produced a marriage certificate from the District of Columbia. The leader of the group, the local sheriff, told them the certificate was not valid in Virginia and arrested them for violating the state's Racial Integrity Act of 1924, which prohibited a white from marrying anyone other than another white person. Richard was white; Mildred, black. Their crime was marrying each other.

At their trial six months later, they waived a jury trial and accepted a deal from the judge. In exchange for a suspended sentence of one year in the state prison, they would leave Virginia for twenty-five years. "Almighty God created the races white, black, yellow, malay and red," the judge explained later when the case came back to him on appeal, "and he placed them on separate continents. And but for the interference with his arrangement there would be no cause for such marriages. The fact that he separated the races shows that he did not intend for the races to mix." This view was by no means an isolated one. A public opinion poll in 1965 revealed that 42 percent of northern whites and 72 percent of southern whites supported laws banning interracial marriages.

The Lovings moved to Washington, D.C., but found it difficult to adjust to urban life. Mildred especially wanted to move back to the county where both she and Richard had family. In desperation, she wrote U.S. Attorney General Robert F. Kennedy, asking for his help. The Justice Department referred the letter to the American Civil Liberties Union (ACLU), which agreed to take the case. It offered the civil rights organization an opportunity to challenge the anti-mixing laws then on the books of sixteen states. The Lovings reluctantly accepted the ACLU's plan. They were private people who preferred to be left alone in their marriage. "We have thought about other people," Richard Loving told a reporter, "but we are doing it for us—because we want to live here."

The marriage of Mildred and Richard Loving in 1958 provided the test case for overturning Virginia's antimiscegenation laws. Virginia was then one of sixteen states to restrict marriage based on racial classifications.

After Virginia's highest court unanimously refused to overturn their convictions, the Lovings appealed to the U.S. Supreme Court. Their argument was straightforward: the statutes were "relics of slavery" and expressions of racism. "There are no laws more symbolic of the Negro's relegation to second-class citizenship.... [T]hey are legalized racial prejudice, unsupported by reason or morals, and should not exist in a good society," their petition argued. In the oral presentation, the Lovings' attorney advanced another, more poignant reason why the justices should void the marriage law. Richard had asked him to "tell the Court I love my wife, and it is just unfair that I cannot live with her in Virginia."

The justices agreed, 9 to 0. "The clear and central purpose of the Fourteenth Amendment was to eliminate all official state sources of invidious racial discrimination in the States," Chief Justice Earl Warren wrote. "There can be no doubt that restricting the freedom to marry solely because of racial classifications violates the central meaning of the equal protection clause." Racial classifications are "so directly subversive of the principle of equality at the heart of the Fourteenth Amendment," he concluded, that they also deprived citizens of liberty without due process of law.

Surprisingly, there was no public backlash to the decision in *Loving* v. *Virginia*, despite the social outrage that historically had attended intimate interracial relationships. Most Americans were sympathetic to the need to redeem the promise of equal protection made by the Fourteenth Amendment, at least when it came to racial classifications. For the Lovings, the result was more immediate and more personal. "I feel free now," Mildred said when she learned of the decision. Soon they returned to Virginia to live among family and friends without fear of going to prison. Their lives had changed, but they never understood why the public should be interested in their case. "All we ever wanted," they claimed, "was to get married, because we loved each other."

In the series of cases from *Brown* to *Loving*, the Supreme Court gave life to the equal protection clause and extended the promise of equality before the law to racial minorities who previously had been denied this right. But in some ways these cases were easy once the justices decided that laws requiring segregation by race violated the Fourteenth Amendment. What followed were issues far more difficult to resolve because they involved not legal discrimination but rather attempts to remedy past wrongs based on race and other suspect classifications such as gender.

Ending legal segregation did not end racial separation. Whether for economic opportunity or prejudice against minorities, many whites moved from cities into suburbs, leaving the inner cities poorer and less integrated. One response was to end segregation in fact and not simply in law. For example, schools were segregated in part because students lived in all-white or all-black neighborhoods, so courts required busing of blacks into white schools to ensure a racial balance approximately equal to the entire community's ratio of back and white citizens.

Another response was to allow affirmative action programs to guarantee minority access to higher education, civil service positions, labor unions, and government contracts. Under these programs, governments could take race into account as a way to increase minority participation. Although many people viewed these efforts as reverse discrimination, the Supreme Court upheld many affirmative action programs, especially in states where legal segregation had been strongest. The most important case was *Regents of the University of California* v. *Bakke* (1978). The Court allowed universities to consider race as a factor in admission decisions as a way of boosting the number of minority students, so long as they did not use strict racial quotas to reach a desirable mix, a result the justices reaffirmed in 2005 in two decisions involving the University of Michigan. The justices also struck down laws that resulted in discrimination, even if the result was unintentional and the law was fair otherwise. Finally, in 1987, in *St. Francis College* v. *Al-Khazraji,* they expanded the legal definition of race beyond its traditional meaning to include "identifiable classes of persons who are subjected to intentional discrimination solely because of their ancestry or ethnic characteristics." Equal protection of laws applied to any person, an Arab in this case, who was a member of one of these classes.

The successful attack on racial discrimination was not lost on women, who looked to the equal protection clause as a way to remove inequalities based on gender. In the 1970s, the Court began to strike down gender classifications as a violation of the Fourteenth Amendment, just as they had done with racial classifications in earlier decades. The justices were responding in both instances to a broad national consensus brought about in the first instance by the civil rights movement and in the second by the women's movement. By the mid-1990s, one of the last male-only bastions fell before the equal protection standard when the Court ruled, in *United States* v. *Virginia,* that Virginia could not deny admission to women at the state-supported Virginia Military Institute. The belief that women would falter under the rigors of military training was a stereotype that could not be used to deny an individual's right to equal protection. Even though an Equal Rights Amendment narrowly failed to win ratification, courts and legislatures at the federal and state level increasingly refused to accept discrimination based on gender.

Equal protection does not mean absolutely equal treatment. By its nature, law relies on classifications, and it treats people differently for good reason. We as a society do not

Attorney General Robert F. Kennedy addresses a crowd of civil rights demonstrators outside the Justice Department building in Washington, D.C., in June 1963. As attorney general, Bobby Kennedy ensured that federal troops protected the Freedom Riders sponsored by the Congress of Racial Equality on voter registration trips through the South, and he was a key adviser to his brother President John F. Kennedy in drafting civil rights legislation.

provide driver's licenses, for example, to people who are blind, and we accept the idea that seniority confers different benefits, such as higher pay or greater privileges, on people who do the same job. What we do not accept is different treatment based solely on race, gender, or other classifications—age, sexual orientation, physical disability, among others—that have no reasonable relationship to the job, admission criteria, eligibility requirements, or the like. Also, equal protection does not apply equally to all groups. Distinctions based on race are more suspect than those based on gender, in part because the Fourteenth Amendment was designed specifically to eliminate the ill effects of racial classifications, even if the Court did not apply it in this fashion until the last half of the twentieth century. Not all our expectations for equal treatment before the law are based on the Fourteenth Amendment, however. The Americans with Disabilities Act (1990) is a federal statute, for instance, and not a constitutional requirement, but it and similar statutes reflect our constitutional commitment to equality.

The late-twentieth-century movement toward equality—the so-called egalitarian revolution—came from a variety of circumstances, but it could not have occurred without a Constitution capable of accommodating new meanings. John Marshall, a member of the founding generation and perhaps the nation's greatest chief justice, reminded his contemporaries that the document they had ratified in 1788 would always have "to be adopted to the various crises of human affairs." A second justice with the same surname but not the same heritage, Thurgood Marshall, the first African American on the Supreme Court, stated it more bluntly two centuries later:

> The men who gathered in Philadelphia in 1787 could not have imagined nor would they have accepted that the document they were drafting would one day be construed by a Supreme Court to which had been appointed a woman and a descendent of an African slave. "We the People" no longer enslaves, but the credit does not belong to the framers. It belongs to those who refused to acquiesce in outdated notions of "liberty," "justice," and "equality" and who strived to better them.

History presents new opportunities to apply—and extend—older concepts. The principle of equal protection of the law is one of the best examples of how our constitutional rights gain meaning from experience.

Americans have always been committed to allowing individuals an equal opportunity to reach their full potential, to engage in the pursuit of happiness on equal terms with each other in the marketplace, in education, and in other parts of society. We have also understood that the ability to compete equally depends upon equality before the law. The idea of equal protection of laws is a fundamental concept of democratic citizenship. With it, each of us can participate in decisions that affect us and our society, and we each bear responsibility for the choices we make. Without it, we would have categories of citizenship, with some members of society enjoying greater rights and power than others. We as a people have rejected this more restricted view of the role and responsibilities of citizenship by embracing, ultimately, a national goal of equality before the law. In doing so, we have acted to redeem the promise of 1776 that all men and women are created equal.

"A Broader Protest Is Made in Behalf of Woman"

Margaret Fuller was a writer, lecturer, early women's right advocate, and one of the most influential literary personalities in the nineteenth century. Daughter of a U.S. congressman and a close friend of Ralph Waldo Emerson, she organized a series of discussion groups in the 1840s around topics such as art, education, and equal rights for women. Many of the leading crusaders for equal rights for women attended these sessions. Fuller developed the ideas from these discussions more fully in a major work, Woman in the Nineteenth Century *(1845), which argued for the independence of women. Fuller was America's first public intellectual woman of letters, and her work helped to shape the early women's rights movement.*

It should be remarked that, as the principle of liberty is better understood, and more nobly interpreted, a broader protest is made in behalf of Woman. As men become aware that few men have had a fair chance, they are inclined to say that no women had a fair chance....

We would have every arbitrary barrier thrown down. We would have every path laid open to Woman as freely as to Man. Were this done, and a slight temporary fermentation allowed to subside, we should see crystallizations more pure and of more various beauty. We believe the divine energy would pervade nature to a degree unknown in the history of former ages, and that no discordant collision, but a ravishing harmony of the spheres, would ensue.

Yet, then and only then will mankind be ripe for this, when inward and outward freedom for Woman as much as for Man shall be acknowledged as a right, not yielded as a concession. As the friend of the negro assumes that one man cannot by right hold another in bondage, so should the friend of Woman assume that Man cannot by right lay even well-meant restrictions on Woman....

What Woman needs is not as a woman to act or rule, but as a nature to grow, as an intellect to discern, as a soul to live freely and unimpeded, to unfold such powers as were given her when we left our common home....

It is therefore that I would have Woman lay aside all thought, such as she habitually cherishes, of being taught and led by men. I would have her, like the Indian girl, dedicate herself to the Sun, the Sun of Truth, and go nowhere if his beams did not make clear the path. I would have her free from compromise, from complaisance, from helplessness, because I would have her good enough and strong enough to love one and all beings, from the fullness, not the poverty of her being.

Arguments about an Opinion

After a Supreme Court case has been decided, the justice assigned to write the majority opinion circulates a draft for comment by the other justices. Chief Justice Earl Warren, who wrote the opinion in Loving v. Virginia *outlawing racial classifications, received the following memo from Justice Byron White, who expressed a reservation about Warren's draft. White told the chief justice that he prefers not to say that any legal classification by race is illegal because he thinks there might be an instance, "although perhaps rare," where it would be rational to do so. In the end, however, he agreed to support the opinion as the chief justice wrote it. The memo, dated May 31, 1967, reveals how the justices confer with each other to reach a decision, especially how they try to persuade other justices.*

Re: No. 395 - Loving v. Virginia

Dear Chief:

I may misunderstand your opinion, but it seems to me that we must meet the second contention made by the State which you mention on page 7 of your opinion—the so-called rationality of the statutory classification—and that you do meet it by saying either that there can be no rational racial classification, at least where criminal liability is concerned, or that the test is much more onerous than mere rationality where racial classification are involved and that this heavier burden has not been met here. I prefer the second approach since I think there are some racial classifications, although perhaps rare, which I would approve, although I see no reason for me or the Court to say so at this point.

Also, if the statute satisfied the Equal Protections Clause, I would not hold it a violation of due process as "arbitrary." On the other hand, since it does not meet equal protection standards, it may automatically be a violation of due process also. All in all, I see no reason to reach the due process question.

Perhaps in the interest of time, I should just concur in the result on the ground that the statute violates the Equal Protection Clause since the heavy burden of justifying the racial classification employed by the statue has not been met by the State in this case.

Sincerely,
Byron

CHAPTER 4

The Right to Free Exercise of Religion

For the American revolutionaries, freedom of the soul was the most precious liberty. It was first among rights because it gave meaning to freedom itself. Without it, truth would perish; without truth, men and women could never be fully free. The war for independence was fought for religious liberty as well as for political liberty, and the First Amendment reflects this premier role. Protecting religious liberty was the first right guaranteed to American citizens, heading the list of other necessary rights of a democratic society—freedoms of speech, press, assembly, and petition. "Congress shall make no law," the amendment proclaims, "respecting an establishment of religion or prohibiting the free exercise thereof."

Free exercise means the right to believe in any religion or in no religion at all. History taught the founders the futility of mandating or suppressing religious beliefs, as well as the bloody consequences of trying to do either. Throughout the European past, governments had sought to control what people could believe and routinely persecuted heretics and other individuals who challenged official religious doctrines. Conformity in all things spiritual was prized by church and state alike, and government used its power to torture, imprison, or execute dissenters. The late-fifteenth-century Spanish Inquisition was the most notorious example of such persecution, but in fact all European nations, including England, suppressed religious dissenters.

The English had direct experience with the dangers of religious division. Its bloody sixteenth-century civil war largely stemmed from attempts of government to suppress religious dissent. Even though the conflict led to greater toleration in religious matters, the English government still did not accept the idea of complete religious freedom. The colonies, too, denied its citizens free exercise of religion. Maryland in 1654 withdrew protection from anyone who professed or practiced the "Popish religion," as Roman Catholicism was called; a few years later, Massachusetts hanged four Quakers on the Boston Common; Presbyterian preachers were thrown in jail in eighteenth-century New York; and as late as 1774, itinerant Baptist preachers in Virginia were imprisoned for declaring their beliefs publicly.

The framers rejected this past. James Madison, the primary author of the Bill of Rights, wrote in the 1780s, "Torrents of blood have been spilt in the old world, by vain attempts of the secular arm to extinguish religious discord. . . . Time has revealed the true remedy." The remedy, of course, was freedom of conscience. This right was central to what the founders understood as the great American experiment in liberty. The Virginia Statute for Religious Freedom gave perfect voice to this view. Passed in 1786, after Virginia voters elected a legislature opposed to state interference in religion, the law became the model

"[R]eligion is a matter which lies solely between man and his God. . . . I contemplate with sovereign reverence that act of the whole American people which declared that their legislature should 'make no law respecting an establishment of religion, or prohibiting the free exercise thereof,' thus building a wall of separation between Church and State."

—Thomas Jefferson, letter to the Danbury Baptist Association, January 1, 1802 for the religion clause of the First Amendment. Its architect was Thomas Jefferson, who listed it, along with the Declaration of Independence and the founding of the University of Virginia, as the legacy he wanted the world to remember. The Virginia Statute guaranteed that "all men shall be free to profess, and by argument to maintain, their opinion in matters of religion." This freedom, the act declared, was one of the "natural rights of mankind," and the statute's preamble made plain that the act was necessary because "Almighty God hath created the mind free."

Embracing this right in theory, however, did not always guarantee it in practice. The United States in the eighteenth and nineteenth centuries was overwhelmingly Protestant. Catholics and Jews experienced intolerance, although not legal interference, because their doctrines were different, as did numerous other groups, such as Quakers, Anabaptists, and Mennonites. Two long-lasting religious revivals, or periods of intense preaching and spiritual renewal known as the first and second Great Awakenings, spawned many new sects and denominations. A number of them held doctrines outside the mainstream of what most Americans believed, and they too suffered ostracism, discrimination, and, at times, violence. Mormons especially were persecuted. The sect developed in the 1820s in an area of upstate New York known as the "burned-over district" because of its intense religious fervor. Mormons soon became targets of suspicion and hostility because their beliefs and practices, including polygamy, or plural marriage, set them apart from most nineteenth-century Americans. Pursued relentlessly, they fled from Ohio to Missouri to Illinois, where their leader, Joseph Smith, was murdered and their temple burned. They finally moved to Utah, then part of what Americans considered the Great American Desert, to find a place where they could practice their faith unmolested. Even then, they had to abandon polygamy—and even its advocacy—before the state could be admitted into the Union.

The nineteenth century witnessed few Supreme Court decisions on the religion clauses of the First Amendment, but the twentieth century found the justices deeply engaged in deciding what free exercise meant. The nation had become more diverse as immigrants from Eastern Europe and Asia arrived in large numbers between the 1890s and 1920s, bringing with them a host of religions other than Protestant Christianity. This new pluralism challenged traditional assumptions about the public role of religion and its relationship to the state. It was not long before these issues reached the Supreme Court.

Beginning in the 1940s the justices defined religious liberty as part of the liberty protected under the due process clause of the Fourteenth Amendment, which meant that the First Amendment now applied to state and federal governments equally. This shift required the Court to consider how far the constitutional protection of free exercise extended. Did it protect, for example, groups who refused to follow a law because it interfered with their right to practice their religion?

Religious minorities were most in danger of having their free exercise limited or denied, and few groups was more persecuted than Jehovah's Witnesses, a pacifist sect that sought to restore Christianity to its primitive beginnings. Their vigorous evangelizing activities offended many Americans, who wanted to use ordinances and other government measures to regulate their door-to-door solicitations or use of public places as pulpits. This issue became especially urgent during the heightened tensions of the depression and World War II because Jehovah's Witnesses would not pledge allegiance to the flag or swear loyalty to any form of national authority. Their beliefs described these acts as worshiping an authority other than God, a practice they rejected. Did the First Amendment protect their right to refuse to do something that the people's elected representatives had decided was clearly in the national interest?

In 1935, the leader of the Jehovah's Witnesses, Joseph Rutherford, went on the radio to praise young Carleton Nichols, a third grader in Lynn, Massachusetts, for refusing to recite the Pledge of Allegiance to the U.S. flag as required by state law. Rutherford told his audience of fellow believers that saluting the flag amounted to worshiping a false idol, which violated God's law and would bring eternal damnation. He held up Witnesses in Nazi Germany as examples of faithfulness. They had refused to salute Adolf Hitler in face of extreme pressure, and now he implored American disciples to show the same courage, which young Carleton had done by keeping his seat.

Listening to the broadcast at their kitchen table were Lillian Gobitas, a twelve-year-old girl, and her ten-year-old brother, William. Lillian was class

Ten-year-old Billy Gobitas explained his refusal to salute the flag in this letter to the Minersville, Pennsylvania, school directors. "I do not salute the flag because I have promised to do the will of God," he wrote.

president and a good student. She knew her classmates would not understand if she, too, refused to salute the flag, but, she recalled later, "I did a lot of reading and checking in the Bible and I really took my own stand." Her brother and two other young Witnesses joined her. The school board voted to expel them. In the process, they rejected the argument of Lillian and William's parents that they loved their country but they could not salute the flag without violating their religious convictions. Every citizen and every child must show proper regard for the flag, the board president declared, or soon the nation would suffer from disrespect and a lack of patriotism. The Gobitas family sued the board, claiming a violation of their First Amendment right to exercise their beliefs freely.

Walter Gobitas escorts his children from U.S. district court in Philadelphia after they testified in their suit against the Minersville school district. The children claimed that saluting the flag was a form of idolatry, which was forbidden by the biblical book of Exodus: "Thou shalt not make unto thee any graven image, nor bow down to them."

The idea of a pledge had existed only since 1892, when the editors of a children's magazine proposed one for the 400th anniversary of Columbus's voyage to the New World. The pledge—the same one we recite now, except that the words "under God" were added in 1952—quickly became popular. In 1907, Kansas was the first state to make its recitation compulsory for schoolchildren; by 1935, forty of the forty-eight states had similar laws. Many people undoubtedly believed these laws were in accord with the founding generation's wishes, but not if George Washington serves as a guide. When some members of the Continental Congress in 1778 suggested a pledge of loyalty be required for soldiers, he wrote in response: "I would not wish in any instance that there should be the least degree of compulsion exercised."

The lower federal courts ruled in favor of the Gobitases, but the Supreme Court did not agree by an 8-to-1 vote. The majority framed the issue as one of nationalism, not religious rights. It was 1940 and the nation was on the verge of war. The justices were uneasy about doing anything that might decrease respect for the flag or interfere with a school board's ability to foster patriotism in its students. "National unity," Justice Felix Frankfurter wrote in the majority opinion, "increases national security." The proper remedy for Lillian and William Gobitas and their parents was to elect a legislature sympathetic to their views.

The lone dissenting member of the Court disagreed sharply with this view. In an unrelated case two years earlier, Justice Harlan Fiske Stone had written a footnote in which he claimed special protection for First Amendment rights. "The Constitution," he argued, "expressed more than the conviction of the people that democratic processes must be preserved at all costs. It also is an expression of faith and a command that freedom of the mind and spirit must be preserved, which government must obey, if it is to adhere to that justice and morality without which no free government can exist." In his dissent in *Minersville School District* v. *Gobitis* (the Court misspelled Gobitas), Stone resurrected this theme and gave it special emphasis by taking the unusual step of reading his dissent aloud before the Court. The role of the Constitution, he said, was to protect individuals, not government: "The very essence of the liberty which [the Bill of Rights] guarantee is the freedom of the individual from compulsion as to what he shall think and what he shall say, at least where the compulsion is to bear false witness to his religion." Asking an unpopular group to lobby the legislature for a change in the law, as the majority had suggested, was no remedy.

The decision exposed Jehovah's Witnesses to public attack, and they became victims of violence in a country worried about Hitler's advance across Europe and its own security. The U.S. Department of Justice counted more than three hundred attacks on Witnesses during the months afterward. A meeting hall was burned in Maine; a Maryland mob, aided by police, broke up a Witnesses' meeting; in Illinois, a Witness was beaten until he kissed the flag; an Indiana crowd drove Witnesses from town, as did a group in Mississippi. In West Virginia, nine Witnesses were forced to swallow large amounts of castor oil, causing severe cramps and bleeding, before a sheriff tied them together, paraded them in front of an angry crowd, painted them with swastikas, and drove them out of town. "It was open season on Jehovah's Witnesses," Lillian Gobitas recalled later.

Two years later, another case came before the Supreme Court. This time West Virginia had passed a law requiring the Pledge of Allegiance in public schools, which Marie Barnette, a Witness, refused to do. The Court reversed its earlier decision, voting 6 to 3, thanks to a change of mind on the part of three justices and the retirement of two other justices. In *West Virginia State Board of Education* v. *Barnette* (1943), Justice Robert Jackson made a powerful defense of personal liberty: if there was any "fixed star in our constitution, it is that no official, high or petty, can prescribe what shall be orthodox in politics, nationalism, religion, or other matters of opinion or force citizens to confess by word or act their faith therein." Other justices supported him in separate opinions. The rights guaranteed by the First Amendment protect unpopular minorities, Justice Hugo Black wrote, because "freedom to speak and write about public questions is as important to government as is the heart to the human body. In fact, this privilege is the heart of our government." While it was necessary and proper to teach patriotism, forcing unity was no different than what Nazi Germany did, Justice Jackson admonished. Those who seek to force an end to dissent, he noted, "soon find them exterminating dissenters." Above all, the Bill of Rights protected the right to individual opinions and beliefs, no matter how unpopular.

The right to believe freely is an absolute right under the First Amendment: government cannot force citizens to accept or reject any religious idea or belief. Taking action on the belief, however, is not an absolute right. Societies in the past believed in human sacrifice as a religious act, yet no one today may claim constitutional protection for this extreme practice. Clearly, the right to free exercise must be balanced with society's need for order, safety, and public welfare. The important question is how we identify what is protected and what is not.

The Supreme Court has addressed this issue by defining religion broadly and by expanding the activities protected by the free exercise language of the First Amendment. Certain religious views might even seem preposterous to most people, but anyone has a right to beliefs that traditional faiths would consider to be lies: "Men may believe what they cannot prove," the Court concluded in a 1944 case. The justices also have restricted governments from limiting the ability of individuals to practice their religion. Laws that require stores to close on Sunday, for example, are unconstitutional if they discriminate against groups, such as Jews or Seventh-Day Adventists, whose sacred times are on other days of the week. More recently, in *Church of the Lukumi Babalu Aye* v. *City of Hialeah* (1993), the Court upheld the right of believers in a folk religion to practice animal sacrifice, even though public health laws forbade it. In an Oregon case in 1990 (*Employment Division* v. *Smith*), however, the government's interest in controlling narcotics outweighed American Indians' right to use peyote, a hallucinatory drug, in their religious ceremonies. Free exercise of religion does not excuse anyone from obeying laws that are neutral and apply to everyone, the Court ruled, but otherwise government must prove a strong need to regulate a religious practice, no matter how slightly.

The peyote decision alarmed religious groups from across a broad spectrum of belief, and they lobbied successfully for the Religious Freedom Restoration Act of 1993, which sought to set a stricter test for government to meet before it could interfere with free exercise. Although the Court later ruled much of the act unconstitutional, the popular response was noteworthy. Protestants, Catholics, Muslims, and Jews, among others, agreed that their separate beliefs were best protected by a common commitment to the right of free exercise.

Today, America is home to the world in all its religious variety. By some estimates, the United States has more than 1,500 organized religious groups, representing all the world's religions. We truly are a pluralistic society, and we value our diversity even as we struggle with the problem of maintaining national unity in the face of so many different beliefs. The issue seems new to us, but in fact the founders understood how attractive freedom of religion would be to the world's people. They recognized their greatest challenge would be to live up to the promise represented by the Latin phrase they chose for the Great Seal of the United States—*E Pluribus Unum* (Out of Many, One). In an era when governments elsewhere enforced conformity, could this new nation allow men and women to live according to their own beliefs? History taught that religion had been a bloody battleground. How could they prevent it from disuniting America?

Their solution was a radical experiment in liberty that remains our practice. They embraced diversity in the conviction that it would lead to truth and freedom. In the *Federalist Papers,* essays written to persuade voters to ratify the

Some Native Americans shake peyote fans to accompany vision songs that are part of their religious rituals. Participants also smoke the hallucinatory peyote weed, bringing them into conflict with antidrug laws.

Constitution, James Madison argued that we as a nation should encourage people to follow their own interests. In *Federalist* No. 10, he claimed that we are more secure in our liberty when a large number of interest groups exist. In such circumstances, no group will ever have enough members to form a permanent majority that can threaten the rights of people who hold unpopular beliefs.

Madison was writing about all sorts of beliefs, political as well as religious, but religion was his model for encouraging such unparalleled diversity. He believed truth would emerge from a vigorous exchange of ideas—but he also understood that, ultimately, every man and woman would have to decide the moral and spiritual truths he or she would live by. For the founding generation, the right to believe and act according to individual conscience was the essence of liberty. It is why the First Amendment lists freedom of religion first among the individual rights that must be protected from government interference. Our unity, they trusted, would come from our common commitment to this first principle of freedom.

The idea of free exercise of religion is, perhaps, even more important today. Violent religious disagreements are as much a part of the twenty-first century as they were of the distant past. Numerous societies throughout the world still do not accept the right of individuals to believe or not to believe as they choose. In the United States, certain groups, fearing that we have become a secular or unreligious society, want to declare America officially to be a Christian nation. Yet our entire history reveals a strong link between the free and unrestrained exercise of religion and religious vitality. With the exception of Ireland, we are the most overtly religious society in the Western world, with more than 90 percent of Americans identifying themselves as believers of one sort or another. Our commitment to the peaceful coexistence of many different beliefs is rare in world history. We do not have citizens taking arms against each other in the name of faith, despite our sharp disagreements over matters of theology and practice. A commitment to the free exercise of belief is what has led to this unusual religious tradition. We have learned from our history, even if imperfectly, that religious freedom is central to freedom itself. The key question now is whether and how we will maintain this commitment.

Religious Tolerance in the Colonies

Free exercise of religion meant different things to seventeenth- and eighteenth-century Americans than it does to us, and that meaning differed among the various colonies. Rhode Island, under the leadership of Roger Williams, was the only colony to embrace completely free exercise of religion. In The Bloody Tenent *(1644), written while Williams was in England to secure a charter for his colony, he argued for tolerance.*

It is the will and command of God that, since the coming of His Son, the Lord Jesus, a permission of the most Paganish, Jewish, Turkish or anti-Christian consciences and worship be granted to all men, in all nations and countries; and they are only to be fought against with that sword which is only, in Soul matters able to conquer, to wit; the sword of the Spirit—the Word of God.

Most colonies adopted a policy of toleration, with the Pennsylvania Charter of Liberties (1682) among the most liberal, but such tolerance extended only to people who believed in one God as an eternal, supreme Creator.

That all persons living in this province, who confess and acknowledge the one Almighty and eternal God, to be the Creator, Upholder and Ruler of the world; and that hold themselves obliged in conscience to live peaceably and justly in civil society, shall, in no ways, be molested or prejudiced for their religious persuasion, or practice, in matters of faith and worship, nor shall they be compelled, at any time, to frequent or maintain any religious worship, place or ministry whatever.

In Common Sense *(1776), a tract that argued for separation from Great Britain, Thomas Paine also advocated free exercise of religion as "the will of the Almighty." He argued that government had an obligation to protect the right of belief.*

As to religion, I hold it to be the indispensable duty of every government, to protect all conscientious professors thereof, and I know of no other business which government hath to do therewith.... For myself, I fully and conscientiously believe, that it is the will of the Almighty, that there should be a diversity of religious opinions among us: it affords a larger field for our Christian kindness. Were we all of one way of thinking, our religious dispositions would want matter for probation; and on this liberal principle, I look on the various denominations among us, to be like children of the same family, differing only, in what is called, their Christian names.

"The Diversity We Profess to Admire"

In Wisconsin *v.* Yoder *(1972), a unanimous Supreme Court held that Wisconsin's compulsory high school attendance law violated the rights of Amish parents to free exercise of their religious beliefs. The Amish, a conservative Christian group, came from Germany originally and settled first in Pennsylvania and later in the Midwest. Since the sixteenth century, they have believed in maintaining a strict separation between themselves and the modern world. In the twentieth century, their religious beliefs led them to maintain their rural traditions and to reject automobiles and electricity. They also refused to marry outside their community. Amish parents permitted their children to attend public schools only through the eighth grade because of concern that attendance at high school would lead to outside marriages. Wisconsin law, however, required school attendance until age sixteen. Writing for the Court, Chief Justice Warren Burger concluded that the Amish right to free exercise of religion trumped the interest of the state in educating its youth.*

We come then to the quality of the claims of the respondents concerning the alleged encroachment of Wisconsin's compulsory school-attendance statute on their rights and the rights of their children to the free exercise of the religious beliefs they and their forebears have adhered to for almost three centuries. In evaluating those claims we must be careful to determine whether the Amish religious faith and their mode of life are, as they claim, inseparable and interdependent. A way of life, however virtuous and admirable, may not be interposed as a barrier to reasonable state regulation of education if it is based on purely secular considerations; to have the protection of the Religion Clauses, the claims must be rooted in religious belief.

The conclusion is inescapable that secondary schooling, by exposing Amish children to worldly influences in terms of attitudes, goals, and values contrary to beliefs, and by substantially interfering with the religious development of the Amish child and his integration into the way of life of the Amish faith community at the crucial adolescent stage of development, contravenes the basic religious tenets and practice of the Amish faith, both as to the parent and the child.

Insofar as the State's claim rests on the view that a brief additional period of formal education is imperative to enable the Amish to participate effectively and intelligently in our democratic process, it must fall. The Amish alternative to formal secondary school education has enabled them to function effectively in their day-to-day life under self-imposed limitations on relations with the world, and to survive and prosper in contemporary society as a separate, sharply identifiable and highly self-sufficient community for more than 200 years in this country. In itself this is strong evidence that they are capable of fulfilling the social and political responsibilities of citizenship without compelled attendance beyond the eighth grade at the price of jeopardizing their free exercise of religious belief. When Thomas Jefferson emphasized the need for education as a bulwark of a free people against tyranny, there is nothing to indicate he had in mind compulsory education through any fixed age beyond a basic education. Indeed, the Amish communities singularly parallel and reflect many of the virtues of Jefferson's ideal of the "sturdy yeoman" who would form the basis of what he considered as the ideal of a democratic society. Even their idiosyncratic separateness exemplifies the diversity we profess to admire and encourage.

CHAPTER 5

Separation of Church and State

The American Revolution was a radical experiment in liberty. Nowhere was its character more evident than in what Thomas Jefferson called a "novel innovation"—the First Amendment's separation of church and state. The language was unmistakably direct: "Congress shall make no law respecting an establishment of religion." The establishment clause, as it is known, forbids government from supporting or favoring religion or any particular religious belief or practice. It also outlaws discrimination in favor of religion. When linked to its companion clause—"Congress shall make no law... prohibiting the free exercise thereof"—the amendment embraces the now-classic American principles of liberty of conscience, freedom of religious expression, religious equality, and separation of church and state.

In adopting the amendment, the framers drew upon their own experience but went beyond it to reject the history they had inherited from Europe. For a thousand years, governments in Western Europe accepted the idea that there was only one true religion, Roman Catholicism, that encompassed the entire society. The state's role was to enforce uniform belief and practice by any means necessary, including the torture and execution of heretics and infidels. Even after the Protestant Reformation, the sixteenth-century revolt against the Catholic Church, governments continued to use their power to uphold the authority of a single national church. Church and state were partners in maintaining the good order of society. Too much was at stake in heaven and on earth to consider any other arrangement.

In England, the most troublesome challenge to conformity came from Puritans and others who believed the Church of England was corrupt. These religious dissenters founded several of the early American colonies, but, despite their alienation from the national church, they rejected neither the idea of a single faith nor a state church. They did not seek religious freedom for everyone but only the right to practice what they believed. Rhode Island was an early exception to this history. Its founder, Roger Williams, insisted on complete religious freedom. The charter for the colony, issued in 1663, promised residents "at all times hereafter, freely and fully [to] have and enjoy... their own judgments and consciences, in matters of religious concernments." Williams advanced an important principle, but his small colony was an isolated outpost in a world that accepted close ties between religion and government as natural. In 1682, Pennsylvania adopted a liberal policy that tolerated or accepted the diverse practice of religion for people who believed in God, but only Rhode Island proclaimed complete religious liberty.

Toleration gradually grew in American soil, despite these early barriers. The European ideal of one church in one nation never fit the circumstances of the

> *"All civil states with their officers of justice, in their respective constitutions and administrations, are... essentially civil, and therefore not judges, governors, or defenders of the Spiritual, or Christian, State and worship.... God requireth not an uniformity of religion to be enacted and enforced in any civil state; which enforced uniformity, sooner or later, is the greatest occasion of civil war, ravishing consciences, persecution of Christ Jesus in His servants, and of the hypocrisy and destruction of millions of souls."*
>
> —Roger Williams, *The Bloody Tenent* (1644)

colonies, where distance and diversity were barriers to conformity. Not all of the colonies were English in origin—New York, for instance, was initially Dutch, with its Reformed tradition—and the Spanish and French settlements, all Catholic, bounded the English on all sides. During the eighteenth century especially, the arrival of new immigrants from different cultures, including non-Anglican or dissenting preachers, led to religious toleration in practice and, increasingly, in law. The first Great Awakening, a colonies-wide religious revival of the 1730s and 1740s, spurred a flowering of new sects. Slowly a new pattern of religious liberty replaced the older European model of a state church and an official creed, even though at the time of Revolution, most colonies still had an established church, usually the Church of England, supported by taxes from members and nonmembers alike.

For the revolutionaries, political liberty was meaningless without religious liberty, and disestablishment, the separation of church and state, was necessary to guarantee freedom of the soul, the most precious of all liberties. Even before the Bill of Rights prohibited a state church, the framers of the Constitution had signaled their radical break with the past by refusing to require officeholders to meet a religious test, that is, to subscribe to certain religious beliefs—or even to believe at all. Earlier, the Virginia Statute for Religious Freedom (1786), the model for much of our language about religious liberty, made clear that the state would not support any churches—or Christianity more generally—much less one faith. Thomas Jefferson, proud author of the law, argued that religion must be protected from the state, and the state from religion, because it was so essential to mankind's happiness and well-being. True religion could spread only by reason and persuasion, never by governmental edict. The First Amendment, Jefferson believed, enshrined this principle by building a "wall of separation" between church and state.

The founding generation embraced the idea, but the nineteenth century proved that old habits were hard to discard. The First Amendment restrained only the central government, and not until 1833 did all state constitutions guarantee full freedom of religion and remove all remnants of earlier religious establishments. For much of the century, state officials promoted common Christian beliefs and practices—in the form of Bible verses and Christian symbols inscribed on public

buildings, for example—and state taxes supported missionaries and religious schools on the American frontier. This general but unofficial conformity weakened over time under pressure from waves of immigrants from Ireland, Germany, and other parts of Europe that did not share a strictly Protestant culture.

In the late nineteenth century, the United States became even more diverse in its population and religious practices, especially with new immigration from Italy, Greece, and eastern Europe, with their Catholic, Orthodox, and Jewish faiths, and from Asia. In response, some states rewrote their constitutions to prohibit such things as direct state aid for religious education. Other states responded by trying to reinforce the traditional, cozy relationship between Protestantism and the state, for instance, by denying Roman Catholics the legal right to establish state-approved schools or by refusing to allow Jehovah's Witnesses to preach on public streets. Denied relief from religious discrimination in state courts, dissenters began to turn to federal courts.

In the nineteenth century, few cases involving religion made it to the Supreme Court, but by the 1940s the justices were responding forcefully to the rights of religious dissenters. Two landmark cases, *Cantwell* v. *Connecticut* (1940) and *Everson* v. *Board of Education* (1947), established free exercise and separation of church and state, respectively, as part of the liberty protected by the Fourteenth Amendment's guarantee of due process of law. By incorporating them into the due process clause, the Court allowed for these protections to restrain both state and federal governments. For the justices, these freedoms, like other First Amendment rights, were essential to the democratic process. Without the liberty to discuss, write, believe, and act, Americans could not participate effectively in governing themselves.

The religion cases often were controversial because they challenged long-standing popular assumptions about the role of religion in public life. Then as now, Americans were an observant people, especially when compared to Europeans. Surveys from the 1940s and 1950s reported that nine in ten respondents believed in God, and five in ten attended worship regularly, figures still true today. The United States, as many citizens understood its history, was divinely blessed. Although keeping church and state separate was part of a prized heritage of liberty, many people believed it was acceptable for the government to honor God in schools, courthouses, and other public places. When the Supreme Court ruled that prescribed prayers did not belong in public schools, a firestorm of criticism erupted, challenging the decision and spurring a decades-long debate that continues today.

The 1950s were a tense decade for Americans. Freedom and security remained at risk a few short years after the defeat of Hitler. The military battlefields of World War II had been replaced by the Cold War, a struggle between two superpowers, the United States and the Soviet Union. The enemy this time was "Godless, atheistic communism," as it was called, an ideology opposed to democracy and one that officially repudiated religion. One response to this threat was to elevate the public role of religion. For example, Congress adopted the slogan "In God We Trust" as the national motto and added "under God" to the Pledge of Allegiance, in part to symbolize differences between the United States and Soviet Union.

In New York the state board of regents, which was responsible for public education, reflected the national mood by crafting a nondenominational prayer for schoolchildren to recite each morning. The prayer seemed innocuous—"Almighty God, we acknowledge our dependence upon Thee, and we beg Thy blessings upon us, our parents, our teachers, and our country"—but when a Long Island school district made it part of the school day, Lawrence Roth objected.

Roth was a manufacturing executive who was actively involved in a local committee for better schools. He also was Jewish, and although not observant personally, he was bothered by Christian symbols in the school his son attended. When the board decided to adopt the regents' prayer, Roth felt something had to be done: "If the state could tell us what to pray and when to pray," he said, "there was no stopping it." With other parents, he asked the board president, William Vitale, Jr., to withdraw the policy, but the board refused, claiming the prayer was voluntary. Children could sit quietly or leave the room, if parents provided an excuse. Board members, who earlier had refused to allow a discussion of Hanukkah during the Christmas season, could

not see the problem. The prayer was ecumenical—it included all religions—so who could object?

Roth requested the New York Civil Liberties Union (NYCLU) to sue the school board for violating the First Amendment's ban on an establishment of religion. In taking the case, the NYCLU asked Roth to find other individuals who were upset by the practice and who would become plaintiffs with him. Although he located more than fifty families who responded, in the end only five people withstood community pressure and joined the lawsuit. Stephen Engel, Roth's next-door neighbor, was one of them. Like the other litigants, he believed that religious instruction was the responsibility of parents, not the duty of the state.

Public sentiment mounted against Roth and the other plaintiffs. Opponents claimed they were anti-Christian, even anti-God, and accused them of being unpatriotic. Roth's two sons experienced anti-Semitic abuse from fellow classmates, and their teachers were antagonistic toward them. All five families received sacks of hate mail, snubs from friends, and threats of various sorts, from unemployment to arson and child kidnapping.

After losing in state courts, Roth, Engel, and the other petitioners appealed to the U.S. Supreme Court. Their argument before the high bench was straightforward: the state, by composing its own prayer for an institution with compulsory attendance, was engaged in an establishment of religion. In response to the school board's claim that the prayer was voluntary, the plaintiffs countered that the practice of isolating children who did not take part placed them under enormous peer pressure, thus making the prayer, in effect, compulsory for this vulnerable population.

The justices agreed. In June 1962, they ruled, 6 to 1, that the regents' prayer was unconstitutional because a government body had placed its "official stamp of approval" on an obvious religious activity. Justice Hugo Black rejected the view that the decision was anti-religion or anti-prayer. The framers of the First Amendment, he wrote, knew that "governmentally established religions and religious persecutions go hand in hand." The Bill of Rights ensured that, in America, government could not "shackle men's tongues to make them speak only the religious thoughts that government wanted them to speak and to pray only to the God that government wanted them to pray to."

A deafening protest greeted the decision in *Engel* v. *Vitale*. The public reaction was among the most hostile in the Court's history. Former President Herbert Hoover lamented the destruction of "a sacred American heritage," and the Catholic cardinal of New York blasted the justices for crippling the "very heart of the godly tradition in which America's children have so long been raised." Congressmen railed against the decision, some claiming that the Court had made God unconstitutional. States in the Bible Belt sought to defy the ruling by allowing teachers to decide whether to pray or not, a practice later ruled illegal.

The controversy did not fade quickly, as the plaintiffs soon discovered. Lawrence Roth received thousands of hate letters; one read, "If you don't like our God, then go behind the Iron Curtain where you belong, Kike, Hebe, Filth!" Threatening telephone calls hounded all the petitioners. Not all the threats were idle. Someone planted a bomb in the Roths' basement; another burned a cross in their lawn. Two busloads of protestors appeared in front of Engel's house, screaming and terrifying his children until neighbors with pitchforks and shovels forced the demonstrators off his property. Through all the public vilification, Roth and his fellow litigants remained satisfied with their role in protecting religious freedom, but their attorney was glad for another reason: "If the First Amendment came up today, it wouldn't pass," he noted thirty years after the decision, "Thank God we are stuck with it."

The debate over government and religion continues today, even though the Supreme Court has hewed close to its position in *Engel* v. *Vitale*. Subsequent decisions have stoked the fires of protest. Reciting the Lord's Prayer and reading from the Bible in public schools also were violations of the First Amendment's establishment clause, the justices decided the year after *Engel*. Other cases forbade public schools from endorsing a religious practice or belief, teaching theology or creationism, displaying the Ten Commandments or Bible verses, or using the facilities of religious schools or the services of religious officials.

In 1971, a threefold test emerged in *Lemon* v. *Kurtzman* to gauge whether a law concerning religion was constitutional: Did it have a secular, or nonreligious,

"I believe in an America where the separation of church and state is absolute—where no Catholic prelate would tell the President (should he be Catholic) how to act, and no Protestant minister would tell his parishioners for whom to vote—where no church or church school is granted any public funds or political preference—and where no man is denied public office merely because his religion differs from the President who might appoint him or the people who might elect him."

—John F. Kennedy, address to the Greater Houston
Ministerial Association, September 12, 1960

purpose? Did the law neither advance nor inhibit religion? Did it foster or encourage no excessive entanglement between church and state? If the answer to each of these questions was yes, then the law was constitutional; answering no to any of them cast doubt on the measure. More recently, the Court has relaxed this standard somewhat to allow laws that affect religious activity but are religiously neutral in their language, intent, and application. Church groups, for example, can use school facilities on an equal basis with nonreligious groups, and states can provide remedial or disability services to students in religious and public schools alike. Still, the basic principle remains: government must be strictly neutral on questions of religion; faith and belief are matters for the individual conscience alone.

This stance continues to cause unease among people who think government should promote morality. With the exception of Ireland, the United States is the most religious society in the Western world, with nearly 90 percent of Americans identifying themselves as religious believers, so why must government remain strictly neutral? Most people who make this argument do not seek an established church, but they desire public policies that foster religious beliefs, regardless of denomination. Some would go further, advocating that government should enshrine traditional, largely Protestant, values in laws governing moral choices.

Even though government support of religion generally might sound appealing, especially in times of unsettling social change, many strongly religious people oppose any level of government involvement. We are too diverse in our religious beliefs, they argue, to make this approach practical, even if it could be done constitutionally. They also note that the separation of church and state is responsible for the vitality of religion in the United States. Without an established faith, denominations and creeds compete with each other for membership, thus increasing the public presence of religion.

Not everyone accepts this conclusion. Some groups claim that a strict separation of church and state has resulted in hostility, not neutrality, toward religion. They want government to take positive steps to ensure that religious groups are not excluded from government funding solely because they are religious. In a case from 1995, for example, a question arose from the University of Virginia, founded by Thomas Jefferson: could a public university refuse to spend student-fee monies to support a magazine that advocated an evangelical Christian point of view, when this funding was available to support a wide range of other student publications, including some antagonistic to religion? In *Rosenberger* v. *University of Virginia*, the Supreme Court, by a 5-to-4 vote, ruled that the establishment clause did not bar the support as long as the distribution of funds was neutral and evenhanded, even though the magazine promoted a particular religious message. More recently, President George W. Bush's administration put into practice what it termed a "faith-based initiative" to allow religious groups to compete equally with other not-for-profit agencies to deliver government-funded social services, such as homeless shelters or child care. A religious group that receives these monies may not require participants to accept its beliefs and it cannot force them to join worship, but neither does it have to hide its religious convictions.

"Three such tests may be gleaned from our cases [to judge that a law does not violate the First Amendment's establishment clause]. First, the statute must have a secular legislative purpose; second, its principal or primary effect must be one that neither advances nor inhibits religion . . . ; finally, the statute must not foster 'an excessive government entanglement with religion.'"

—Chief Justice Warren Burger, *Lemon* v. *Kurtzman* (1971)

The modern debate about the meaning and purpose of the separation of church and state is dressed in new language, but it fundamentally is the same debate we have had since the adoption of the First Amendment. Competition of ideas, including religious ideas, was central to the thought of the framers. It was the free pursuit of ideas, no matter how strange they may seem to others, that promised truth—and from truth came liberty. The framers believed as well that truth came from the application of reason and logic, and they sought to ensure that government was powerless to interfere with its pursuit. Religion was necessary for democracy, they argued, but only if individual citizens had freedom of thought without any governmental pressure to believe certain things and disbelieve others. Here was the heart of their opposition to government entanglement with religion.

As a society we have accepted this view for practical as well as philosophical reasons. Competing religious groups realize that it is better to keep the government neutral in matter of religion than it is to have their opponents gain control over government. Today, we have more than 1,500 organized religious groups in the United States, representing all the world's faith traditions. How could government choose among them? Who is to say which religion, if any, holds such truth that government should endorse it and give it protection? Even some advocates of a faith-based initiative began to waver or lose enthusiasm when they learned that denominations they did not favor were eligible to compete for government grants.

We cannot base our understanding of the separation of church and state—or any other right—solely on the views of the framers, but neither should we dismiss them casually. The religious contention we witness today is an age-old problem. Official neutrality toward religion, we have learned, works both to enhance democratic government as well as to foster religious vitality. We have also discovered that the separation of church and state does not mean a denial of all public expressions of religion. What is new—or, at least, what is more pronounced now—is the presence in our society of all the world's religions. We are no longer a nation of Protestants, Catholics, and Jews, as sociologists described the United States in the 1950s and earlier. We are also a nation of Muslims, Buddhists, Confucians, Hindus, Sikhs, and countless other faith traditions, as well as millions of people who do not subscribe to any faith. How we respond to these new circumstances—how we define the relationship between church and state, as well how we understand the public role of religion—will help to determine whether our great experiment in liberty and democracy continues to thrive.

An Argument against State-Supported Religion

In 1785, the Virginia General Assembly considered a bill to levy an assessment, or general tax, to support teachers of Christian religions. The measure, supported by a group of citizens led by Patrick Henry, sought to use public funds to encourage a plural establishment, that is, a state that supported all Christian religions. Henry and others believed the law would help to create a virtuous citizenry.

James Madison and Thomas Jefferson opposed the bill because it violated their belief in the separation of church and state. In 1779, Jefferson had drafted the Virginia Act for Establishing Religious Freedom, but the general assembly had not adopted it. Madison submitted his "Memorial and Remonstrance against Religious Assessments" in 1785, in opposition to the tax bill, and the legislature then tabled the proposed tax and adopted Jefferson's bill for religious liberty.

The "Memorial and Remonstrance" remains a powerful argument against state-supported religion. In the three sections below, Madison argues that state power used to favor religion can also force people to conform to a particular religion (number 3). He then argues that it violates the principle of equality on which the new nation was founded (number 4). Finally, he believes it will destroy the harmony among religions that distinguished American experience from the religious warfare of Europe.

3. Because it is proper to take alarm at the first experiment on our liberties. We hold this prudent jealousy to be the first duty of Citizens, and one of the noblest characteristics of the late Revolution. The free men of America did not wait till usurped power had strengthened itself by exercise, and entangled the question in precedents. They saw all the consequences in the principle, and they avoided the consequences by denying the principle. We revere this lesson too much soon to forget it. Who does not see that the same authority which can establish Christianity, in exclusion of all other Religions, may establish with the same ease any particular sect of Christians, in exclusion of all other Sects? that the same authority which can force a citizen to contribute three pence only of his property for the support of any one establishment, may force him to conform to any other establishment in all cases whatsoever?

4. Because the Bill violates the equality which ought to be the basis of every law, and which is more indispensible, in proportion as the validity or expediency of any law is more liable to be impeached. If "all men are by nature equally free and independent," all men are to be considered as entering into Society on equal conditions; as relinquishing no more, and therefore retaining no less, one than another, of their natural rights. Above all are they to be considered as retaining an "equal title to the free exercise of Religion according to the dictates of Conscience." Whilst we assert for ourselves a freedom to embrace, to profess and to observe the Religion which we believe to be of divine origin, we cannot deny an equal freedom to those whose minds have not yet yielded to the evidence which has convinced us. If this freedom be abused, it is an offence against God, not against man: To God, therefore, not to man, must an account of it be rendered. As the Bill violates equality by subjecting some to peculiar burdens, so it violates the same principle, by granting to others peculiar exemptions. Are the Quakers and Menonists [Mennonites] the only sects who think a compulsive support of their Religions unnecessary and unwarrantable? Can their piety alone be entrusted with the care of public worship? Ought their Religions to be endowed above all others with extraordinary privileges by which proselytes may be enticed from all others? We think too favorably of the justice and good sense of these denominations to believe that they either covet pre-eminences over their fellow citizens or that they will be seduced by them from the common opposition to the measure....

11. Because it will destroy that moderation and harmony which the forbearance of our laws to intermeddle with Religion has produced among its several sects. Torrents of blood have been split in the old world, by vain attempts of the secular arm, to extinguish Religious discord, by proscribing all difference in Religious opinion. Time has at length revealed the true remedy. Every relaxation of narrow and rigorous policy, wherever it has been tried, has been found to assuage the disease. The American Theatre has exhibited proofs that equal and compleat liberty, if it does not wholly eradicate it, sufficiently destroys its malignant influence on the health and prosperity of the State. If with the salutary effects of this system under our own eyes, we begin to contract the bounds of Religious freedom, we know no name that will too severely reproach our folly. At least let warning be taken at the first fruits of the threatened innovation. The very appearance of the Bill has transformed "that Christian forbearance, love and charity," which of late mutually prevailed, into animosities and jealousies, which may not soon be appeased. What mischiefs may not be dreaded, should this enemy to the public quiet be armed with the force of a law?

"A Wall between Church and State"

A 1941 New Jersey law authorized boards of education to reimburse parents, including those whose children went to Catholic schools, for the cost of transportation to and from school. Arch Everson was a Trenton resident and taxpayer who believed this practice violated the First Amendment's establishment clause. By a 5-to-4 vote, the U.S. Supreme Court did not agree, and it upheld the New Jersey law. Writing for the majority in Everson v. Board of Education *(1947), Justice Hugo Black cited James Madison's "Memorial and Remonstrance" of 1785, in which Madison successfully fought against a tax to support a state church in Virginia. In his opinion, Black argued that the First Amendment requires the state to be strictly neutral, neither supporting nor inhibiting religion, but it does not require the state to be an adversary of religion.* Everson *remains good law today.*

The "establishment of religion" clause of the First Amendment means at least this: Neither a state nor the Federal Government can set up a church. Neither can pass laws which aid one religion, aid all religions, or prefer one religion over another. Neither can force nor influence a person to go to or to remain away from church against his will or force him to profess a belief or disbelief in any religion. No person can be punished for entertaining or professing religious beliefs or disbeliefs, for church attendance or non-attendance. No tax in any amount, large or small, can be levied to support any religious activities or institutions, whatever they may be called, or whatever from they may adopt to teach or practice religion. Neither a state nor the Federal Government can, openly or secretly, participate in the affairs of any religious organizations or groups and vice versa. In the words of Jefferson, the clause against establishment of religion by law was intended to erect "a wall of separation between Church and State."...

[The First] Amendment requires the state to be neutral in its relations with groups of religious believers and non-believers; it does not require the state to be their adversary. State power is no more to be used so as to handicap religions, than it is to favor them....

The First Amendment has erected a wall between church and state. That wall must be kept high and impregnable. We could not approve the slightest breach. New Jersey has not breached it here.

CHAPTER 6

The Right to Freedom of Speech

Free speech is our most fundamental—and our most contested—right. It is an essential freedom because it is how we protect all of our other rights and liberties. If we could not speak openly about the policies and actions of government, then we would have no effective way to participate in the democratic process or protest when we believed governmental behavior threatened our security or our freedom. Although Americans agree that free speech is central to democratic government, we disagree sharply about what we mean by *speech* and about where the right begins and ends. Speech clearly includes words, but does it also include conduct or symbols? Certainly, we have the right to criticize the government, but can we also advocate its overthrow? Does the right to free speech allow us to incite hate or use foul language in public?

The framers of the Bill of Rights understood the importance of free expression and protected it under the First Amendment: "Congress shall make no law…abridging the freedom of speech." Both English history and their own colonial past had taught them to value this right, but their definition of free speech was much more limited than ours. Less than a decade after the amendment's ratification, Congress passed the Sedition Act of 1798, making it a crime to criticize the government. Many citizens believed government could forbid speech that threatened public order, as witnessed by numerous early-nineteenth-century laws restricting speech against slavery. During the Civil War, thousands of antiwar protestors were arrested on the theory that the First Amendment did not protect disloyal speech. Labor unrest in the 1800s and 1890s brought similar restraints on the right of politically unpopular groups, such as socialists, to criticize government's failure to protect working people from the ills of industrialization and economic depression.

Freedom of speech did not become a subject of important court cases until the twentieth century when the Supreme Court announced one of the most famous principles in constitutional law, the clear and present danger test. The test was straightforward: government could not restrict speech unless it posed a known, immediate threat to public safety. The standard sought to balance the need for order with the right to speak freely. At its heart was the question of proximity, or closeness, and degree. If speech brought about an action that was dangerous under the immediate circumstances, such as falsely yelling "fire" in a crowded theater, then it did not enjoy First Amendment protection. With this case, *Schenck* v. *United States* (1919), the Court began a decades-long process of seeking the right balance between free speech and public safety.

The balance, at first, was almost always on the side of order and security. Another case decided in 1919, *Debs* v. *United States,* illustrates how restrictive the test could be. Eugene Debs was a labor leader from Indiana who had run

> *"The free communication of thoughts and opinions is one of the invaluable rights of man; and every citizen may freely speak, write and print on any subject, being responsible for the abuse of that liberty."*
>
> —Pennsylvania Constitution (1790)

for President four times as the candidate of the Socialist Party of America, once polling more than one million votes. At a June 1918 rally in Chicago, while U.S. troops were fighting in World War I, he told the working-class crowd, "You need to know you are fit for something better than slavery and cannon fodder." He was sentenced under an existing federal statute to twenty years in prison for inciting disloyalty and obstruction of military recruitment, which the Supreme Court upheld.

For the next five decades, the Court wrestled with the right balance between speech and order. Much of what defined freedom of speech emerged from challenges to the government's ability to regulate or punish political protest. Each case brought a new set of circumstances that allowed the justices an opportunity to modify or extend the clear and present danger test. Many decisions recognized the abstract right of individuals to speak freely, but each one hedged this right in important ways. Always in the background were conditions that pointed to disorder, dissension, and danger—the Great Depression, World War II, and the Cold War, among them—so the justices were cautious in expanding a right that would expose America to greater threats. These cases, however, gradually introduced a new perspective on the value of free speech in a democracy, namely, the belief that truth is best reached by the free trade in ideas.

The belief that society is best served by a marketplace of ideas open to all opinions, no matter how radical, ultimately prevailed. In 1927, the Court had endorsed what came to be called the bad tendency test: if officials believed speech was likely to lead to a bad result, such as urging people to commit a violent act, it was not protected under the First Amendment even if no violence occurred. By 1969, however, similar facts produced a different outcome. Ku Klux Klan members in Ohio invited a television station to film their rally. Waving firearms, they shouted racist and anti-Semitic slurs and threatened to march on Congress before their leader was arrested and later convicted under a state law banning speech that had a tendency to incite violence. The Supreme Court overturned his conviction in

Eugene V. Debs and Ben Hanford were the Socialist Party of America's candidates for President and Vice President in 1904 and 1908. Debs wanted to reorganize American society, telling workingmen that if they would "march together, vote together and fight together," they would secure their rights. Many Americans viewed the radical reform platform of the socialists as a threat to national security.

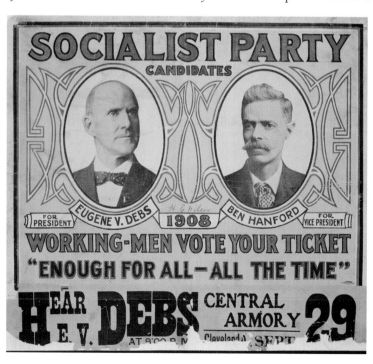

Brandenburg v. *Ohio* and established the rule still in effect today: the First Amendment protects the right to advocate the use of force or violence, but it does not safeguard speech likely to incite or produce an immediate unlawful act. The *Brandenburg* test has allowed Nazis to march, Klan members to hold rallies, and other extremist groups to promote views far outside the mainstream of public opinion. With few exceptions—fighting words and obscenity, for example—government today cannot regulate the content of speech.

Even as society was coming to accept a wide range of political ideas, opposition to an unpopular war raised other questions about the limits and forms of free speech. By the mid- to late 1960s, the Vietnam War divided Americans. Although many citizens supported the use of U.S. troops to stop communism in Asia, a growing minority, including many draft-age young people, took to the streets to oppose the war. The protestors did not limit their efforts to anti-war speeches; they also wore shirts with obscene slogans, burned draft cards, and desecrated American flags. Using these symbols to protest, they argued, was a form of free speech. Soon, the Supreme Court faced the question squarely in a case involving a youthful protestor from the nation's heartland: is symbolic speech—messages using symbols or signs, not words—protected by the First Amendment?

The first large-scale American demonstration against the Vietnam War occurred in November 1965 when more than 25,000 protestors converged on the nation's capital. Fifty Iowans made the long bus ride, and on the way home they decided to make their opposition known locally by wearing black armbands to work and school. One member of the peace contingent was Lorena Tinker, the wife of a Des Moines Methodist minister and mother of five children. Mary Beth Tinker, a thirteen-year-old eighth grader, followed her mother's suggestion and became one of a handful of local public school students who wore this symbol of protest to school. This act placed her in the middle of a national controversy about student rights and freedom of expression.

In many ways, Mary Beth was a normal eighth grader. She was a good student who enjoyed singing, spending time with her friends, and taking part in church activities. What made her different was a commitment to social justice, a passion encouraged by her parents, both of whom were known for their activism. Her parents wanted their children to share their moral and social values, and Mary Beth responded eagerly to their invitation to participate with them. By the time she became a teenager, she already had attended her first protest, accompanying her father to a rally about fair housing.

Mary Beth Tinker, her brother, John, and a handful of Des Moines students planned their demonstration for December 16, 1965. The students' aim was not to protest the war but to mourn its casualties, Vietnamese and American, and to show support for proposed peace talks. School officials, however, promised to suspend anyone who came to school wearing the armbands, and the school principal suspended Mary Beth and sent her home. She was one of five students suspended that day for wearing the offending cloth. Significantly, the school ban applied only to armbands, in other words, to students who opposed the Vietnam War; a number of students that day wore an array of other symbols, including the Iron Cross, a Nazi medal.

The War Production Board Office for Emergency Management produced this poster during World War II to encourage American citizens to be wary of betraying sensitive information to the enemy. It epitomizes the inherent conflict between the free-speech rights of Americans and the necessity for protecting national security.

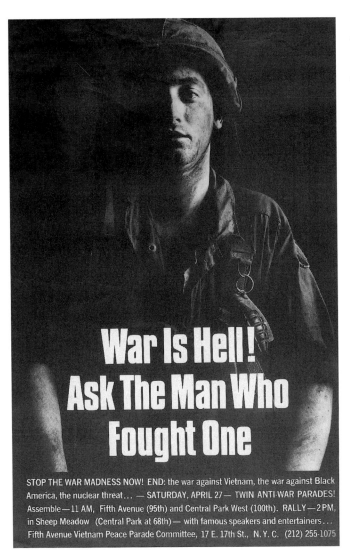

STOP THE WAR MADNESS NOW! END: the war against Vietnam, the war against Black America, the nuclear threat… — SATURDAY, APRIL 27 — TWIN ANTI-WAR PARADES! Assemble — 11 AM, Fifth Avenue (95th) and Central Park West (100th). RALLY — 2 PM, in Sheep Meadow (Central Park at 68th) — with famous speakers and entertainers… Fifth Avenue Vietnam Peace Parade Committee, 17 E. 17th St., N.Y.C. (212) 255-1075

The Fifth Avenue Vietnam Peace Parade Committee produced this poster to advertise an antiwar march in New York City. Some veterans found such protests distasteful or even disloyal to the servicemen who had died in the conflict, while others supported the protestors' constitutionally protected right to free speech.

When the school board upheld the suspensions, the Tinkers persuaded the Iowa Civil Liberties Union to take the case to federal court. Two lower federal courts agreed with the school's action, rebuffing the argument that the policy violated the First Amendment guarantee of free speech. The Supreme Court decided otherwise. In its 7-to-2 decision, announced in February 1969, the justices held that the wearing of armbands is a symbolic act akin to "pure speech" and protected by the right to free expression. The protesting students posed no threat to the order required for effective instruction, nor did the wearing of armbands interfere with the school's educational mission. In this instance, the balance between order and liberty was weighted on the side of the First Amendment. Students and teachers, the Court concluded, do not "shed their constitutional rights to freedom of speech or expression at the schoolhouse gate."

Symbolic speech has been the focus of some of our greatest constitutional drama. Words may be powerful and provocative, but symbols are often more inflammatory because they are visual and evoke an emotional response. We live in an age when we use pictures and symbols to convey important messages, whether in politics or the marketplace. For these reasons, the Supreme Court's recognition of symbolic speech as a right protected by the First Amendment has been a significant development.

Twenty-five years after Mary Beth Tinker put on her armband in remembrance of the war dead, *Life* magazine featured a handful of civil liberties cases to celebrate the bicentennial of the Bill of Rights. Mary Beth's case was included, even though the rights of students remained, and still are, more limited than those of adult citizens. But her actions as an eighth grader expanded our conception of constitutionally protected speech to include the symbols we use to express our convictions.

More than most other recent decisions, cases involving symbolic speech have revealed how contentious the right of free speech remains in our society. In 1989, the Supreme Court ruled that the First Amendment protected individuals who burned the American flag in protest. This decision was highly controversial, and it has resulted in numerous attempts to amend the Constitution to protect the flag and, in effect, limit speech in this circumstance. The outcome of this effort is uncertain, but the debate raises important questions: What role does this right play in our democracy? How does it contribute to our liberty as Americans?

The right to speak freely, without restraint, is essential to democratic government because it helps us develop better laws and policies through challenge, rebuttal, and debate. When we all have the ability to speak in the public forum, offensive opinions can be combated with an opposing argument, a more inclusive approach, a more effective idea. We tolerate offensive speech and protect the right to speak even for people who would deny it to us because we believe that exposing their thoughts and opinions to open debate will result in the discovery of truth. This principle is an old one in Western thought. U.S. Supreme Court Justice Oliver Wendell Holmes's dissent in *Abrams* v. *United States,* a 1919 case suppressing free speech, is a classic statement of this view: "The best test of truth is the power of thought to get itself accepted in the competition of the market, and that truth is the only ground upon which [the public's] wishes safely can be carried out."

Governmental actions to deny differing points of view, even distasteful or unpopular opinions, rob us of the range of ideas that might serve the interests of society more effectively. In a case decided almost a decade before *Tinker* v. *Des Moines,* the Supreme Court found this rationale especially applicable to the classroom. "The Nation's future," the justices wrote, "depends upon leaders trained through wide exposure to that robust exchange of ideas which discovers truth out of a multitude of tongues." As a nation, we are willing to live with the often bitter conflict over ideas because we believe it will lead to truth and to improved lives for all citizens. We recognize that freedom of speech is the first freedom of democracy, as the English poet John Milton argued during his own seventeenth-century struggle to gain this right: "Give me the liberty to know, to utter, and to argue freely according to conscience, above all liberties." The ability to speak freely allows us to pursue truth, to challenge falsehoods, to correct mistakes—all are necessary for a healthy society.

Free speech also reflects a commitment to individual freedom and autonomy, the right to decide for ourselves and to pursue our own destiny. Throughout our history, we have been so committed to individual choice that many foreign observers believe it is our most characteristic trait. We see it reflected daily in everything from advertising slogans—"Have It Your Way"— to fashion statements, but fail to recognize how closely freedom is tied to the right to speak freely. Free speech guarantees us an individual voice, no matter how far removed our opinions and beliefs are from mainstream society. With this voice we are free to contribute as individuals to the marketplace of ideas or a marketplace of goods, as well as to decide how and under what circumstances we will join with others to decide social and governmental policies.

A commitment to free speech, of course, will not resolve all conflict, not if our history is any guide. The debate is most contentious during times of war or other moments when national security is at stake. Even then—perhaps especially then—we will continue to fight over words and symbols because they express our deepest hopes and our most worrisome fears. This contest over what speech is acceptable and what is not has been a constant theme of our past. Rarely do these struggles produce a neat consensus. More often, intemperate rhetoric and bitter division have been their legacy, and this angry clamor is one of the basic noises of our history. What makes the struggle to protect free speech worthwhile is its ability to serve as a lever for change. When we practice our right to speak openly, we are defining the contours of our democracy. It is messy work, but through it, we keep the Constitution alive and, with it, our dreams of a just society.

"Restriction of free thought and free speech is the most dangerous of all subversions. It is the one un-American act that could most easily defeat us."

—Justice William O. Douglas, "The One Un-American Act" (1953)

"Free Trade in Ideas"

Jacob Abrams was a Russian immigrant and anarchist convicted of violating the Sedition Act of 1918, which made it a crime to advocate anything that would impede the war effort during World War I. In 1917 Justice Oliver Wendell Holmes, Jr., had written the Court's opinion in Schenck v. United States, *upholding similar convictions because Congress had a right to regulate speech that posed a "clear and present danger" to public safety. But by the time Abrams's appeal reached the Court in 1919, Holmes had modified his views. Disturbed by antiradical hysteria, he dissented from the majority's decision upholding Abrams's conviction in* Abrams v. United States. *His eloquent discussion of the connection between freedom of speech and the search for truth soon became the standard used by the Supreme Court to judge free speech cases until* Brandenberg v. Ohio *in 1972. The First Amendment, Holmes reasoned, protected the expression of all opinions "unless they so imminently threaten immediate interference with the lawful and pressing purposes of the law that an immediate check is required to save the country."*

But as against dangers peculiar to war, as against others, the principle of the right to free speech is always the same. It is only the present danger of immediate evil or an intent to bring it about that warrants Congress in setting a limit to the expression of opinion where private rights are not concerned. Congress certainly cannot forbid all effort to change the mind of the country. Now nobody can suppose that the surreptitious publishing of a silly leaflet by an unknown man, without more, would present any immediate danger that its opinions would hinder the success of the government arms or have any appreciable tendency to do so....

Persecution for the expression of opinions seems to me perfectly logical. If you have no doubt of your premises or your power and want a certain result with all your heart you naturally express your wishes in law and sweep away all opposition. To allow opposition by speech seems to indicate that you think the speech impotent, as when a man says that he has squared the circle, or that you do not care whole heartedly for the result, or that you doubt either your power or your premises. But when men have realized that time has upset many fighting faiths, they may come to believe even more than they believe the very foundations of their own conduct that the ultimate good desired is better reached by free trade in ideas—that the best test of truth is the power of the thought to get itself accepted in the competition of the market, and that truth is the only ground upon which their wishes safely can be carried out. That at any rate is the theory of our Constitution. It is an experiment, as all life is an experiment. Every year if not every day we have to wager our salvation upon some prophecy based upon imperfect knowledge. While that experiment is part of our system I think that we should be eternally vigilant against attempts to check the expression of opinions that we loathe and believe to be fraught with death, unless they so imminently threaten immediate interference with the lawful and pressing purposes of the law that an immediate check is required to save the country.... Only the emergency that makes it immediately dangerous to leave the correction of evil counsels to time warrants making any exception to the sweeping command, "Congress shall make no law abridging the freedom of speech." Of course I am speaking only of expressions of opinion and exhortations, which were all that were uttered here, but I regret that I cannot put into more impressive words my belief that in their conviction upon this indictment the defendants were deprived of their rights under the Constitution of the United States.

"Malicious Words" versus "Free Communication"

In response to fears about imminent wars with France in 1798, the Federalist-controlled Congress passed a series of four acts known collectively as the Alien and Sedition Acts. Section 2 of the Sedition Act made it a crime to make defamatory statements about the government or President. (Sedition is an action inciting resistance to lawful authority and tending to lead to the overthrow of the government.) The act was designed to suppress political opposition. Its passage by Congress reveals how limited the definition of the right of free speech was for some Americans only a few years after the ratification of the First Amendment.

Sec. 2.... That if any person shall write, print, utter, or publish, or shall cause or procure to be written, printed, uttered or published, or shall knowingly and willingly assist or aid in writing, printing, uttering or publishing any false, scandalous and malicious writing or writings against the government of the United States, or either house of the Congress of the United States, or the President of the United States, with intent to defame the said government, or either house of the said Congress, or the said President, or to bring them, or either of them, into contempt or disrepute; or to excite against them, or either or any of them, the hatred of the good people of the United States, or to stir up sedition within the United States, or to excite any unlawful combinations therein, for opposing or resisting any law of the United Sates, or any act of the President of the United States, done in pursuance of any such law, or of the powers in him vested by the constitution of the United States, or to resist, oppose, or defeat any such law or act, or to aid, encourage or abet any hostile designs of any foreign nation against the United States, their people or government, then such person, being thereof convicted before any court of the United States having jurisdiction thereof, shall be punished by a fine not exceeding two thousand dollars, and by imprisonment not exceeding two years.

James Madison, congressman from Virginia, and Thomas Jefferson, the sitting Vice President, secretly drafted resolutions protesting the Sedition Act as unconstitutional. The Virginia and Kentucky legislatures passed these resolutions in 1798. Both resolutions especially pointed to the act's violation of First Amendment protections, as seen in the Virginia Resolution here.

Resolved,... That the General Assembly doth particularly protest against the palpable and alarming infractions of the Constitution in the two late cases of the "Alien and Sedition Acts" passed at the last session of Congress; the first of which exercises a power no where delegated to the federal government, and which by uniting legislative and judicial powers to those of executive, subverts the general principles of free government; as well as the particular organization, and positive provisions of the federal constitution; and the other of which acts, exercises in like manner, a power not delegated by the constitution, but on the contrary, expressly and positively forbidden by one of the amendments thereto; a power, which more than any other, ought to produce universal alarm, because it is levelled against that right of freely examining public characters and measures, and of free communication among the people thereon, which has ever been justly deemed, the only effectual guardian of every other right.

That this state having by its Convention, which ratified the federal Constitution, expressly declared, that among other essential rights, "the Liberty of Conscience and of the Press cannot be cancelled, abridged, restrained, or modified by any authority of the United States," and from its extreme anxiety to guard these rights from every possible attack of sophistry or ambition, having with other states, recommended an amendment for that purpose, which amendment was, in due time, annexed to the Constitution; it would mark a reproachable inconsistency, and criminal degeneracy, if an indifference were now shewn, to the most palpable violation of one of the Rights, thus declared and secured; and to the establishment of a precedent which may be fatal to the other.

The Sedition Act expired in 1801 but not until a number of the Federalists' opponents, including Congressman Matthew Lyon of Vermont, had been convicted of violating the law. Today, historians consider the Sedition Act to have been a gross misuse of government power. In 1798, the Kentucky Resolutions focused on the rights of states to determine the limits of free speech.

Resolved, that it is true as a general principle, and is also expressly declared by one of the amendments to the Constitution, that "the powers not delegated to the United States by the Constitution, nor prohibited by it to the States, are reserved to the States respectively, or to the people;" and that no power over the freedom of religion, freedom of speech, or freedom of the press being delegated to the United States by the Constitution, nor prohibited by it to the States, all lawful powers respecting the same did of right remain, and were reserved to the States or the people: that thus was manifested their determination to retain to themselves the right of judging how far the licentiousness of speech and of the press may be abridged without lessening their useful freedom, and how far those abuses which cannot be separated from their use should be tolerated, rather than the use be destroyed.

CHAPTER 7

The Right to Freedom of the Press

The founders of the United States believed a free press was a prerequisite for a free society. James Madison, often called the Father of the Constitution, said it was "one of the great bulwarks of liberty." Thomas Jefferson said if he had a choice between government without newspapers or newspapers without government, he would choose newspapers. It was not mere coincidence, then, that the First Amendment guarantees the right to a free press—"Congress shall make no law abridging freedom of the press"—and links it closely to the right to free speech. To the founders, they were twin pillars of American freedom.

The relationship between a free press and liberty was not an issue before the invention of movable type in the mid-1400s. The printing press provided rulers a new way to spread their authority more quickly and over a wider area, but it also gave opponents the same ability to criticize government. To minimize this threat, the British Crown licensed printers and required official approval before publication. (This form of censorship is commonly called prior restraint.) Even when the licensing law expired in England in 1694, it continued in the colonies, thereby allowing officials to suppress ideas or information they considered harmful. Printers could be punished criminally, for example, if they published unapproved criticisms of the church or state.

During the struggle with Great Britain, colonists used pamphlets, broadsides, and newspapers to make their protests, debate their differences, and rally support for independence. The press was valuable to the revolutionary cause because the printed word reached a much wider audience than sermons, speeches, or letters, the other main avenues for communication. As a result, constitutions in the young states included the right to a free press as a limit on governmental power. The revolutionary generation believed this right was part of their heritage as Englishmen. Greater press freedom had been one result of the seventeenth-century struggle between king and Parliament for supremacy, and the colonists thought the right extended to them through their charters of settlement. An important commentary on the common law at the time of independence declared that "the liberty of the press is...essential to the nature of a free state...[and] consists in laying no previous restraints upon publications." This understanding served as the foundation for the First Amendment protection.

As with free speech, however, people disagreed almost immediately with the meaning of this right. The 1790s was an especially troublesome decade for press freedom. The nation was on the brink of war with France when Congress passed the Sedition Act in 1798 to punish journalists who criticized, or libeled, the government. Under the claim of protecting national security, more than twenty-five people went to jail, convicted of criminal libel. Critics charged the

> *"That the freedom of the press is one of the great bulwarks of liberty, and can never be restrained but by despotick governments."*
>
> —Virginia Declaration of Rights (1776)

In August 1775, following the battles of Lexington and Concord, King George III declared that the colonies were officially in rebellion. He decreed that any British subject who failed to report information about rebellion and sedition would be severely punished.

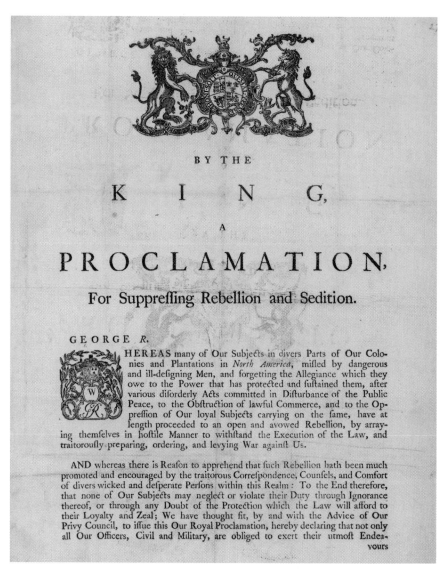

BY THE

KING,

A

PROCLAMATION,

For Suppressing Rebellion and Sedition.

GEORGE *R.*

HEREAS many of Our Subjects in divers Parts of Our Colonies and Plantations in *North America*, misled by dangerous and ill-designing Men, and forgetting the Allegiance which they owe to the Power that has protected and sustained them, after various disorderly Acts committed in Disturbance of the Public Peace, to the Obstruction of lawful Commerce, and to the Oppression of Our loyal Subjects carrying on the same, have at length proceeded to an open and avowed Rebellion, by arraying themselves in hostile Manner to withstand the Execution of the Law, and traitorously preparing, ordering, and levying War against Us.

AND whereas there is Reason to apprehend that such Rebellion hath been much promoted and encouraged by the traitorous Correspondence, Counsels, and Comfort of divers wicked and desperate Persons within this Realm: To the End therefore, that none of Our Subjects may neglect or violate their Duty through Ignorance thereof, or through any Doubt of the Protection which the Law will afford to their Loyalty and Zeal; We have thought fit, by and with the Advice of Our Privy Council, to issue this Our Royal Proclamation, hereby declaring that not only all Our Officers, Civil and Military, are obliged to exert their utmost Endeavours

government with using its power to put down political opposition, but the act expired before the Supreme Court could consider its constitutionality.

The nineteenth century witnessed an explosion in the number and spread of newspapers and magazines. This rapid increase in publications and a subsequent decline in the price of a newspaper—one penny by the 1850s—changed the nature of journalism. Attacks on parties and politicians declined in favor of human-interest and crime stories. The emergence of the Associated Press, a news-gathering collective, in 1848 and Western Union's transcontinental telegraph in 1861 opened a national market for news. By the end of the century, newspapers had become big businesses, with rival publishers competing for a share of an expanding audience. The power of the press could be seen during the Spanish-American War in 1898, when newspapers owned by William Randolph Hearst and Joseph Pulitzer published vivid accounts of Spanish atrocities in Cuba to stir war fever. Such news sold papers, as did shocking stories about the sordid side of private lives. The popular term for this kind of reporting was "muckraking," but in fact many of the scandalous accounts of the day exposed official graft and corruption, as well as the dire living conditions in urban slums. Some newspapers claimed to avoid the excesses of investigative reporting—the *New York Times,* for example, sought to be objective by offering only "All the News That's Fit to Print"—but increasingly, journalism was about creating news and not simply reporting it.

This change brought calls for legal restraints, which went unheeded because the popular press enjoyed wide readership. More at risk were papers that challenged the power of the state. Many were progressive and socialist publications that campaigned for reforms considered extreme at the time—labor laws, for example—but which were adopted in later decades. State laws sought to control these publications under "criminal anarchy" statutes, especially after an anarchist assassinated President William McKinley in 1901. Communist party and other leftist newspapers were targets, as were ethnic newspapers, because they challenged strongly held American values. World War I brought further concern about the press, especially when newspapers published items thought to threaten national security, even if the government's definition of threats was overly broad. It was not long before serious-minded people were asking whether the press was too free or too powerful: what, exactly, did the First Amendment protect?

The Supreme Court considered this important question in the early 1930s. An anti-Semitic publisher from the upper Midwest printed a scandal sheet filled with ethnic slurs, and the government sought to shut the paper down. Did hate-mongers enjoy the protection of the First Amendment? For the first time since the ratification of the Bill of Rights, the justices faced squarely the question of what freedom of the press means.

Corruption was common in Minneapolis during the 1920s, as it was in numerous other American cities. It was the era of Prohibition; bootlegging, speakeasies, and gambling were common, and to protect their illegal interests, gangsters paid off local police and politicians. In Minneapolis, the mayor, chief of police, and district attorney were all reputed to be on the mob's payroll. The city's respectable newspapers ignored these rumors, and scandal sheets soon filled the void, luridly describing the prostitution, gambling, and sexual adventures of the city's upper crust who, many people believed, profited from crime and disorder.

The *Twin City Reporter* was one of these tabloids, or rags. Its owners, Howard Guildford and Jay Near, practiced a brand of journalism that teetered on the edge of legality and propriety. They had a nose for corruption, but exposing wrongdoing was frequently a way to further their own self-interests. Jay Near was a pen for hire. His favorite targets were the elites of society, the rich and powerful, whom he always portrayed in the worst light. At the *Reporter,* he found a paper willing to pay for his anti-Semitic, antiblack, and antilabor screeds. For several years, Guildford and Near plied their trade, bribing police for tip-offs and publishing stories under headlines such as "Smooth Minneapolis Doctor with Woman in St. Paul Hotel" and "White Slavery Trade: Well-Known Local Man Is Ruining Women and Living Off Their

An angel walks across the wires of the newly completed transcontinental telegraph, carrying the first coast-to-coast telegram, an appeal for national unity. The cartoon ran in Harper's Weekly *in 1861. The telegraph made it possible for news to travel quickly across the country and made freedom of the press more important than before.*

THE FIRST TELEGRAPHIC MESSAGE FROM CALIFORNIA.

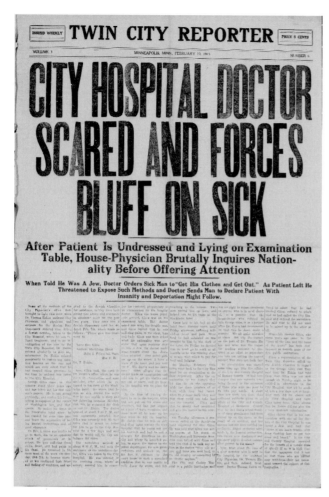

TWIN CITY REPORTER

ISSUED WEEKLY   PRICE 6 CENTS

VOLUME 1   MINNEAPOLIS, MINN., FEBRUARY 19, 1915   NUMBER 6

CITY HOSPITAL DOCTOR SCARED AND FORCES BLUFF ON SICK

After Patient Is Undressed and Lying on Examination Table, House-Physician Brutally Inquires Nationality Before Offering Attention

When Told He Was A Jew, Doctor Orders Sick Man to "Get His Clothes and Get Out." As Patient Left He Threatened to Expose Such Methods and Doctor Sends Man to Declare Patient With Insanity and Deportation Might Follow.

Sensational newspaper headlines reveal the pervasive nature of the xenophobia (fear of foreigners) that swept the United States in the World War I era. Jews, Catholics, and blacks were particular targets, but so were members of ethnic minorities.

Earnings." Minority groups and most institutions were attacked as well, usually in crude and hostile terms.

By 1917, the two men tired of their work and left Minneapolis, only to return ten years later with another entry in the weekly newspaper game. They created the *Saturday Press* and, for their first issue, made plans to report on an alliance with police that allowed the current owner of the *Twin City Reporter* to run an illegal gambling joint. The police chief got wind of their scheme and shut down the paper before it could publish the story. His authority for this action was simply the power of his office.

When the *Saturday Press* finally appeared on newsstands, it reported on mob threats and official misconduct. In retaliation, Guildford was gunned down by two assailants. While recovering, he and Near put out an issue that spewed forth hate and bitterness, blaming Jewish mobsters for the corruption and violence that infected the city. "There have been too many men in this city and especially those in official life, who have been taking orders and suggestions from JEW GANGSTERS. . . . It is Jew, Jew, Jew," they wrote, "as long as one cares to comb over the records."

The diatribe persuaded the county attorney, later a three-term governor, to "put out of business forever the *Saturday Press* and other sensational weeklies." He relied upon a 1925 state law, known as the "gag law," that declared such newspapers to be public nuisances and stopped them from publishing unless the stories were not only true but also "published with good motive and for justifiable ends." A local judge granted an injunction, a legal order forbidding Guildford and Near from distributing any paper that attacked public officials. The order was upheld on appeal by the Minnesota Supreme Court, which defended freedom of the press as an ideal even as it denied the *Saturday Press* a right to publish. "In Minnesota," the state chief justice wrote, "no agency can hush the sincere and honest voice of the press, but our [state] constitution was never intended to protect malice, scandal, and defamation when untrue or published with bad motives or without justifiable ends." Truth alone was not a defense: "There is no constitutional right to publish a fact merely because it is true," the court declared. The law protected the press's liberty, not its right to offend.

Near sought help for an appeal to federal courts from two unlikely allies—Roger Baldwin, liberal founder of the American Civil Liberties Union, a new organization dedicated to promoting individual rights, and Robert McCormick, the conservative publisher of the *Chicago Tribune*. Baldwin especially disagreed with the *Saturday Press*'s content and style, whereas McCormick shared Near's anticommunism and bigotry against immigrants. McCormick and Baldwin agreed on one thing, however—the First Amendment gave Near the right to publish without government censorship.

The Supreme Court decided *Near v. Minnesota* in 1931. Near won. Writing for the 5-to-4 majority, Chief Justice Charles Evans Hughes announced his view of the Minnesota law: "This is the essence of censorship." He acknowledged that the press could make false accusations and damage reputations, but the proper remedy was to sue later under libel laws for monetary damages. It harmed democracy to give government the power to censor because government was often a target of the criticism it sought to suppress. Without the vigorous public debate spurred by the press, truth would be hard to find and liberty would suffer. Of course, the freedom to publish was not absolute, the chief justice continued. During war, for example, government could restrain the press in the interests of national security, but Near's case did not pose this threat. The government could not prevent him from publishing, no matter how offensive or reckless his views were.

After the decision, the *Saturday Press* reappeared under a new masthead, "The Paper That Refused to Stay Gagged." Jay Near's triumph notwithstanding, the newspaper folded within twelve months; two years later, he died. His legacy did not come from his sensational stories but from the news he made while pursuing a right to publish his often reckless charges. The case involving his paper established the legal principle that has defined freedom of the press in the United States ever since. The right to a free press means the government cannot censor what the press chooses to publish. Once the press has information it considers newsworthy, the government seldom, if ever, can prohibit its dissemination. At the heart of the First Amendment, in brief, lies hostility to prior restraint—the idea that government officials must approve a story before it can be published.

Recent decades have witnessed a number of cases involving free press claims. Most have focused on the adversarial relationship between the government and the press that emerged during the civil rights movement and Vietnam War. Then and now, state and federal officials at times try to control access to information or to use the threat of libel to stop the press from reporting the news. The Supreme Court generally has rejected these efforts. For example, when a Montgomery, Alabama, official sued the *New York Times* for libel and sought damages based on minor mistakes made when reporting the truth about the desegregation struggle in the South in the 1960s, the Supreme Court ruled in favor of the press. The First Amendment, the unanimous justices concluded in *New York Times Co.* v. *Sullivan* (1964), protected the press not only from prior restraint but also from any punishment—imprisonment, fines, or civil damage awards—for reports about a public official's conduct unless actual malice was involved. "Erroneous statement is inevitable in public debate," the Court wrote, and even false statements must "be protected if the freedoms of expression are to have the 'breathing space' that they . . . 'need to survive.'" Giving a wide berth to the press serves a vital public purpose: it preserves open government and allows citizens to hold officials accountable for their actions.

What if the public's right to know runs up against government claims of secrecy for reasons of national security? *Near* v. *Minnesota* recognized that protecting the nation might trump the right to publish, but under what conditions? This question came up in 1971 when the *New York Times* decided to publish the stolen Pentagon Papers, a secret study proving the government had misinformed the public about its war goals in Southeast Asia and the prospects for victory. President Richard Nixon, for the first time in the nation's history,

"The fact that the liberty of the press may be abused by miscreant purveyors of scandal does not make any the less necessary the immunity of the press from previous restraint in dealing with official misconduct."

—Chief Justice Charles Evans Hughes, *Near* v. *Minnesota* (1931)

instructed the government to go to court to stop their publication on grounds that it put the nation's security at risk. The Supreme Court refused this request, in a 6-to-3 vote, in *New York Times Co.* v. *United States;* it held that the government had not demonstrated a need to stop publication. Prior restraint, a majority of the justices agreed, required extraordinary circumstances. Without a free press, the government could hide its actions from the public, making it difficult for people to hold officials accountable.

How this principle will play out in the aftermath of the events of September 11, 2001, or whether the threat of terrorism requires a different balance between freedom and security, is still unresolved. How do we as a society balance our need for protection against plots to bring us harm with our need for information that allows us to judge whether government's actions are proper? We have reached no fixed answer to this question, and perhaps these issues will have to be addressed case by case, at least initially, until we understand more about the threat we face. Also unsettled is the effect of new technology, such as the Internet, on our understanding of freedom of the press. To date, we continue to embrace open access to information and with it the right of people to publish without restraint in this new medium. This position contrasts sharply with other societies. For instance, in 2006, China banned Internet search firms, such as Google and Yahoo, from doing business in the country unless they blocked access to information the government considered dangerous.

New threats and new technologies have always led to new questions about the extent of our rights. No right is absolute, of course. The right to a free press does not apply equally to obscenity or to a reporter's protection of confidential sources, for example. Student-run publications do not enjoy full First Amendment protection against prior restraint. We impose certain fairness restrictions on television and radio because they use a limited public resource, the airwaves, to broadcast the news. We also recognize that rights at times are in conflict, as when the right to a trial by an impartial jury clashes with the right of a free press to report on an investigation and trial. This issue was a concern in both the trials of O. J. Simpson, who was acquitted in 1995 of killing his ex-wife and another man, and Scott Peterson, convicted of killing his pregnant wife in 2004, to mention two well-known examples. But even as we search for the right balance between rights and responsibilities, we have always held firm on one principle: prior restraints on the press are unconstitutional.

In doing so, we have endorsed the people's right to know as a fundamental liberty in a free and democratic society. We also have kept faith with our history. When the First Congress was debating the amendments that became the Bill of Rights, a continuing theme was the deep and abiding link between knowledge and freedom. Without the ability to know what was happening, without a free press, self-government was not possible—and without self-government, liberty was not possible. Public knowledge made government accountable to the people, the final authority in a democratic republic. It was this understanding that prompted Edmund Randolph, a revolutionary leader from Virginia, to remind James Madison of how indispensable this right was to the nation's future. "The liberty of the press," he wrote, "ought not to be surrendered but with blood."

"Democracy Must Know the Truth"

J. P. Tumulty was secretary to the President during Woodrow Wilson's administration. In this role, he served as Wilson's liaison to the press. When Congress was debating the Espionage Bill of 1917, Tumulty warned Wilson that the bill, which made it a crime to publish reports that interfered with U.S. military success or gave encouragement to the enemy, was perceived as an attempt to control the press. In a letter dated May 8, 1917, he reminded the President about the bad experience with the Alien and Sedition Acts of 1798 and argued that "the more completely the attempt to censor the press is killed, the better for the cause of freedom." Tumulty's advice notwithstanding, the act passed and resulted in numerous convictions, especially of antiwar socialist editors and writers. The tension noted by Tumulty in 1917—press freedom versus protection of war secrets—continues today, as witnessed by the debate over a New York Times *revelation in 2006 of the mining of telephone records by the National Security Agency as part of the federal government's antiterrorism efforts.*

The path of the Espionage Bill will be made more difficult by the memorandum issued yesterday by the State Department and distributed broadcast, warning all officials not to talk with newspapermen "even on insignificant matters of fact or detail."

I know how strongly you feel on the matter of a strict censorship but I would not be doing my full duty to you and the Administration if I did not say to you that there is gradually growing a feeling of bitter resentment against the whole business, which is daily spreading. The experience of the Administration of President Adams in fostering the Alien and Sedition Laws bids us beware of this whole business. Of course there is a great difference between the situation that confronts us and that which confronted some of your predecessors; but the whole atmosphere surrounding the Espionage Bill is hurtful and injurious, because of the impression which has gained root with startling intensity that the bill is really a gigantic machine, erected for the despotic control of the press and that the power provided for in the bill must of necessity be delegated by the President and that the press will be controlled by a host of small bureaucrats who will interpret the president's instructions according to their own intellects.

I have gathered during the last week editorial comment from various journals throughout the country which have been our firmest supporters and they are unanimous in condemning what they consider to be the unjust features of this legislation....

The American people are called to a mighty effort to save the world from an attempt at autocratic domination. Great sacrifices are before them. They are ready to endure whatever is necessary for the work in hand. But if they are to try their hardest, they must know that no effort is wasted; that public offices are administered with faith and efficiency. Public judgment must be passed on those who are weak and those who are strong in the Government. When a department requires reorganization, the people must know it, other wise it might not be reorganized.

In fight for the truth, democracy must know the truth. The more completely the attempt to censor the press is killed, the better for the cause of freedom. The press has no desire to expose military secrets. It wants America to win....

Sincerely yours,
Tumulty

First Amendment Violations

In June 1971, the New York Times *published the first installment of the so-called Pentagon Papers, a classified 7,000-page document on the conduct of the Vietnam War, which had begun in 1964. The report revealed that the government had kept information about the conduct of the war from the American public. The Nixon administration secured a lower court order temporarily restraining publication of further installments, but the judge denied a permanent injunction, or order to stop publication. The government appealed, contending that publication would endanger the troops and undermine the peace talks then underway. The Supreme Court heard the case immediately and voted 6 to 3 to deny the government's request. In* New York Times Co. v. United States *and* United States v. Washington Post Co. *(1971), Justice William Brennan wrote a concurring opinion in which he argued that even halting publication temporarily to review the issues constituted an unconstitutional prior restraint of the press.*

The entire thrust of the Government's claim throughout these cases has been that publication of the material sought to be enjoined "could," or "might," or "may" prejudice the national interest in various ways. But the First Amendment tolerates absolutely no prior judicial restraints of the press predicated upon surmise or conjecture that untoward consequences may result. Our cases, it is true, have indicated that there is a single, extremely narrow class of cases in which the First Amendment's ban on prior judicial restraint may be overridden. Our cases have thus far indicated that such cases may arise only when the Nation "is at war,"…during which times "[n]o one would question but that a government might prevent actual obstruction to its recruiting service or the publication of the sailing dates of transports or the number and location of troops." Even if the present world situation were assumed to be tantamount to a time of war, or if the power of presently available armaments would justify even in peacetime the suppression of information that would set in motion a nuclear holocaust, in neither of these actions has the Government presented or even alleged that publication of items from or based upon the material at issue would cause the happening of an event of that nature. "[T]he chief purpose of [the First Amendment's] guaranty [is] to prevent previous restraints upon publication."…Thus, only governmental allegation and proof that publication must inevitably, directly, and immediately cause the occurrence of an event kindred to imperiling the safety of a transport already at sea can support even the issuance of an interim restraining order. In no event may mere conclusions be sufficient: for if the Executive Branch seeks judicial aid in preventing publication, it must inevitably submit the basis upon which that aid is sought to scrutiny by the judiciary. And therefore, every restraint issued in this case, whatever its form, has violated the First Amendment—and not less so because that restraint was justified as necessary to afford the courts an opportunity to examine the claim more thoroughly. Unless and until the Government has clearly made out its case, the First Amendment commands that no injunction may issue.

CHAPTER 8

The Right to Freedom of Assembly

In the 1830s, a French visitor named Alexis de Tocqueville toured the United States to learn why the American Revolution had created a functioning democracy whereas the French Revolution had failed. His classic book, *Democracy in America*, listed a number of reasons for this success, including one still considered a national trait: "Americans of all ages, all stations in life, and all types of dispositions are forever forming associations." They gathered for every sort of civic purpose, and in the process, he concluded, they were fulfilling the promise of self-government.

We remain a nation of joiners. Every day and at all ages, we come together voluntarily in civic groups, religious institutions, benevolence societies, sports leagues, service societies, and school clubs, among thousands of other organizations. In doing so, we exercise the fundamental freedoms of assembly and association, rights protected by the First Amendment, which states that "Congress shall make no law...abridging...the right of the people peaceably to assemble."

The founding generation understood the value of the freedom of assembly because they had relied on it during their struggle for independence. The colonists used a variety of methods to protest British violations of their liberties; chief among them were assemblies of people, such as the Sons of Liberty, willing to make their grievances known publicly. English law allowed these gatherings unless they endangered public safety, and royal authorities often labeled colonial protests as dangerous to public order. Not all of the assemblies

The Coterie Club of Findlay, Ohio, a women's literary club founded in the 1890s, provided its members with an intellectual and social outlet. Americans have typically joined a variety of civic and social organizations, practicing their rights of association and assembly.

were peaceful, of course; the colonists resisted British attempts to suppress their protests, sometimes with force.

The revolutionary creation of a government based on popular consent carried with it an obligation to provide a way for citizens to express their views and protest against authority collectively as well as individually. This notion seemed so obvious to many people that they thought it was not necessary to list it as a protected right. "If people converse together they must assemble for that purpose," noted one member of the First Congress. "It is a self-evident, inalienable right which the people possess." But the framers of the First Amendment, remembering their recent experience, thought otherwise. If they did not protect it, officials might do as the British had done and try to deny collective protests against the government. They knew the right of peaceful assembly gave meaning to the other rights of expression. Individual citizens had limited ability to influence the government, but people acting together could exercise great power to protect their liberty from abuse.

Throughout U.S. history, demonstrations, marches, and rallies have been common ways to pressure legislators to change laws and provide remedies for intolerable conditions. Striking workers, antiwar protesters, civil rights marchers, and woman suffragists are among the hundreds of groups that have filled streets and public squares, challenging what they judged to be unequal treatment or misguided policies. Many of these events still carry great emotional or symbolic significance. Martin Luther King's "I Have a Dream" speech during the civil rights March on Washington in 1963, the large antiwar protests of the late 1960s, and the 1995 Million Man March, organized by Nation of Islam leader Louis Farrakhan, remain vivid memories for many Americans, in large measure because they were among the first televised demonstrations in the nation's history. All these various forms of assembly were

On Memorial Day 1933, communist protestors in San Diego, home to several military bases, participate in an antiwar demonstration. They were denied a parade permit because they would not promise not to show a red flag. Nevertheless, they rallied in New Town Park, bearing banners criticizing the "imperialistic war" and the capitalist system. When they attempted to form a parade, police officers moved in to stop them and rioting ensued.

protected by the First Amendment. Riots and other violent acts do not have the same guarantee, even if the underlying grievances are the same as protests of peaceful assemblies.

Until the twentieth century, the First Amendment limited only the federal government, not the states. A right of assembly also appeared in many state constitutions, but minority groups often discovered its protections did not apply equally to them. The word *peaceable* had come to be interpreted as "legal," or whatever the lawmakers or police officers allowed. Courts and legislators, in the name of ensuring public safety, outlawed any gatherings with a "bad tendency" to produce disorder. The right of assembly did not protect these assemblies. Socialists, communists, labor unions, and other so-called radical groups were prosecuted routinely under laws that forbade demonstrations deemed to threaten public safety.

A dockworker in Portland, Oregon, named Dirk DeJonge was a communist who sought an end to capitalism by organizing a labor union. He received a seven-year prison sentence for advocating an industrial and political revolution. Significantly, a state law also forbade voluntary assemblies for the purpose of advocating these activities. In 1937, the Supreme Court reversed DeJonge's conviction and gave new force to the right to assemble peacefully. Free speech, free press, and free assembly were necessary "for free political discussion, to the end that government may be responsive to the will of the people and that changes, if desired, may be obtained by peaceful means. Therein," the justices concluded, "lies the security of the Republic." In *DeJonge* v. *Oregon,* the U.S. Supreme Court recognized assembly as a right incorporated, or included, in the due process clause of the Fourteenth Amendment as a limit on state power.

Four decades later, the right of assembly faced another test, but this time the challenge was more difficult. It involved a group who sought to parade its message of hate before an especially vulnerable population. The question at issue was simple: did the Constitution protect neo-Nazis who viciously taunted elderly Holocaust survivors?

Frank Collins was the son of Max Cohen, a Jewish survivor of Dachau, a Nazi concentration camp. He was also the leader of the National Socialist Party of America. Frank Collins, in short, was a neo-Nazi. He led a party of about fifty members who goose-stepped about their Chicago headquarters, dressed in brown-shirted uniforms and black boots. They were a ragtag group of anti-Jew and antiblack hate-mongers who worshiped Adolf Hitler and proclaimed the resurrection of the Third Reich.

Few people gave them much notice. The American Jewish Committee kept tabs on the group but considered it politically impotent and capable only of spewing vicious propaganda. Even a Nazi publication in Europe called its American members "dead-beats, right wing kooks, and religious nuts." But in 1978, it would have been difficult to find anyone in Skokie, Illinois, who shared this view. This Chicago suburb had a substantial Jewish population, including more than six hundred survivors of the Holocaust. Many residents were either related to or knew one or more of these survivors. The World War II death camps of Buchenwald, Bergen-Belsen, and Auschwitz were not names in a history book to the citizens of Skokie. They were painful memories.

HELENA, MONTANA   March 20, 1960 MAR 2 3 1960

American Civil Liberties Union,

Sirs:

    For forty years I have been a member of the A.C.L.U. because I have wanted to "defend to the death his right to say it". Now I read that we are defending the right of persons in Washington, D.C., to advocate putting all Jews in gas chambers.

    Do we also defend a campaign to kill all Christians? Or to commit murder in general? Or to advocate theft? Or rape? I have always thought of myself as "liberal". But I find myself unable to "defend to the death" the right to violate the laws of decency.

    In a specific case of theft, or murder, or rape, in which the defendant may or may not be guilty, by all means let's defend him! But a campaign for murder is quite another thing.

    In 1930 I might have seen this situation in a purely theoretical light. But today, in 1960, we know that Auschweitz started this way. As a practical matter, what is "free speech"?

    Yours, greatly disturbed,

Belle F. Winestine

P.S. I have seen Auschwitz!

WINESTINE
105-11th AVENUE
HELENA, MONTANA

In 1960, a period of fervent public protest, a longtime member of the American Civil Liberties Union voiced her concerns about the tension between complete free speech and the perils of extremist movements. Like many American Jews, she was particularly frightened by the specter of the Nazi concentration camps such as Auschwitz.

When Collins sought a permit to hold a rally in a Skokie city park, government officials told him he would have to get a $350,000 bond; they knew he could not satisfy this requirement. In response, he planned to assemble his followers in front of the village hall, wearing full Nazi uniform, and hand out literature protesting the infringement of his right to speak. The village council wanted to ignore the group, but the Jewish community was adamantly opposed and convinced the council to block the rally, even though many Jewish organizations, such as B'nai B'rith, normally were strong supporters of free expression. "These weren't ideas being discussed," the village attorney argued in response to newspaper inquiries. "The swastika was not an expression of free speech. It amounted to an assault [on the Holocaust survivors]."

The Skokie council passed three ordinances to put their case on firmer footing, including bans on hate literature and demonstrations by persons wearing military-style uniforms. When the village used these ordinances to stop the Nazi rally, Collins enlisted help from the American Civil Liberties Union (ACLU). It was a difficult moment for the ACLU. It abhorred the Nazis' rants, but it believed even their hate-filled speech and rallies fell under the protection of the First Amendment. If government could stop a Nazi demonstration, it also could stop a Jewish one, the civil liberties organization argued.

By now the case was receiving national attention, and lower state courts tried vainly to find a way through the emotionally charged battlefield. The Illinois Appellate Court, citing a U.S. Supreme Court approval of a criminal conviction for "fighting words" or words likely to provoke a fight, ruled that the Nazis could march but only in clothing stripped of the swastika. But the state supreme court reversed the lower court's decision: the ban on the demonstration violated the First Amendment. The federal district court upheld the ban; the ordinances were invalid. Acknowledging that it was tempting to look for an exception to the guarantee of free speech and assembly in this instance, the court decided that "it was better to allow those who preach racial hate to expend their venom in rhetoric than to be panicked into embarking on a dangerous course of permitting the government to decide what its citizens must say and hear." The Supreme Court refused to hear the case, which meant it left intact the lower court's ruling that "the freedom of thought carries with it the freedom to speak and to publicly assemble to express one's thought." These rights were at the heart of democratic government.

Collins revived his plan to demonstrate, but now he faced a massive counterdemonstration announced by his opponents. Seizing an opportunity to save face, the neo-Nazi leader changed his mind and shifted his rally to an all-white suburb of Chicago to avoid what he called "a mob of howling creatures." He also announced a demonstration in downtown Chicago. Both events proved to be anticlimactic: the downtown rally drew twenty-five Nazi demonstrators, two thousand police, and far more people who screamed their opposition. The suburban demonstration attracted more than two hundred Nazi sympathizers, but they too were outnumbered by police and vocal opponents. With all the noise, few people at either event heard Collins's speeches. Within minutes, the spectacles were over.

Following the rallies, representatives from Skokie's religious bodies held an interfaith memorial service in memory of the Holocaust victims. Soon life in the village returned to normal, but with one major difference. The opponents of hate realized they were victorious after all. The Holocaust survivors, the village attorney noted, "felt that now they finally had stood up to a symbol and that they had defeated it." True to its promise, freedom of assembly, in the end, had promoted the cause of truth.

The right of assembly appears in the same amendment with other basic rights of democracy—the freedoms of religion, speech, press, and petition. We consider these rights fundamental because they allow citizens to express their views and participate freely in government without subscribing to certain beliefs or belonging to approved parties. The protection of assembly differs from the other rights in its wording, however. It is the only one in the First Amendment that has an adverb attached to it—"peaceably." It also implicitly contains another guarantee, the right to associate freely.

In many ways the right to associate with anyone for legitimate, or noncriminal, purposes has been more controversial—and more at risk—than the right to assemble peacefully. Dirk DeJonge's case in 1937 was as much about his membership in the Communist party as it was about his right to rally his fellow dockworkers to support a labor union. In the late 1940s and early 1950s, widespread fear of communism led Congress to pass laws requiring the Communist party and other so-called radical groups to register with the federal government. Congressional committees, most notably one headed by Senator Joseph McCarthy of Wisconsin, conducted investigations into alleged communist activity in government, the entertainment industry, and elsewhere. Actors, teachers, writers, and others who refused to testify about their associations,

"This Court has recognized the vital relationship between freedom to associate and privacy in one's associations.... Inviolability of privacy in group association may in many circumstances be indispensable to preservation of freedom of association, particularly where a group espouses dissident beliefs."

—Justice John Marshall Harlan II, *NAACP* v. *Alabama* (1958)

Robert Thompson and Benjamin Davis are surrounded by supporters as they emerge from federal court in New York City. They were two of the ten national board members of the Communist Party USA convicted in 1949 of violating the Smith Act, which prohibited membership in an organization deemed to advocate violent overthrow of the federal government.

even when citing their Fifth Amendment privilege against self-incrimination, soon found their names on "blacklists" that prevented them from working.

The Supreme Court initially ruled that Congress could limit the right of association for communists because of the group's announced desire to overthrow the government. Four justices dissented strongly, however, warning that this action placed the nation in danger of tyranny. Banning people from associating because of their ideas, the minority argued, made the First Amendment's protection of speech and assembly meaningless. Soon the Court began to reconsider its position. In a series of cases in the 1960s, it reversed the earlier ruling, and by 1967 it had decided that the freedom of association, part of the right of assembly, even allowed communists to work in the nation's defense plants.

Other cases during this period made it clear why the right of association was vital to democratic government. During the struggles for civil rights in the 1950s, state governments in Alabama and Arkansas tried to compel antisegregation groups such as the National Association for the Advancement of Colored People (NAACP) to reveal their membership lists. The organizations refused. Making these names public would subject their members to harassment and violence, they claimed—and their fears were not without reason, as events throughout the South tragically revealed. The Supreme Court unanimously upheld these refusals. The right to associate for peaceful purposes, as well as the right to keep these associations private, were protected by the First Amendment. This right was implicit, or included, in the right of assembly.

Today, the freedoms of assembly and association continue to be contested rights. As a society, we have embraced these freedoms as necessary for a vital democratic government, but we disagree on the balance between these rights and the legitimate protection of public safety or promotion of public order. Free expression generally, including free assembly and association, must follow laws regulating health, safety, and welfare of the general public, such as regulations on traffic, litter, noise abatement, and use of private property. At times, the interests of public safety and the rights of assembly and association may be in conflict—for example, keeping picketers a safe distance away from an abortion clinic or enacting a curfew or anti-loitering laws—and it is in these cases we struggle to find the right balance. The events since the terrorist attacks of September 11, 2001, have also called into question how far the right of association extends. Illegal and criminal associations clearly are not protected, but it is not easy to identify which associations threaten national security and which do not.

Our history provides the best assurance of the worth of free assembly and association to our society. The ability to come together voluntarily has produced changes we now consider essential to a healthy democracy. Associations of powerful voices have called for the inclusion of women and blacks in our political process; groups have pushed successfully for the end to segregation and wars; demonstrations have reminded us to safeguard our natural environment; and organizations have worked tirelessly for improved health, education, working conditions, and public safety in neighborhoods, towns, and cities across the nation. Most important, the rights of assembly and association have given meaning to the right of free expression, which ultimately is a catalyst for change.

The right to speak as an individual is a prerequisite for self-government, but it is our ability to act together that makes it possible for self-government to improve our lives and extend our freedom. We should not fear the opinion that disagrees with us. If we insist on harmony in our society, we deny human nature and we also deny the potential of liberty to produce greater good. "Conformity," President John Kennedy reminded us, "is the jailor of freedom." When we guarantee the right of assembly and association, no matter how unpopular the cause, we are in fact protecting our own liberty and our future as a free people.

The Power of Association

In 1831, Alexis de Tocqueville, an aristocratic Frenchman, visited the United States to study its prison system. His classic work Democracy in America *(1835) described the essential character of Americans and their government. Tocqueville believed the strength of the new nation was its voluntary associations, which the First Amendment right of assembly protected.*

An association consists simply in the public assent which a number of individuals give to certain doctrines and in the engagement which they contract to promote in a certain manner the spread of these doctrines. The right of association in this fashion almost merges with freedom of the press, but societies thus formed possess more authority than the press. When an opinion is represented by a society, it necessarily assumes a more exact and explicit form. It numbers its partisans and engages them in its cause; they, on the other hand, become acquainted with one another. And their zeal is increased by their number. An association unites into one channel the efforts of divergent minds and urges them vigorously towards the one end which it clearly points out.

The second degree in the exercise of the right of association is the power of the meeting. When an association is allowed to establish centers of action at certain important points in the country, its activity is increased and its influence extended. Men have the opportunity of seeing one another; means of execution are combined; and opinions are maintained with a warmth and energy that written language can never attain.

Lastly, in the exercise of the right of political association there is a third degree: the partisans of an opinion may unite in electoral bodies and choose delegates to represent them in a central assembly. This is, properly speaking, the application of the representative system to a party....

The most natural privilege of man, next to the right of acting for himself, is that of combining his exertions with those of his fellow creatures and of acting in common with them. This right of association therefore appears to me almost as inalienable in its nature as the right of personal liberty.

"The Opportunity for Free Political Discussion"

In 1937, the U.S. Supreme Court overturned the conviction of Dirk DeJonge, who had been prosecuted under an Oregon statute that outlawed criminal syndicalism, or organizing to bring about a change in the form of government or in industrial ownership or control. DeJonge had helped to conduct a meeting organized by the Communist party to protest police shootings of striking workers. The meeting was peaceful, and the Oregon court had held that a person could be convicted for nothing more than participating in a party meeting. In reversing the conviction, Chief Justice Charles Evans Hughes wrote in DeJonge v. Oregon *(1937), "[P]eaceable assembly for lawful discussion cannot be made a crime." It was a major First Amendment case. The right to assemble peaceably was guaranteed against state interference by the Fourteenth Amendment's due process clause.*

Freedom of speech and of the press are fundamental rights which are safeguarded by the due process clause of the Fourteenth Amendment of the Federal Constitution. The right of peaceable assembly is a right cognate to those of free speech and free press and is equally fundamental.... The First Amendment of the Federal Constitution expressly guarantees that right against abridgment by Congress. But explicit mention there does not argue exclusion elsewhere. For the right is one that cannot be denied without violating those fundamental principles of liberty and justice which lie at the base of all civil and political institutions—principles which the Fourteenth Amendment embodies in the general terms of its due process clause....

These rights may be abused by using speech or press or assembly in order to incite to violence and crime. The people through their Legislatures may protect themselves against that abuse. But the legislative intervention can find constitutional justification only by dealing with the abuse. The rights themselves must not be curtailed. The greater the importance of safeguarding the community from incitements to the overthrow of our institutions by force and violence, the more imperative is the need to preserve inviolate the constitutional rights of free speech, free press and free assembly in order to maintain the opportunity for free political discussion, to the end that government may be responsive to the will of the people and that changes, if desired, may be obtained by peaceful means. Therein lies the security of the Republic, the very foundation of constitutional government.

It follows from these considerations that, consistently with the Federal Constitution, peaceable assembly for lawful discussion cannot be made a crime. The holding of meetings for peaceable political action cannot be proscribed. Those who assist in the conduct of such meetings cannot be branded as criminals on that score. The question, if the rights of free speech and peaceable assembly are to be preserved, is not as to the auspices under which the meeting is held but as to its purpose; not as to the relations of the speakers, but whether their utterances transcend the bounds of the freedom of speech which the Constitution protects. If the persons assembling have committed crimes elsewhere, if they have formed or are engaged in a conspiracy against the public peace and order, they may be prosecuted for their conspiracy or other violation of valid laws. But it is a different matter when the State, instead of prosecuting them for such offenses, seizes upon mere participation in a peaceable assembly and a lawful public discussion as the basis for a criminal charge.

A Privilege of Citizenship

The Committee for Industrial Organization (CIO) was a coalition of five labor unions that left the American Federation of Labor (AFL) in 1938 in order to boost pay and improve job conditions and security for workers in heavy industries, such as steel manufacturing. Its members included a number of communists who favored more aggressive policies than practiced by the older, more conservative unions of the AFL.

In 1937, the CIO began a campaign to promote its cause and enlist new members. Organizers often used public parks to their rallies, but in Jersey City, New Jersey, the mayor, Frank "Boss" Hague, used a city ordinance regulating the parks to prevent these meetings and the distribution of literature. The CIO sued in federal court, claiming that the ordinance violated the First Amendment right to freedom of assembly. In 1939, the U.S. Supreme Court upheld its claim. Justice Pierce Butler, the most conservative justice on the Court, wrote the opinion in Hague v. Committee for Industrial Organization *(1939), which ruled that the right of assembly was a right of national citizenship and therefore protected under the Fourteenth Amendment from abridgement by the states.*

Although it has been held that the Fourteenth Amendment created no rights in citizens of the United States, but merely secured existing rights against state abridgment, it is clear that the right peaceably to assemble and to discuss these topics, and to communicate respecting them, whether orally or in writing, is a privilege inherent in citizenship of the United States which the Amendment protects. . . .

Citizenship of the United States would be little better than a name if it did not carry with it the right to discuss national legislation and the benefits, advantages, and opportunities to accrue to citizens therefrom. All of the respondents' proscribed activities had this single end and aim. . . .

What has been said demonstrates that, in the light of the facts found, privileges and immunities of the individual respondents as citizens of the United States, were infringed by the petitioners, by virtue of their official positions, under color of ordinances of Jersey City, unless, as petitioners contend, the city's ownership of streets and parks is as absolute as one's ownership of his home, with consequent power altogether to exclude citizens from the use thereof, or unless, though the city holds the streets in trust for public use, the absolute denial of their use to the respondents is a valid exercise of the police power. . . .

Wherever the title of streets and parks may rest, they have immemorially been held in trust for the use of the public and, time out of mind, have been used for purposes of assembly, communicating thoughts between citizens, and discussing public questions. Such use of the streets and public places has, from ancient times, been a part of the privileges, immunities, rights, and liberties of citizens. The privilege of a citizen of the United States to use the streets and parks for communication of views on national questions may be regulated in the interest of all; it is not absolute, but relative, and must be exercised in subordination to the general comfort and convenience, and in consonance with peace and good order; but it must not, in the guise of regulation, be abridged or denied.

CHAPTER 9

The Right to Petition

Many legal observers consider the right to petition to be uninteresting. It has spurred no landmark cases, and the First Amendment's language is plain and straightforward: Congress shall make no law abridging the "right of the people . . . to petition the Government for a redress of grievances." It guarantees citizens the right to complain and ask officials to correct a problem or right a wrong, but where is the controversy in exercising this right? It is an obvious right in a democratic society.

The founding generation no doubt would have been surprised and pleased to hear this response because their experience had taught them not to take the right to petition for granted. In the Declaration of Independence, they had justified their separation from Great Britain in part because King George III had refused to heed their petitions: "We have petitioned for Redress in the most humble terms: Our repeated petitions have met with repeated injury. A Prince, whose character is thus marked by every act which may define a Tyrant, is unfit to be the ruler of a free people." The king's indifference to the colonists' complaints had proved to be his undoing. The framers of the Bill of Rights sought to avoid the same mistake by ensuring that the political process would be receptive to the people's concerns.

The right to petition, like the guarantee of due process, was an old privilege by the time of the Revolution. It has roots in the constitutional development of England, where the first mention of redress, a word that means correcting an error or providing a remedy, occurred in the tenth century. In 1215, the Magna Carta, the Great Charter of English liberties, formally recognized the right of barons to petition the king. Over several tumultuous centuries, the act of petitioning the monarch for personal relief from laws or punishments became an entrenched tradition. The right was not unlimited, however. During the mid-seventeenth century, for example, Parliament prohibited petitions with more than twenty signatures, a number its members thought reflected a demand rather than a request. It also restricted petitions likely to provoke public unrest. The Glorious Revolution of 1689, which marked the final triumph of Parliament over the king in practical matters of governing, removed these limits and fully implemented the right by banning "all commitments and prosecutions for such petitioning."

Englishmen by then had carried the right with them to the New World and enacted it in their charters and local laws. From early settlement to independence, colonial assemblies received thousands of petitions from every rank in society, including groups normally excluded from government, such as women, slaves, and Indians. The complaints ranged widely and prayed for relief in matters of debt, property, divorce, taxes, criminal punishments, and a host of other actions. They were, in many ways, a gauge of the public mood in a time before mass media and opinion surveys. Petitioning served as a form of public dia-

> *"Every man whether Inhabitant or forreiner, free or not free shall have libertie to come to any publique Court, Councel, or Towne meeting, and either by speech or writeing to move any lawfull, seasonable, and materiall question, or to present any necessary motion, complaint, petition, Bill or information, whereof that meeting hath proper cognizance, so it be done in convenient time, due order, and respective manner."*
>
> —Massachusetts Body of Liberties (1641)

logue with elected or appointed rulers. Royal governors and colonial legislatures, however, often viewed them as a nuisance and at times discouraged petitions by charging fees and punishing petitioners who filed a false complaint—for example, a fabricated claim that the government owed a debt or denied a right. Appeals to the king and Parliament remained open to aggrieved colonists, but in the years preceding the Revolution, colonists increasingly found their petitions rejected by an imperial government eager to assert its authority over them.

These experiences made the revolutionary generation especially keen to guarantee the right to petition. The framers recognized that popular sovereignty, the authority of the people to rule, depended upon the ability of individual citizens to discuss their concerns openly and to communicate directly with officials. They included the right of petition, along with the closely related rights of speech, press, and assembly, in the First Amendment to ensure that the national government heard the people's complaints.

Ironically, it was Congress itself that first denied the right of Americans to petition for a redress of grievances. At stake was the future of slavery in the District of Columbia. When antislavery advocates began to petition Congress in the 1830s for abolition of slavery in the nation's capital, the House of Representatives tabled these grievances without reading them. Outraged, a seventy-six-year-old congressman from Massachusetts set forth on an often lonely eight-year campaign to remove this "gag" that prevented the people's voice from being heard. What made the crusade memorable was not simply his tenacity in making Congress abide by the Constitution but the fact that he was a former President of the United States whose only term in office had been universally judged a failure.

Short, bald, paunchy, plagued by physical problems, and forever failing to control a fierce temper, John Quincy Adams in 1830 was a man old before his time. He remained bitter over his defeat for reelection as President two years earlier, especially because he considered the victor, Andrew Jackson, to be his inferior on every count. "My whole life has been a succession of disappointments," he confided to his diary. "I have no plausible motive for wishing to live when everything I foresee and believe [about the future] makes death desirable."

What makes this statement remarkable was Adams's life itself, which seemed to be a succession of triumphs, not disappointments. Eldest son of John

Former President John Quincy Adams sat for this portrait in 1843, while serving as a congressman from Massachusetts. Adams was an impassioned advocate of citizens' right to petition the government. The rigid pose of the daguerrotype perhaps does not convey the charismatic oratory of this influential statesman, known popularly as Old Man Eloquent.

Adams, the nation's second President, John Quincy was ambassador to the Netherlands at age twenty-six, U.S. senator from Massachusetts at thirty-five, and then minister to Russia. But it was as secretary of state that his talents shone. He favored an aggressive expansion of the United States across the continent and was one of the chief architects of the Monroe Doctrine, which called for an end to European interference in the Americas. His record earned him a reputation among future historians as perhaps the greatest occupant of the office. In all of these positions, he embodied his father's dedication to public service, as well as his own ambition. John Quincy's successes were no accident: John Adams had written his wife, Abigail, that their job as parents was to "Fix their [children's] Attention upon great and glorious Objects, . . . [and] make them great and manly."

Despite this history, John Quincy Adams's Presidency was a failure. The country rejected his view of a strong national government, in part because southerners believed it threatened their ability to hold slaves. He left Washington a dejected and disillusioned man, convinced that slavery had defeated liberty in a struggle for the nation's soul. Then, he had an opportunity for political rebirth when supporters persuaded him to run for the U.S. House of Representatives. His victory in 1830 made him the only former President to date to hold elective national office after his White House years, although a twentieth-century President, William Howard Taft, later became chief justice of the United States.

Adams soon faced a controversy that would consume the remainder of his life and restore his reputation. By 1834, the American Anti-Slavery Society had begun a major campaign to flood Congress with petitions seeking the abolition of slavery and the slave trade in the District of Columbia. Adams presented each of these petitions to the House of Representatives for consideration—50 on one day, 350 a few days later—to the growing distress of southern congressmen. Finally, in 1836, pro-slavery representatives succeeded in passing a resolution directing that all petitions relating to slavery would be tabled immediately without discussion. Slavery was too volatile an issue, they warned, and could not be discussed publicly without wrecking the Union. This "gag rule" would be renewed each session for the next eight years. Under it, Congress effectively denied antislavery forces a right guaranteed by the Constitution.

An angry Adams protested loudly, claiming the action violated the Constitution and the rights of his constituents. Ridiculed and rebuffed, the ex-President took on the entire House. He used every parliamentary tactic he could to keep the antislavery debate alive, "creeping through this rule and skipping over that," in the words of one observer, until ordered to stop. He also insulted his colleagues when they refused to rescind the rule, attacking one for his "rotten breath" and another for having "the very thickest skull of all New

Hampshire." Under a barrage of abuses and threats—from Georgia, "Your damned guts will be cut out in the dark"; from Alabama, "I promise to cut your throat from ear to ear"—Adams held firmly to his charge that Congress had abandoned the First Amendment's guarantee of the right to petition.

Adams became a funnel for all antislavery petitions to Congress. The number of these petitions was staggering: the Anti-Slavery Society collected more than 2 million signatures on hundreds of petitions from 1838 to 1839 alone, an eye-popping number in a nation with a population of less than 17 million, including slaves; studies have shown that men and women from all classes signed these petitions. The congressman from Massachusetts personally introduced them all. One occasion was especially memorable. Adams asked the speaker if it would be in order to introduce a petition from twenty-two slaves. Outraged southern congressmen were on their feet immediately, threatening to censure him and burn the petition. Then Adams let it be known that the petitioners were in favor of slavery. Recognizing that Adams had outwitted them, in part because he had forced them to consider a petition from slaves, who legally were property and without rights, the pro-slavery members sought to censure Adams for having "trifled with the House." This attempt failed, but not before Adams took the floor and savaged his opponents for their suppression of the Constitution. His grand defense of the right to petition soon earned him popular acclaim in the North, where he became known, admiringly, as Old Man Eloquent.

Year after year, session after session, Adams fought a lonely battle in the House. His campaign was not aimed at eliminating what he knew to be an evil institution. Rather, he sought to preserve what he called the "four freedoms,"

GREAT MASSACHUSETTS PETITION.

To the Senate and House of Representatives of the State of Massachusetts:
The undersigned citizens of the State of Massachusetts, earnestly desiring to free this commonwealth and themselves from all connection with domestic slavery and to secure the citizens of this state from the danger of enslavement, respectfully pray your honorable body,

1. To forbid all persons holding office under any law of this state from in any way officially or under color of office, aiding or abetting the arrest or detention of any person claimed as a fugitive from slavery.

2. To forbid the use of our jails or public property of any description whatever within the Commonwealth, in the detention of any alleged fugitive from slavery.

3. To propose such amendments to the Constitution of the United States as shall forever separate the people of Massachusetts from all connection with slavery.

NAMES.

The GREAT MASSACHUSETTS PETITIONS have been sent to Postmasters and known friends of human liberty in every town in the State. Many thousands have been printed. Let every freeman into whose hands they may fall, constitute himself an agent to obtain signatures. See that your own town and all the neighboring towns are supplied. Return them by forefather's day, Dec. 22d, or at any rate by Jan. 1, 1843. Hold your town meetings on the 22nd of December, and your county meetings on the first of January, throughout the state. Direct to the Latimer Committee, at their Head Quarters No. 3, Amory Hall, Boston. Let the parcels come, if possible, post paid, or free of expense. Sign under the word names, in a SINGLE Column.

GREAT PETITION TO CONGRESS.

To the Senate and House of Representatives of the United States of America:
The undersigned citizens of the State of Massachusetts, earnestly desiring to free their commonwealth and themselves from all connection with domestic slavery and to secure the citizens of their state from the danger of enslavement, respectfully pray your honorable body,

To pass such laws and to propose such amendments to the Constitution of the United States as shall forever separate the people of Massachusetts from all connection with slavery.

NAMES.

In 1842, residents of Massachusetts circulated this printed petition to Congress in an effort to influence it to pass antislavery legislation and to amend the Constitution to ban slavery throughout the country. Congress routinely tabled these petitions until John Quincy Adams's successful campaign to end the Gag Rule in 1844.

FRANK LESLIE'S

ILLUSTRATED

WEEKLY

NEW YORK, MAY 3, 1894. [PRICE, 10 CENTS.

THE WOMAN-SUFFRAGE MOVEMENT IN NEW YORK CITY.

In 1904, society leaders in New York City collect signatures on petitions to be presented to the constitutional convention considering an amendment to the Constitution to permit women to vote.

anticipating the phrase used by Franklin Roosevelt a century later: freedom of speech, freedom of press, freedom of petition, and freedom of debate in Congress. They were the "first principles of civil liberty." The right to petition, to make government accountable, was vitally important. Without it, this son of the Revolution argued, the republican government established by the Constitution would not survive.

The climax of Adams's efforts came in 1842 when the House again tried to censure him, this time for introducing a petition, not related to slavery, from poet John Greenleaf Whittier calling for the Union to be dissolved. He was now seventy-five but never had he been so commanding in his own defense—and in defense of the right to petition. When urged by his friends to rest, he replied, "No, no, not at all. . . . I am ready for another heat." The effort to silence the ex-President failed. Two years later, in 1844 at the beginning of another Congress, Adams once more moved to abandon the gag rule. This time, he succeeded. Finally, Americans could petition their government again.

Adams served in the House of Representatives for four more years, his constituents affirmed in their right to submit their grievances against slavery. In February 1848, he was sitting at his House desk as usual, when he suddenly reddened and collapsed, felled by a stroke. He died two days later. His burial in Boston drew the largest crowd the nation had seen since Benjamin Franklin's funeral. As mourners entered Faneuil Hall to view the body, they passed under a sign: "Born a citizen of Massachusetts. Died a citizen of the United States."

The words recognized a man who was one of the last links to the Revolutionary generation, but Adams already had revealed how he wanted to be remembered, at least in part. After he won his war against the gag rule, he received a beautiful walking cane etched with lines from the Roman poet Horace, extolling "A man just and tenacious in purpose." Later, Old Man Eloquent added his own inscription: "Right of Petition Triumphant."

Petitioning has a broader meaning today than it did in the days of John Quincy Adams. It includes all open expression of issues, interests, and grievances designed to cause the government to act. Letter writing, e-mail campaigns, ballot initiatives, testifying before government committees, and numerous other means all fall under the protection of the First Amendment right of petition. These methods, of course, also invoke the rights of free speech, press, and assembly, and most often the Supreme Court decides cases involving petition by reference to these other guarantees. In this sense, then, petition is less visible than its sister freedoms.

The right to petition, like the other rights covered in the First Amendment, is not unlimited, nor does it cover all activities that fall under petition's broader modern meaning. In a 1985 case, the justices rejected any special constitutional status for the right, which means that lawmakers may require petitioners to follow rules to ensure public order and safety. For example, some cities make petitioners show identification when going door to door. These regulations must be neutral, however, and cannot restrict the right unreasonably. Also, the act of petitioning carries with it no guarantee that government will act on complaints or even reply to the petitioners. Government officials cannot prevent individuals and groups from submitting a grievance, but then it is up to the petitioners to work through the democratic process to ensure an appropriate response or action. Many states, especially in the West, allow citizens to circulate petitions to propose new laws for direct approval by voters. California voters in 1978, for example, limited increases in their property taxes because antitax petitioners gathered enough signatures to put Proposition 13 on the ballot.

If the right to petition seems uninteresting to modern commentators, perhaps it is because the right works so well. It serves important goals in a democracy by creating a flow of information from the public to officials, a flow not governed by what the media considers important. It is a source of public opinion and frequently provides a safety valve for inflammatory issues. It is when we deny citizens the right to express their grievances that democracy suffers, or as President John Kennedy said, "Those that make peaceful revolution impossible will make violent revolution inevitable." Our form of government and our individual liberty require the right to petition for redress of grievances. John Quincy Adams recognized this truth. "The stake in the question," he argued at one point in his long campaign, "is your right to petition, your freedom of thought and action."

"Let every lover of freedom rejoice! The absurd and tyrannical XXVth (formerly the XXIst) Rule of the House which required the rejection of all petitions relating to slavery has been repealed by a decisive vote! The Sage of Quincy has won a proud victory for the Rights of Humanity. May he long live to rejoice over it! Here is a motion which will not go backward. There will be no more Gag-Rules."

—*New York Tribune* editorial, December 5, 1844

The local petition was still alive and well in the 1980s, when residents of Bryant Pond, Maine, formed the Don't Yank the Crank Committee to save their hand-cranked phone system. Brad Hooper displays the signed petitions near the village's sole crank phone booth, outside the Hooper family's general store. Petitions remain an important part of many protest movements.

Debating an Abolition Petition

Southerners in Congress during the 1830s were determined not to allow debate over the possible abolition of slavery. In both the Senate and House of Representatives, they blocked efforts to receive petitions from constituents or voted to table them immediately upon their introduction. The 1836 Senate debate between James Buchanan of Pennsylvania, later the fifteenth President, and John C. Calhoun of South Carolina, Vice President from 1829 to 1832, reveals the different positions of North and South regarding the meaning of the right to petition.

Mr. Buchanan. The proposition [the right to petition] is almost too plain for argument, that, if the people have a constitutional right to petition, a corresponding duty is imposed upon us to receive the petitions. From the very nature of things, rights and duties are reciprocal. The human mind cannot conceive of the one without the other. They are relative terms. If the people have a right to command, it is the duty of their servants to obey. If I have a right to a sum of money, it is the duty of my debtor to pay it to me. If the people have the right to petition their representatives, it is our duty to receive their petition.

Mr. Calhoun. The first amended article of the Constitution, which provides that Congress shall pass no law to prevent the people from peaceably assembling and petitioning for a redress of grievances, was clearly intended to prescribe the limits within which the right might be exercised. It is not pretended that to refuse to receive petitions, touches, in the slightest degree, on these limits. To suppose that the framers of the Constitution—no, not the framers, but those jealous patriots who were not satisfied with that instrument as it came from the hands of the framers, and who proposed this very provision to guard what they considered a sacred right—performed their task so bunglingly as to omit any essential guard, would be to do great injustice to the memory of those stern and sagacious men.

Chapter 10

The Right to Freedom from Racial Discrimination

In 1938, the Carnegie Corporation of New York asked Nobel Prize–winning Swedish economist Gunnar Myrdal and his wife, Alva, who later received the Nobel Peace Prize, to investigate the problems faced by African Americans. The result was a landmark study, *An American Dilemma: The Negro Problem and Modern Democracy*. The problem they described was a conflict between the high ideals of American society, as expressed in its founding documents, and the continuing reality of racial discrimination. It was a dilemma with a long history in America.

Slavery is the ultimate form of discrimination, and racial slavery had been part of the American landscape since the mid-seventeenth century. By the time of the Revolution, holding human beings as property was allowed in all thirteen states. It was also recognized in the Constitution in five places, including a clause that prevented Congress from abolishing the slave trade until twenty years after the document's ratification. Even though most delegates to the Constitutional Convention favored an immediate end to the traffic in slaves, slaveholders were confident that the Constitution did not grant the national government any power to emancipate slaves. They were correct in the short run. Because of these provisions, William Lloyd Garrison, a fiery abolitionist leader, later called the document "a covenant with death."

During the decades before the Civil War, cases involving slavery flooded federal courts. Many of the disputes involved the return of runaway slaves, slavery in the national territories, and the journeys of slaves through free states. All of these issues were highly inflammatory and contributed to the growing tension between increasingly antislavery northern states and southern states committed to the defense of the "peculiar institution." Hardly a year passed without an incident that called attention to a society that, in Abraham Lincoln's later characterization, was "half slave and half free."

By the 1850s, the antislavery crusade had resulted in a new Republican party determined to halt the spread of slavery, if not eliminate it altogether. An attempt by the pro-southern majority of the U.S. Supreme Court to resolve the controversy over slavery in favor of the South resulted in one of the Court's most inflammatory and controversial decisions. Led by Chief Justice Roger B. Taney, the Court ruled 7 to 2 that Dred Scott, a slave who sought his freedom after living in free territory and in Illinois, did not have access to the federal courts because he was black and therefore could not be a citizen of the United States. The Court claimed that, at the time of the Constitution's adoption, blacks were not citizens and universally were considered "beings of an inferior order, and altogether unfit to associate with the white race." It also held that the Fifth Amendment guaranteed the slaveholder's right to own another person. Taney had hoped to end the controversy over slavery and also destroy the Republican party, but *Scott* v. *Sandford* (1857) had the opposite effect. A hostile northern reaction to the decision strengthened both the antislavery and Republican causes. Three years later, Lincoln's election to the Presidency brought the impending crisis to its head and resulted in the attempted southern secession and civil war.

The aim of the war, in Lincoln's original view, was the preservation of the nation, not the elimination of slavery, but this understanding began to change after he issued the Emancipation Proclamation in 1863, which freed slaves in territories not under the control of Union forces. Ultimately, the Union's military victory made it possible to pass the Thirteenth Amendment, which formally ended slavery upon its ratification in 1866. When southern states then passed so-called Black Codes to deprive former slaves of any meaningful liberty—and when they blocked, in practice, the rights they had been required to extend to blacks formally—Congress followed with two more amendments. The Fourteenth Amendment (1868) conferred both national and state citizenship on blacks and forbade states from depriving "any person of life, liberty, or property, without due process of law" or denying to "any person. . . the equal protection of the laws." The Fifteenth Amendment (1870) prohibited the denial of the right to vote because of race. Congress also passed a series of civil rights acts intended to enforce the amendments and prevent racial discrimination.

Throughout the nineteenth century and much of the twentieth, the Supreme Court interpreted the amendments and civil rights acts narrowly. Lawmakers had clearly intended to prevent abuses, but the Court rejected a view that the amendments changed the historical relationship between the states and the central government. Federalism, or the division of power between state and national governments, was part of the original Constitution. States traditionally had responsibility for such things as criminal justice and the health and education of their citizens, whereas the central government had authority for those activities that affected the nation at large. Had the amendments changed this relationship? Until the mid-twentieth century, the Court generally thought not, at least for most individual rights. A series of cases in the 1870s and 1880s effectively curtailed the ability of Congress to improve the condition of former slaves. These matters, the justices decided, were for states to decide. Although the Court conceded that the object of the amendments, especially the Fourteenth Amendment, was to enforce the "absolute equality of races before the law," it also concluded in *Plessy* v. *Ferguson* (1896) that the amendments "could not have been intended to abolish distinctions based on color." "Separate but equal," or legal segregation, was acceptable under the Constitution, the Supreme Court decided.

Occasionally, however, the Court took a broader view of the amendments. One such case involved an unusually broad interpretation of racial discrimination. The decision, while advanced for its day, actually had little impact initially, although a century later, it became a powerful weapon in the modern civil rights revolution. What made the case unusual, however, was the plaintiff who pursued the issue to the Supreme Court. He was not African American but a member of another minority group that had suffered racial discrimination. He was Chinese.

"When the rights of even one human being are held in contempt the rights of all are in danger. . . . Our Government is founded on the equality of human rights—on the idea, the sacred truth that all are entitled to life, liberty and the pursuit of happiness. Our country is an asylum for the oppressed of all nations—of all races."

—Attorney Robert G. Ingersoll, "Should the Chinese Be Excluded?"
North American Review (1893)

Yick Wo went to San Francisco in 1861, lured, as were many Chinese immigrants before him, by the prospect of a better life. China was home to wars, unrest, natural disasters; California promised greater comfort and easy wealth, thanks to the gold rush that began in 1848 when prospectors struck pay dirt at Sutter's Mill.

Within three years, Yick Wo had established a laundry, a common occupation for Chinese immigrants who found themselves shut out of the more lucrative jobs in mining, manufacturing, or fishing. Racial discrimination, he had discovered quickly enough, was part of the culture of this American paradise. Chinese immigrants were prominent targets. In 1850, the state legislature taxed all foreign miners twenty dollars a month; in 1860, another bill required Chinese fishermen to buy a special license; two years later, legislators passed a law to discourage all Chinese immigration into the state. Chinese children could not attend public schools. As soon as a new opportunity arose, someone put forward a new measure to prevent Chinese from taking advantage of it. They could not even claim citizenship, the most basic American right. Legal documents

Most Chinese in California during the late nineteenth and early twentieth centuries lived in Chinatowns, such as that of San Francisco. They were repeated targets of discriminatory legislation and law enforcement. At its height, San Francisco's Chinatown had some 20,000 residents.

usually described them as "subjects of the Empress of China." The Chinese were a people set apart, legally and culturally, from the promise of American life.

In response, the Chinese created a variety of self-help organizations. One of these groups represented the interests of Chinese laundries, including Yick Wo's. San Franciscans described it as a "wealthy and powerful association" that threatened the municipal government—and, of course, the hundred or so laundries in the city that were not owned by Chinese. They pressured the board of supervisors to require all laundries in the city to get the board's consent to stay in business, unless the laundry was "located in a building constructed either of brick or stone." Almost all of the Chinese laundries were made of wood, as were most of the city's homes and businesses.

The board refused Yick Wo's application, as it did those of all the other Chinese owners. Eighty laundries in wooden buildings were allowed to remain open because, the board determined, they did not have drying scaffolds on their roofs and therefore posed no danger to their neighbors. None of the owners of these laundries was Chinese.

With the backing of the laundrymen's association, the Chinese continued to operate their businesses without the required permission. After he was arrested, Yick Wo refused to pay the fine and was sentenced to ten days in jail, which he appealed, unsuccessfully, to the California Supreme Court. Meanwhile, a second test case involving Wo Lee, a laundryman in another part of the city, was heard by a federal district court, with a different result. The judge agreed that the ordinance, while neutral on its face, was in fact applied arbitrarily by the supervisors and discriminated against the Chinese.

The Supreme Court decided to hear the two cases together, and in May 1886 the justices ruled in favor of Yick Wo and Wo Lee. In their order to discharge the petitioners from custody, the justices noted that the laundrymen had complied with every requirement of the law to protect against fire and guard the public health. The facts demonstrated "hostility to the race and the nationality." No one offered any reason "except the will of the supervisors" why the laundrymen should not be allowed to practice "their harmless and useful occupation." Discrimination did not occur only in the text of statutes, the majority opinion concluded. Laws can be fair on their face, "yet, if it is applied and administered by public authority with an evil eye and an unequal hand, so as practically to make unjust and illegal discriminations between persons in similar circumstances...the denial of equal justice is still within the prohibition of the constitution."

The ordinance and its enforcement were violations of the Fourteenth Amendment's guarantee of equal protection of the laws, which applied to all persons in the United States, not just citizens. The Constitution did not "leave room for the play and action of purely personal and arbitrary power.... For the very idea that one man may be compelled to hold his life, or the means of living, or any material right essential to

In 1881, Harper's Weekly *lambasted the Chinese immigrants who were becoming an increasing presence in the western part of the country. Although welcomed at first, they soon were viewed as an economic threat. As early as 1852, a report in California lamented U.S. immigration policies "by which the surplus and inferior population of Asia may be brought into competition with the labor of our own people."*

The integration of Anacostia High School in Washington, D.C., in the late 1950s was the result of the Supreme Court's ruling in Brown v. Board of Education. *Court-ordered racial desegregation was often accomplished by busing students to distant neighborhoods.*

the enjoyment of life, at the mere will of another, seems to be intolerable in any country where freedom prevails, as being the essence of slavery itself."

Yick Wo v. *Hopkins* (1886) established an important principle that lay dormant for almost a century before becoming a central part of modern civil rights law. Even if a law is expressed in completely neutral terms—even if its language is not discriminatory—it will be judged unconstitutional if it results in discrimination. The Fourteenth Amendment protects individuals against a statistically significant unequal result and not simply intentional discrimination. Known as disparate impact, this standard was important in overturning statutes passed after *Brown* v. *Board of Education* (1954), the case that declared segregation of the races to be inherently unequal.

Civil rights are rights that belong to us by virtue of our citizenship. They include the fundamental rights guaranteed by the Constitution, as well as by congressional acts. Much of what we identify today as our right to be free from racial discrimination stems from a series of national laws passed since the 1950s. The Civil Rights Act of 1964 was the most comprehensive civil rights law in U.S. history. Two provisions—Title II and Title VII—were especially important because they prohibited racial discrimination in public accommodations, or any place open to the public, such as hotels, swimming pools, and public transportation, and in employment. Other acts, such as the Voting Rights Act of 1965, gave rights to individuals based on the concept of equal treatment.

The Court has interpreted these protections broadly, accepting, for example, that any employment practice that results in racial discrimination is unconstitutional, even if there is no intent to discriminate, which, of course, was the argument of Yick Wo and his fellow laundrymen. The Civil Rights Act of 1991 strengthened this principle even more by eliminating any claim by businesses that they needed to discriminate in order to remain competitive or viable. Significantly, these acts also allow individuals to collect damages from anyone who acts illegally to deny their rights. The Supreme Court generally has affirmed these laws, announcing in a 1989 case, for example, "Neither our words nor our decisions should be interpreted as signaling one inch of retreat from Congress's policy to forbid discrimination in the private, as well as the public, sphere."

One result of the various civil rights laws was affirmative action programs that required employers or labor unions to make a serious effort to hire members of racial minorities who had traditionally been excluded because of discrimination. Such programs were necessary, many people concluded, to erase old patterns of discrimination. But these attempts to remedy the ill effects of past practices were controversial, especially because they first appeared during a period of economic stagnation. Opponents claimed that affirmative action programs resulted in reverse discrimination, or bias against one group (whites) in order to make up for past discrimination against another group (blacks). They also argued that these programs, while not imposing racial quotas, violated American beliefs that merit, not race, should determine who is hired or wins a contract or is admitted to college.

The Supreme Court finally addressed this issue in 1978 in *Regents of the University of California* v. *Bakke.* The medical school at the University of California, Davis, with no history of racial discrimination, set aside sixteen of one hundred seats in its entering class for minorities, some of whom had lower grades and test scores than white applicants. One person denied admission was Allan Bakke, an aerospace engineer in his thirties. He sued, claiming that the program was a form of racial discrimination prohibited by the Fourteenth Amendment. By a narrow 5-to-4 vote that reflected the division in public opinion, the Court ruled in favor of Bakke and decided that although race could be one criterion for making decisions, specific racial quotas were illegal unless there was a history of racial discrimination. In 2003, in *Grutter* v. *Bollinger,* the justices upheld the use of race in making admission decisions if the purpose was to achieve "the educational benefits that flow from a diverse student body."

The Court has also upheld flexible affirmative action programs in other areas, such as a requirement that 10 percent of all the federal funds spent on public works projects go to minority contractors. Affirmative action opened opportunities for blacks in business, government, and the professions and helped spur the rapid growth of the black middle class in the late twentieth century. The same has been true for other racial and ethnic minorities who have experienced discrimination, as well as for women and people with disabilities.

Race remains an American dilemma, but it has never been expressed solely in terms of black and white. Most ethnic minorities have experienced discrimination. American Indians, Hispanics, Chinese, Japanese—the historical list is a long one, and the examples are too numerous to recount. We are not unique in this record of discrimination based on race, of course, but we are acutely aware of our shortcomings because our aspirations as a nation embrace the goal of equality of all people.

The Thirteenth, Fourteenth, and Fifteenth Amendments enshrined equality before the law for all citizens as a fundamental right, and the various civil rights acts have sought to redeem this promise for all Americans. The Constitution is color-blind, but regrettably we as citizens often are not. The

Many Americans believed that the Supreme Court's 1978 decision in Regents of the University of California v. Bakke, *in which it ruled that the University of California at Davis could not bar Allan Bakke from its medical school on the basis of racial preferences, was a case of reverse discrimination. The ruling divided Americans over the issue of equal opportunity.*

issues we face in eliminating racial discrimination are complex, and proposed solutions at times appear to conflict with other important values, such as freedom of association or rewards based on individual merit.

We have not yet created a society where, as Martin Luther King, Jr., so eloquently stated in his 1963 "I Have a Dream" speech, people are judged not by the color of their skin but by the content of their character. Yet our history, troubled as it has been, affirms that Americans have taken seriously the promise of the Declaration of Independence that all people are created equal. What should be reassuring is how the quest to eliminate racial barriers has revitalized our sense of liberty and democracy. The concept of equal protection under the law, present at the creation of the American republic, now includes people who, by definition, did not enjoy this fundamental right in 1787. We as a nation have grown in our understanding of liberty, rights, and social responsibility, and it is the potential for an even fuller sense of human equality that keeps the Constitution a vital document more than two hundred years after its adoption.

Discrimination on Public Transportation

Racial discrimination has been a constant theme of American history. Free blacks in the North before the Civil War did not have to endure the bonds of slavery, but they still had to deal with a highly segregated society. In the following account published in the New York Tribune *in 1854, Elizabeth Jennings, an African American schoolteacher in New York City recounts her forcible expulsion from a streetcar reserved for whites. This situation existed well into the twentieth century in a large part of the country. One hundred years after Elizabeth Jennings gave her account, Rosa Parks, a seamstress in Montgomery, Alabama, refused to give up her seat to a white passenger and move to the back of the bus. Her action began the bus boycott that propelled Martin Luther King, Jr., and the civil rights movement to national prominence and led to the end of legal segregation in public transportation, housing, education, and other areas of American life.*

Sarah E. Adams and myself walked down to the corner of Pearl and Chatham Sts. to take the Third Ave. cars. I held up my hand to the driver and he stopped the cars, we got on the platform, when the conductor told us to wait for the next car: I told him I could not wait, as I was in a hurry to go to church (the other car was about a block off). He then told me that the other car had my people in it, that it was appropriated for that purpose. I then told him I had no people. It was no particular occasion; I wished to go to church, as I had been going for the last six months, and I did not wish to be detained. He insisted upon my getting off the car; I told him I would wait on the car until the other car came up; he again insisted on my waiting in the street, but I did not get off the car; by this time the other car came up, and I asked the driver if there was any room in his car. He told me very distinctly, "No, that there was more room in my car than there was in his." Yet this did not satisfy the conductor; he still kept driving me out or off of the car; said he had as much time as I had and could wait just as long. I replied, "Very well, we'll see." He waited some few minutes, when the drivers becoming impatient, he said to me, "Well, you may go in, but remember, if the passengers raise any objections you shall go out, whether or no, or I'll put you out." I answered again and told him I was a respectable person, born and raised in New York, did not know where he was born, that I

had never been insulted before while going to church, and that he was a good for nothing impudent fellow for insulting decent persons while on their way to church. He then said I should come out or he would put me out. I told him not to lay his hands on me; he took hold of me and I took hold of the window sash and held on; he pulled me until he broke my grasp and I took hold of his coat and held on to that. . . . He then ordered the driver to fasten his horses, which he did, and come and help him put me out of the car; they then both seized hold of me by the arms and pulled and dragged me flat down on the bottom of the platform. . . . I went again in the car, and the conductor said you shall sweat for this; then told the driver to drive as fast as he could and not take another passenger in the car; to drive until he saw an officer or a Station House. They got an officer on the corner of Walker and Bowery, whom the conductor told that his orders from the agent were to admit colored persons if the passengers did not object, but if they did, not to let them ride. When the officer took me there were some eight or ten persons in the car. Then the officer, without listening to anything I had to say, thrust me out, and then pushed me, and tauntingly told me to get redress if I could; this the conductor also told me, and gave me some name and number of his car; he wrote his name Moss and the car No. 7, but I looked and saw No. 6 on the back of the car.

"Every Possible Protection against Espionage"

After the bombing of Pearl Harbor in Hawaii and the U.S. declaration of war against Japan in late 1941, concern arose about the loyalty of Japanese Americans. Many residents of the West Coast worried about an attack from Japanese bombers, and the military feared that citizens of Japanese ancestry might aid the enemy. President Franklin D. Roosevelt issued the following executive order in 1942 authorizing the removal of 120,000 Japanese Americans, more than two-thirds of them native-born U.S. citizens, and their placement into concentration camps. The Supreme Court upheld the executive order and subsequent federal legislation in Hirabayashi v. United States *(1943) and* Korematsu v. United States *(1944). Most scholars today consider the forced incarceration and the Supreme Court cases that approved it to have been America's worst wartime mistake concerning civil rights.*

Whereas, The successful prosecution of the war requires every possible protection against espionage and against sabotage to national defense material, national defense premises and national defense utilities...:

Now, therefore, by virtue of the authority vested in me as President of the United States, and Commander in Chief of the Army and Navy, I hereby authorized and direct the Secretary of War, and the Military Commanders whom he may from time to time designate, whenever he or any designated Commander deem such action necessary or desirable to prescribe military areas in such places and of such extent as he or the appropriate Military Commander may determine, from which any or all persons may be excluded, and with respect to which, the right of any person to enter, remain in, or leave shall be subject to whatever restriction the Secretary of War or the appropriate Military Commander may impose in his discretion. The Secretary of War is hereby authorized to provide for residents of any such area who are excluded therefrom. such transportation, food, shelter, and other accommodations as may be necessary, in the judgment of the Secretary of War or the said Military Commander and until other arrangements are made, to accomplish the purpose of this order. The designation of military areas in any region or locality shall supersede designation of prohibited and restricted areas by the Attorney General under the Proclamation of December 7 and 8, 1941, and shall supersede the responsibility and authority of the Attorney General under the said Proclamation in respect of such prohibited and restricted areas.

I hereby further authorize and direct the Secretary of War and the said Military Commanders to take such other steps as he or the appropriate Military Commander may deem advisable to enforce compliance with the restrictions applicable to each Military area herein above authorized to be designated. including the use of Federal troops and other Federal Agencies, with authority to accept assistance of state and local agencies.

I hereby further authorize and direct all Executive Department, independent establishments and other Federal Agencies, to assist the Secretary of War or the said Military Commanders in carrying out this Executive Order, including the furnishing of medical aid, hospitalization, food, clothing, transportation, use of land, shelter, and other supplies, equipment, utilities, facilities and service.

This order shall not be construed as modifying or limiting in any way the authority granted under Executive Order 8972, dated December 12, 1941, nor shall it be construed as limiting or modifying the duty and responsibility of the Federal Bureau of Investigation, with response to the investigation of alleged acts of sabotage or duty and responsibility of the Attorney General and the Department of Justice under the Proclamation of December 7 and 8, 1941, prescribing regulations for the conduct and control of alien enemies, except as such duty and responsibility is superseded by the designation of military areas thereunder.

CHAPTER 11

The Right to Vote

We cannot imagine a modern democracy without adult citizens having the right to vote freely. It is a basic right of citizenship in a democratic society. Yet nowhere in the Constitution is the right to vote granted explicitly. At a time when even dictatorial governments formally (and fraudulently) hold elections, it seems remarkable that the world's leading democracy does not mention the right to vote in the main body of its most important document.

The creation of a federal system that divided power between state and central governments explains this strange omission. The framers left it to states to determine qualifications of voters in state and national elections, which at the time meant that only white men who owned property could vote. This limitation proved unacceptable, and beginning in the nineteenth century, states gradually opened the door to widespread participation in elections. By the 1970s, changes in voter qualifications opened the ballot to nearly all adult citizens.

Today, we tend to think of new rights as results of Supreme Court decisions. We often forget that rights also stem from political action and constitutional amendment. The extension of the right to vote to all adult citizens falls into this latter category. Property restrictions disappeared in the 1820s and 1830s when, under political pressure, new state constitutions extended the right to vote—also called suffrage and the franchise—to free white males older than twenty-one. Changes to the federal constitution occurred after the Civil War. The Fifteenth Amendment (1870) prohibited states from denying the right to vote on account of "race, color, or previous condition of servitude." The Nineteenth Amendment (1920) enfranchised women. The Twenty-fourth Amendment (1964) banned poll taxes meant to discourage blacks from voting in federal elections. The Twenty-sixth Amendment (1971) lowered the voting age to eighteen. Collectively, the voting amendments represent the greatest addition of rights to the Constitution since the Bill of Rights was adopted in 1791.

Few of these changes came easily. Opponents were fearful that new voters would threaten their political power or challenge the values they prized. In each instance a shift in social attitudes preceded the adoption of the amendment and made it possible. Many of the major expansions of the franchise have also occurred during or in the aftermath of wars because it was difficult to ask people to bear the demands of war while denying them the vote. But even when most people agreed the time had come to extend the franchise, stiff opposition remained, making it difficult to claim victory, as illustrated by the final act—the so-called War of the Roses—in the long battle to enact the Nineteenth Amendment.

August 1920 was hot and muggy in Nashville, Tennessee. Normally, it was a month when residents left the capital city for the highlands of Kentucky or the Smoky Mountains to the east. But this August was not typical. The Tennessee legislature was in session to ratify the Nineteenth Amendment and

Tennessee's first woman suffrage organization was founded in Memphis in 1889 and was succeeded by many other such groups over the next three decades. In addition to holding rallies and business meetings and distributing literature, suffragists hosted such social events as a barbecue that featured a race between an automobile with a female driver and an airplane with a female pilot.

extend the vote to women. Thirty-five states had passed it, one short of the three-fourths of states required for its adoption. Yet suffragists, supporters of the amendment, were uneasy. Connecticut, the state they had counted on for victory, suddenly appeared unlikely to ratify the amendment. Now they had to fight the battle in the conservative, unsympathetic South. A defeat in Tennessee, they feared, might kill the amendment.

The town was thick with celebrities and reporters from around the nation. Carrie Chapman Catt, head of the National Woman Suffrage Association, had arrived from New York two months earlier to team with prominent Tennessee women to organize rallies and letter-writing campaigns, enlisting support from women of urban and rural backgrounds, different social classes, and different races. To demonstrate their unity, the pro-amendment forces adopted the yellow rose as a symbol. In response, opponents chose the red rose. The ensuing campaign became known, naturally, as the War of the Roses, recalling the fifteenth-century civil war among the nobility in England.

Initially, legislators appeared to favor passage, but they soon began to waver under relentless pressure from opponents of the amendment. Suffragists feared the worst, even after the Tennessee senate voted overwhelmingly to ratify. The state's lower house appeared to be leaning the other way. Legislators wore either yellow roses or red roses to signal their position on the vote, and a simple count of roses, 49 red and 47 yellow, forecast defeat for the amendment. "We are up to the last half of the last state," Catt wrote, "[and] opposition of every sort is fighting with no scruple.... [They] are appealing to Negrophobia and every other cave man's prejudice.... It's hot, muggy, nasty, and this last battle is desperate.... We are low in our minds.... Even if we win, we who are here will never remember it but with a shudder."

The road to ratification that was reaching its climactic moment in Tennessee had begun in 1848 in New York State at the Seneca Falls Women's Rights Convention. The Declaration of Rights of Women, the document produced by the convention, contained the first serious proposal that women be allowed to vote. Twenty years later, in 1868, a woman suffrage amendment was first intro-

Antisuffragists in Tennessee, including Mrs. James S. Pinckard (left), president general of the Southern Women's League for the Rejection of the Susan B. Anthony Amendment and a niece of Senator John C. Calhoun, a fervent nineteenth-century supporter of states' rights, pose for a tableau. The antisuffrage movement was associated with the traditional values of the Old South, represented by the Confederate veteran and flag, and was supported by powerful business interests in the state.

duced, unsuccessfully, in Congress. In the 1870s, suffragists tried again, this time proposing the so-called Anthony amendment, named for Susan B. Anthony, the century's leading campaigner for women's rights, and modeled after the Fifteenth Amendment, which forbade states from denying the right to vote based on race or color. (Even though that amendment does not refer to gender, in effect it applied to men only.) The Anthony amendment provided that "the right of citizens of the United States to vote shall not be denied or abridged by the United States or by any State on account of sex," words that became the language of the Nineteenth Amendment forty-two years later.

Stymied in their attempts to get a constitutional amendment passed by Congress in the 1860s and 1870s, suffragists resorted to the courts, with no success. In what was termed the "new departure," they looked to the Fourteenth Amendment's language that all persons born in the United States are citizens who enjoy the privileges and immunities of citizenship. Voting was one of those

"But to have drunkards, idiots, horse-racing, rum-selling rowdies, ignorant foreigners, and silly boys fully recognized, while we ourselves are thrust out from all the rights that belong to citizens, it is too grossly insulting to the dignity of woman to be longer quietly submitted to. The right is ours. Have it, we must. Use it, we will. The pens, the tongues, the fortunes, the indomitable wills of many women are already pledged to secure this right."

—Elizabeth Cady Stanton, speech, Waterloo, New York (1848)

privileges, they argued. But the Supreme Court did not agree, rejecting the attempt of a reformer, Virginia Minor, to register to vote in Missouri. Advocates of women's right to vote were more successful in persuading some states, especially western states, to grant the franchise to women. Other suffragists, tired of the slow progress, began using more radical tactics: picketing the White House, staging large marches and demonstrations, and going to jail. During World War I, women played important roles in the war effort, and they used their new influence to pressure the President and Congress for a reward of political equality. Their tactics paid off. In 1918, President Woodrow Wilson asked Congress to submit the Nineteenth Amendment to the states, which it did in 1919.

All the arguments advanced in Tennessee for and against the amendment had been part of the national debate for decades. Supporters focused on two themes—equality and responsibility. Women were citizens, and the American ideals of citizenship, as expressed in the Declaration of Independence and reinforced in the Fourteenth Amendment, required equal treatment under law. The Fifteenth Amendment had extended the vote to previously excluded African Americans, so women, too, were due this right. Unfortunately, this argument sometimes was accompanied by the ugly claim of white women's superiority over black men as potential voters. Women also pointed to their contributions to the nation's economy; increasingly they worked in factories and had begun to enter the professions. Even so, women were denied opportunities to fulfill their civic obligation. They could not serve on juries, for instance, because jurors were chosen from voting rolls, an exclusion that denied women defendants the right to be tried by their peers.

Opponents of female suffrage focused attention on what they claimed would threaten the family. A woman's place was in the home; it was her separate sphere, a world of motherhood and domesticity where she exerted a naturally superior moral influence. Placing women in the nasty arena of partisan politics would sully them, dragging them to the level of the men who were less refined morally and ethically. Ironically, many feminists accepted the notion that women played a superior domestic role, but they argued in rebuttal that by voting women would uplift the nation's political and moral tone.

The critical Tennessee vote on the amendment came in the state's house of representatives on August 18. Supporters were two votes shy of passage, but a legislator abandoned his hospital bed to close the gap to one vote. Then, unexpectedly, an opponent switched sides, leaving the legislature deadlocked. A second vote on the amendment produced another tie. Tensions mounted as each side lobbied furiously to change legislators' minds. Suddenly, on the third roll call, the youngest member of the legislature, twenty-four-year-old Harry Burns, whose district opposed the amendment, dramatically announced his support. In his pocket was a telegram from his mother, a staunch suffragist, who urged him to vote yes, writing, "I have been watching to see how you stood, but have noticed nothing yet. Be a good boy and help Mrs. Catt put 'Rat' in Ratification." Joined by another member who also changed his vote, the amendment passed, 49 to 47.

With the certification of Tennessee's decision, the Nineteenth Amendment—and a new right—became part of the Constitution. Only one delegate from the

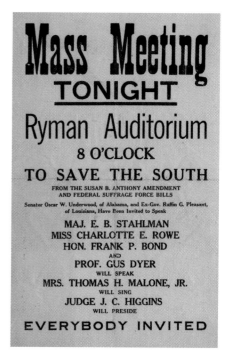

Antisuffragists in Tennessee feared that giving women the right to vote would alter the traditional southern way of life and would inspire conflict between the races. During World War I, antisuffragists also argued that women should not be allowed to vote because they could not contribute to national defense.

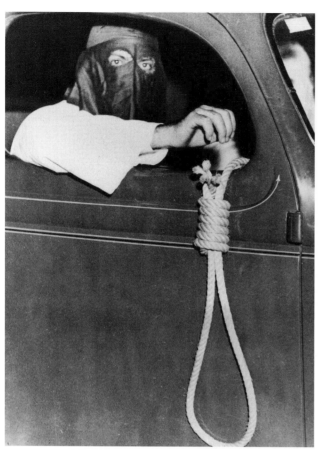

The Ku Klux Klan in Florida and elsewhere in the South was serious in its attempts to intimidate black voters. This Klan member in Miami dangles a noose from his car window during a 1939 primary election; nevertheless, 616 blacks exercised their right to vote.

Seneca Falls convention was still alive when the amendment passed. Charlotte Woodward had been nineteen years old in 1848. When finally eligible to cast her first ballot, she was ninety-one. It had taken a lifetime for women to achieve the right to vote.

The Nineteenth, Twenty-fourth, and Twenty-sixth Amendments contain clear directives and have required little or no judicial interpretation. The Fifteenth Amendment is in a class by itself, even though it, too, contained a similar directive extending the vote to black citizens. This new constitutional protection did not guarantee access to the polls as many states, especially in the South, found other ways to discourage black men, and then women, from exercising their rights. Literacy tests, poll taxes, and intimidation were just some of the obstacles African Americans had to overcome. White voting registrars, for instance, required potential black voters to read and explain complex constitutional texts and then denied the vote even when the applicant demonstrated his knowledge. White men were given a pass under so-called "grandfather" clauses that allowed them to register if their ancestors had voted. Not until the 1960s were most of these barriers removed by law.

Today, the franchise is nearly universal in the United States. Only juveniles, aliens (foreign-born residents who are not yet citizens), convicted felons, and insane persons cannot vote in most states. Not all questions related to voting are settled, however. In Georgia, for example, all counties, regardless of size, had a single representative in the legislature. A series of cases in the 1960s addressed these problems when the Supreme Court adopted what is known as the "one man, one vote" principle to judge how fairly state legislatures created voting districts, based on the Fourteenth Amendment's requirement of equal protection of the laws for different groups of people. These decisions corrected some gross inequities, but they raised other questions. In redrawing districts, for example, could legislatures create predominately black or Latino districts for the purpose of ensuring the election of minority officeholders? The underlying question was an important one—is voting an individual right or a group right? These issues are still being debated, although Americans remain true to the tradition that legislators represent individual voters, not groups. Also unsettled is how far political parties may go to redraw voting districts to make it more likely their candidates will win—and whether these districts can be redrawn at times other than the years immediately following a census conducted every decade.

A more significant modern problem is the number of eligible voters who choose not to exercise their right. Many people fail to register, even though recent laws allow registration by mail or when applying for governmental services, including a driver's license. Only about half of all registered voters participate in the national election for President, and even fewer people vote in other elections. This low turnout places the United States near the bottom of all

"The vote . . . is the most powerful instrument ever devised by man for breaking down injustice and destroying the terrible walls which imprison men because they are different from other men."

—President Lyndon B. Johnson, upon signing the
Voting Rights Act of 1965

Western democracies. The group that votes least is eighteen- to twenty-four-year-olds, thereby giving young adults less influence over government policy even though, as the largest group in the military, they are the citizens whose lives are most at risk from political decisions.

What difference does voting make—and more important, what is its relationship to other individual rights? Each vote counts, sometimes in ways unimagined when they are cast. The Presidential election of 2000, for example, was one of the closest contests in U.S. history. Less than three hundred votes separated winner from loser in Florida, the state whose electoral votes tipped the election to George W. Bush. But what difference does voting make to our individual rights under the Constitution? The most direct relationship comes in the laws passed by Congress and the various state legislatures. We elect the senators and representatives who pass measures that may extend or limit our rights. We also vote for the President and governors who administer and enforce these statutes. The selection of federal and state judges has a less direct but equally important relationship with voting. The U.S. Senate, elected by popular vote, approves the President's appointments for federal judgeships. These judges interpret our constitutional guarantees, which is why the confirmation of Supreme Court nominees attracts such attention.

Voting is a fundamental right—and a responsibility—of citizens in a democracy. It is, in fact, a right that gives special meaning to the First Amendment rights of freedom of speech, press, and assembly that we deem essential for our liberty. These rights and the right to vote are required for a government "of the people, by the people, for the people," in Abraham Lincoln's words. One of the original contributions made by the founding generation, a generation raised in a world of monarchies, was the theory of popular sovereignty, where power resides in the people and not the government. Our constitution expresses this concept in its opening phrase, "We the People." When we exercise our right to vote, we affirm the value of this revolutionary ideal and, in the process, revitalize our democracy.

Are All Citizens Necessarily Voters?

Virginia Minor of Missouri was the first person to take the cause of women's right to vote to the U.S. Supreme Court. In 1869, she developed an argument called the "New Departure" in which she claimed that women already had the right to vote as a consequence of the adoption of the Fourteenth Amendment and its citizenship clause. Women were citizens of the United States, she claimed, and were entitled to all the "privileges and immunities" of citizens, as protected by the amendment. One of these privileges was the right to vote. When she tried to register to vote in Missouri, however, the county election judge, Reese Happersett, refused to enroll her on the list of eligible voters. In 1875, a unanimous U.S. Supreme Court rejected her appeal. It reasoned that because a person could be a citizen without being a voter, therefore voting was not a privilege or right of citizenship protected by the Fourteenth Amendment. Chief Justice Morrison R. Waite wrote the opinion in Minor v. Happersett.

The question is presented in this case, whether, since the adoption of the fourteenth amendment, a woman, who is a citizen of the United States and of the State of Missouri, is a voter in that State, notwithstanding the provision of the constitutional and laws of that State, which confine the right of suffrage to men alone....

The direct question is...whether all citizens are necessarily voters.

The [fourteenth] amendment did not add to the privileges and immunities of a citizen. It simply furnished an additional guaranty for the protection of such as he already had....

It is clear...that the Constitution has not added the right of suffrage to the privileges and immunities of citizenship as they existed at the time it was adopted. This makes it proper to inquire whether suffrage was coextensive with the citizenship of the States at the time of its adoption. If it was, then it may with force be argued that suffrage was one of the rights which belonged to citizenship, and in the enjoyment of which every citizen must be protected. But if it was not, the contrary may with propriety be assumed.

[A]ll the citizens of the States were not invested with the right of suffrage. In all, save perhaps New Jersey, this right was only bestowed upon men and not upon all of them....

Women were excluded from suffrage in nearly all States by the express provision of their constitutions and laws....

But we need not particularize further. No new State has ever been admitted to the Union which has conferred the right of suffrage upon women, and this have never been considered a valid objection to her admission. On the contrary...the right of suffrage was withdrawn from women as early as 1807 in the State of New Jersey, without any attempt to obtain the interference of the United States to prevent it. Since then the governments of the insurgent States have been reorganized under a requirement that before their representatives could be admitted to seats in Congress they must have adopted new constitutions, republican in form. In no one of these constitutions was suffrage conferred upon women, and yet the States have all been restored to their original position as States in the Union.

Certainly, if the courts can consider any question settled, this is one. For nearly ninety years the people have acted upon the idea that the Constitution, when it conferred citizenship, did not necessarily confer the right of suffrage....Our province here is to decide what the law is, not to declare what it should be.

We have given this case the careful consideration its importance demands. If the law is wrong, it ought to be changed; but the power for that is not with us.

"No Person Shall Be Kept from Voting Because of His Race"

Prior to the passage of the Voting Rights Act in 1965, the federal government responded to claims of racial discrimination in voting in the South on a case-by-case basis. The civil rights march from Selma to Birmingham, Alabama, in March 1965 dramatized the injustices and brutality inflicted on blacks who sought to vote. The use of police dogs and fire hoses to stop the marchers and the murders of several civil rights workers led to public outrage and a decision by Lyndon Johnson's administration to seek a national voting rights act. President Johnson outlined his reasons for the request in a nationally televised speech (below) to a joint session of Congress while the Selma march was still in progress. The act passed quickly. In 2006, the act was extended for another twenty-five years.

Our fathers believed that if this noble view of the rights of man was to flourish, it must be rooted in democracy. The most basic right of all was the right to choose your own leaders. The history of this country, in large measure, is the history of the expansion of that right to all of our people.

Many of the issues of civil rights are very complex and most difficult. But about this there can and should be no argument. Every American citizen must have an equal right to vote. There is no reason which can excuse the denial of that right. There is no duty which weighs more heavily on us than the duty we have to ensure that right.

Yet the harsh fact is that in many places in this country men and women are kept from voting simply because they are Negroes.

Every device of which human ingenuity is capable has been used to deny this right. The Negro citizen may go to register only to be told that the day is wrong, or the hour is late, or the official in charge is absent. And if he persists, and if he manages to present himself to the registrar, he may be disqualified because he did not spell out his middle name or because he abbreviated a word on the application.

And if he manages to fill out an application he is given a test. The registrar is the sole judge of whether he passes this test. He may be asked to recite the entire Constitution, or explain the most complex provisions of State law. And even a college degree cannot be used to prove that he can read and write.

For the fact is that the only way to pass these barriers is to show a white skin.

Experience has clearly shown that the existing process of law cannot overcome systematic and ingenious discrimination. No law that we now have on the books—and I have helped to put three of them there—can ensure the right to vote when local officials are determined to deny it.

In such a case our duty must be clear to all of us. The Constitution says that no person shall be kept from voting because of his race or his color. We have all sworn an oath before God to support and to defend that Constitution. We must now act in obedience to that oath.

CHAPTER 12

The Right to a Fair Trial

The image is an old one in Western history: accuser versus accused, each summoning witnesses publicly in front of a judge to present their different versions of the truth. If the contest is equal and the judge impartial, then we deem the outcome fair and the verdict just, one that speaks the truth.

An adversarial process is central to our notion of criminal justice, and it extends deep into our past. In Anglo-Saxon England, one person would accuse another person publicly, and representatives of the community decided what form of trial would best determine the truth. The choices involved oaths by witnesses, a physical test known as an ordeal, or a winner-take-all physical contest or battle. Beginning with the arrival of William the Conqueror in 1066, the system became more formal: a grand jury investigated a crime and issued an indictment, or formal accusation, government prosecutors presented evidence supporting the accusation, and a trial jury determined the defendant's guilt or innocence. Procedures developed to ensure fairness and to protect the innocent. Among these rules was a guarantee that the accused could confront witnesses against him and challenge their testimony.

Colonists brought these rights with them to the New World and expanded them. By the time of the American Revolution, the list of procedural rights guaranteed in charters and statutes was more extensive than its English counterpart. Chief among them were rights to ensure that accused persons could defend themselves in court, including the right to know the charges against them, to confront their accusers, to challenge jurors, and to compel witnesses to testify. The colonists regarded these procedures as part of their birthright as English citizens and objected when new imperial regulations in the mid-eighteenth century threatened to limit or eliminate them. The rights were considered essential to due process of law, the most ancient and best guarantee of liberty, so their violation justified independence.

Protections for the accused received major emphasis in the new nation's Bill of Rights. Four of the ten amendments addressed matters of criminal process

"THAT in all capital or criminal prosecutions a man hath a right to demand the cause and nature of his accusation, to be confronted with the accusers and witnesses, to call for evidence in his favour, and to a speedy trial by an impartial jury of his vicinage, without whose unanimous consent he cannot be found guilty, nor can he be compelled to give evidence against himself; that no man be deprived of his liberty except by the law of the land, or the judgment of his peers."

—Virginia Declaration of Rights (1776)

so completely that scholars have called them a miniature code of criminal procedure. The Sixth Amendment was especially important for a fair trial. In addition to its guarantee of a speedy and public trial by an impartial local jury, the amendment requires defendants "to be informed of the nature and cause of the accusation; to be confronted with the witnesses against him; to have compulsory process for obtaining witnesses in his favor; and to have the Assistance of Counsel in his defense." This constellation of rights embodies basic notions of fairness and balance. It gives the defendant the same rights as the government. For instance, the state uses a lawyer to prosecute; the accused can have a lawyer to assist in the defense. The prosecuting attorney can compel witnesses to testify; so can the defendant.

In making rights to a fair trial so prominent, the framers were not inventing new principles of justice—earlier English laws had included such things as compulsory process for the accused—but they were proclaiming them fundamental to liberty itself. History warned against the dangers of arbitrary government. Despotism flourished when government could act in secret and outside the law. The founding generation relied in part upon public trials and fair process—procedures that balanced the power of government with the rights of individuals—as safeguards against tyranny.

During the nineteenth century, criminal justice was primarily the responsibility of the states, not the central government. State constitutions incorporated similar guarantees, such as trial by jury and protections against warrantless search and seizure. Before the Civil War, judges were especially alert to attempts by state legislatures to erode these protections in efforts to control crime. Elaborate rules governed such things as subpoenas (legal orders used to compel witnesses to testify) and the language of indictments. Soon, criminal procedure was a highly specialized subject, with separate courses of study and treatises to explain its complex rules to lawyers. The rules were specific to each state, which meant that the rights of the accused were to a large extent dependent upon geography. A person charged with the same crime in Alabama and New Jersey might have the same rights in theory, but the court procedures protecting these rights could vary widely. Criminal law in some states, for example, allowed courts to assign an attorney to assist poor defendants, whereas in other states it imposed no such obligation. The rules in practice reflected as well the individual decisions of thousands of local officers and courts, as well as the expectations and prejudices of the people they served. The right to a fair trial also often depended on who you were and where you lived.

This situation changed in the twentieth century when the Supreme Court began to interpret the Fourteenth Amendment's due process clause as a limit on the power of the state, as well as federal, governments. Due process, the justices decided, included many of the specific provisions of the Bill of Rights. This process of incorporation, as it is called, began early in the century but reached its highpoint in the 1960s. In what became known as the "due process revolution," the Bill of Rights became a national code of criminal procedure. The promise of a fair trial applied equally to all citizens everywhere.

Television series and reality shows, such as those on Court TV, highlight the adversarial nature of criminal justice, but they sometimes obscure how constitutional guarantees of a fair trial work in ordinary cases. Instead of a dramatic clash of good versus evil, what happens in most courtrooms often appears boring and uneventful; the vast majority of cases are not sufficiently compelling for television. Sometimes, the routine nature of many trials hides the way constitutional guarantees shape the administration of justice. Close examination reveals a complicated picture, one nearer to the founding generation's conception of rights at trial in some ways and further from it in others, as illustrated by a murder trial from New York.

In a South Bronx subway station on June 28, 1972, John Skagen, a white off-duty policeman, without apparent provocation, stopped James Richardson, a twenty-eight-year-old black man on his way to work at a local hospital, and ordered him to get against a wall and put his hands up. Maybe he thought Richardson was one of the unlicensed street peddlers that area merchants had complained about; perhaps it was the snub-nosed .32-caliber revolver Richardson had tucked into his pants. Whatever the reason, Skagen pocketed his badge and began a search. Suddenly, Richardson turned, his gun drawn. The two men faced each other for a split second, followed by four shots in quick succession—two bullets hit Skagen's shoulder, one struck Richardson in the groin, and the fourth lodged in a bystander's forearm.

Richardson fled down the street, yelling "He's shooting. A crazy man's shooting at me." Skagen appeared at the top of the stairs and fired, hitting Richardson in the shoulder but not halting him. A nearby patrolman, not recognizing his fellow officer, fired at Skagen, not stopping until his clip was empty. Richardson continued to run, now with several cops in pursuit, and threw his gun away before finally being slammed against a fence and handcuffed. Skagen was rushed to a hospital—the one where Richardson worked—but his wounds were fatal. In searching the scene, officers discovered a blue leather case Richardson had discarded before running. On it was a gold correction officer's badge stolen in the robbery of a bar several days earlier.

Few crimes stir more public response than the killing of a policeman. Such cases are rich in symbolism: the officer represents law and order; the accused, violent disorder. Coming as it did so soon after the urban riots of the late 1960s, this case offered authorities good opportunity to slight the procedures that define a fair trial.

But this did not happen. Richardson received all the rights guaranteed under the U.S. Constitution. Each time he was questioned at the hospital, an officer read him his rights, the so-called Miranda warning ("you have the right to remain silent") based on the Fifth Amendment. His arrest was based on probable cause, or a reasonable belief that he committed a crime, which is a Fourth Amendment requirement. The district attorney took the evidence before a grand jury, which issued an indictment with seven counts, or criminal acts the government alleged Richardson had committed. (The Fifth Amendment requires a grand jury for capital crimes in federal courts, so in this state case the right to a grand jury came from the New York constitution.) The indictment provided Richardson with several important protections. It told him what the prosecution would try to prove. Each crime had a precise legal meaning, and the government would have to demonstrate beyond a reasonable doubt that his actions met this definition. Also, the indictment fixed a legal boundary around the case; at trial, the prosecutor could not attempt to prove other crimes. The indictment, formally provided to Richardson at his arraignment, satisfied the Sixth Amendment's stipulation that the accused "be informed of the nature and cause of the accusation."

Within days, a James Richardson Defense Committee had formed in the South Bronx, where the suspect lived along with many of the city's African Americans. The case's notoriety attracted the attention of William Kunstler, a skillful yet flamboyant lawyer who had won a national reputation for defending individuals from what he believed was government persecution: the idea of "one cop killing another cop, and then charging a black bystander with the crime," as he put it, appealed to his sense of injustice. Kunstler asked to be the court-appointed counsel for the indigent Richardson, a right the Sixth Amendment guaranteed. He successfully lobbied for lower bail—the Eighth Amendment forbids excessive bail—but it still took seven months before Richardson's supporters could raise the $10,000 required for his release while awaiting trial. The trial clearly would not be speedy, as the Sixth Amendment prescribed, but the delay was not unusual; urban courts faced a flood of crimes and typically took eighteen months to move a case from arraignment to verdict. In this instance, it took twenty-seven months, in part because the defense requested more time to prepare.

During the interim, the prosecutor, Stephen Phillips, a young assistant district attorney who was trying one of his first cases, met with Kunstler to learn if Richardson would be willing to enter into a plea bargain, or plead guilty in exchange for a lesser sentence. He was not. If he had accepted the prosecutor's offer, Richardson would have waived the public trial required by the Sixth Amendment. During these negotiations, Phillips revealed the state's case. Under the Supreme Court's interpretation of the Fourteenth Amendment's due process clause, the prosecutor has to disclose exculpatory evidence, that is, evidence that could be interpreted to demonstrate the defendant's innocence. Phillips did not have to reveal all the evidence, however, although in this instance he did.

Further protection for the accused came later at a pretrial hearing. Judge Ivan Warner, an experienced and scrupulously fair jurist, examined the evidence to determine if it had been gathered properly; this step protects the defendant from police abuses. William Kunstler argued that the statements Richardson made in the hospital were forced confessions, illegal under the Fifth Amendment, because his client was in too much pain to understand his rights. After hearing testimony from the attending policemen and doctors, including Kunstler's cross-examination, which he would repeat at trial, the judge concluded that six of the seven statements met the constitutional test for allowable evidence and could be admitted at trial. Richardson had been in trouble with the law on earlier occasions, and the prosecution wanted to use several outstanding warrants for his arrest to suggest that Skagen might have stopped him for this reason. But the prosecutor could not prove the policeman knew about these warrants, so Judge Warner excluded this evidence. Introducing it might prejudice the jurors against Richardson.

Passengers wait for a train on the Lexington Avenue subway line in New York City, a mode of transportation considered inherently dangerous in the 1960s and 1970s. Plagued by petty crime and panhandlers, subway riders had little sympathy for those responsible for the high crime rate in the subway and were not necessarily concerned about defendants' legal rights.

Both the prosecutor and defense counsel took part in the selection of the jury. They considered two hundred potential jurors. Each side challenged several for cause, claiming that something in their background or their answers demonstrated that they could not reach a just verdict. Each lawyer could have dismissed up to twenty potential jurors, the number allowed by New York law, without offering a reason at all. The goal of this process, known as *voir dire* (from the French, meaning "to say the truth"), is to seat an impartial jury, as mandated by the Sixth Amendment. Kunstler used all of his twenty peremptory challenges, as they are called, to exclude jurors he believed would automatically favor a police version of events. Phillips used fourteen of his challenges to keep people with antigovernment attitudes off the panel. Finally, after eight days, the two sides settled on the twelve jurors and four alternates who would hear the case and reach a verdict.

The trial took two weeks. A full courtroom first heard witnesses for the prosecution—police officers, bystanders, doctors, and others—describe what happened, as they remembered it. To prove the primary count, murder, Phillips had to demonstrate that Richardson, acting with premeditation, fired the fatal shot. Ballistics evidence was inconclusive; Skagen had bled to death and one of the defendant's bullets had nicked an artery, but the officer might have died from shots fired by his fellow officer. Other counts described lesser offenses and had other standards of proof. Through his attorney, the defendant could confront the witnesses, a Sixth Amendment guarantee, and challenge their testimony. Kunstler's cross-examination tried to suggest a racially motivated police conspiracy to protect the officer who shot Skagen. Following the prosecution's presentation, Kunstler called witnesses for the defense—bystanders, acquaintances, and doctors who testified to a different view of the crime. Phillips, in turn, had the opportunity to cross-examine these witnesses. Richardson did not testify in his own defense, which was his right under the Fifth Amendment.

Judge Warner's roles were to enforce the rules of procedure and to establish the official record of the case. He allowed neither the prosecution nor defense to wander from the charges or the testimony because he knew that his actions could be reviewed by a higher court upon appeal. Once, he stopped Kunstler from asking whether the officer who shot Skagen felt remorse over a black man's death in another notorious police-shooting case, a question that had nothing to do with the charge against Richardson. The judge also had two other important roles. After testimony had ended, he had to decide if the evidence established all the legal elements of the crime. If it did not, then he had an obligation to dismiss the case. In this instance it did, so the jury would decide if the prosecution had proven guilt beyond a reasonable doubt. Then Judge Warner charged the jury, a second role he played during the trial. He reminded jurors that the indictment was merely an accusation and that the state had the burden of proof. Richardson did not have to prove his innocence. Warner also instructed them on the law involved in the case, including a definition of reasonable doubt, so they could determine whether or not the evidence, as they believed it, supported the indictment.

The jury found Richardson guilty of three of the seven counts—second-degree manslaughter, felony possession of a handgun, and possession of stolen property. The state had not proven the charge of murder or the other three counts; there was no conclusive evidence that Richardson fired the fatal shot or that he acted with premeditation. The jurors had taken their time in reaching a decision. It had taken them three days of long, intense deliberations, and several times they had returned to court to have Judge Warner explain the law again or to hear particular parts of the court record.

Sentenced to a prison term of up to ten years, Richardson remained free on bail while pursuing an appeal. Appeal of a conviction is not a constitutional right, but federal and state laws typically provide at least one review of the case by a higher court that looks only at the record of the case to determine if serious, irreversible errors occurred. In an appeal, the burden of proof—the responsibility for proving a claim—shifts from the state to the convicted defendant. Richardson no longer was assumed to be innocent. He had been convicted, so now he had to prove that serious errors had occurred at trial. He was able to do this, but only in part. He convinced the judges that his reckless conduct did not cause Skagen's death and therefore it did not meet the legal definition of manslaughter. Although the court reversed his conviction on this charge, it affirmed the felony-gun and stolen-property verdicts and sent the case back for re-sentencing. The court rejected the claim that Richardson had been denied a fair trial.

On May 27, 1976, almost four years after the death of John Skagen, James Richardson was sentenced to three years in the state prison. The Fifth Amendment's prohibition against double jeopardy prevented the state from retrying him for murder.

A criminal trial is a search for truth, but, as *People* v. *Richardson* demonstrates, truth is not the only value at stake. The need to uphold public order and to punish wrongdoing also are important. Overriding these values, however, is the requirement to protect individual liberty. The Bill of Rights especially insists that government respect the rights of individuals. Nowhere do we see these limits on official power more clearly than in criminal trials.

Individuals charged with crimes stand alone against the enormous power of the state. They face a loss of liberty or, in extreme cases, life. Our sense of

The county clerk swears in a trial jury in a local courthouse. The photograph was used by the U.S. Information Agency in foreign publications to demonstrate the merits of the American system of justice, which guarantees persons accused of a crime a fair trial by a jury of one's peers.

justice rejects this imbalance of power as unfair. It provides too much opportunity for this power to be used improperly, and it holds too much potential for punishing the innocent, an unacceptable outcome. Over time, therefore, we have devised elaborate procedures to guard the defendant's rights and make the contest between government and citizen more equal. In doing so, we trust that only the guilty will suffer a loss of freedom.

James Richardson's trial operated under these rules. At every stage of the process, constitutional protections of his liberty came into play. Occasionally, people voice concerns that strict adherence to these rights results in injustice because it "lets criminals go free" or it violates the interests of victims who, quite naturally, want their attacker punished. We all are concerned with public safety, but what is noteworthy is that protecting the rights of James Richardson did not result in his freedom. In fact, most criminal trials end in conviction. Numerous studies reveal that the chances of a lasting conviction increase greatly when police and prosecutors pay strict regard to the procedures that define a fair trial.

People v. *Richardson* was unusual because it went to trial. The vast majority of prosecutions today end with plea bargains. The Supreme Court has decided that, properly administered, plea negotiations are an acceptable part of modern criminal justice. Caseloads are too high to try every case, and most defendants, in truth, are guilty. But to satisfy the constitutional definitions of due process, plea agreements must be voluntary. The defendant waives, or does not claim, several important protections—the right against self-incrimination, the right to a jury trial, and confrontation of witnesses, among others—which is one reason the Court in the 1960s extended the right to assistance of counsel to all parts of the criminal process, and not simply the courtroom alone. Although the presence of counsel helps to ensure fair process, it is no guarantee that the defendants receive all their constitutional rights, especially if they are poor. Most court-appointed attorneys or public defenders, lawyers whose job it is to represent indigent defendants, are overworked and underpaid. They also work in an environment where the normal assumptions about innocence and guilt are turned on their head: plea bargaining presumes guilt, not innocence. Although plea bargaining may be efficient or even necessary, it has the potential to foster two systems of justice—one for the middle and upper classes, with legal protections for defendants, and one for the lower class, where the right to a fair trial is a paper promise.

In the criminal process of a free society, a proper concern for fair procedures—a fair trial—is crucial. Individual liberty is especially vulnerable to arbitrary governmental power, and without freedom from official capriciousness, no other human right can exist. The founding generation was especially alert to the need to protect the rights of defendants, which is why they devoted so much of the Bill of Rights to guarantees of a fair trial. They were realistic men who did not expect these rights to prevent all injustices. But they expected, at a minimum, that the formal expression of these rights, especially the guarantee of a fair trial, would serve, in the words of James Madison, as a "good ground for an appeal to the sense of the community" when threatened by arbitrary government or oppressive majorities. But Madison also recognized how communities could be seized by their concerns for safety, so he also trusted courts and judges to consider themselves "in a peculiar manner the guardian of these rights."

It is worth considering whether we still accept this view. After all, we live in a different world from the framers. Murders, robberies, assaults, and other threats to our safety and the security of our property are unfortunate facts of our daily lives. In response, numerous people call for stricter law enforcement and demand that lenient judges quit hamstringing the police and prosecutors by coddling criminals. It seems like such an easy solution—until we consider whether or not we want to be without these rights in the event we are accused. The rights that define a fair trial are available to individuals charged with driving under the influence, possessing banned drugs, breaking the tax laws, or being an accessory after the fact, as much as they are to defendants accused of first-degree murder. Rights rarely appear important until we need them.

Law and order. Fair trial. Many people see these slogans at opposite ends of an ideological spectrum, but in truth they both are part of what we expect in a democratic society. Throughout our history, we have learned that one depends upon the other. Fairness in our criminal process and respect for the rights of the accused are the things that persuade us to follow the law, which in turn assures us of the order we need to live freely and without fear. Our rights, ultimately, are the best guarantees of our liberty and our security. By honoring them, even when it is most difficult to do so, we all become the greatest defenders of our freedom and the servants of our highest ideals of justice.

A Heritage of Rights

In 1641, the Puritan colony of Massachusetts Bay adopted a code of laws called the Body of Liberties that spoke in terms of rights of citizens rather than restrictions on them. The list of liberties was comprehensive for its time. Blending Puritan theology and English common law, many of its guarantees anticipated the protections contained over a century later in the federal Bill of Rights. A primary protection of the Body of Liberties was the right to a fair trial, which included the right of counsel, trial by jury, right of appeal, and right to bail.

Every man that findeth himselfe unfit to plead his owne cause in any Court shall have Libertie to imploy any man against whom the Court doth not except, to helpe him, Provided he give him noe fee or reward for his paines. This shall not exempt the partie him selfe from Answering such Questions in person as the Court shall thinke meete to demand of him. . . .

In all Actions at law it shall be the libertie of the plantife and defendant by mutual consent to choose whether they will be tried by the Bench or by a Jurie, unlesse it be where the law upon just reason hath otherwise determined. The like libertie shall be granted to all persons in Criminall cases. . . .

It shall be in the libertie of every man cast condemned or sentenced in any cause in any Inferior Court, to make their Appeale to the Court of Assistants, provided they tender their appeale and put in securitie to prosecute it before the Court be ended wherein they were condemned, And within six days next ensuing put in good securitie before some Assistant to satisfie what his Adversarie shall recover against him; And if the cause be of a Criminall nature, for his good behaviour, and appearance, And everie man shall have libertie to complaine to the Generall Court of any Injustice done him in any Court of Assistants or other.

Obstacles to a Speedy Trial

The right to a fair trial includes the right to a speedy trial, as guaranteed by the Sixth Amendment. In modern America, increased crime, crowded courts, and the need to honor all other constitutional rights (such as the right to counsel) has lengthened considerably the time from indictment, the formal accusation of a crime, to trial. The U.S. Supreme Court has addressed this issue on several occasions, including Barker v. Wingo *(1972), in which Justice Lewis Powell outlined the reasons why trials experience delays and offered a balancing test to determine when the right to a speedy trial has been denied. This passage from the* Barker *opinion reveals the complexity of American criminal justice and the difficulty of applying rights of the accused according to a mechanical formula.*

The right to a speedy trial is generically different from any of the other rights enshrined in the Constitution for the protection of the accused. In addition to the general concern that all accused persons be treated according to decent and fair procedures, there is a societal interest in providing a speedy trial which exists separate from, and at times in opposition to, the interests of the accused. The inability of courts to provide a prompt trial has contributed to a large backlog of cases in urban courts which, among other things, enables defendants to negotiate more effectively for pleas of guilty to lesser offenses and otherwise manipulate the system. In addition, persons released on bond for lengthy periods awaiting trial have an opportunity to commit other crimes.... Moreover, the longer an accused is free awaiting trial, the more tempting becomes his opportunity to jump bail and escape. Finally, delay between arrest and punishment may have a detrimental effect on rehabilitation.

If an accused cannot make bail, he is generally confined.... This contributes to the overcrowding and generally deplorable state of those institutions. Lengthy exposure to these conditions "has a destructive effect on human character and makes the rehabilitation of the individual offender much more difficult." At times the result may even be violent rioting. Finally, lengthy pretrial detention is costly.... In addition, society loses wages which might have been earned, and it must often support families of incarcerated breadwinners.

A second difference between the right to speedy trial and the accused's other constitutional rights is that deprivation of the right may work to the accused's advantage. Delay is not an uncommon defense tactic. As the time between the commission of the crime and trial lengthens, witnesses may become unavailable or their memories may fade.... Thus, unlike the right to counsel or the right to be free from compelled self-incrimination, deprivation of the right to speedy trial does not per se prejudice the accused's ability to defend himself.

Finally, and perhaps most importantly, the right to speedy trial is a more vague concept than other procedural rights. It is, for example, impossible to determine with precision when the right has been denied.... As a consequence, there is no fixed point in the criminal process when the State can put the defendant to the choice of either exercising or waiving the right to a speedy trial....

A balancing test necessarily compels courts to approach speedy trial cases on an ad hoc basis. We can do little more than identify some of the factors which courts should assess in determining whether a particular defendant has been deprived of his right. Though some might express them in different ways, we identify four such factors: Length of delay, the reason for the delay, the defendant's assertion of his right, and prejudice to the defendant.

The length of the delay is to some extent a triggering mechanism. Until there is some delay which is presumptively prejudicial, there is no necessity for inquiry into the other factors that go into the balance....

Closely related to length of delay is the reason the government assigns to justify the delay.... A deliberate attempt to delay the trial in order to hamper the defense should be weighted heavily against the government. A more neutral reason such as negligence or overcrowded courts should be weighted less heavily.... Finally, a valid reason, such as a missing witness, should serve to justify appropriate delay....

Whether and how a defendant asserts his right is closely related to the other factors we have mentioned. The strength of his efforts will be affected by the length of the delay, to some extent by the reason for the delay, and most particularly by the personal prejudice, which is not always readily identifiable, that he experiences. The more serious the deprivation, the more likely a defendant is to complain....

A fourth factor is prejudice to the defendant. Prejudice, of course, should be assessed in the light of the interests of defendants which the speedy trial right was designed to protect. This Court has identified three such interests: (i) to prevent oppressive pretrial incarceration; (ii) to minimize anxiety and concern of the accused; and (iii) to limit the possibility that the defense will be impaired. Of these, the most serious is the last, because the inability of a defendant adequately to prepare his case skews the fairness of the entire system. If witnesses die or disappear during a delay, the prejudice is obvious. There is also prejudice if defense witnesses are unable to recall accurately events of the distant past. Loss of memory, however, is not always reflected in the record because what has been forgotten can rarely be shown....

[T]hese factors have no talismanic qualities; courts must still engage in a difficult and sensitive balancing process. But, because we are dealing with a fundamental right of the accused, this process must be carried out with full recognition that the accused's interest in a speedy trial is specifically affirmed in the Constitution.

CHAPTER 13

The Right to Due Process

I n the Magna Carta (1215), the great charter of English liberty, noblemen forced King John to abide by the "law of the land" in his dealings with them. Under this agreement, the king accepted the idea that his power was not absolute. He could act only as the law permitted him to act. Although English kings had far more authority to do as they pleased than do modern democratic governments, the Magna Carta introduced the idea that no man was above the law. When we say the United States is a nation of laws, we reaffirm this ancient principle called due process.

When drafting the Constitution and Bill of Rights, the framers thought of due process as central to their liberty. At first they believed the appearance of this guarantee in state constitutions offered sufficient protection, so the phrase does not appear in the U.S. Constitution as ratified in 1788. Opponents of the Constitution argued that the concept needed to restrain the federal government as well, and they succeeded in making it one of the rights guaranteed by the Bill of Rights. It appears in the Fifth Amendment (ratified in 1791) as a restraint on the central government; it also appears in the Fourteenth Amendment (ratified in 1868) as a restraint on the power of state governments.

The goal of due process is to prevent arbitrary government. It requires the state and federal governments to follow fair procedures when they act to deprive an individual of life, liberty, or property. The meaning of fairness has varied over time, but historically the guarantee has referred to procedures that protected individuals against arbitrary arrest and punishment—no arrest without a warrant, the right to counsel, indictment before a grand jury, and so forth. Many of these rights also are protected separately under the Bill of Rights.

Due process in its earliest form was significant primarily in criminal procedures, although at the end of the nineteenth century, it was also used briefly to protect certain property interests against regulation by government. Under criminal due process, state governments could—and did—establish their own procedures to ensure a fair trial. These procedures varied from state to state, a result that was permitted under existing interpretations of the Constitution. For the most part, states took seriously their responsibility to ensure due process. Even crimes involving slaves required strict adherence to procedures. But people on the margins of society—the poor or ethnic minorities, for example—often found that the law on paper was not the law in practice.

The year 1931 was a hard one for many Americans. The nation was in the second year of the Great Depression. One in every four workers was unemployed, and thousands of people were abandoning their homes to look for work elsewhere. Lacking cars and money, many men became transients, or hoboes, who hitched rides on trains that would take them to California and other places where life was rumored to be easier.

"Article 39. No free man shall be seized or imprisoned, or stripped of his rights or possessions, or outlawed or exiled, or deprived of his standing in any other way, nor will we proceed with force against him, or send others to do so, except by the lawful judgment of his equals or by the law of the land."

—Magna Carta (1215)

On March 25, 1931, a group of white hoboes complained to a deputy sheriff near Scottsboro, Alabama, that a "bunch of negroes" on a Memphis-bound train had attacked them. The charge was a serious one, especially in the racially oppressive atmosphere of the Deep South. The matter became explosive when a hastily gathered posse discovered two white girls dressed in men's clothing in the same railroad car as nine black youths. The teenaged girls realized they had committed a serious breach of race relations by being together, unsupervised, with black males, and to protect themselves and their reputations, they claimed that the boys, ranging in age from thirteen to nineteen, had repeatedly raped them. Word of the incident spread quickly around the rural county. By the time the youths reached the Scottsboro jail, only the judge's promise of speedy punishment kept an angry mob from lynching them.

In the aftermath of slavery, African Americans, especially in the South, continued to suffer from discrimination and often found themselves outside the protection of the law. Southern legal officials—sheriffs, judges, and jurors—were white men. In the segregated society of the 1930s, these officials almost always believed the word of a white person, any white person, over that of a black. When blacks were charged with crimes against whites, judges and jurors discounted the testimony of black witnesses and readily convicted black defendants, even when the evidence was weak. Blacks accused of heinous crimes, such as murder or rape, often faced scores of white men who tortured and executed them before large, cheering crowds that included women and children. The horror of these grisly spectacles was deeply etched in black culture. The Scottsboro boys knew this awful history: from the 1890s to the 1930s, more than 3,000 blacks died at the hands of lynch mobs, primarily in the South and Midwest.

The trial was a sham. Under Alabama law, anyone accused of a capital crime—a crime punishable by death—had to be represented by counsel. The judge appointed all seven members of the Scottsboro bar as defense attorneys. One by one, the lawyers withdrew from the case; they knew their future practice would suffer by taking this assignment. Only an unreliable seventy-one-year-old lawyer, appointed on the morning of the trial, was left to defend the nine boys. Aiding the defense was an alcoholic white attorney from Chattanooga, hired by a group of concerned black ministers because he had on occasion taken cases on behalf of African Americans. This team did not consult with the defendants—the lawyers met them for the first time a mere thirty minutes before the court opened—and they offered little resistance to the courtroom charade. They did not even give a closing statement.

Facing popular demands that white womanhood be avenged, the trial—actually four separate cases—proceeded swiftly. The testimony of the girls was contradictory, and statements from the examining physicians strongly suggested that the women had not been raped. In fact, within a year, one of the so-called victims would admit no assault had occurred. But this evidence mattered little. Four days after the trial began, the all-white jury gave its expected verdict of guilty, and eight of the nine defendants stood before the judge to hear the death sentence pronounced; the ninth, only thirteen years old, received a life term in prison. The verdict was immensely satisfying to the crowd of 3,000 that

"[T]he fundamental requisite of due process of law is the opportunity to be heard."

—Justice Mahlon Pitney, *Grannis* v. *Ordean* (1914)

Judge James E. Horton listens intently as Dr. R. R. Bridges testifies at the first retrial of the Scottsboro boys, in April 1933. The physician stated that one of the two white girls they were alleged to have attacked, Victoria Price, had only superficial bruises and scratches. The girls admitted much later that they had lied to protect their reputations.

flooded the small county seat to witness the trial, a throng considered so volatile that the state National Guard mounted machine guns on the courthouse steps to control it.

The case was not over, however. Widespread newspaper coverage and the novelty of eight men sentenced to death for the same crime on the same day had attracted the attention of important national groups, including the National Association for the Advancement of Colored People (NAACP), which appealed the verdict on behalf of the defendants. In the process, the case became the cause célèbre of the decade. The nation had entered an age of national mass media, and this case had all the elements to make a good story— sex, race, and claims of injustice.

In 1932, the Supreme Court ruled on the Scottsboro case, formally known as *Powell* v. *Alabama* (the case took the name of Ozie Powell, one of the defendants). The defendants sought to overturn the verdict for three reasons: the trial was not fair; there were no blacks on the jury; and they were poorly represented by their counsel. They claimed that the state had violated both the Sixth and Fourteenth Amendments to the U.S. Constitution. The Sixth Amendment, part of the Bill of Rights, guaranteed a right to counsel in criminal trials, and the Fourteenth Amendment prohibited states from depriving any person of life, liberty, or property, without due process of law.

The Court ruled only on the issue of representation of counsel. The justices agreed that the defense of the Scottsboro boys was unacceptably casual. Previous decisions (or precedents) at both state and federal levels agreed that the right to counsel was central to the meaning of due process. Any action to deny this right would also deny defendants the due process promised by the Constitution. The flabby, almost nonexistent defense presented in this case did not meet the test of fairness. In a later case arising from the same circumstances, *Norris* v. *Alabama* (1935), the justices ruled that it was also a denial of due process to exclude blacks from the jury that tried Clarence Norris, another Scottsboro defendant.

The two Scottsboro cases were important because they were among the first ones to declare that all states had to honor constitutional guarantees of due process in their criminal trials. In this instance, the guarantee of a right to counsel in capital cases was judged essential to a fair trial. Previous to *Powell* v. *Alabama,* the U.S. Supreme Court followed tradition by deciding that the Bill of Rights, including the Fifth Amendment, restricted the federal government only. It did not change its position in the Scottsboro case—this shift would come later—but it did rule that the Fourteenth Amendment's guarantee of due process applied to the states as well as to the central government. In criminal trials, at least, all defendants charged with a capital offense now had a right to counsel, although states could decide how to honor this requirement.

The story of the Scottsboro boys had no happy ending, however. For most of them, the Supreme Court decision did not end their troubles. Their cases went back to the Alabama court for retrial, and they again were convicted. For much of the rest of the 1930s, their fate was a matter of public debate, political maneuvering, and legal wrangling. The first trials were followed by a long and confusing series of appeals, retrials, additional convictions, reduced charges, and secret negotiations for release of the boys (now men). Although advocates for the Scottsboro boys secured the release of all but one of the prisoners between 1937 and 1950, their experiences had been devastating.

Consider the case of Clarence Norris. On three occasions between 1931 and 1937, Norris was tried, convicted, and sentenced to death for rape. In 1938, his sentence was commuted to life imprisonment, but his incarceration was only marginally less depressing. Of those eight years, Norris said, "I believe if there is a God he forgot about me and my companions in the case. I don't know about heaven but there damn sure is a hell. I lived there from 1938 until 1946."

Although the efforts of supporters saved him from the electric chair, Norris never knew who or what to believe or trust. He was especially resentful over the deal struck between Alabama authorities and defense lawyers in 1937 that resulted in the release of four defendants, while five others remained in prison under a sentence of death or life imprisonment. Years later he said, "I never understood it, and nobody ever explained it to me." Paroled for a second time in 1946, he escaped to Cleveland, Ohio, where his mother lived, and he assumed the identity of his brother to avoid detection by local police. Finally, in 1976, Governor George Wallace signed a pardon for Clarence Norris, who for the first time since 1931 was truly a free man.

By the twentieth century, it was apparent that notions of fairness depended upon who you were and where you lived. The Scottsboro case is important

Clarence Norris, one of the nine African Americans convicted in the Scottsboro case, leaves Kilby Prison in Montgomery, Alabama, in September 1946. He was paroled after serving nine years of a life sentence. In 1976, Alabama governor George Wallace signed a pardon for Norris in recognition of the injustice of his conviction and imprisonment.

because it marked the beginning of a movement toward national standards of due process. In a wide range of cases since the 1930s, the U.S. Supreme Court expanded the meaning of due process, sometimes to the point of raising questions about whether its guarantee of individual rights has come at the expense of government's ability to protect public safety.

Today, we are much more aware of our procedural rights in criminal trials, in large measure because of the popularity of police and courtroom dramas on television. We are not as alert to the wide array of other procedural guarantees in other areas of our lives, but we expect people in authority to follow established procedures before imposing a burden or penalty on us. We require notices to be given before officials seize property—a car, for example—for non-payment of debts; schools must follow established procedures if they act to expel a student; and so forth.

"The history of American freedom is, in no small measure, the history of procedure." Justice Felix Frankfurter's telling comment expresses a fundamental article of faith about our constitutional heritage: liberty and rights cannot exist without due process of law. Procedural fairness and consistency are essential elements of due process, a concept that has long been the touchstone of our law. Whatever else due process might mean, procedural fairness, in the words of Justice Robert Jackson, "is what it most uncompromisingly requires."

In the criminal law of a free society, a proper concern for due process is crucial. Without it, individual liberty is especially vulnerable to arbitrary governmental power. Freedom from official capriciousness is essential to all other human rights. This ideal is an old one, and its significance in Western thought can scarcely be overstated. Government holds enormous power. It alone has the

A banner hung from its Fifth Avenue headquarters in New York City in 1936 was one of many efforts by the NAACP to call attention to the epidemic of lynchings taking place in the American South. In 1919, the group had published Thirty Years of Lynching in the United States: 1889–1918, *and it lobbied hard for the passage of antilynching legislation.*

A large group of hoboes rides a flat car between Bakersfield and Fresno, California, probably in search of work during the Great Depression. The Scottsboro defendants were hoboes when two white girls accused them of rape.

legitimate authority to accuse, prosecute, and punish individuals. As a result, any criminal trial between the government and the citizen is inherently unequal. Our conception of justice balances the contest between government and the individual by restraining official power.

Many of the requirements of modern due process are controversial because they appear to make government inefficient. They delay actions that most people agree are the right ones to take. The most difficult issues arise whenever we perceive the nation's security is at risk, and historically we have not been so insistent on following due process during these times, sometimes to our regret. More often, however, we as a society have usually decided that the individual's right to fair treatment generally outweighs the government's need to act quickly. Achieving the right balance is never easy, of course, yet the debate itself is evidence of a vibrant democracy. It is also testimony to a central belief of the nation's founders: the protection of liberty requires limits on the power of government. In a democratic society, these limits are embodied in law, which government must obey, and without a commitment to due process of law, our freedom itself is at risk.

Denial of Due Process

Four years after the Scottsboro case, the U.S. Supreme Court again considered the meaning of due process in Brown v. Mississippi *(1936). Three African American tenant farmers, including Ed Brown, were convicted of the murder of a white planter. During the trial, prosecution witnesses freely admitted using force to extract confessions from the defendants. Despite their testimony, the trial court admitted the evidence, and an all-white jury convicted the men and sentenced them to death by hanging. Declaring that "the rack and torture chamber may not be substituted for the witness stand," the Supreme Court reversed the conviction "for want of essential elements of due process." Following its decision in* Brown, *written by Chief Justice Charles Evans Hughes, the Court decided a line of cases that expanded the requirements of due process that states must follow in their administration of criminal justice.*

The question in this case is whether convictions, which rest solely upon confessions shown to have been extorted by officers of the state by brutality and violence, are consistent with the due process of law required by the Fourteenth Amendment of the Constitution of the United States....

The state is free to regulate the procedure of its courts in accordance with its own conceptions of policy, unless in so doing it "offends some principle of justice so rooted in the traditions and conscience of our people as to be ranked as fundamental."...The state may abolish trial by jury. It may dispense with indictment by a grand jury and substitute complaint or information....But the freedom of the state in establishing its policy is the freedom of constitutional government and is limited by the requirement of due process of law. Because a state may dispense with a jury trial, it does not follow that it may substitute trial by ordeal. The rack and torture chamber may not be substituted for the witness stand. The state may not permit an accused to be hurried to conviction under mob domination—where the whole proceeding is but a mask—without supplying corrective process....Nor may a state, through the action of its officers, contrive a conviction through the pretense of a trial which in truth is "but used as a means of depriving a defendant of liberty through a deliberate deception of court and jury by the presentation of testimony known to be perjured."...And the trial equally is a mere pretense where the state authorities have contrived a conviction resting solely upon confessions obtained by violence. The due process clause requires "that state action, whether through one agency or another, shall be consistent with the fundamental principles of liberty and justice which lie at the base of all our civil and political institutions."...It would be difficult to conceive of methods more revolting to the sense of justice than those taken to procure the confessions of these petitioners, and the use of the confessions thus obtained as the basis for conviction and sentence was a clear denial of due process....

In the instant case, the trial court was fully advised by the undisputed evidence of the way in which the confessions had been procured. The trial court knew that there was no other evidence upon which conviction and sentence could be based. Yet it proceeded to permit conviction and to pronounce sentence. The conviction and sentence were void for want of the essential elements of due process, and the proceeding thus vitiated could be challenged in any appropriate manner....It was challenged before the Supreme Court of the State by the express invocation of the Fourteenth Amendment. That court entertained the challenge, considered the federal question thus presented, but declined to enforce petitioners' constitutional right. The court thus denied a federal right fully established and specially set up and claimed, and the judgment must be reversed.

Preventing Oppressive Practices

In 1948, the United States and its Western allies were in the early years of a decades-long Cold War with the Soviet Union and nations under its control. Fears of spying and infiltration of the government by communist agents led federal officials to monitor and restrict access to the United States by foreign nationals. In 1948, a Hungarian immigrant (Ignatz Mezei) who had lived in the United States since 1923 traveled to Europe on personal business. Upon his return, he was denied reentry based on the tip of an informant who evidently accused him of spying, although the government would not confirm the accusation. He was held on Ellis Island, a port of entry into the United States, without a hearing for two years before he could appeal his detention to the Supreme Court. The majority opinion upheld the government's action in Shaughnessy v. Mezei *(1953), but Justice Hugo Black, along with William Douglas and Robert Jackson, objected in dissent and claimed that the failure to provide a hearing was a denial of due process.*

MR. JUSTICE BLACK, with whom MR. JUSTICE DOUGLAS concurs, dissenting.

Mezei came to this country in 1923 and lived as a resident alien in Buffalo, New York, for twenty-five years. He made a trip to Europe in 1948 and was stopped at our shore on his return in 1950. Without charge of or conviction for any crime, he was for two years held a prisoner on Ellis Island by order of the Attorney General. Mezei sought habeas corpus in the District Court. He wanted to go to his wife and home in Buffalo. The Attorney General defended the imprisonment by alleging that it would be dangerous to the Nation's security to let Mezei go home even temporarily on bail. Asked for proof of this, the Attorney General answered the judge that all his information was "of a confidential nature" so much so that telling any of it or even telling the names of any of his secret informers would jeopardize the safety of the Nation. Finding that Mezei's life as a resident alien in Buffalo had been "unexceptionable" and that no facts had been proven to justify his continued imprisonment, the District Court granted bail. The Court of Appeals approved. Now this Court orders Mezei to leave his home and go back to his island prison to stay indefinitely, maybe for life.

MR. JUSTICE JACKSON forcefully points out the danger in the Court's holding that Mezei's liberty is completely at the mercy of the unreviewable discretion of the Attorney General. I join MR. JUSTICE JACKSON in the belief that Mezei's continued imprisonment without a hearing violates due process of law.

No society is free where government makes one person's liberty depend upon the arbitrary will of another. Dictatorships have done this since time immemorial. They do now. Russian laws of 1934 authorized the People's Commissariat to imprison, banish and exile Russian citizens as well as "foreign subjects who are socially dangerous."...Our Bill of Rights was written to prevent such oppressive practices. Under it this Nation has fostered and protected individual freedom. The Founders abhorred arbitrary one-man imprisonments. Their belief was—our constitutional principles are—that no person of any faith, rich or poor, high or low, native or foreigner, white or colored, can have his life, liberty or property taken "without due process of law." This means to me that neither the federal police not federal prosecutors nor any other governmental official, whatever his title, can put or keep people in prison without accountability to courts of justice. It means that individual liberty is too highly prized in this country to allow executive officials to imprison and hold people on the basis of information kept secret from courts. It means that Mezei should not be deprived of his liberty indefinitely except as the result of a fair open court hearing in which evidence is appraised by the court, not by the prosecutor.

CHAPTER 14

The Right to Habeas Corpus

Most individual rights of Americans are based on the Bill of Rights or another amendment to the Constitution. Habeas corpus is an exception. This ancient legal procedure commands government to show cause—to provide a legal reason—for holding an individual in detention. The literal meaning of *habeas corpus,* from Latin, is "you should have the body." This term comes from the opening words of the document, or writ, used during the medieval period in England to require the jailor to bring a suspect to court. This Great Writ, as it became known, is the undeniable right of every American citizen. It receives mention in Article I, Section 9, of the Constitution as one of the limits on the power of Congress: "The Privilege of the Writ of Habeas Corpus shall not be suspended, unless when in Cases of Rebellion or Invasion the public Safety may require it." The framers judged it so essential to liberty that they ensured it could not be abridged except in the gravest circumstances.

The origin of habeas corpus is unclear, but it dates at least to 1215, when King John, under pressure from noblemen, issued the Magna Carta, the Great Charter of English liberty; it was part of the law of the land the king was bound to obey. The original use of habeas corpus was to bring a prisoner into court for trial, but gradually it became a right available to protect individuals against arbitrary detention by the state. During the religious and political turmoil of the seventeenth century, concern grew in England about abuse of power, especially in ecclesiastical or church courts and in royal tribunals such as the Star Chamber, the secret agency used to punish enemies of the state. When abuses continued even after the Star Chamber's demise in 1641, the Habeas Corpus Act, passed in 1679, reinforced the power of courts to issue the writ and made officials personally liable for disobeying the law.

The colonists brought habeas corpus with them as part of their rights and privileges under English common law. The refusal to grant habeas corpus was a grievance during the decades before independence, so the revolutionary generation wrote guarantees of the right into both state and federal constitutions. The first statute ever passed by Congress, the Judiciary Act of 1789, empowered all federal courts "to grant writs of habeas corpus for the purpose of an inquiry into the cause of commitment." State legislatures also passed similar laws. Significantly, anyone—not simply the person under detention—could petition a court to issue a writ. Antislavery advocates took advantage of this feature to bring cases before judges sympathetic to their cause, hoping to secure freedom for slaves who were journeying through free states. Such was the result with Med Maria, a six-year-old slave girl traveling with her mother in Massachusetts in 1836. Abolitionists used a writ of habeas corpus to gain a court ruling that she was being detained illegally by her master because Massachusetts had no law allowing slavery to exist. A more famous use of the writ for the same purpose, but with a different outcome, occurred in the Dred Scott case, with the U.S. Supreme Court ultimately deciding that Scott was not a person under the meaning of the Constitution and therefore had no rights.

The Civil War was an important test of the writ of habeas corpus because it raised questions about how far individual rights extend in a national emergency. Soon after Confederate troops fired on Fort Sumter, off the coast of Charleston, South Carolina, in April 1861, pro-secession mobs in northern cities tried to prevent the passage of Union troops, and in border states, southern sympathizers recruited and trained armed volunteers. The law of treason was too muddy to permit confident prosecution of such activity, and state criminal statutes were irrelevant. In response to the crisis, President Abraham Lincoln, claiming extraordinary emergency powers, suspended the writ of habeas corpus and ordered the arrest and detention of persons "dangerous to the public safety." Military authorities, federal marshals, and Secret Service agents detained hundreds of suspected subversives, often without sufficient evidence to make a definite charge. Civilian judges frequently sought the release of such prisoners, but military officers disregarded their orders.

In 1862, federal officials arrested James B. Merryman, a Confederate recruiter in Maryland, and imprisoned him without trial as a threat to national security. Chief Justice Roger B. Taney, a fellow Marylander and a slaveholder, issued a writ of habeas corpus, and when the President rejected it, he wrote an opinion declaring Lincoln's suspension of habeas corpus to be unconstitutional, arguing that Congress alone had this power. Lincoln ignored Taney's protests and continued to suspend the writ in areas where resistance to the war threatened Union victory, including places far removed from the battlefield.

In 1863, Congress retroactively authorized the suspension of habeas corpus but ordered that prisoners be released if grand juries failed to indict them. But what

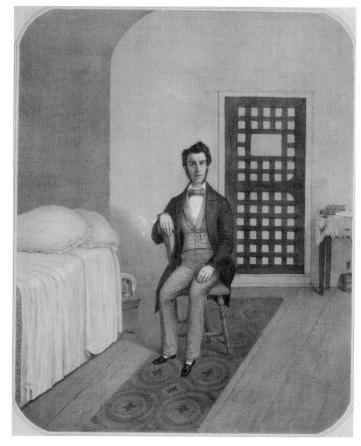

Passmore Williamson, secretary of the Pennsylvania Abolition Society, sits in his cell in Moyamensing Prison after he was convicted of contempt of court in a habeas corpus case in 1855. The charges involved Williamson's evasive testimony regarding the freeing of three slaves owned by the U.S. minister to Nicaragua, and the case ignited a controversy about the status of slaves traveling through free territory.

Martial or Military Commission:

Second—That the Writ of Habeas Corpus is suspended in respect to all persons arrested, or who are now, or hereafter during the rebellion shall be, imprisoned in any fort, camp, arsenal, military prison, or other place of confinement by any military authority, or by the sentence of any Court Martial or Military Commission.

In witness whereof, I have hereunto set my hand, and caused the seal of the United States to be affixed.

Done at the City of Washington this twenty fourth day of September, in the year of our Lord one thousand eight hundred and sixty two, and of the Independence of the United States the 87th.

Abraham Lincoln.

By the President:

William H Seward,
Secretary of State.

With this proclamation, dated September 24, 1862, President Abraham Lincoln suspended the right of habeas corpus "in respect to all persons arrested, or who are now, or hereafter during the rebellion shall be, imprisoned in any fort, camp, arsenal, military prison, or other place of confinement by any military authority or by the sentence of any Court Martial or Military Commission."

if the military authorities, worried that local courts might release dangerous men, ignored this law? What was the extent of government's power during wartime? Could it bypass constitutional guarantees of civil liberty, such as the writ of habeas corpus, to protect the nation's security?

Late in 1864, an arrest and conviction by a military court of an accused traitor from Indiana tested these fundamental questions. The outcome was a decision that still ranks as one of the most important statements of our rights ever issued by the Supreme Court.

Lambdin P. Milligan was an Ohio native who moved to Indiana in the 1830s and turned to law because he could not make a living as a farmer. A respected member of the state bar, he became involved in the anti-war faction of the Indiana Democratic party. Known as Copperheads, after the treacherous snake, these southern sympathizers in the North were Jeffersonian Democrats who believed in states' rights and in an agricultural society as the best means to preserve liberty. They especially distrusted New Englanders, whom they associated with industrialization, and they had no sympathy with abolition. Milligan, like other Peace Democrats, believed New England capitalists were using the war to enhance their own economic interests, while placing the military burden on common men from the western states.

In the elections of 1862, Indiana Democrats gained strength as public opinion became unsettled about the war, which was not going well for the Union. This sentiment emboldened Milligan, who became convinced that the Emancipation Proclamation was proof that Lincoln had fallen under the influence of abolitionist New Englanders. Believing that the South and West had economic interests in common, he began to campaign for an armistice (truce) and urged Democrats to defend their rights "at all costs." His movement, however, had reached its high point. Union victories in 1863 convinced voters that the tide had turned against the Confederacy, and the Peace Democrats began to lose public support. As a result, Milligan failed to capture his party's nomination for governor in 1864.

Embittered, Milligan joined with sympathizers to form secret societies, clubs designed to further the antiwar cause. One of these societies, the Sons of Liberty, named Milligan an officer, perhaps without his knowledge. The activities of the society did not remain secret for long, and the Republican governor and the commander of the Indiana district of the Union Army employed spies to learn more about its inner workings. The information the agents collected was exaggerated—much of it was based on hearsay—but the reports led to Milligan's arrest for treason. The key evidence was an 1864 speech in which Milligan opposed Lincoln's conduct of the war. Milligan and five others were accused of conspiring to seize arms and ammunition at federal arsenals and to liberate Confederate prisoners held in several northern camps.

The men were tried before a military tribunal, even though civil courts were open and operating in Indiana. Four of the men were found guilty of treason; the military court sentenced three of them to hang. Milligan was one of the three condemned men. After Lincoln's assassination, the new President, Andrew Johnson, commuted Milligan's sentence to life imprisonment, but Milligan refused to compromise. He petitioned a federal circuit court to grant a writ of habeas corpus, arguing that the military had no authority to try him. When the two judges disagreed on the decision, Milligan appealed to the Supreme Court.

The Court agreed unanimously with Milligan. The military court lacked jurisdiction, the justices concluded; the Constitution was not suspended in times of war, and a military trial of civilians while domestic courts were open denied the accused of their rights to a grand jury indictment and trial by jury. Justice David Davis wrote in the Court's opinion: "The Constitution of the United States is a law for rulers and people, equally in war and peace, and covers with the shield of its protection all classes of men, at all times, and under all circumstances. No doctrine, involving more pernicious consequences, was ever invented by the wit of man than that any of its provisions can be suspended during any of the great exigencies [crises] of government."

A state of war did not suspend the Constitution or its guarantee of individual rights. The framers knew the nation likely would be involved in wars, but they still chose to restrict what the President could do alone because "unlimited power, wherever lodged at such a time, was especially hazardous to free men."

Released from prison in April 1866, Milligan sought damages for the time he spent behind bars. He successfully sued the governor, members of the military commission, and others he believed were responsible for his imprisonment, but a recently passed state law limited his award to five dollars. The jury's verdict mattered most to Milligan, who saw it as vindication of his antiwar belief and actions. He returned home a hero, convinced that his case had established a vital principle of American liberty: government must honor the rights of individuals, even during national emergencies.

Although *Ex Parte Milligan* ("in the matter of Milligan") was a landmark decision, a federal law passed a year after the Court's decision gave the writ of habeas corpus much of its modern importance. Congress worried, with good reason, that southern state courts would not protect the rights of newly freed slaves, so it passed the Habeas Corpus Act of 1867. This measure allowed individuals imprisoned or detained under state authority to seek a writ of habeas corpus from a federal court if they believed the state had violated their constitutional rights. The act changed the nature of the writ itself. Previously, it had applied only to questions about the legality of detention before trial; now habeas corpus could be invoked by federal judges to review detention after conviction in both federal and state courts. It marked a significant expansion of federal power and was the most important means of protecting federal constitutional rights until the Supreme Court began to interpret these safeguards as part of the Fourteenth Amendment's due process clause.

Lambdin P. Milligan (below) appealed his conviction on conspiracy charges by a military tribunal, on the grounds that civilian courts were functioning in Indiana at the time. In upholding Milligan's appeal, Justice David Davis of the U.S. Supreme Court wrote, "By the protection of law Human rights are secured; withdraw that protection, and they are at the mercy of wicked rulers, or the clamor of an excited people."

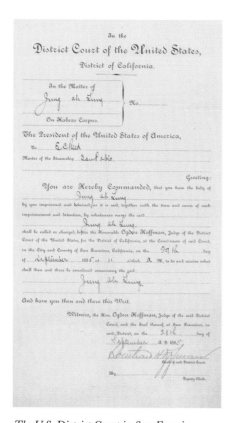

The U.S. District Court in San Francisco issued this writ of habeas corpus in the case of Jung Ah Lung, a Chinese immigrant, in September 1885. The U.S. government sought to prohibit Lung, who had established U.S. residency but had returned briefly to China, from returning to the United States. In Re Jung Ah Lung became a case of major significance for constitutional due process.

The twentieth century witnessed increased use of habeas corpus in all areas of law, largely because of the expansion of constitutionally protected rights under the Fourteenth Amendment. Its use by prisoners is an especially controversial modern use of the habeas petition. Death row inmates often seek post-conviction relief, which is a review after a final judgment to determine whether the trial was fair. The review conducted under a habeas petition is not the same as an appeal. It involves such questions as: Was the defendant informed of his rights? Did he have access to counsel? Was she tried by an impartial jury? These questions address the lawfulness of procedures used in the pretrial, trial, sentencing, or appeal; the petition for a review cannot claim simply that the defendant is innocent. This use of habeas corpus in this manner raises popular concern about delays in the finality of justice. The petitions clog federal court dockets, prompting questions about how far the federal judiciary should be involved in criminal justice, historically a responsibility of the states. In response, both Congress and the Supreme Court in recent years have restricted habeas petitions in capital cases. For all the controversy surrounding their use, however, the vast majority of petitions fail to prove a legal or factual error.

Habeas corpus is an old remedy for testing the lawfulness of all detentions, but its primary importance in American history has been to challenge the power of the executive. When drafting the Constitution, the framers were mindful of their heritage as Englishmen. The history of the mother country had taught them to fear the unchecked power of the executive, so they wrote a document that separated government's power among three branches—legislative, executive, and judicial. They also provided means to challenge the unauthorized use of power, especially by the branch directly responsible for administering the law. The writ of habeas corpus was one of those means. It could not be suspended, they agreed, except when necessary to preserve the nation itself.

This principle, of course, is the central meaning of *Ex Parte Milligan.* The Court repeatedly has upheld its declaration that the President cannot suspend the Constitution without the express approval of Congress. Even though it has not applied the decision consistently, as the internment of Japanese Americans during World War II reveals, the justices have never repudiated *Milligan.* Its principles remain central to our democracy, as a 2004 case from the Iraq-Afghanistan conflict demonstrated.

Under the congressional resolution authorizing the use of force, the U.S. military captured an American citizen in Afghanistan, classified him as an enemy combatant, and denied him access to a lawyer or courts. The suspect's father used a writ of habeas corpus to challenge this detention. The justices, in a 6-to-3 vote, rejected the executive's authority to deny access to courts without a congressional suspension of the writ. *Hamdi* v. *Rumsfeld* recognized the importance of giving the President wide latitude to defend the nation's security but concluded, "it is equally vital that our calculus not give short shrift to the values that this country holds dear or to the privilege that is American citizenship. It is during our most challenging and uncertain moments that our Nation's commitment to due process is most severely tested; and it is in those times that we must preserve our commitment at home to the principles for which we fight abroad." American citizens have a fundamental right, the Court declared, "to be free from involuntary confinement by [their] own government without due process of law."

Today, we struggle to reconcile liberty and security, but the constitutional balance point is clear: we value liberty above all else, so we expect any use of governmental power to meet strict tests. One standard is that government must act according to the law. The writ of habeas corpus assures us that we have a means of enforcing this requirement. Its protection of the freedom of the person, Thomas Jefferson noted, is an "essential principle of our government" because it "secures every man here, alien or citizen, against everything which is not law." Arbitrary, unlawful confinement of any citizen is an assault on our individual and collective liberty, and its price is too steep for a free society to pay for its safety. Benjamin Franklin, like other founders, knew this. "They who would give up an essential liberty for temporary security," he wrote, "deserve neither liberty or security." The constitutional privilege of habeas corpus assures us that, in acting lawfully, we have the greatest protection of our security and our freedom.

Japanese American evacuees arrive by train at the War Relocation Authority center in Poston, Arizona. The relocation and internment of more than 100,000 people of Japanese ancestry during World War II raised questions about the proper use of executive power and is generally considered a violation of the Fourteenth Amendment's due process requirements.

"This Is a Great Bulwark"

In 1788, ratifying conventions were held in each state to consider whether to approve the new constitution proposed by the convention in Philadelphia the previous year. Voters elected delegates who debated each provision of the document before agreeing to give or withhold consent. The right of habeas corpus, especially the power of Congress to suspend it during times of emergency, drew the attention of these conventions. In this transcript of the Massachusetts debate, delegates voiced their concerns about this power of suspension.

Judge Sumner said, that this was a restriction on Congress, that the writ of *habeas corpus* should not be suspended, except in cases of rebellion or invasion. The learned judge then explained the nature of this writ. When a person, said he, is imprisoned, he applies to a judge of the Supreme Court; the judge issues his writ to the jailer, calling upon him to have the body of the person imprisoned before him, with the crime on which he was committed. If it then appears that the person was legally committed, and that he was not bailable, he is remanded to prison; if

illegally confined, he is enlarged. This privilege, he said, is essential to freedom, and therefore the power to suspend it is restricted. On the other hand, the state, he said, might be involved in danger; the worst enemy may lay plans to destroy us, and so artfully as to prevent any evidence against him, and might ruin the country, without the power to suspend the writ was thus given. Congress have only the power to suspend the privilege to persons committed by their authority. A person committed under the authority of the states will still have a right to this writ.

Later during the Massachusetts convention, a delegate named Samuel Nasson argued that citizens should not give up the right of habeas corpus too easily.

Samuel Nasson: The paragraph that gives Congress power to suspend the writ of habeas corpus, claims a little attention—This is a great bulwark—a great privilege indeed—we ought not, therefore, to give it up, on any slightest pretence. Let us see—how long

it is to be suspended? As long as rebellion or invasion shall continue. This is exceeding loose. Why is not the time limitted [*sic*] as in our Constitution? But, sir, its design would then be defeated—It was the intent, and by it we shall give up one of our greatest privileges.

"The Most Celebrated Writ"

In 1963, the Supreme Court extended the right of habeas corpus, which had been applicable only to federal courts, to individuals who had been convicted in state courts with its decision in Fay v. Noia. *Previously, a respect for federalism, especially the states' primary responsibility for criminal justice, meant that a defendant convicted in state court could be brought before a federal court under a writ of habeas corpus only if he had exhausted all avenues for appeal under state procedures. Under the new rule, the federal judiciary assumed a greater role for protecting the rights of prisoners. In the majority opinion, Justice William Brennan discussed the role of the writ of habeas corpus in protecting individual liberty.*

We do well to bear in mind the extraordinary prestige of the Great Writ, habeas corpus ad subjiciendum, in Anglo-American jurisprudence: "the most celebrated writ in the English law." . . . It is "a writ antecedent to statute, and throwing its root deep into the genius of our common law. . . . It is perhaps the most important writ known to the constitutional law of England, affording as it does a swift and imperative remedy in all cases of illegal restraint or confinement. It is of immemorial antiquity, an instance of its use occurring in the thirty-third year of Edward I." . . . Received into our own law in the colonial period, given explicit recognition in the Federal Constitution, Art. I, . . . habeas corpus was early confirmed by Chief Justice John Marshall to be a "great constitutional privilege." . . .

These are not extravagant expressions. Behind them may be discerned the unceasing contest between personal liberty and government oppression. It is no accident that habeas corpus has time and again played a central role in national crises, wherein the claims of order and of liberty clash most acutely, not only in England in the seventeenth century, but also in America from our very beginnings, and today. Although in form the Great Writ is simply a mode of procedure, its history is inextricably intertwined with the growth of fundamental rights of personal liberty. For its function has been to provide a prompt and efficacious remedy for whatever society deems to be intolerable restraints. Its root principle is that in a civilized society, government must always be accountable to the judiciary for a man's imprisonment: if the imprisonment cannot be shown to conform with the fundamental requirements of law, the individual is entitled to his immediate release.

CHAPTER 15

The Right to Protection against Illegal Search and Seizure

The Bill of Rights is a miniature code of criminal procedure. These ten amendments list seventeen rights designed to guarantee fairness to individuals accused of crimes. The Fourth Amendment contains the first of these protections: "The right of the people to be secure in their persons, houses, papers, and effects, against unreasonable searches and seizures, shall not be violated, and no Warrants shall issue, but upon probable cause." The right had its roots in English history, but the American struggle for independence gave it special significance for the new nation.

One of the colonial grievances against the British government concerned warrants (written authorization) that officials in charge of trade used to search colonists' property for smuggled goods. These documents, called writs of assistance, gave officers broad power to conduct searches and seize property based only on their general suspicion of unlawful actions. First introduced during the reign of Henry VIII (1513–47), the British government claimed that general search warrants, which did not allege a specific crime, were necessary for effective law enforcement, especially against publications the government considered dangerous. This practice was controversial, however, and Parliament began to limit the power after it forced King James II from the throne in the Glorious Revolution of 1688. By the eve of the American Revolution, general warrants had declined dramatically as a tool to restrain the press, but they continued to be used unchecked in the enforcement of customs law. Britons did not object to broad search and seizure powers in this area because the writs were used infrequently in the search for smuggled goods in England. The American experience was dramatically different.

Opposition to general warrants came to a head in Boston, one of the busiest ports in the colonies and center of the smuggling trade. In Massachusetts, as elsewhere, customs officials could enter and search buildings simply on the authority of their royal appointments. In 1761, Boston merchants hired lawyer James Otis to challenge the legality of these writs. His presentation in court electrified the colonists because he asserted the supremacy of fundamental law, such as individual rights, over legislative power. A man's home and property, he argued, were sacred; his privacy could not be invaded on the whim of government officials. Here, Otis anticipated Sir William Pitt, a prominent member of Parliament who gave eloquent voice to this right two years later. "The poorest man may in his cottage bid defiance to all the force of the Crown," Pitt thundered. "It may be frail—its roof may shake—the wind may blow through it—the storm may enter—the rain may enter—but the King of England cannot enter: all his forces dare not cross the threshold of that ruined tenement." This sentiment, expressed in the seventeenth-century maxim "A man's home is his castle," embodied a central tenet of liberty for the colonists.

Otis lost his case, but not his cause. Colonial mobs thwarted efforts of officials to search and seize suspicious goods, and colonial courts refused to grant the writ. Americans found in this issue a fundamental right of the accused; protecting individuals from unreasonable searches and seizures was a right they deemed essential to liberty. Significantly, it was a right not previously included in colonial charters, laws, or declarations.

The framers of the Bill of Rights intended the Fourth Amendment to ensure that their new government could not resort to the high-handed search measures and abuses of power they had experienced as colonists. But the language they used, although pregnant with meaning, lacked specific definition. What was an unreasonable search? How much detail did a warrant have to include in its description of suspected goods? The colonial and revolutionary experience provided examples to guide interpretation, but it left no settled answers.

For almost a century, the Supreme Court was relatively silent on these questions, leaving state courts to wrestle with similar protections listed in their separate constitutions. In 1886, however, the justices considered *Boyd* v. *United States*, a case in which the Fourth Amendment loomed large even though the offense was minor. Two brothers, both New York City merchants, were found guilty of importing goods illegally after the judge required them to produce the evidence that convicted them. They appealed, claiming the order violated the Fourth Amendment. What made the issue complicated was the absence of a physical search. The brothers were accused of avoiding taxes by importing plate glass illegally, so the judge required them to produce their invoices as evidence of payment, which of course proved the charge against them.

In its decision, the U.S. Supreme Court agreed that this order was an illegal seizure because no official had provided sufficient evidence, or probable cause, to justify a warrant. The justices also linked the warrantless seizure of evidence to the Fifth Amendment's protection against self-incrimination. The order to produce the invoice meant the brothers were compelled to give evidence that incriminated them. "Unconstitutional practices get their first footing...by silent approaches and slight deviations from legal modes of procedure," the

Massachusetts lawyer James Otis made powerful arguments against the general search warrants imposed by the British. The writs of assistance were, he said, "the worst instrument of arbitrary power, the most destructive to English liberty, and the fundamental principles of the Constitution." John Adams said of his courtroom artistry, "Otis was a flame of fire!...American independence was then and there born; the seeds of patriots and heroes were then and there sown."

"The 'unreasonable searches and seizures' condemned in the fourth amendment are almost always made for the purpose of compelling a man to give evidence against himself, which in criminal cases is condemned in the fifth amendment; and compelling a man 'in a criminal case to be a witness against himself,' which is condemned in the fifth amendment, throws light on the question as to what is an 'unreasonable search and seizure.'"

—Justice Joseph P. Bradley, *Boyd* v. *United States* (1886)

majority opinion declared. "It is the duty of the courts to be watchful for the constitutional rights of the citizen, and guard against any stealthy encroachments thereon." The case was significant because it gave life to the Fourth Amendment and kept it, as Justice William Brennan said almost a century later, from becoming "a dead letter in the federal courts."

The Court's impassioned defense of individual rights overshadowed its failure to address the question of how to enforce the right. Under previous practice, even illegally seized evidence could be admitted as proof of a crime. The solution was obvious: exclude such evidence from trial. The Court took this step three decades later in 1914 in the case of *Weeks* v. *United States.* Weeks had been convicted of using the mails to transport lottery tickets, but the evidence against him came from a warrantless search. He argued that this illegally obtained evidence should be excluded from trial, and the Supreme Court agreed. The decision announced what came to be known as the exclusionary rule: federal courts must exclude, or not use, evidence obtained through unconstitutional searches. The rule applied only to U.S. courts, and even then there was one exception. If state or local police turned over illegally obtained evidence to federal prosecutors, the evidence could be used in federal courts. The practice, appropriately called the "silver platter" exception because evidence figuratively came to investigators the way servants once delivered invitations to a ball, too often was a routine method of investigation for federal officials. It continued even after the Court decided in 1948 that the ban on illegal searches, but not the exclusionary rule, applied to states under the Fourteenth Amendment. Two-thirds of the states chose to continue the practice of allowing improperly seized evidence at trial.

The Fourth Amendment, it appeared, gave Americans a right but not a complete remedy. Finally in 1960, the justices abandoned the silver platter doctrine. More significantly, the next year they abruptly applied the exclusionary rule to state as well as federal courts. The case began with a future national celebrity, a woman who possessed obscene materials, and an impatient police force. It would end with angry protests that the Supreme Court was willing to let criminals go free simply because law officers had made a mistake.

On May 20, 1957, Don King was not yet the boxing promoter and celebrity he would become; he ran an illegal lottery in Cleveland, Ohio—and his house had just been bombed. His call to a local policeman set in motion a case that would affect every station house in America.

Three days later, an anonymous tip led plainclothes police to the home of Dollree Mapp, who rented out rooms in her house to boarders from the fight game and illegal betting or numbers racket. When she appeared after several hours, the detectives asked for permission to search her house. She called her lawyer, who advised her not to let the cops in without a search warrant. Soon the plainclothesmen were back, this time accompanied by uniformed officers. They claimed to have a warrant, and when Mapp denied them entry, they broke open the door, waving a piece of paper that she grabbed and stuffed down her sweater. A struggle followed, during which police recovered the paper and handcuffed Mapp. By this time her lawyer had arrived, but they prevented him from entering the house.

After dragging her upstairs, officers began to search the entire house. In the basement, they opened a trunk containing pictures of nude males and females, "lewd" books, and betting materials. They arrested her for violating Ohio's obscenity law, despite her protests that the materials belonged to a former tenant. Convicted of possessing the betting equipment and pornographic books, Mapp received a one-to-seven year sentence in the Ohio State Reformatory for Women.

She appealed, arguing that the police violated her Fourth Amendment rights by seizing items not listed specifically in the search warrant. The prosecution, in fact, could not produce a warrant—it had been lost, the state said—but argued that, even if the search was improper, Ohio law still allowed illegally seized evidence to be admitted at trial. On this point, the state was correct. The U.S. Supreme Court had ruled that a police search without a specifically worded warrant was illegal. Rather than impose the exclusionary rule, however, the Court had allowed individual states to correct the wrong done by an illegal search in whatever manner they chose. Ohio decided to accept improperly seized evidence at trial but to punish the offending police officer as a trespasser.

In 1961, the Supreme Court reversed Mapp's conviction by a vote of 6 to 3. Writing for the majority, Justice Tom Clark noted that the law excluded illegally seized evidence in federal courts but not in state courts. The result, he concluded, defied logic: "The state, by admitting evidence unlawfully seized, serves to encourage disobedience of the Federal Constitution which it is bound to uphold." Applying the exclusionary rule to both state and federal courts "is not only the logical dictate of prior cases, but it also makes very good sense. There is no war between the Constitution and common sense." Clark acknowledged that criminals could go free "because the constable blundered," in the words of an earlier justice, Benjamin Cardozo, but "it is the law that sets him free. Nothing can destroy a government more quickly than its failure to observe its own laws, or worse, its disregard of the charter of its own existence."

Dollree Mapp won her case, but her troubles did not end. She moved to New York City, where she dabbled unsuccessfully in several businesses before being convicted in 1971—after a proper search—on charges of receiving stolen

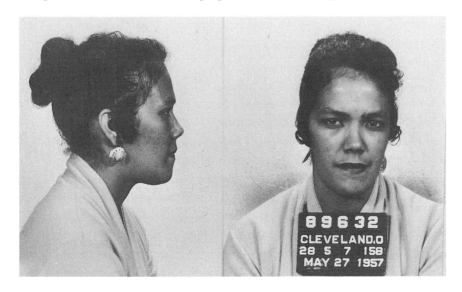

The Cleveland police department took this mug shot of Dollree Mapp after she was arrested for possession of obscene pictures. Her determination to fight the unjust search of her house is evident in the photographs. She said later, "You have to be man enough or woman enough to stand and fight if it's something worth fighting for."

Members of the Tampa, Florida, police department's QUAD (Quick Uniform Attack on Drugs) Squad execute a search warrant. Their actions were authorized in advance by a judge, based on preliminary evidence that there was reasonable presumption of a crime.

property. Sentenced to twenty years in prison, she was pardoned after serving nine years. Later she recalled her role in the case that changed police practices: "I know right from wrong, and I knew I was right in this case. You have to be man enough or woman enough to stand and fight if it's something worth fighting for. And *Mapp* v. *Ohio* was worth fighting for."

The decision in *Mapp* infuriated police and prosecutors because it had important practical consequences: any evidence seized in violation of the Constitution would no longer be admissible at any criminal trial, federal or state. The exclusionary rule would handcuff them in fighting crime, they claimed, and it would let criminals go free. These concerns certainly were legitimate, but as it turned out, they were largely unfounded. Numerous studies have demonstrated that few criminals go unpunished because of the rule. Instead, law enforcement officers became more careful and more professional in their work. "Cops learned to obtain warrants, secure evidence, and prepare cases," the police chief of Minneapolis reported later. "Arrests that had been clouded by sloppiness, illegality, and recklessness were now much tidier." The result was better law enforcement.

The Supreme Court also recognized instances when circumstances made it impractical or unnecessary to obtain a warrant. In a series of cases since *Mapp* v. *Ohio,* the justices allowed exceptions to the exclusionary rule. For example, if prosecutors prove that the discovery of otherwise illegal evidence was inevitable, then courts can admit it at trial. This situation might arise if law officers discovered a murder victim after they obtained evidence illegally. They could claim an exception to the exclusionary rule if they could prove that they would have searched the area anyway and thereby discovered the body. The justices also recognized a "good faith" exception if an unintentional mistake occurs, as when, for example, an officer obtains a warrant but the warrant contains an error in its description.

Other circumstances may not require a warrant at all. Police do not need court permission to search whenever an individual consents voluntarily or when the officer is acting legally and spots something in plain view. They may also search an area under the defendant's immediate control, as well as conduct searches to protect themselves, when making an arrest. With these exceptions, the Court has tried to fit its guidelines to the real-life situations police encounter. It has sought to balance the rights of individuals with the need for order. The central questions are always the same: when does privacy give way to a more important public purpose, and for what reasons?

Cases about search and seizure are, in fact, cases about privacy and security. The great object of the Fourth Amendment is to protect privacy. The amendment's language signals the value the framers placed on protecting our right to be left alone unless there is a strong and justifiable reason to invade that privacy. We are free to live in private and to possess things in private. As a society, we believe the right to "to be secure in [our] persons, houses, papers, and effects" is an essential liberty, one equally necessary for our individual happiness and for the common good. But we also recognize that this right is not absolute. The amendment provides a way for society to ensure its security against individuals who would use their privacy to harm others. It allows the government to invade our privacy for probable cause if it can demonstrate to an independent authority— a judge—good and legitimate reasons for doing so.

Today, questions surrounding security and privacy are more complicated than ever. The September 11, 2001, terrorist attacks on the World Trade Center and the Pentagon gave the issue a special urgency. New technologies also raise new problems. The Supreme Court has always taken into account new means of communication when considering the Fourth Amendment, as when it decided in the 1920s that monitoring telephone conversations through wiretaps required a warrant even though no physical intrusion on privacy occurred. Now we have instruments that can see inside buildings, powerful computers that collect and manipulate vast amounts of personal information, machines that permit us to communicate instantly with people all over the globe. These technologies make our private lives more comfortable and more flexible; they also have the potential to make our society more vulnerable. How do we balance our right to privacy with our need for security?

Although the framers never could have imagined these new technologies, they gave us an amendment flexible enough to adapt to them. They left us no formula to apply in any and all circumstances, but they did provide us with a vital principle of liberty and a durable achievement. The principle? We live under a government of laws, not of men, and the role of government and of law is to protect and promote our individual rights and not simply our collective security. Justice Felix Frankfurter, in the 1950s, said it eloquently: "A knock on the door, whether by day or by night, as a prelude to a search, without authority of law but solely on the authority of the police...[is] inconsistent with the conception of human rights enshrined in the history and the basic constitutional documents of English-speaking peoples." The durable achievement? We live in a society where we do not fear a knock on the door.

"We think that obtaining by sense-enhancing technology any information regarding the interior of the home that could not otherwise have been obtained without physical 'intrusion into a constitutionally protected area,'... constitutes a search—at least where (as here) the technology in question is not in general public use. This assures preservation of that degree of privacy against government that existed when the Fourth Amendment was adopted."

—Justice Antonin Scalia, *Kyllo* v. *United States* (2001)

The Exclusionary Rule

The case of Weeks v. United States *(1914) marked the beginning of the federal exclusionary rule that bars improperly seized evidence from being used at trial. Prior to this decision, courts operated on the premise that the need for justice outweighed the search and seizure protections of the Fourth Amendment, so they regularly admitted evidence taken without a proper warrant. In the Supreme Court's majority opinion, Justice William Day emphasized the obligation of federal courts and law officers to respect the constitutional rights of individuals. He concluded that the essential violation of the Fourth Amendment was the invasion of Weeks's right of personal security, personal liberty, and private property. The illegally seized evidence, the Court ruled, could not be used in a federal trial. The decision did not restrict the states, however. Not until* Mapp v. Ohio *(1961) did the Court apply the exclusionary rule to state criminal trials.*

The defendant was arrested by a police officer, so far as the record shows, without warrant, at the Union Station in Kansas City, Missouri, where he was employed by an express company. Other police officers had gone to the house of the defendant, and being told by a neighbor where the key was kept, found it and entered the house. They searched the defendant's room and took possession of various papers and articles found there, which were afterwards turned over to the United States marshal. Later in the same day police officers returned with the marshal, who thought he might find additional evidence, and, being admitted by someone in the house, probably a boarder, in response to a rap, the marshal searched the defendant's room and carried away certain letters and envelops found in the drawer of a chiffonier. Neither the marshal nor the police officer had a search warrant. . . .

The effect of the 4th Amendment is to put the courts of the United States and Federal officials, in the exercise of their power and authority, under limitations and restraints as to the exercise of such power and authority, and to forever secure the people, their persons, houses, papers, and effects, against all unreasonable searches and seizures under the guise of law. This protection reaches all alike, whether accused of crime or not, and the duty of giving to it force and effect is obligatory upon all entrusted under our Federal system with the enforcement of the laws. The tendency of those who execute the criminal laws of the country to obtain conviction by means of unlawful seizures and enforced confessions, the latter often obtained after subjecting accused persons to unwarranted practices destructive of rights secured by the Federal Constitution, should find no sanction in the judgments of the courts, which are charged at all times with the support of the Constitution, and to which people of all conditions have a right to appeal for the maintenance of such fundamental rights. . . .

The efforts of the courts and their officials to bring the guilty to punishment, praiseworthy as they are, are not to be aided by the sacrifice of those great principles established be years of endeavor and suffering which have resulted in their embodiment in the fundamental law of the land. . . .

We therefore reach the conclusion that the letters in question were taken from the house of the accused by an official of the United States, acting under color of his office, in direct violation of the constitutional rights of the defendant; that having made a seasonable application for their return, which was heard and passed upon by the court, there was involved in the order refusing the application a denial of the constitutional rights of the accused, and that the court should have restored these letters to the accused. In holding them and permitting their use upon the trial, we think prejudicial error was committed.

New Means of Invading Privacy

In the late 1920s, Roy Olmstead was convicted of unlawfully transporting and selling liquor in violation of the National Prohibition Act. His appeal offered the Supreme Court the first opportunity to consider whether the use of illegal wiretapping to gather evidence could be used in federal trials. The majority ruled 5 to 4 in Olmstead v. United States *(1928) that wiretapping did not involve the physical invasion of a defendant's home, which meant that it fell outside the Fourth Amendment's requirement of a warrant for a legal search. In his dissent below, Justice Louis Brandeis argued that the Fourth and Fifth Amendments were linked and together they protected a general right to privacy, which illegal wiretapping violated. Later, both the Supreme Court and Congress agreed with Brandeis's position, with the result that law officers must secure a warrant before using this means of search and seizure.*

When the Fourth and Fifth Amendments were adopted, "the form that evil had theretofore taken" had been necessarily simple. Force and violence were then the only means known to man by which a government could directly effect self-incrimination.... Protection against ... invasion of "the sanctities of a man's home and the privacies of life" was provided in the Fourth and Fifth Amendments by specific language.... But "time works changes, brings into existence new conditions and purposes." Subtler and more far-reaching means of invading privacy have become available to the government. Discovery and invention have made it possible for the government, by means far more effective than stretching upon the rack, to obtain disclosure in court of what is whispered in the closet. Moreover, "in the application of a Constitution, our contemplation cannot be only of what has been, but of what may be." The progress of science in furnishing the government with means of espionage is not likely to stop with wire tapping.... Can it be that the Constitution affords no protection against such invasions of individual security?

The makers of our Constitution undertook to secure conditions favorable to the pursuit of happiness. They recognized the significance of man's spiritual nature, of his feelings and of his intellect. They knew that only a part of the pain, pleasure and satisfactions of life are to be found in material things. They sought to protect Americans in their beliefs, their thoughts, their emotions and their sensations.

They conferred, as against the government, the right to be let alone—the most comprehensive of rights and the right most valued by civilized men. To protect, that right, every unjustifiable intrusion by the government upon the privacy of the individual, whatever the means employed, must be deemed a violation of the Fourth Amendment. And the use, as evidence in a criminal proceeding, of facts ascertained by such intrusion must be deemed a violation of the Fifth.

By the laws of Washington, wire tapping is a crime.... To prove its case, the government was obliged to lay bare the crimes committed by its officers on its behalf. A federal court should not permit such a prosecution to continue....

Decency, security, and liberty alike demand that government officials shall be subjected to the same rules of conduct that are commands to the citizen. In a government of laws, existence of the government will be imperiled if it fails to observe the law scrupulously. Our government is the potent, the omnipresent teacher. For good or for ill, it teaches the whole people by its example. Crime is contagious. If the government becomes a lawbreaker, it breeds contempt for law; it invites every man to become a law unto himself; it invites anarchy. To declare that in the administration of the criminal law the end justifies the means—to declare that the government may commit crimes in order to secure the conviction of a private criminal—would bring terrible retribution. Against that pernicious doctrine this court should resolutely set its face.

CHAPTER 16

The Right to Protection against Double Jeopardy

No rule of criminal procedure is older than the one forbidding the government to try defendants twice for the same offense. It was considered so fundamental to due process that its appearance in the Bill of Rights is not surprising. The Fifth Amendment language seems clear—"nor shall any person be subject for the same offense be put in jeopardy of life or limb"—but in fact the protection is one of the least understood rights of the accused.

The principle that no person can be put in jeopardy, or in danger, twice for the same crime dates back to ancient Greek and Roman law. In England, the protection was part of the common law, or the body of judge-made law used in royal courts, but in the United States it became a part of the Constitution. The language used to describe double jeopardy differed between the two countries. English law included what its most influential commentator, Sir Edward Coke, called the "universal maxim . . . that no man is to be brought into jeopardy of his life, more than once, for the same offense." For double jeopardy to apply, however, a trial had to result in a verdict. The Fifth Amendment broadened this language by adding "or limb" to the ban on "jeopardy of life," which meant it applied in less serious criminal cases and not simply felonies, as was true in Great Britain, but the new language also was less precise. In America, a trial did not have to result in a verdict to bar a second prosecution, so it was unclear when a defendant was in jeopardy. Was it upon indictment, the formal accusation of a crime? When the trial began? When the trial ended?

Complicating the law of double jeopardy in the United States was the division of power between the states and the central government, a system known as federalism. For most of American history, states have been responsible for criminal justice on the theory that violations of law were best judged by the community in which they occurred. Many state constitutions contained a double jeopardy clause, but not all did. States that did not make it part of their constitutional law, however, still included it in their law of criminal procedure. The language of the ban differed somewhat from state to state, however, so from the beginning the potential existed for various interpretations of what everyone agreed was a fundamental right.

By the early nineteenth century, two primary standards existed for applying the ban on double jeopardy. Some states adopted the practice of allowing a second trial on the same offense if the jury could not agree on a verdict or if the defendant consented to a motion to dismiss, or discharge, the jury before it reached a verdict. A verdict of guilty or innocent was the test to determine whether a person had been tried once. Other states believed this standard did not protect the defendant sufficiently. For these courts, a defendant was in

"No man shall be twise sentenced by Civill Justice for one and the same Crime, offence, or Trespasse."

—Massachusetts Body of Liberties (1641)

jeopardy when a jury was sworn and charged to try the case. Only then would the accused be protected from multiple prosecutions for the same offense. As the Indiana supreme court explained it, "If a Court has the right, during the trial, capriciously to discharge the jury, and continue the case until the next term, the liberty of [the defendant] would be completely in the hands of the judge. He might, at every term, empanel, discharge, and continue, and thus rob the prisoner of his liberty, by preventing a final determination."

Other questions plagued the interpretation of double jeopardy. An especially troublesome one was whether a person could be tried for the same crime in both federal and state courts. For most of its history, the Fifth Amendment prohibition applied to the federal government only. This situation changed in the twentieth century, however, when federal law enforcement increasingly moved into areas once reserved almost exclusively for the states and as the U.S. Supreme Court nationalized the Bill of Rights protections, thereby enforcing national standards, for criminal defendants. More urgent was another question. Did the Fourteenth Amendment include a ban on double jeopardy in its guarantee of due process of law, thus making protection uniform across the nation rather than one that varied from state to state?

This latter issue came up in an important case in 1937. A Connecticut grand jury had charged Frank Palko with the first-degree murder of two policemen, but the trial jury found him guilty of second-degree murder. After Palko was sentenced to life imprisonment, the state appealed the conviction. It asked for a new trial because the indictment was for first-degree murder, whereas the jury gave a verdict only on the lesser, included charge of second-degree murder. The state supreme court agreed and ordered a new trial. This time, a jury found Palko guilty of first-degree murder, and the judge sentenced him to death. Palko appealed to the U.S. Supreme Court. He argued that the Fourteenth Amendment incorporated, or included, the Fifth Amendment prohibition of double jeopardy as a restriction on the power of the states. Justice Benjamin Cardozo, writing for the majority, rejected this position. Some rights, such as the right to free speech or religious freedom, were so basic as to be "of the very essence of a scheme of ordered liberty," but double jeopardy was not one of these rights, Cardozo wrote. "The state is not attempting to wear the accused out by a multitude of cases, [but only] that the case against him shall go on until there shall be a trial free from the corrosion of legal error." Frank Palko died in the electric chair several months later.

The Court's decision did not allow states to ignore the principle of double jeopardy, but the justices were unwilling to make it part of a national standard of due process and fair trial. Over the next few decades, they would consider the issue case by case. But this course did not mean the Court was backing away from the ancient ban on double jeopardy; indeed, in some ways its commitment was stronger than ever, as a case from the 1950s revealed.

Everett Green was a mild-mannered man in his early sixties when District of Columbia police arrested him in 1953 for the murder of his longtime friend Bettie Brown. They lived in the same boardinghouse, and Green looked after Brown as her health began to fail. No one had any reason to suspect him of anything other than devotion, but when firefighters found the elderly woman dead

In this 1959 cartoonist's comment on two Supreme Court cases concerning double jeopardy, a hangman representing the federal courts pulls on a rope while a justice tells him to give someone else a turn. In the background a man wearing a sheriff's badge who represents state courts waits with his noose.

in a burning house, with Everett unconscious in a bloody bathtub upstairs, they uncovered disturbing conflicts between the evidence and his account of what happened.

At the hospital where he had been taken, Green told investigators about an intruder who had attacked him with a knife. He could not explain how the man had gotten into the locked house, which still was bolted when the firemen arrived, nor why his assailant had set fires in five locations throughout the residence. Later, the detectives returned with damning evidence that pointed directly to him as the murderer of Bettie Brown. In a letter postmarked the day of the fire, Green had written to an acquaintance about his friend's death, saying "we both want it this way." He asked that his ashes be thrown on Chesapeake Bay and had included forty dollars to buy flowers for Brown's grave.

Green acknowledged the letter. He said he had found Bettie Brown dead when he checked on her the night before the fire; she had died in her sleep, and, depressed, he contemplated suicide. Then the intruder attacked him. He stuck with this story when testifying in his own defense at his trial for arson and murder, even though a medical examiner said Brown had died of smoke inhalation. Upon cross-examination, however, he revealed that both he and Brown had been threatened with eviction more than once, including the day before the fire. They believed they soon would be institutionalized.

The jury found Green guilty of arson and second-degree murder, and the judge sentenced him to one to three years in prison for arson and five to twenty years for murder. Given his age, the term could be a life sentence. Dissatisfied with the verdict, the defense attorney combed the trial record for a mistake to justify a reversal of the conviction. He found it in the judge's instructions to the jury, which allowed jurors to find Green guilty of murder in either the first or second degree. This instruction was wrong; the criminal code required a verdict on the charge of first-degree murder if the death was caused by arson. Now Everett Green had to make a critical decision. If he succeeded in overturning the verdict, the state might try him for first-degree murder; if found guilty in a new trial, he could be put to death. Green was willing to take the risk because, he told his lawyer, his current sentence meant he likely would die in prison.

The trial judge erred, the court of appeals agreed; Green would have a new trial. But before the second trial began, his attorney advanced a new defense.

Green had already been tried once on the charge of first-degree murder, and when the jury found him guilty of second-degree murder, it implicitly found him not guilty of the more serious crime. Trying him again would be a violation of his Fifth Amendment protection against double jeopardy. It was a novel argument, and even his attorney doubted its success. In fact, the U.S. Supreme Court had rejected a similar argument in 1905, and no court had upheld a case on the grounds proposed by Green's lawyer.

The trial judge rejected the double jeopardy claim, and this time the jury found Everett Green guilty of murder in the first degree. His gamble had failed; now he faced death by electrocution. When the court of appeals rejected his petition for a new trial, noting he had been warned about the possible consequences of his actions, Green asked the Supreme Court to hear his case.

The justices heard arguments in the case on two different occasions—they could not reach a decision the first time—before issuing their opinion in fall 1957. The retrial, they concluded, violated the Fifth Amendment ban on double jeopardy. Green was in direct peril of being convicted and punished for first-degree murder at his first trial, but the jury refused to convict him. He did not waive his double jeopardy right by appealing his conviction. "The State with all its resources and power," the Court stated, "should not be allowed to make repeated attempts to convict an individual." Protection against double jeopardy, it continued, is "a vital safeguard in our society, one that was dearly won and one that should continue to be highly valued. If such great constitutional protections are given a narrow, grudging application they are deprived of much of their significance." Everett Green had been required to take a "desperate chance." He had risked his freedom and his life for a principle guaranteed by the Constitution. "The law should not," the justices decided, "place the defendant in such an incredible dilemma."

After years of anxiety, frustration, and expense, Everett Green was a free man, even if he remained poor and sick. Four years later, he died in a veterans' home in Virginia, having left the District of Columbia on the one-way bus ticket provided to all released felons.

In *Green* v. *United States,* the Supreme Court made a strong statement about the value of the ban on double jeopardy, and because of it, Everett Green had his freedom. But this was one case. How long would the justices continue to accept appeals one by one before they concluded that this "vital safeguard" would become a guarantee in all criminal trials at all levels, as part of the Fourteenth Amendment's due process clause?

In 1969, they reached this result in *Benton* v. *Maryland.* Throughout the 1960s the Court had been engaged in what became known as the due process revolution. It interpreted the Bill of Rights protections for defendants as restraints on state, as well as federal, criminal process. Protections against search and seizure, the right to counsel, the privilege against self-incrimination—all had been incorporated into the due process language of the Fourteenth Amendment. With *Benton* v. *Maryland,* the ban on double jeopardy joined the list. In its 1937 *Palko* decision, the Court had allowed states the freedom to deny rights to defendants so long as the denial was not shocking to a universal sense of justice. Now, the justices specifically rejected this vague

> *"[The guarantee against double jeopardy] consists of three separate constitutional protections. It protects against a second prosecution for the same offense after acquittal. It protects against a second prosecution for the same offense after conviction. And it protects against multiple punishments for the same offense."*
>
> —Justice Potter Stewart, *North Carolina* v. *Pearce* (1969)

standard and ruled that states must extend those guarantees of the Bill of Rights that are fundamental to an American sense of justice. The ban on double jeopardy was one of them.

Stripped to its essence, the Fifth Amendment right against double jeopardy seems clear—a person cannot be tried twice for the same crime—but in practice many questions remain. What about a case in which the same crime can be prosecuted under two separate laws, such as a kidnapping that results in a murder? Does a conviction for murder bar a prosecution for kidnapping? Generally, the Supreme Court has ruled that in this case the ban would apply if the same facts are used to prove guilt in each trial. What about a mistrial or a dismissal of charges before the jury reaches a verdict? Does this bar another prosecution? Here the rules are a bit more complicated. A defendant is in danger, or in jeopardy, when the jury is sworn in—or when the first witness is sworn in a trial by judge alone (a bench trial)—but not if the jury cannot reach a verdict (a hung jury). Also, the protection against double jeopardy usually does not bar a retrial when the verdict is reversed on appeal. Significantly, protection against double jeopardy applies to civil as well as criminal trials because the same issue—subjecting a person to possible penalties twice for the same act—is at stake.

The most difficult question, however, is whether a defendant may be tried in both federal and state courts for the same crime. The double jeopardy clause does not prevent such prosecutions because we have a federal system of government in which both state and national governments have the power to define criminal acts. Occasionally, the result may appear unjust. Should both state and federal authorities prosecute someone for the same act of bank fraud, for example? But sometimes this dual sovereignty corrects an injustice. When some southern states in the 1960s conducted sham trials of individuals who had killed or abused civil rights workers, the federal government prosecuted the same crime under national statutes and convicted racist thugs who otherwise would have escaped punishment.

Modern double jeopardy law is complicated. Chief Justice William Rehnquist once characterized it as "a veritable Sargasso Sea which could not fail to challenge the most intrepid judicial navigator." What is not complicated, however, is the reason for the doctrine. Although any society requires a high degree of public order to function properly—and we trust government to enforce laws to ensure our safety—as a nation we have chosen first to protect individual liberty. We do not allow government to hammer away, trial after trial, at individuals for the same offense because it would violate our commitment to fairness. The ban on double jeopardy is no mere technicality. This ancient principle is essential to our definition of a fair trial and to our sense of justice, and our commitment to these ideals provides us one of our best guarantees of liberty.

Freedom from Anxiety and Insecurity

Everett Green faced a cruel dilemma when he sought a new trial after he had been convicted of second-degree murder and arson in the death of his friend in 1953, because a successful appeal meant the state could try him for first-degree murder and sentence him to death. Green made the choice to appeal, however, and the Supreme Court, in Green v. United States *(1957), accepted his contention that he already had been placed in jeopardy once. Justice Hugo Black explained for the 5-to-4 majority why the protection against double jeopardy is essential to American conceptions of justice.*

The constitutional prohibition against "double jeopardy" was designed to protect an individual from being subjected to the hazards of trial and possible conviction more than once for an alleged offense....

The underlying idea, one that is deeply ingrained in at least the Anglo-American system of jurisprudence, is that the State with all its resources and power should not be allowed to make repeated attempts to convict an individual for an alleged offense, thereby subjecting him to embarrassment, expense and ordeal and compelling him to live in a continuing state of anxiety and insecurity, as well as enhancing the possibility that even though innocent he may be found guilty.

In accordance with this philosophy it has long been settled under the Fifth Amendment that a verdict of acquittal is final, ending a defendant's jeopardy, and even when "not followed by any judgment, is a bar to a subsequent prosecution for the same offence."... Thus it is one of the elemental principles of our criminal law that the Government cannot secure a new trial by means of an appeal even though an acquittal may appear to be erroneous....

Moreover it is not even essential that a verdict of guilt or innocence be returned for a defendant to have once been placed in jeopardy so as to bar a second trial on the same charge. This Court, as well as most others, has taken the position that a defendant is placed in jeopardy once he is put to trial before a jury so that if the jury is discharged without his consent he cannot be tried again.... This prevents a prosecutor or judge from subjecting a defendant to a second prosecution by discontinuing the trial when it appears that the jury might not convict. At the same time jeopardy is not regarded as having come to an end so as to bar a second trial in those cases where "unforeseeable circumstances...arise during [the first] trial making its completion impossible, such as the failure of a jury to agree on a verdict."...

At common law a convicted person could not obtain a new trial by appeal except in certain narrow instances. As this harsh rule was discarded courts and legislatures provided that if a defendant obtained the reversal of a conviction by his own appeal he could be tried again for the same offense.... [W]hatever the rationalization, this Court has also held that a defendant can be tried a second time for an offense when his prior conviction for that same offense had been set aside on appeal....

Green was in direct peril of being convicted and punished for first degree murder at his first trial. He was forced to run the gantlet once on that charge and the jury refused to convict him. When given the choice between finding him guilty of either first or second degree murder it chose the latter. In this situation the great majority of cases in this country have regarded the jury's verdict as an implicit acquittal on the charge of first degree murder. But the result in this case need not rest alone on the assumption, which we believe legitimate, that the jury for one reason or another acquitted Green of murder in the first degree. For here, the jury was dismissed without returning any express verdict on that charge and without Green's consent. Yet it was given a full opportunity to return a verdict and no extraordinary circumstances appeared which prevented it from doing so. Therefore it seems clear, under established principles of former jeopardy, that Green's jeopardy for first degree murder came to an end when the jury was discharged so that he could not be retried for that offense....In brief, we believe this case can be treated no differently, for purposes of former jeopardy, than if the jury had returned a verdict which expressly read: "We find the defendant not guilty of murder in the first degree but guilty of murder in the second degree."...

The right not to be placed in jeopardy more than once for the same offense is a vital safeguard in our society, one that was dearly won and one that should continue to be highly valued. If such great constitutional protections are given a narrow, grudging application they are deprived of much of their significance.

States Cannot Make Repeated Attempts at Conviction

In Palko v. Connecticut *(1937), the Supreme Court concluded that the Fifth Amendment protection against double jeopardy did not apply to the states under the due process clause of the Fourteenth Amendment. The justices considered the question again in 1969 in* Benton v. Maryland. *Benton had been charged with larceny and burglary but convicted only of burglary, while being found not guilty of larceny. When he sought a new trial because of a problem with the way the jury had been selected, the state sought to try him again on both crimes. Benton agreed that he had waived his right to claim double jeopardy on the burglary charge, but he argued that the jury had acquitted him of larceny and therefore the state could not retry him for that crime. Writing for the 5-to-4 majority, Justice Thurgood Marshall agreed and reversed* Palko, *applying the ban on double jeopardy to the states as well as the federal government.*

Our recent cases have thoroughly rejected the Palko notion that basic constitutional rights can be denied by the States as long as the totality of the circumstances does not disclose a denial of "fundamental fairness." Once it is decided that a particular Bill of Rights guarantee is "fundamental to the American scheme of justice,"...the same constitutional standards apply against both the State and Federal Governments. Palko's roots had thus been cut away years ago. We today only recognize the inevitable....

Today, every State incorporates some form of the prohibition in its constitution or common law. As this Court put it in *Green* v. *United States,* "[t]he underlying idea, one that is deeply ingrained in at least the Anglo-American system of jurisprudence, is that the State with all its resources and power should not be allowed to make repeated attempts to convict an individual for an alleged offense, thereby subjecting him to embarrassment, expense and ordeal and compelling him to live in a continuing state of anxiety and insecurity, as well as enhancing the possibility that even though innocent he may be found guilty." This underlying notion has from the very beginning been part of our constitutional tradition. Like the right to trial by jury, it is clearly "fundamental to the American scheme of justice."

CHAPTER 17

The Privilege against Self-Incrimination

"You have the right to remain silent." These words are as well known as any phrase in American law. We hear them spoken on countless television dramas whenever the police make an arrest. They represent the privilege against self-incrimination, a right guaranteed by the Fifth Amendment, which states, "No person...shall be compelled in any criminal case to be a witness against himself." This protection against forced confessions is essential to our conception of liberty, but the right also raises fundamental questions about how to balance individual liberty with society's need for security, questions that are as current as today's headlines.

The privilege against self-incrimination goes back to the fourth century, but its most dramatic early expression can be found in medieval controversies between the English king and the church. Royal courts used a system of justice that employed public accusations and jury trials. Defendants knew the charges against them, and they were tried in public by members of the community. Church courts, by contrast, favored a system in which accusations were often made in secret, and the judge was also the prosecutor. These courts did not inform defendants of the accusation against them but required that they take an oath to tell the truth and to answer all questions fully. Defendants then faced a series of questions based on the prior examination of witnesses and informants. Contradictory answers were used against the defendants in an effort to break them down and force confessions of guilt. Failure to take the oath justified torture to learn the truth. In this process, defendants could be forced to incriminate themselves. The oath used to begin the process, the oath *ex officio* (from Latin, meaning "by virtue of the office"), became known as a self-incriminating oath.

The two systems of justice had different goals. The church's inquisitorial system formed the basis of European criminal justice and focused on proving the accused guilty. It was better that the innocent should suffer than the guilty escape. The opposite was true for the accusatorial system of England—it sought to protect the innocent above all else. In the words of Sir John Fortescue, a fifteenth-century chief justice, "One would much rather that twenty guilty persons should escape the punishment of death, than that one innocent person should be condemned, and suffer capitally."

The sixteenth and seventeenth centuries witnessed a shift in English practice. Secret proceedings and torture became mainstays of the Star Chamber, the court that tried enemies of the state. In theory, the oath *ex officio* and torture were extraordinary powers required to protect national security, but more often they were used against religious dissenters. One such case involved John Lilburne, a Puritan arrested for smuggling religious pamphlets into England in 1637. He refused to take the self-incriminating oath, claiming that it was

John Lilburne's unpopular opinions led to Parliament's declaration that he and his followers "shall be esteemed as Traytors to the Commonwealth, and be proceeded against accordingly." "Accordingly" meant imprisonment in the Tower of London.

"against the very law of nature, for nature is a preserver of itself....But if a man takes this wicked oath, he undoes and destroys himself." Over the next three years, Lilburne was repeatedly jailed, fined, and tortured, but he became a hero to Englishmen for his defense of liberty. In response, Parliament abolished the Star Chamber in 1641, concluding that Lilburne's sentence was "illegal, unjust, against the liberty of the subject and law of the land, and Magna Carta."

The American colonists were well aware of this history of royal abuse when they came to the New World, and they brought with them a firm conviction that no man should be required to testify against or accuse himself. They considered this privilege part of their rights under common law. In 1641, for example, the Massachusetts Puritans included prohibitions against torture and self-incriminating oaths in their earliest law code, the Body of Liberties, even though the magistrates still sought confessions in religious trials. By the time of the Revolution, these protections were considered to be so essential to liberty that they appeared in the various state constitutions; in 1791, the privilege against self-incrimination became part of the Fifth Amendment to the U.S. Constitution.

During the nineteenth century, American courts excluded evidence from confessions that had resulted from official violence or trickery. Interrogation was acceptable, however, as was the use of deception and psychological pressure applied by friends, family, or community. The key was whether the confession was made voluntarily; if not, the evidence was considered unreliable. Courts usually accepted a confession as voluntary unless evidence demonstrated that a law officer used a clear and unmistakable threat, so law officers frequently pushed the bounds of what was acceptable. Their aim was to make defendants admit guilt and to create an efficient system of justice. A growing fear of crime and disorder from the "dangerous classes" of immigrants and urban poor added to the pressure to use whatever methods were necessary to gain a confession. The extent of lawlessness in law enforcement became apparent in the 1920s when a national commission revealed the routine use of police brutality, the so-called "third degree," to force confessions and remove suspected criminals from the streets.

The U.S. Supreme Court during this period extended Fifth Amendment protection to civil cases in which testimony might lead to criminal prosecution, but it also rejected a universal or national privilege against self-incrimination. In *Twining* v. *New Jersey* (1908), the president of an investment bank enriched himself at his company's expense. When he refused to testify on his own behalf at trial, the judge told the jury that it could draw a negative inference from his silence. New Jersey's constitution allowed this conclusion, even though the practice vio-

"No man shall be forced by Torture or confesse any Crime against himselfe nor any other unless it be in some Capitall case where he is first fullie convicted by cleare and suffitient evidence to be guilty, After which if the cause be that of nature, That it is very apparent there be other conspiratours, or confederates with him, Then he may be tortured, yet not with such Tortures as be Barbarous and inhumane."

—Massachusetts Body of Liberties (1641)

lated the defendant's Fifth Amendment privilege. The U.S. Supreme Court upheld Twining's conviction. The protection against self-incrimination was "a wise and beneficent rule of evidence," the justices concluded, but it was not an essential part of due process. States were free to set their own standards. New Jersey's position, in many ways, reflected popular attitudes toward anyone who claimed the privilege. During the various congressional hearings in the 1950s to root out communism in the United States, for instance, "taking the Fifth," shorthand for refusing to testify for fear of self-incrimination, was often seen as an indication of guilt. For many Americans, concerns for order and national security trumped the rights of individuals to remain silent.

Finally in 1964, the Court decided that the privilege against self-incrimination was an essential part of due process as protected by the Fourteenth Amendment, thereby restricting the states as well as the federal government. But how far did the right extend? It clearly bound legal proceedings, but did it apply to investigations and other pretrial actions as well? Two years later, it became clear that it did when the justices reviewed a conviction for rape. Their decision embroiled the Court in the most famous and bitterly criticized confession case in the history of American law.

Around midnight on March 2, 1963, an eighteen-year-old woman closed her refreshment stand at a Phoenix, Arizona, movie theater and walked home. A short distance from her house, a car pulled in front of her, blocking the sidewalk. The driver grabbed her and forced her into the back seat. Tying her hands and feet, he threatened her with a sharp object and drove her into the nearby desert, where he raped her. He dumped her, hysterical and disheveled, near her house, where she lived with her mother and married sister.

Less than two weeks later, the police arrested Ernesto Arturo Miranda, a twenty-three-year-old Mexican American dockworker who lived with his girlfriend in Mesa, a Phoenix suburb. Miranda was known to the police. He had a record of six arrests and four imprisonments by the time he was eighteen. He also had a history of sexual problems: one of the arrests was for attempted rape; another was for Peeping Tom activities.

When he was brought in for questioning, Miranda was in constitutionally unprotected territory. In 1963, the rights that protected a defendant in the courtroom—the right to remain silent, the right to counsel, the right to confront witnesses, and other protections for the criminally accused—did not extend to the police station. Most people believed law officers needed wide

The wives of communist conspiracy defendants are joined in a mass demonstration protesting a judge's decision to send their husbands to jail for contempt of court. The rights of Communist party members were fiercely debated during the Red Scare of the 1950s.

latitude to investigate and prosecute crime. This certainly was the case in Arizona, where the state's constitutional convention in 1910 had rejected a ban on third-degree interrogations. "Do you intend to array yourselves on the side of the criminals," one delegate argued, "do you intend to put the State of Arizona on the line protecting criminals?" The goal of criminal justice was to protect the public, not criminals. This view was widely shared in the 1960s.

By all accounts, Miranda's interrogation was routine. He was alone with the police, without a lawyer. No one kept a record, and memories differed about what occurred. Miranda claimed the officers promised to drop an unrelated charge of robbery if he admitted the rape; the police denied making this offer. No one used physical force or unusual psychological tactics. In the end, Miranda confessed to the rape, writing his account of the crime by hand. The entire affair took less than two hours.

The police did not force Miranda to confess, but a question remained about whether he had confessed voluntarily. After all, he was in a highly stressful

> *"Coercing the supposed state's criminals into confessions and using such confessions so coerced from them against them in trials has been the curse of all countries. It was the chief iniquity, the crowning infamy of the Star Chamber, and the Inquisition, and other similar institutions. The Constitution recognized the evils that lay behind these practices and prohibited them in this country."*
>
> —Mississippi Supreme Court, *Fisher* v. *State* (1926)

environment—confined in a small room with harsh lighting, surrounded by armed men who wore badges of authority, and without legal assistance. He also suffered from mental illness, according to two psychiatrists who examined him later. Given these circumstances, could his confession be considered freely given and therefore reliable? If not, it could not be used at trial.

Miranda's court-appointed attorney was unsuccessful in persuading the court to exclude the confession. He then sought to discredit the victim, claiming that she had not resisted—a circumstance that, even if true, would be irrelevant under today's law—and that she was only trying to protect her reputation. The jury rejected these claims and found Miranda guilty of kidnapping and rape. The court sentenced him to a prison term of up to fifty-five years.

In November 1965, the U.S. Supreme Court agreed to hear his appeal. The question before the justices was straightforward: did the failure of police to inform Miranda of his rights violate his Fifth Amendment guarantee against forced confessions? With Chief Justice Earl Warren writing for the majority, the Court extended the right to an attorney and the privilege against self-incrimination to the pretrial interrogation of a suspect. The justices also ruled that, prior to questioning, a suspect must be informed of these rights by using the now-familiar formula: he "has a right to remain silent, that any statement he does make may be used as evidence against him, and that he has a right to the presence of an attorney, either retained or appointed."

The opinion joined the Fifth Amendment's privilege against self-incrimination with the Sixth Amendment's guarantee of a right to counsel and, for the first time in U.S. history, applied both to the police station. Simply informing a person of his rights without also allowing the assistance of counsel would place the police at an unfair advantage, Warren wrote. The atmosphere of the interrogation room, where the suspect stood isolated and alone, carried "its own badge of intimidation." Even if no physical brutality occurred, it was "destructive of human dignity" and violated the constitutional requirement of fairness. The accused may choose to waive the assistance of a lawyer, but the Constitution requires that he be reminded of his right to have one. "Incommunicado interrogation [questioning without benefit of counsel]," the chief justice's opinion concluded, "is at odds with one of our Nation's most cherished principles—that the individual may not be compelled to incriminate himself."

Four justices disagreed vehemently with the decision. Their arguments varied, but the strongest objections centered on

Ernesto Miranda looks grim in his mug shot, taken in an Arizona police station where he confessed to kidnapping and rape. His case led to a requirement that police warn suspects of their rights. The statement, which begins, "You have the right to remain silent," is known as a Miranda warning.

FEDERAL BUREAU OF INVESTIGATION, UNITED STATES DEPARTMENT OF JUSTICE
WASHINGTON, D.C.

CURRENT ARREST OR RECEIPT

DATE ARRESTED OR RECEIVED	CHARGE OR OFFENSE (If code citation is used it should be accompanied by charge)	DISPOSITION OR SENTENCE (List FINAL disposition only. If not now available submit later on FBI Form R-84 for completion of record.)
7-5-1963 MARICOPA COUNTY	COUNT I-KIDNAPPING COUNT II-RAPE(FIRST DEGREE) TO RUN CONCURRENTLY	20 yrs. to 30 yrs.

OCCUPATION	RESIDENCE OF PERSON FINGERPRINTED
TRUCK DRIVER	WIFE: TWILA MIRANDA 157 E. COMMONWELL CHANDLER, ARIZONA

If COLLECT wire reply or COLLECT telephone reply is desired, indicate here

☐ Wire reply   ☐ Telephone reply

Telephone number

FOR INSTITUTIONS USE ONLY

Sentence expires... 7-5-1993

INSTRUCTIONS
1. FORWARD ARREST CARDS TO FBI IMMEDIATELY AFTER FINGERPRINTING FOR MOST EFFECTIVE SERVICE
2. TYPE or PRINT all information.
3. Note amputations in proper finger squares
4. REPLY WILL QUOTE ONLY NUMBER APPEARING IN THE BLOCK MARKED "CONTRIBUTOR'S NO."
5. Indicate any additional copies for other agencies in space below—include their complete mailing address

SEND COPY TO:

Joe N. Rodriguez, Secretary
ARIZONA STATE PRISON
Florence, Arizona

Justices William O. Douglas, Stanley Reed, Earl Warren, Hugo Black, and Felix Frankfurter pause for a photo with President Dwight Eisenhower (third from right) on the White House steps in 1953, the year Warren was appointed chief justice. Within eight months of his appointment, Warren would preside over the first of many historic decisions concerning our rights in Brown v. Board of Education.

the fear that the new rules would hamper police unduly. "We do know that some crimes cannot be solved without confessions," warned Justice John Marshall Harlan II, "and that the Court is taking a real risk with society's welfare in imposing its new regime on the country." The result of the decision, other justices agreed, inevitably would weaken the capacity of law enforcement to convict dangerous criminals. "In some unknown number of cases," Justice Byron White argued, "the Court's rule will return a killer, a rapist or other criminal to the streets . . . to repeat his crime whenever it pleases him."

The decision did not free Ernesto Miranda, who was serving a separate sentence for robbery. He won a retrial but was convicted a second time, this time without the use of his confession as evidence. Paroled in 1972, he became a minor celebrity, selling autographed cards containing preprinted Miranda warnings on the streets of downtown Phoenix. After a three-year re-imprisonment for a parole violation, he died in 1975 in a barroom brawl over a three-dollar bet, one month after winning another release. During the investigation, police questioned the two suspects who eventually were charged with the crime. Their notes revealed that the detectives had dutifully warned both men of their right to remain silent.

Police officers, prosecutors, commentators, and politicians were quick to denounce the Miranda warnings, which they believed "handcuffed" the police. National data revealed a sustained rise in crime since the 1950s, and this decision, critics charged, would worsen the problem. This response was understandable, but its fears proved to be exaggerated. Numerous studies have since demonstrated that the decision did not restrain police unduly and had little effect on their work. A 1998 study, for example, found that less than 1 percent of all criminal cases had to be dismissed because police failed to give a warning before the accused confessed. In fact, more than 90 percent of all criminal convictions today involve plea bargains, with voluntary confessions, by defendants in exchange for a reduced sentence.

The *Miranda* decision did not halt voluntary confessions; it only defined proper methods of interrogation. One outcome has been increased professionalism in police practices. In response to *Miranda,* many departments raised standards for employment, adopted performance guidelines, and improved training and supervision. The result vindicated the view of the majority justices, first voiced by Justice Louis Brandeis in the 1920s, that hard work and respect for the law, not deception or lawbreaking, were the requirements for effective law enforcement. "Our government," Brandeis wrote in *Olmstead* v. *United States* (1928), "teaches the whole people by its example. If the government becomes the lawbreaker, it breeds contempt for law; it invites every man to become a law unto himself; it invites anarchy."

Miranda v. *Arizona* was a revolutionary decision. It extended the protection of the Bill of Rights beyond the courtroom to an important pretrial procedure, custodial interrogation. Even though numerous political campaigns have promised to overturn the decision, in fact the warnings have become part of American culture. Subsequent courts have noted exceptions to the rules—the rules do not apply to on-the-scene questioning, for example—but the justices have always reaffirmed the requirement that suspects be informed of their rights. The 1966 decision, the Court noted in a later case, "embodies a carefully crafted balance designed to protect *both* the defendant's and the society's interests."

Today, we continue to wrestle with finding the appropriate balance between public order and individual rights. Since the terrorist attacks of September 11, 2001, the issues have taken on added significance. The Constitution, as Justice Robert Jackson reminded Americans in 1949, is not a suicide pact, but neither are its requirements meaningless because of a threat to national security. The Fifth Amendment's privilege against self-incrimination achieves its importance, however, not in this extreme circumstance but in the more ordinary working of our legal system. The right is necessary for our sense of justice because it helps to ensure fairness. We assume the innocence of an individual until the government proves otherwise. Government has vast power, so we balance the scales of justice by, among other things, protecting the individual from a forced confession, an involuntary admission of guilt. Without it, there can be no due process of law.

The privilege against self-incrimination is also essential to our understanding of individual liberty. As a society, we believe freedom rests upon a fundamental right to privacy and human dignity. Central to our conception of privacy is the need for men and women to be custodians of their own consciences, thoughts, feelings, and sensations. Forcing us to reveal these things, making us confess without our consent, robs us of the things that make us individuals. No one and no power has the right to take something so precious from us, and the Fifth Amendment exists to ensure that we guarantee to each citizen the dignity and self-respect that allows us all to be free.

Crafting an Opinion

After the Supreme Court hears arguments in a case, the justices meet in conference to discuss the case and take a preliminary vote. If the chief justice is in the majority, he assigns a justice who voted with the majority to draft an opinion for comment by all the justices. (If the chief is in the minority, the assignment is made by the justice with the most seniority who also voted with the majority.) The draft opinion is an opportunity for the majority justices to make their most persuasive arguments in the hope of gaining additional support. In Miranda v. Arizona *(1966), Chief Justice Earl Warren assigned the draft opinion to himself. Justice William Brennan, who voted in conference with the majority, read the chief's draft and sent him a twenty-one-page memo suggesting changes. On the first page of the memo, Brennan recommended an important change in wording.*

Dear Chief:

I am writing out my suggestions addressed to your *Miranda* opinion with the thought that we might discuss them at your convenience. I feel guilty about the extent of the suggestion but this will be one of the most important opinions of our time and I know that you will want the fullest expression of my views.

I have one major suggestion. It goes to the back thrust of the approach to be taken. In your very first sentence you state that the root problem is "the *role* society must *assume*, consistent with the federal Constitution, in prosecuting individuals for crime." I would suggest that the root issue is "the *restraints* society must *observe*, consistent with the federal Constitution, in prosecuting individuals for crime."

In the final opinion for Miranda v. Arizona, *Chief Justice Earl Warren accepted Brennan's modification. He used his colleague's language—"the* restraints *society must* observe*"—instead of his own less forceful and less clear phrase, "the* role *society must* assume.*"*

The cases before us raise questions which go to the roots of our concepts of American criminal jurisprudence: the restraints society must observe consistent with the Federal Constitution in prosecuting individuals for crime. More specifically, we deal with the admissibility of statements obtained from an individual who is subjected to custodial police interrogation and the necessity for procedures which assure that the individual is accorded his privilege under the Fifth Amendment to the Constitution not to be compelled to incriminate himself.

"Protecting Constitutional Rights Does Not in Any Way Prevent Law Enforcement"

Miranda v. Arizona resulted in widespread protests that the Supreme Court had exceeded its authority and had begun to legislate rules of police conduct instead of decide cases. Many critics warned that the decision would handcuff police and let criminals go free. Lost among the outrage were the voices of supporters of what came to be called the "Miranda warnings." Senator Wayne Morse of Oregon was a strong advocate of civil liberties and endorsed the decision on the Senate floor. His following speech was recorded in the Congressional Record *in 1966. Later studies of law enforcement revealed that the requirement to notify defendants of their rights did not lead to the direful results predicted by critics of the decision.*

As the RECORD shows, I have argued over and over again that the guilty have exactly the same constitutional rights as the innocent. I have argued that you cannot have constitutional rights for some but not for others. I have spoken out over the years, against arrests for investigation and against third-degree tactics on the part of police departments—and they continue to exist... in a variety of forms....

One has only to read this landmark opinion... in Miranda against Arizona, to appreciate how sound have been the arguments throughout the years of those of us who have been opposing the denial of constitutional rights when arrested....

We cannot maintain a government by law within the framework of our Constitution if we countenance what would be the effect of the minority views expressed in this case: the sanctioning of arbitrary and capricious discretion in the police....

[A]s one who worked a good many years in the field of research on law-enforcement policy, and as editor in chief of a five-volume work put out by the Department of Justice when I was an assistant to the Attorney General, I wish to say that it is in times of stress that it is so important that there be no transgression on constitutional rights by the police or by the courts, or we will cease to be freemen and freewomen....

To these chiefs of police, prosecutors, and others who would have constitutional rights of arrested persons transgressed upon, I wish to say, as pointed out by the Chief Justice in this case, that protecting constitutional rights does not in any way prevent law enforcement on the part of an efficient police department or an efficient prosecutor's office and recognizes their duty to stay within the framework of the Constitution.

CHAPTER 18

The Right to Trial by Jury

Among all abuses of governmental power, we may fear the secret trial most. Trial by jury guards against this practice, and for this reason juries have long occupied an important place in our understanding of individual rights. English colonists identified trial by jury as one of the three rights central to their definition of liberty; the other two were due process of law and representative government. A local jury chosen from one's peers, or equals, guarded against vindictive and overbearing judges and distant government. Jurors from the neighborhood came to their task with knowledge about the events on trial and about the reputation of the accused and accuser. Their general verdict—a simple reply of guilty or not guilty to a charge of wrongdoing—was the people's most effective weapon against tyranny. The jury, quite simply, was the best available method of assuring justice and protecting liberty.

The struggle for independence convinced Americans that their confidence in the jury was not misplaced. The most troublesome actions of Great Britain

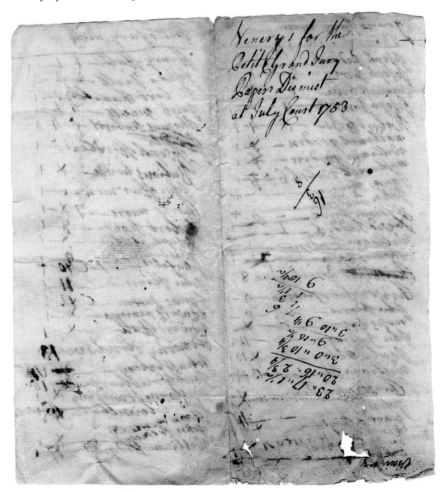

This 1753 list of jurors from North Carolina is divided into two columns (on opposite page). The left column lists names of grand jurors. A grand jury determines whether it is reasonable to prosecute the suspect for a felony based on the evidence. The right lists members of a petit jury (or trial jury), a group of citizens that sits in judgment at civil and criminal trials.

centered on attempts to limit the use of jury trial in cases involving colonial protests against imperial laws. One of the provisions of the Stamp Act of 1765, for example, shifted trials of alleged violators to a court where a judge alone decided guilt or innocence; in 1774, another parliamentary statute denied the right to a trial by a jury from the neighborhood. To many colonists, these actions, when considered with other threats to liberty, were sufficient to justify separation from the mother country.

The Constitution and Bill of Rights testify to the importance the framers placed on trial by a local jury. Article 3, which outlines the functions of the judiciary, requires that the "Trial of all Crimes, except in Cases of Impeachment, shall be by Jury; and such Trial shall be held in the State where the said Crimes shall have been committed." The guarantee of this right appears twice more in the Bill of Rights. The Sixth Amendment defines the right more extensively: "In all criminal prosecutions, the accused shall enjoy the right to a speedy and public trial, by an impartial jury of the State and district wherein the crime shall have been committed." The Seventh Amendment extends this right to civil cases, that is, noncriminal cases such as disputes over contracts, in which the amount in dispute is more than twenty dollars, a figure that has not changed over time even though a dollar was worth much more then. These amendments spelled out carefully the founders' criteria for fair trials: they must be speedy and public; the jury must be local; and jurors must be impartial. Underlying these criteria was a belief

> *"The great value of the trial by jury certainly consists in its fairness and impartiality. Those who most prize the institution, prize it because it furnishes a tribunal which may be expected to be uninfluenced by an undue bias of the mind."*
>
> —Chief Justice John Marshall, *United States* v. *Burr* (1807)

that justice in a republic depended upon the active involvement of virtuous citizens in the public affairs of a community. Juries were a means to this end.

The nineteenth century witnessed a decline in the jury's role in both civil and criminal trials, even though commentators continued to laud its virtues. In theory, jurors were considered to be the judges of both law and fact, which meant they not only determined what the facts of a case were but also decided how to interpret the law. This practice was an old one that reflected the belief that justice required jurors to use their local knowledge to fit the law to the circumstances of their communities. For instance, a statute may forbid trespass on private property, but if it was long-standing practice in an area to cut across a field, then a local jury would know this and refuse to convict a person who simply was doing what everyone else did. But the nineteenth century witnessed a change in the jury's role: jurors could determine the facts, but they had to accept the law as interpreted by the judge. Civil juries, which decided noncriminal cases, especially felt this restriction because commerce required standards that did not vary from place to place. The goal was consistent and equal application of the law, an unlikely result if civil and criminal juries were free to determine in each case what the law meant.

Other changes affected the criminal jury primarily. In a pattern that continues today, many criminal prosecutions never reached trial. Plea bargaining and negotiated punishments became the typical way of managing the increase in crime that resulted from overcrowded cities. Citizens began to avoid jury duty, aided by state laws that excused entire groups, usually business and professional men, from this civic duty. (Women were not eligible for jury duty because they could not vote; also, some men considered them "too delicate" for this task.) Soon, juries were thought to be composed primarily of the least virtuous citizens rather than pillars of the community. By the end of the century, trial by jury was still praised formally as a bulwark against tyranny, but increasingly it was satirized in practice, as evidenced by Mark Twain's characterization that it "put a ban on intelligence and honesty, and a premium on ignorance, stupidity and perjury."

Despite this history, most Americans continued to believe that the right to a speedy public trial by an impartial jury of peers was a bedrock principle of American freedom. They were buoyed in this conviction by laws and court decisions, most of them in the twentieth century, that broadened the jury pool to include blacks and women, making juries, in theory, more representative of the community than ever. But with the rise of highly competitive mass media since the 1950s, a different issue has claimed our attention: does extensive media coverage undermine the constitutional promise of an impartial jury? Consider the 1995 trial of African American former football star and Hollywood celebrity O. J. Simpson, who was accused of killing his ex-wife and another man. For months, Americans watched as a drama of sex, race, and violence played itself out on national television. Simpson's acquittal divided the nation into racial camps, with blacks generally applauding the jury's decision and many whites condemning it. Commentators wondered whether juries were capable of reaching an objective verdict in a case so heavily promoted by Court TV and 24-hour news channels. Perhaps, they suggested, we should try such cases before judges alone.

Forty years earlier, another notorious trial focused national attention on this issue. The case involved a prominent Ohio doctor accused of murdering his wife. It, too, raised important questions about the trust we place in juries.

On July 4, 1954, residents of Cleveland, Ohio, awoke to read about the grisly murder of a prominent doctor's wife in one of the idyllic suburbs around Lake Erie. After entertaining neighbors at a holiday party, thirty-one-year-old Marilyn Sheppard had gone to bed while her neurosurgeon husband fell asleep on the couch. Sometime later Sam Sheppard heard her calling him. He ran to the bedroom where he saw an intruder—a "bushy haired man"—fighting with his wife. Before he could save her, he was struck on the head from behind and knocked unconscious. Regaining his senses, he found his wife dead, her face bloody and unrecognizable. His son, sleeping in a nearby room, was unharmed. Sheppard found the back door open, saw someone moving toward the lake, and gave chase. The two men began to fight and Sheppard again lost consciousness; the intruder escaped.

In front-page stories, the three major Cleveland daily newspapers at first described the events as a brutal tragedy that shattered a model family and horrified the community. They speculated that drug thieves were responsible and reported in detail on the police investigation. Within a week, however, doubts emerged about the doctor's story, even though he never changed his account under repeated questioning. There were too many holes in it, people thought: Why was there no evidence of a break-in? How had Sheppard's son slept through the violent struggle? Why didn't the dog bark? The only answer the doctor gave was, "I don't know."

The police suspected Sheppard from the outset, with a detective telling him, "I think you did it," less than twenty-four hours after the crime. No physical evidence linked Sheppard to the crime, and the injuries he suffered were consistent with his story, but police thought his motive was a sexual affair Sheppard denied for several days before admitting it. They also believed the family was failing to cooperate fully.

A 1954 editorial calls for police to "quit stalling and bring" Sam Sheppard, widower of a murdered wife, in for questioning. Although the text of the editorial seems reasonable enough, the headline's exclamation point and the photo of Sheppard, who appears to be hiding behind dark sunglasses, suggest that he is guilty.

Reporting this story was an openly skeptical press, encouraged at every step by police leaks. A reporter traveled with the lead detective to Los Angeles to bring Sheppard's girlfriend back for questioning, with the story running on page one. The editorial pages began calling for Sheppard's arrest, culminating in a *Cleveland Press* editorial on July 29 that ran across the top of the front page, "Quit Stalling and Bring Him In!" That evening, the police charged the doctor with the murder of his wife.

Massive publicity accompanied the trial, which began almost four months later. The judge denied a motion to move the case to another venue because of prejudicial pretrial publicity and required the lawyers to agree on a jury from the sixty-four-person jury pool, all of whom were local celebrities because the newspapers published their names and addresses. He also made extraordinary efforts to accommodate press interest in the trial, setting up a table for local reporters in the space normally reserved for the judge, jurors, and lawyers only and assigning most of the spectator seats to out-of-town reporters. Sheppard's lawyers protested this "trial by newspaper," adding, "If you read a story like this about the People's Court in China . . . it would raise hair on your head." The judge ignored their pleas to restrain the press, and after six weeks of testimony, the jurors found Sheppard guilty of second-degree murder.

Sentenced to life in prison, Sheppard appealed in the first of more than a dozen unsuccessful attempts to overturn the verdict. In 1961, he got a new lawyer—a flamboyant young attorney named F. Lee Bailey, who would make his reputation from this case—and finally in 1966, the U.S. Supreme Court agreed to hear him. Three years earlier, a new television series had begun, featuring a husband wrongly accused of killing his wife and his subsequent quest for the mysterious one-armed stranger he believed had killed her. Although the creator of "The Fugitive" denied any connection to Sheppard's case, the resemblance was striking, and pundits wondered whether its popularity influenced the justices to hear the case.

The Supreme Court reversed Sheppard's conviction. "The massive, pervasive, and prejudicial publicity attending the petitioner's prosecution prevented him from receiving a fair trial," the justices concluded. The litany of errors at trial was long, with most focusing on the courtroom's carnival atmosphere. The judge too easily accommodated the press at the expense of the defendant's rights and failed to sequester, or isolate, the jury, allowing them to go home at night without strong reminders that they should not read, watch, or listen to any account of the trial or testimony. The hostile coverage by the Cleveland press and the proceedings at trial prejudiced the jury against Sheppard and made a fair trial impossible. "Due process," the Court ruled, "requires that the accused receive a trial by an impartial jury free from outside influences." Sheppard's trial had not met this constitutional standard.

Sam Sheppard had spent ten of the previous twelve years in prison based on the verdict of a biased jury, but his ordeal was not over. The state tried him again, this time governed by rules that guaranteed an impartial panel. Judged not guilty, he was finally free from his legal nightmare, although not his personal one. He became an alcoholic and died in 1970, a broken man. Seeking to restore his reputation through a declaration of innocence, his son unsuccessfully sued the state in a civil trial in 2000. In this case gone wrong, the failure to provide an impartial jury had resulted in a bitter irony: Sheppard's family ultimately believed it had to prove his innocence instead of the state having to prove his guilt.

In *Sheppard* v. *Maxwell*, the right to a public trial by an impartial jury and freedom of press were in conflict. In such instances, the Court decided, nothing prevented the press from reporting on the trial, but judges had a duty to ensure that the balance between this right and an impartial jury "is never weighed against the accused." Although the circumstances of the Sheppard case were decidedly modern, the measure used by the justices was an old one. The founding generation adopted a Bill of Rights to protect individual liberty against governmental power, including governmental actions (or inactions) that allowed the abuse of power by other parties, even if the result met popular approval.

Juries have unique roles in protecting our rights. No other institution of government places so much power—the power literally to decide issues of life and freedom—directly in the hands of average citizens. Juries by definition require government to prove guilt before taking away life, liberty, or property. Although rarely done, jurors can refuse to convict a defendant when they believe the law is wrong or when they believe following the law will lead to a greater injustice, such as when antebellum northern juries refused to send runaway slaves back to their masters despite the law's command. The acceptance of this practice, often called jury nullification, predates the Constitution. An American jury's refusal to follow the British government's instructions to convict printer John Peter Zenger of libel (after he had published criticisms of New York's colonial governor) was evidence to America's founders that this institution protected liberty even when it disobeyed the law. We have faith in such jury power for a variety of reasons: we trust the judgment of twelve members of the community over that of a single judge; juries exercise limited power, operating only in one case; and verdicts are subject to review on matters of law. We also believe jurors will be true to their oath to follow the law as they understand it.

The jury is among our most democratic institutions, especially now that we insist that its membership be as diverse as our pluralistic society, a true cross section of the population. Also, jury service is the primary way most of us participate directly in government. Open to all adult citizens, the jury embodies a belief that each of us is equally competent to do justice.

Ironically, some observers believe this recent democratization of the jury has not solved its problems but only made them worse. Critics of the jury system argue that juries make decisions based on emotion, prejudice, and sympathy rather than law

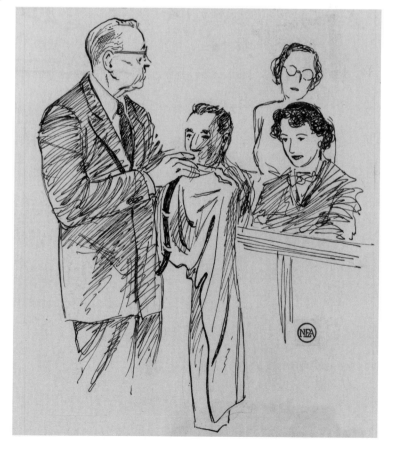

Defense chief William J. Corrigan shows the jury the pants Sam Sheppard was wearing the night his wife, Marilyn, was murdered. Corrigan calls attention to a rip near the right-hand pocket in this courtroom sketch. Until recently many states did not allow cameras in the courtroom—and some still do not permit it—because of fear it would distract jurors or lessen the solemn atmosphere of the trial.

and evidence. They believe modern cases, especially complex civil lawsuits, are too technical for lay people to understand; in medical cases, for instance, they fear juries will award extraordinary damage awards for negligence or error that make the practice of medicine even more expensive. Insurance companies often make this complaint; patients who have been harmed by negligent acts hold an opposite view. Other critics worry about the ability of jurors to ignore the laws of democratically passed legislatures, which, they charge, makes the jury itself a lawless institution. They are also concerned that too much emphasis on ethnically balanced juries results either in deadlocked panels or different standards of justice for different groups. For these reasons and more, we hear periodic calls to reform or abolish the jury system.

Research on juries allays most of these concerns and strengthens our faith in this institution. Overall, jurors are competent and effective. They listen carefully and take seriously the charge not to discuss the evidence or reach a decision until the judge passes the case to them for deliberation and a verdict. They do not rush to judgment; instead, they reach a verdict through analysis of the evidence, not as experts but by judging its trustworthiness with common sense. They seek to persuade each other but also are open to persuasion. They do not reach perfect verdicts but, on the whole, they act as we hope and expect them to act—deliberately and fairly.

Ultimately, the jury's impartiality does not rest upon its ignorance or its superior knowledge; guided by careful judicial instructions, it stems instead from experiences that differ from juror to juror, thereby reflecting the variety of circumstances and opinions we find in real life. Jurors bring their prejudices into the jury room because they cannot do otherwise, but their deliberations, when conducted honestly, expose these prejudices, test them, and allow jurors to set them aside in an effort to be fair. Miscarriages of justice still occur, yet most often juries try to meet the constitutional test of fairness. In doing so, they help to realize the promise of the Bill of Rights and affirm Thomas Jefferson's belief that trial by jury is the "only anchor ever yet imagined by man, by which government can be held to the principles of its constitution."

"The Most Grievous Innovation of All"

In 1764, the Sugar Act transferred the prosecution of smugglers from local courts to vice admiralty courts. The British government was seeking to improve the collection of taxes, or customs duties, owed on imported goods, and Parliament believed that colonial juries too often refused to convict the violators of these imperial trade laws. The vice admiralty court did not have a jury. A judge alone decided guilt or innocence—and he received part of the fines assessed to individuals convicted of smuggling.

The colonists protested vehemently that the loss of trial by jury denied them one of their basic rights as Englishmen, as evidenced by John Adams's "Instructions of the Town of Braintree on the Stamp Act" (1765), in which he attempted to persuade the Massachusetts town to petition the king for a redress, or correction, of this grievance.

But the most grievous Innovation of all, is the alarming Extension of the Power of Courts of Admiralty. In these Courts, one Judge presides alone! No Juries have any Concern there!—The Law, and the Fact, are both to be decided by the same single Judge, whose Commission is only during Pleasure, and with whom, as we are told, the most mischievous of all Customs has become established, that of taking Commissions on all Condemnations; so that he is under a pecuniary Temptation always against the Subject. Now, if the Wisdom of the Mother Country has thought the Independency of the Judges, so essential to an impartial Administration of Justice, as to render them independent of every Power on Earth, nay independent of the King, the Lords, the Commons, the People, nay independent, in Hope and Expectation, of the Heir apparent, by continuing their Commissions after a Demise of the Crown; What Justice and Impartiality are we, at 3000 Miles distance from the Fountain to expect from such a Judge of Admiralty?

The same complaint—denial to the colonists of the right of trial by jury—was also part of the Declaration and Resolves issued by the Continental Congress in 1774. The First Continental Congress met in Philadelphia during the months of September and October in 1774 to protest British policies.

Resolved, . . . That the respective colonies are entitled to the common law of England, and more especially to the great and inestimable privilege of being tried by their peers of the vicinage, according to the course of that law.

The several acts . . . which impose duties for the purpose of raising revenue in America, extend the power of the admiralty courts beyond their ancient limits, deprive the American subject of trial by jury, authorise the judges certificate to indemnify the prosecutor from damages, that he might otherwise be liable to, requiring oppressive security from a claimant of ships and goods seized, before he shall be allowed to defend his property, and are subversive of American rights.

Prejudicial Publicity

In Sheppard *v.* Maxwell *(1966), Justice Tom Clark's majority opinion reviewed some of the newspaper coverage surrounding the murder of Marilyn Sheppard and the trial (and conviction) of her husband, Sam Sheppard. The evidence Clark cites reveals a press engaged in sensationalism. The Court ruled that Sheppard had not been tried by an impartial jury and reversed his conviction.*

Throughout this period the newspapers empha- sized evidence that tended to incriminate Sheppard and pointed out discrepancies in his state- ments to authorities....

A front-page editorial on July 30 asked: "Why Isn't Sam Sheppard in Jail?" It was later titled "Quit Stalling—Bring Him In." After calling Sheppard "the most unusual murder suspect ever seen around these parts" the article said that "[e]xcept for some superficial questioning during Coroner Sam Gerber's inquest he has been scot-free of any official grilling...." It asserted that he was "surrounded by an iron curtain of protection [and] concealment."

That night at 10 o'clock Sheppard was arrested at his father's home on a charge of murder. He was taken to the Bay Village City Hall where hundreds of people, newscasters, photographers and reporters were await- ing his arrival. He was immediately arraigned—having been denied a temporary delay to secure the presence of counsel—and bound over to the grand jury.

The publicity then grew in intensity until his indictment on August 17. Typical of the coverage during this period is a front-page interview entitled: "DR. SAM: 'I Wish There Was Something I Could Get Off My Chest—but There Isn't.'" Unfavorable publicity included items such as a cartoon of the body of a sphinx with Sheppard's head and the legend below: "'I Will Do Everything In My Power to Help Solve This Terrible Murder.'—Dr. Sam Sheppard." Headlines announced, inter alia, that: "Doctor Evidence is Ready for Jury," "Corrigan Tactics Stall Quizzing," "Sheppard 'Gay Set' Is Revealed By Houk," "Blood Is Found In Garage," "New Murder Evidence Is Found, Police Claim," "Dr. Sam Faces Quiz At Jail On Marilyn's Fear Of Him." On August 18, an article appeared under the headline "Dr. Sam Writes His Own Story." And reproduced across the entire front page was a portion of the typed state- ment signed by Sheppard: "I am not guilty of the murder of my wife, Marilyn. How could I, who have been trained to help people and devoted my life to saving life, commit such a terrible and revolting crime?" We do not detail the coverage further. There are five volumes filled with similar clippings from each of the three Cleveland newspapers covering the period from the murder until Sheppard's conviction in December 1954. The record includes no excerpts from newscasts on radio and television but since space was reserved in the courtroom for these media we assume that their coverage was equally large.

CHAPTER 19

The Right to Counsel

Television courtroom dramas have made the assistance of counsel during criminal proceedings one of the most recognizable of all rights guaranteed by the Constitution. We witness countless scenes of defendants refusing to cooperate without the presence of an attorney and of defense lawyers jousting in court with prosecutors to win an acquittal for their client. On "Law and Order" and "Boston Legal," it also does not matter whether the defendants are rich or poor, well-known or anonymous, members of a majority group or not. They all have a lawyer representing them, as we now understand the Sixth Amendment to require.

This unremarkable scene in which every defendant has a lawyer has not always been present throughout American history. Most often, class and race have influenced, if not governed, access to counsel. Still, the idea that defendants needed the assistance of counsel was an early addition to the list of American rights. English law did not provide this guarantee until 1836, yet twelve of the thirteen colonies long before had adopted some form of this protection. State constitutions in the new nation included the right to retain a lawyer for all persons accused of crimes; however, none required the appointment of counsel for poor defendants. This limited understanding, while advanced for its time, is what appears in the Sixth Amendment: "In all criminal cases, the defendant shall enjoy the right…to have the Assistance of Counsel for his defense." The framers recognized access to a lawyer was necessary for a fair trial, but the guarantee meant only that those who could afford a lawyer could have one.

With the rise of a professional bar of lawyers in the nineteenth century, criminal cases began to resemble trials we recognize today, with prosecuting attorneys for the state and defense attorneys for the accused. Questions remained, however, about the extent of the right to a lawyer. How did it apply, for instance, to defendants who could not afford an attorney? Some states assigned counsel at public expense to indigent defendants in felony trials. The Indiana Supreme Court in 1854 was the first to recognize this protection as one of the "principles of a civilized society." But most states did not go this far, and many people who were accused faced the justice system without the advice of a lawyer. Did a fair trial require states to provide a defender at public expense? The emergence of plea bargaining as the typical way to process offenders through the legal system raised another question. What is the right to counsel when the location of criminal justice moves from the courtroom to the police station, which is what happens when suspects confess during interrogation in exchange for more lenient punishment? Do defendants have a right to counsel during police interrogations and other pretrial stages of the criminal process?

The American system of divided government, federalism, has complicated answers to these questions. For most of our history, the control and punishment of crime was a state responsibility. State law defined crimes, and each state

> "Every man that findest himselfe unfit to plead his owne cause in any Court shall have Libertie to imploy any man against whom the Court doth not except, to helpe him, Provided he give him noo fee or reward for his paines. This shall not exempt the partie him selfe from Answering such Questions in person as the Court shall thinke meete to demand of him."
>
> —Massachusetts Body of Liberties (1641)

established its own rules for a fair trial. Although most states agreed on the basic elements of due process, no national standard existed until the 1930s when, in *Powell* v. *Alabama,* the Supreme Court recognized a right to counsel in capital cases. This decision began a series of cases that tested what this obligation meant in practice, but judges produced no uniform rule on when states were required to provide a lawyer. Finally, two cases in the 1960s, one from Florida and one from Illinois, helped to establish the national standards we see portrayed in television dramas. One of them met widespread approval; the other began criticism still heard today.

Clarence Earl Gideon was a habitual thief. A runaway at fourteen, he stole some clothes, and upon his mother's request, went to a reform school for three years. Shortly after his release, he was convicted of robbery and drew a ten-year prison term. Soon, his life fell into a pattern common to habitual criminals— release from prison, another crime, another term, another release, another crime. All the convictions were for small-scale robbery. In between his stints in prison, he married three times and had five children. An alcoholic, he never held a job for long and could not provide for his family.

On June 3, 1961, Gideon was arrested once again, this time for breaking into a bar in Panama City, Florida, where he had moved hoping for a fresh start. He requested the court to appoint counsel to represent him, but the judge refused, citing state law that granted it only to defendants in capital cases. Lacking funds, Gideon defended himself, but he was outmatched. He questioned witnesses inexpertly, and he did not raise a single objection. The attorney who later represented him on appeal characterized his effort as pitiful, concluding, "A lawyer—not a great lawyer, just an ordinary lawyer—could have made ashes of this case." Convicted of breaking and entering with intent to commit a misdemeanor, the court sentenced him to five years in prison.

Sitting in prison, Gideon petitioned the Supreme Court in longhand on five pieces of lined paper, asking the justices to take the case because he did not get a fair trial. "The question is very simple," he wrote, "I requested the court to appoint me an attorney and the court refused." Gideon filed as a pauper, and, as an indication of the importance of the questions at issue, the Court appointed a highly regarded Washington lawyer, Abe Fortas, to represent him on appeal. (Fortas later became a Supreme Court justice.) The case ultimately rested on the straightforward argument that for all serious crimes, the due process clause of the Fourteenth Amendment, which applied to all states, incorporated (or included) the right to counsel as required by the Sixth Amendment. If defendants were too poor to afford a lawyer, then states had to provide one for them. More than twenty state attorneys general urged the justices to adopt this rule because previous decisions had left the law too confused. The Court agreed, even though the justices had to abandon earlier decisions that left this matter to state discretion. It was "an obvious truth," the Court ruled, that otherwise a defendant too poor to hire a lawyer could not be guaranteed the fair trial guaranteed by the Constitution.

Gideon won a new trial, this time with a public defender paid for by the state. An effective cross-examination persuaded the jury to return a verdict of not guilty, and finally Clarence Earl Gideon was a free man. The decision made little difference in his life; he continued to get in trouble with the law. He died

Abe Fortas waits outside the Senate Judiciary Committee as it considers his nomination to the Supreme Court in 1965. As a partner at a leading Washington law firm, he was appointed by the Supreme Court to handle the appeal of Clarence Gideon. Fortas's brilliant argument convinced the Court to require states to provide free counsel for the poor in every serious criminal case.

as he lived, a pauper, but his appeal made history, as he appeared to recognize in a letter to his attorney while waiting for the Supreme Court to decide his case. In a phrase now on his tombstone, he wrote, "Each era finds an improvement in the law for the benefit of mankind."

Gideon v. *Wainwright* (1963) was a call for a new definition of fair trial, and most people agreed with its conclusion: at a minimum, due process required an attorney for poor defendants, regardless of where they lived. Another case, decided the next year, *Escobedo* v. *Illinois,* also extended the right to counsel but was far more controversial.

Danny Escobedo was a twenty-two-year-old laborer of Mexican descent who was accused of the murder of his brother-in-law in January 1960. He had no previous police record. Questioned for fifteen hours, he was released only to be picked up ten days later after another suspect told police that Escobedo had done the shooting. An officer told Escobedo he might as well confess because "we have you sewed up pretty tight," but Escobedo refused to talk and asked to speak with his attorney. Even though the lawyer came to the station to consult with his client, as allowed by Illinois law, the police kept the two men apart and continued to use standard interrogation tactics to get his confession. Finally, Escobedo made incriminating statements after police implied he would get immunity, a claim the police denied later. Based on his "confession," he was convicted of murder and sentenced to twenty years in the state penitentiary. No one had told Escobedo of his right to remain silent.

Like Gideon, Escobedo filed an appeal as a pauper, but unlike Florida law, state law in Illinois provided a public defender assigned from a pool of lawyers. Drawing the case was a former military lawyer from Chicago who, when arguing the case before the Supreme Court, quickly focused on the critical issue: "[Danny Escobedo] convicted himself in that police station....What could [his lawyer] do?" To have the effective assistance of counsel, he told the justices, "you've got to have the assistance at the time you need it."

Representing Illinois was James Thompson, assistant state's attorney and later governor. He sought to persuade the justices that the police and prosecutors needed wide latitude in their investigations to be effective in protecting society against criminals. If the Supreme Court ruled that a suspect had the right to an attorney during questioning at the precinct house, the result would be no more confessions. Police would become less efficient in putting criminals away; society would not be as safe. Law enforcement officials echoed this concern: if the court decides police cannot talk to a suspect before giving him a lawyer, a Houston police chief said, "you're going to see a lot of killers and rapists walking out of police stations with thumb to nose."

The Court divided 5 to 4 in deciding that the Sixth Amendment guaranteed a right to counsel during interrogations. The majority opinion swept aside warnings

On prison stationery, Clarence Gideon petitioned the Supreme Court from his jail cell. He claimed he had been denied his constitutional right to counsel.

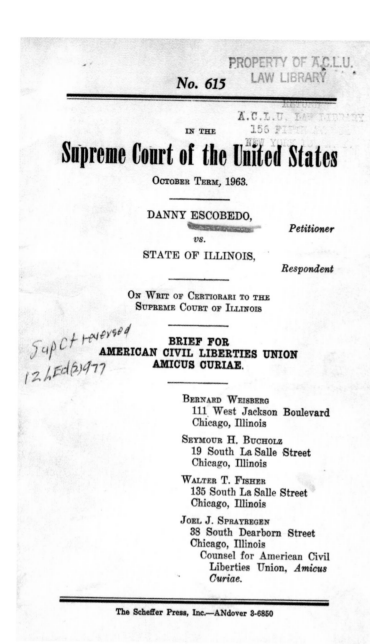

No. 615

IN THE

Supreme Court of the United States

OCTOBER TERM, 1963.

DANNY ESCOBEDO, *Petitioner*

vs.

STATE OF ILLINOIS, *Respondent*

ON WRIT OF CERTIORARI TO THE
SUPREME COURT OF ILLINOIS

*Sup Ct reversed
12 LEd(2)977*

BRIEF FOR
AMERICAN CIVIL LIBERTIES UNION
AMICUS CURIAE.

BERNARD WEISBERG
111 West Jackson Boulevard
Chicago, Illinois

SEYMOUR H. BUCHOLZ
19 South La Salle Street
Chicago, Illinois

WALTER T. FISHER
135 South La Salle Street
Chicago, Illinois

JOEL J. SPRAYREGEN
38 South Dearborn Street
Chicago, Illinois
Counsel for American Civil
Liberties Union, *Amicus
Curiae.*

The Scheffer Press, Inc.—ANdover 3-6850

The ACLU filed an amicus curiae ("friend of the court") brief in the Escobedo *case, and it took an active role in the many appeals that were based on* Escobedo. *It argued that the right to counsel must be available to an accused person at all times, from arrest to appeal, and that the suspect's privilege against self-incrimination can be protected only by a lawyer, not simply by warnings from the police.*

of disaster: history taught that "law enforcement which depends on the 'confession,' will, in the long run, be less reliable and more subject to abuse" than one which depends on vigorous investigation. No system of criminal justice should fear the exercise of a defendant's rights, the justices concluded. If constitutional protections thwart the effectiveness of law enforcement, "then there is something very wrong with that system."

Unlike *Gideon,* strong public disapproval greeted the decision. In the first case, most Americans agreed that a defendant too poor to hire a lawyer could not be assured a fair trial unless the state provided counsel for him. But *Escobedo* seemed different to many people who were becoming increasingly concerned about rising crime rates, urban riots, racial conflict, and youthful challenges to middle-class values. Restraining the police—"handcuffing" was the term used most often by critics of the decision—would encourage criminals and lead only to more crime and greater disorder.

Danny Escobedo's later life provided support for this public alarm. Drifting from job to job, he repeatedly got into trouble with the law. By the time he was arrested in Mexico City in 2001 for parole violations and flight from a warrant in a 1983 stabbing death, he had gained a spot on the U.S. marshal's list of its fifteen most-wanted fugitives. During his adult life, Escobedo had been arrested twenty-five times on charges from narcotics to murder. With such records, opponents of this and later decisions asked, why would we as a society guarantee a right that put public safety at risk by increasing the chance that habitual offenders would go free? Although numerous studies have revealed that insistence on this right has not hampered law enforcement unduly, it is a reasonable question—and it is one the framers answered when they drafted the Constitution.

In its Anglo-American meaning, a fair trial rests upon a unique foundation, the adversarial process, which pits two sides against each other in a legal contest judged or decided by representatives from the community, the jury. It is quite unlike the European inquisitorial system, with a judge or panel of judges empowered to question the accused and decide guilt and innocence. The adversarial process allows each side—prosecution and defense—to lay out its strongest arguments, and it trusts the jury to decide between them. The primary goal of this process is not simply to convict the guilty but also to protect the innocent who are wrongfully accused. Americans at the time of the Constitution's creation understood and endorsed this goal. They accepted the maxim of English law

"An unskilled layman may be able to defend himself in a nonjury trial before a judge experienced in piecing together unassembled facts, but before a jury the guiding hand of counsel is needed to marshal the evidence into a coherent whole consistent with the best case on behalf of the defendant. If there is no accompanying right to counsel, the right to trial by jury becomes meaningless."

—Justice Lewis Powell, *Argersinger* v. *Hamlin* (1972)

since the fifteenth century that "one would rather twenty guilty individuals should escape punishment…than one innocent person should be condemned." Without this assurance, the founders believed, no one could truly be free.

Without an attorney, this adversarial process is a mismatch that puts the defendant at a disadvantage. The reason for this result is twofold. Not having the aid of counsel, the Supreme Court has noted, a defendant "may be put on trial without a proper charge and convicted upon improper evidence. He lacks both the skill and the knowledge to prepare his defense, even though he may have a perfect one." But another reason goes far beyond the legal knowledge required to navigate the court system. Government by definition has great power. It alone has the authority to accuse, prosecute, and punish. It can marshal a vast array of resources to carry out these responsibilities. Officials can use their power, at times, for less noble purposes, such as benefiting themselves and their supporters or persecuting their opponents. The founding generation knew this, and they limited governmental power, in part, by protecting the rights of individuals. They insisted that government follow due process and abide by the rules that guarantee a fair investigation and a fair trial. The presence of counsel to represent the accused and to insist that the government follow its own rules helps to protect us against the abuse of power.

Since the decisions in *Gideon* and *Escobedo*, the Supreme Court has extended the right to counsel to virtually all parts of the criminal process, including when juveniles are charged in delinquency proceedings, in misdemeanor cases when there is potential for a loss of liberty, and in lineups, pretrial hearings, and plea negotiations. In the process, it has tied the right to another guarantee of the Bill of Rights, the Fifth Amendment's protection against self-incrimination. These two rights operate together to guard against the chance that people accused of crime will be forced or tricked into confessing a crime and thereby sacrifice their right to a fair trial.

Ultimately, the right to counsel is essential to our conception of fairness in criminal proceedings. "Of all the rights that an accused person has," the Supreme Court has written, "the right to be represented by counsel is by far the most pervasive right for it affects his ability to assert any other rights he may have." The Sixth Amendment lists the elements of a fair trial—a speedy and public trial, an impartial jury, the right to confront witnesses, and the right to compel testimony. The final clause of the amendment, the right to an attorney, offers assurance that we as a society will keep this promise of fairness.

The San Diego County Public Defender's Office is a large operation with five offices. It provides legal assistance to individuals charged with a crime in state court who are financially unable to retain private counsel. Its staff includes not only experienced trial attorneys but specialists in mental health and juvenile court matters and a professional investigative staff.

The Right to Be Heard

In the Scottsboro case of Powell v. Alabama *(1932), the Supreme Court had to decide if the state's failure to provide effective counsel violated the due process clause of the Fourteenth Amendment. Writing for the 7-to-2 majority, Justice George Sutherland noted that the counsel designated for the defense had actually been a member of the prosecution a short time earlier. He concluded that "the defendants did not have the aid of counsel in any real sense, although they were as much entitled to such aid during that period [before trial] as at the trial itself." Justice Sutherland then discussed the reasons why a fair trial depended upon the assistance of counsel.*

The question, however, which it is our duty, and within our power, to decide, is whether the denial of the assistance of counsel contravenes the due process clause of the Fourteenth Amendment to the Federal Constitution....

It never has been doubted by this court, or any other so far as we know, that notice and hearing are preliminary steps essential to the passing of an enforceable judgment, and that they, together with a legally competent tribunal having jurisdiction of the case, constitute basic elements of the constitutional requirement of due process of law.... Mr. Justice Field... said that the rule that no one shall be personally bound until he has had his day in court was as old as the law, and it meant that he must be cited to appear and afforded an opportunity to be heard....

What, then, does a hearing include? Historically and in practice, in our own country at least, it has always included the right to the aid of counsel when desired and provided by the party asserting the right. The right to be heard would be, in many cases, of little avail if it did not comprehend the right to be heard by counsel. Even the intelligent and educated layman has small and sometimes no skill in the science of law. If charged with crime, he is incapable, generally, of determining for himself whether the indictment is good or bad. He is unfamiliar with the rules of evidence. Left without the aid of counsel he may be put on trial without a proper charge, and convicted upon incompetent evidence, or evidence irrelevant to the issue or otherwise inadmissible. He lacks both the skill and knowledge adequately to prepare his defense, even though he have a perfect one. He requires the guiding hand of counsel at every step in the proceedings against him. Without it, though he be not guilty, he faces the danger of conviction because he does not know how to establish his innocence. If that be true of men of intelligence, how much more true is it of the ignorant and illiterate, or those of feeble intellect. If in any case, civil of criminal, a state or federal court were arbitrarily to refuse to hear a party by counsel, employed by and appearing for him, it reasonably may not be doubted that such a refusal would be a denial of a hearing, and, therefore, of due process in the constitutional sense....

[I]n a capital case, where the defendant is unable to employ counsel, and is incapable adequately of making his own defense because of ignorance, feeble-mindedness, illiteracy, or the like, it is the duty of the court... to assign counsel for him... and that duty is not discharged by an assignment at such a time or under such circumstances as to preclude the giving of effective aid in the preparation and trial of the case....

The United States by statute and every state in the Union by express provision of law, or by the determination of its courts, make it the duty of the trial judge, where the accused is unable to employ counsel, to appoint counsel for him. In most states the rule applies broadly to all criminal prosecutions, in others it is limited to the more serious crimes, and in a very limited number, to capital cases. A rule adopted with such unanimous accord reflects, if it does not establish, the inherent right to have counsel appointed at least in cases like the present, and lends convincing support to the conclusion we have reached as to the fundamental nature of that right.

"You Cannot Have a Fair Trial without Counsel"

Future Supreme Court justice Abe Fortas was a prominent Washington attorney who agreed to represent Clarence Gideon in his appeal to the Supreme Court. Gideon won his appeal in Gideon v. Wainwright *(1963), which established the right to counsel as a guarantee of the Sixth Amendment that was incorporated as a restraint on the states through the Fourteenth Amendment. Fortas made the case in his oral argument that under our adversarial system of justice, assistance of counsel is necessary to ensure fairness.*

I believe that this case dramatically illustrates the point that you cannot have a fair trial without counsel. Indeed, I believe that the right way to look at this... is that a court, a criminal court, is not properly constituted—and this has been said in some of your opinions—under our adversary system of law, unless there is a judge and unless there is a counsel for the prosecution and unless there is a counsel for the defense. Without that, how can a civilized nation pretend that it is having a fair trial, under our adversary system, which means that counsel for the state will do his best within the limits of fairness and honor and decency to present the case for the state, and counsel for defense will do his best, similarly, to present the best case possible for the defendant, and from that clash there will emerge the truth. That is our concept, and how can we say, how can it be suggested that a court is properly constituted, that a trial is fair, unless those conditions exist.

CHAPTER 20

The Rights of Juvenile Defendants

In his great work of political philosophy, *Leviathan*, published in 1651, Thomas Hobbes characterized life in the state of nature as "solitary, poor, nasty, brutish, and short." This description was distressingly true for children even after societies formed. Throughout most of Western history, childhood lasted from birth until six or eight years of age. In fact, the idea of childhood as a time set aside for gradual maturation into adulthood was a foreign concept. Labor came quickly in a young person's life, with many children, on farms and in towns alike, put to work for lengthy periods each day. Schooling was a luxury reserved for wealthy families or, at times, exceptionally gifted children who attracted the attention of a patron. Early death was not uncommon, with as many as one-third to a half of all children failing to reach the age of twenty.

This miserable experience began to change, albeit slowly, during the sixteenth and seventeenth centuries. New wealth and the beginnings of industrialization made life less difficult for an increasing number of people. It also made it possible for England's emerging middle class to develop a sense of childhood that was markedly different from older notions. State- or church-supported schooling became more common, at least through the early years, because commerce required basic literacy. The poorest children still worked at a young age, but it became more frequent to speak of childhood as separate from the adult world.

The legal separation between children and adults was still hazy at the time of American independence, especially in criminal law. One central issue concerned the age when children formed consciences sufficient to hold them responsible for their actions. The common law presumed that a child younger than seven years of age lacked criminal capacity, or the capability to act with intent to cause harm. Children older than seven who were accused of crimes were tried in adult courts, and if convicted, could be sentenced to an adult prison or, in capital cases, condemned to die. In some states, children as young as twelve were executed for murder. Criminal juries faced difficult choices: try youthful offenders as adults and sentence them to jail with hardened criminals or refuse to convict them even for minor offenses.

To avoid such stark alternatives, nineteenth-century reformers developed new institutions, known as houses of refuge, to separate children from adults in matters of criminal punishment. They believed that most criminals were capable of reform if put in the proper environment, which for adults was the penitentiary, a place designed for repentance, and for young offenders, it was the reformatory. The separate juvenile facility also reflected a new view of children. No longer were they seen as young adults, but as vulnerable, corruptible innocents who required special attention to protect them from the wider society while molding them for success as adults. By the end of the century, this sense of children as different from adults led to the division of childhood into three phases—infants, children, and adolescents or juveniles. It also spurred child-centered reforms, such as prohibition of child labor, compulsory school attendance, and social welfare, all aimed at helping parents rear children capable of creating a more just and humane world.

Chief among these reforms was the juvenile court. Reformers (or "child-savers," as they were called) wanted to separate young offenders from the adult criminal justice system and to use the state as a surrogate parent in order to supervise, treat, and reform them. The reformers relied on a legal doctrine known as *parens patriae* (from Latin, "parent of his country"), an old concept that refers to the state as guardian of minors and incompetent people. This idea assumed that the state was helping the child, so the juvenile courts used informal procedures and a different vocabulary to avoid any suggestion that the child was being punished. The age of criminal responsibility was set at sixteen years, and these juvenile courts conducted civil, not criminal, proceedings. Objectionable behaviors were known as "status" offenses, not crimes, a term that conveyed the status of the offender, thus tagging the action as one characteristic of children. Offending children were "delinquent," not guilty; they were given "dispositions," not sentences. There were no lawyers and no juries, and the courts followed none of the procedures used in criminal courts to assure due process. Juvenile judges alone were responsible for deciding how to rehabilitate offenders, and they exercised wide discretion by supervising all youthful conduct, including smoking, sexual behavior, and skipping school (truancy), for example. The goal was to act in the "best interests" of each individual child, and there were few limits on what judges could do to achieve this end.

The reality of juvenile justice, however, never approached its ambitious goal of providing a nurturing environment in which young offenders could reform their lives. Juvenile institutions rarely functioned as centers of rehabilitation but were primarily custodial and punitive. Most juvenile judges and probation officers were poorly trained individuals who lacked the expertise and resources to assist young people. Delinquents often left state care with few skills and bitter memories, ill-prepared for adult life.

After World War II, public trust in this system of juvenile justice eroded. A rise in crimes committed by youth, often associated with urban poverty, led to calls for stronger measures to protect the public. The civil rights movement challenged the juvenile system's segregation of youthful offenders by race and the often harsher dispositions received by black teenagers. Distrust of professionals and government fairness also grew, especially in the late 1950s and 1960s, and led to calls for change across broad areas of American life, including juvenile justice.

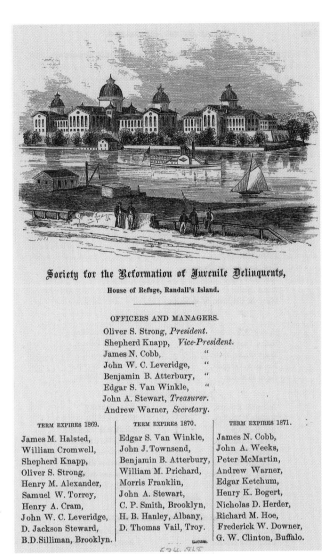

By the mid-nineteenth century, government was expected not to punish juvenile offenders but to reform them. The "reformatory" activities at the so-called House of Refuge on Randall's Island in New York City included a hoop-skirt factory, a shoemaking shop, and recreational activities.

Boys await court action at the Halls of Justice, commonly known as "The Tombs," New York City's main jail in downtown Manhattan, in the 1870s. There were separate sections for women and boys. About thirty boy prisoners were responsible for kitchen work, cleaning chores, and light repair jobs.

Supreme Court decisions reflected these concerns, and nowhere were shifts in law more apparent than in criminal justice. Bill of Rights protections for the accused, now defined as part of due process guaranteed by Fourteenth Amendment, applied to state as well as federal criminal justice. Courts at all levels placed greater emphasis on ensuring meaningful due process to defendants. At first, the new requirements applied only to adult offenders, but by the mid-1960s, concern about the lack of accountability in the juvenile justice system led to questions about whether youthful offenders could claim the protections of the Bill of Rights. In 1967, the justices said yes, and in the process they dramatically reshaped the nation's practice of juvenile justice.

Paul and Marjorie Gault lived with their two teenaged sons, Louis and Gerald, in a new mobile home park in Globe, Arizona, a once-prosperous mining town about seventy-five miles from Phoenix. To make ends meet, Paul worked out of town, while Marjorie worked as a baby-sitter. Louis and Gerald were often on their own during the day, not unlike teenagers in many American families where both parents work.

In 1962, Gerald had his first run-in with the Gila County Juvenile Court when another boy accused him of stealing a baseball glove. Two years later, he was before the court again for being in the company of another boy who allegedly had stolen a woman's wallet. The judge placed Gerald on six months' probation and warned him to stay out of trouble. Two months before his probation ended, he was in court once more. This time a woman had accused him of making an obscene phone call to her.

Arizona's juvenile justice system was typical: it granted juveniles a right to special treatment and protected them from criminal proceedings. It also acted on the principle that juveniles possessed a right to protective custody, not liberty. The purpose of the court hearing was to determine what type of custody—parental or state—was in the best interest of the child. The hearing was informal, with no records kept and no attorneys present. The judge listened to the parties, asked questions, and made a decision about whether the state needed to take corrective action, and if so, what was required to help the child become a responsible citizen. Sometimes, the court consulted psychologists or behavioral specialists; sometimes, it acted on its knowledge or intuition.

Gerald Gault's case was handled routinely. After taking the statement of the woman who reported the obscene call, an officer took Gerald into custody and signed him into the juvenile detention center. The sheriff failed to notify his parents, but Marjorie Gault eventually learned about a hearing scheduled for the following day. She was present to hear the officer ask the judge to declare her son delinquent and place him in protective custody. Three days later, there was a second hearing with both parents in attendance; they had been informed by a handwritten note. Gerald admitted dialing the number but claimed that "a friend had done the talking." The woman who had accused him was not present. No one gave sworn testimony. No one kept a record at either hearing, nor were Gerald or his parents informed of their rights. They were not even informed of what part of the juvenile code he was charged with violating. Although not acceptable in adult trials, this informal process was usual for the juvenile court. So, too, was the result. The judge found Gerald to be a "child in need of supervision" because he had been "habitually involved in immoral matters" and committed him to the Arizona Industrial School at Fort Grant for an indeterminate period, not to exceed six years. If Gerald Gault had been an adult convicted of the same misdemeanor, he would have faced a maximum sentence of two months in jail or a fine of fifty dollars.

Arizona law did not allow an appeal in juvenile proceedings, so the Gaults, with the help of an attorney, filed a writ of habeas corpus. This writ, guaranteed by both federal and state constitutions, commands any person who detains another person to bring the individual to court so a judge can determine whether the detention is legal. The judge who heard the habeas petition dismissed it and sent Gerald back to Fort Grant. But unlike the original hearing, the Gaults could appeal the denial of habeas corpus to the Arizona Supreme Court, which they did, with the support of the American Civil Liberties Union. They claimed the system violated their due process rights as parents; it arbitrarily and unfairly deprived them of custody. When the Arizona high court rejected this argument, the Gaults appealed to the U.S. Supreme Court. This time, however, they chose not to focus on the custody rights of parents, but on the right of Gerald Gault to have the protection of due process.

When the Supreme Court agreed to hear *In re Gault* ("in the matter of Gault"), the justices were halfway through a series of decisions extending Bill of Rights protections to persons accused under state criminal law. Now they would consider whether these due process rights extended to juveniles as well: did the Fourteenth Amendment's guarantee of due process require states to ensure youthful defendants the same rights to counsel, notice of the charge against

In his juvenile court chambers in the mid-1920s, Judge Benjamin Barr Lindsey of Denver congratulates young people who have successfully served probation after being convicted of crimes. Probation suspends a sentence and allows the offender to avoid jail by demonstrating good behavior to a court-appointed supervisor or probation officer.

them, the right to confront their accusers, and other protections of the Bill of Rights? Five months after oral arguments, the justices decided, 8 to 1, that juvenile court proceedings fell within the protections of the Fourteenth Amendment.

Writing for the majority, Justice Abe Fortas, who had joined the Court only two years earlier, concluded that "unbridled discretion [in the judge], however benevolently motivated" and "departures from established principles of due process have frequently resulted not in enlightened procedure, but in arbitrariness." The lack of procedure undermined justice and resulted in resistance, not rehabilitation. Juvenile courts often operated on inaccurate and incomplete information, which proper procedure could correct, and their decisions frequently alienated the youthful offender they were supposed to serve. More important, delinquency proceedings could result in involuntary confinement, which meant that the juvenile's right to liberty was at stake. Delinquency hearings, therefore, must "measure up to the essentials of due process and fair treatment." Due process embodied the rule of law, which was the "primary and indispensable foundation of individual freedom." The fact that the accused are not adults, Fortas declared, "does not justify a kangaroo court." The Bill of Rights, in sum, protects youth as well as adults.

In defining due process for juvenile courts, the justices did not include all the rights of the accused contained in the Bill of Rights. They focused instead on the rights to counsel, confrontation of one's accusers, cross-examination of witnesses, and the privilege against self-incrimination. Juvenile defendants had the protection of these rights, just as adult defendants did. In later cases, the Court clarified the limits of juvenile due process. It required that the juvenile court determine a youth's involvement beyond a reasonable doubt before ordering assignment to a detention facility, but it also decided that a jury trial was not an essential part of due process for juvenile proceedings. Even though young people were entitled to constitutional protections, the systems of justice for adults and juveniles served separate purposes, so the rights of the accused were not identical.

The purpose of *In re Gault* and later decisions was to make juvenile proceedings fairer, but it also made them more adversarial. They now resembled criminal trials rather than the benevolent civil proceedings initially envisioned by progressive reformers in the late nineteenth and early twentieth centuries. This result, most observers believe, was an unintended consequence of the Supreme Court's decision. Although many participants in the system welcomed the changes, state legislatures, pressured by voters to control juvenile crime, enacted so-called "just deserts" laws. These measures allowed the transfer of serious cases from juvenile to criminal court and required juvenile judges to impose more severe sentences for certain crimes, all in an attempt to "fit the punishment to the crime." Other changes were more advantageous to at-risk youth, especially so-called diversion programs that allowed cases of relatively minor misbehavior to be handled outside of a formal court process.

Cases involving the rights of youth have been important in extending definitions of our constitutional rights. Mary Beth Tinker, an eighth-grade student in Des Moines, Iowa, won recognition for the right to protest an unpopular war as a freedom protected by the First Amendment guarantee of free speech.

Twelve-year-old Lillian Gobitas claimed a right to free exercise of religion that expanded our definition of this important liberty when she refused, on religious grounds, to salute the American flag at school. Our view of cruel and unusual punishment, outlawed by the Eighth Amendment, changed when the Supreme Court decided that executing anyone under the age of eighteen was unconstitutional. Federal and state courts have also found consistently that other protections of the Bill of Rights, such as the right to privacy or the guarantee against illegal search and seizure, apply with certain exceptions to young people.

The rights of youth, however, are not as complete as those enjoyed by adults because the courts recognize the different expectations we as a society have of these different groups. Young people are in the process of developing into adults, and we trust parents, schools, and community organizations, among others, to guide and protect them as they mature. We expect young people to learn how to make decisions and accept responsibility so that they can enjoy the full set of rights and privileges as adults in a free society, but until they are able to accept full responsibility, the rights they enjoy will be more limited.

U.S. Department of Justice
Office of Justice Programs
Office of Juvenile Justice and Delinquency Prevention

Combating Violence and Delinquency:
The National Juvenile Justice Action Plan

Summary

Coordinating Council on Juvenile Justice and Delinquency Prevention

For most states, this age of accountability is eighteen, although it comes earlier if a person marries or enters the military before that age.

We form our understanding of freedom from the past, but we apply it with an eye to the future. Our concern for the rights that protect freedom is not simply for our own sake but also for new generations of Americans. Each generation entrusts freedom to the next generation to preserve. Through acknowledging the rights of youth, adult members of society affirm the belief that young people also share the nation's heritage of liberty.

The Coordinating Council on Juvenile Justice and Delinquency Prevention, a coalition of attorneys, mental health professionals, scholars, judges, police, and other government officials chaired by then–Attorney General Janet Reno, issued this report in 1996. It called both for intensified prosecution of serious, violent, and chronic juvenile offenders and for increased efforts to break the cycle of violence by addressing child abuse and neglect.

A Substitute for Parental Authority

Early in the twentieth century, states began to establish separate juvenile courts to safeguard the welfare of young people accused of crimes. Reformers made changes to the justice system to assert state responsibility for the lives of its young offenders before crime became a way of life for them. The juvenile justice system exercised its authority within a "parens patriae" (state as parent or guardian) role. The following decision in a 1905 Pennsylvania case reveals the thinking behind the development of a separate system of juvenile justice.

The act is not for the trial of a child charged with a crime, but is mercifully to save it from such an ordeal, with the prison or penitentiary in its wake, if the child's own good and the best interests of the state justify such salvation.... The act is but an exercise by the state of its supreme power over the welfare of its children....

The design is not punishment, nor the restraint imprisonment, any more than is the wholesome restraint which a parent exercises over his child.... There is no probability, in the proper administration of the law, of the child's liberty being unduly invaded. Every statute which is designed to give protection, care, and training to children, as a needed substitute for parental authority and performance of parental duty, is but a recognition of the duty of the state, as the legitimate guardian and protector of children where other guardianship fails. No constitutional right is violated.

In 1909, the Harvard Law Review *published an article by Judge Julian Mack entitled "The Juvenile Court." Later appointed as a U.S. circuit judge at large, Mack was an appellate judge in Illinois when he wrote this article, which suggests that a judge should assume the role of comforting parent in administering juvenile justice.*

The child who must be brought into court should, of course, be made to know that he is face to face with the power of the state, but he should at the same time, and more emphatically, be made to feel that he is the object of its care and solicitude. The ordinary trappings of the courtroom are out of place in such hearings. The judge on a bench, looking down upon the boy standing at the bar, can never evoke a proper sympathetic spirit. Seated at a desk, with the child at his side, where he can on occasion put his arm around his shoulder and draw the lad to him, the judge, while losing none of his judicial dignity, will gain immensely in the effectiveness of his work.

The Death Penalty Is Unconstitutional for Juveniles

In 2005, the Supreme Court ruled in Roper v. Simmons *that executing juveniles for crimes they committed while under the age of eighteen violated the Eight Amendment's ban on "cruel and unusual punishments," as applied to the states through the Fourteenth Amendment. This decision reversed the Court's conclusion in 1989 that the practice was constitutional. Writing for the majority, Justice Anthony Kennedy pointed to three general differences between juveniles and adults as one reason to treat juvenile offenders differently. He also noted that no state had reinstated the death penalty for juveniles since the 1989 decision, and he observed that the United States stood alone among the nations of the world in condoning execution of youths under eighteen. This case reveals how the meaning of the Constitution changes in response to new conditions.*

This case requires us to address, for the second time in a decade and a half, whether it is permissible under the Eighth and Fourteenth Amendments to the Constitution of the United States to execute a juvenile offender who was older than 15 but younger than 18 when he committed a capital crime. In *Stanford* v. *Kentucky* (1989), a divided Court rejected the proposition that the Constitution bars capital punishment for juvenile offenders in this age group. We reconsider the question....

Since *Stanford*, no State that previously prohibited capital punishment for juveniles has reinstated it. This fact, coupled with the trend toward abolition of the juvenile death penalty, carries special force in light of the general popularity of anticrime legislation...and in light of the particular trend in recent years toward cracking down on juvenile crime in other respects....

Three general differences between juveniles under 18 and adults demonstrate that juvenile offenders cannot with reliability be classified among the worst offenders. First, as any parent knows and as the scientific and sociological studies respondent and his *amici* cite tend to confirm, "[a] lack of maturity and an underdeveloped sense of responsibility are found in youth more often than in adults and are more understandable among the young."...

The second area of difference is that juveniles are more vulnerable or susceptible to negative influences and outside pressures, including peer pressure....

The third broad difference is that the character of a juvenile is not as well formed as that of an adult. The personality traits of juveniles are more transitory, less fixed....

These differences render suspect any conclusion that a juvenile falls among the worst offenders. The susceptibility of juveniles to immature and irresponsible behavior means "their irresponsible conduct is not as morally reprehensible as that of an adult."... Their own vulnerability and comparative lack of control over their immediate surroundings mean juveniles have a greater claim than adults to be forgiven for failing to escape negative influences in their whole environment....The reality that juveniles still struggle to define their identity means it is less supportable to conclude that even a heinous crime committed by a juvenile is evidence of irretrievably depraved character. From a moral standpoint it would be misguided to equate the failings of a minor with those of an adult, for a greater possibility exists that a minor's character deficiencies will be reformed....

Our determination that the death penalty is disproportionate punishment for offenders under 18 finds confirmation in the stark reality that the United States is the only country in the world that continues to give official sanction to the juvenile death penalty. This reality does not become controlling, for the task of interpreting the Eighth Amendment remains our responsibility....

As respondent and a number of *amici* emphasize, Article 37 of the United Nations Convention on the Rights of the Child, which every country in the world has ratified save for the United States and Somalia, contains an express prohibition on capital punishment for crimes committed by juveniles under 18....

[O]nly seven countries other than the United States have executed juvenile offenders since 1990: Iran, Pakistan, Saudi Arabia, Yemen, Nigeria, the Democratic Republic of Congo, and China. Since then each of these countries has either abolished capital punishment for juveniles or made public disavowal of the practice....In sum, it is fair to say that the United States now stands alone in a world that has turned its face against the juvenile death penalty.

Over time, from one generation to the next, the Constitution has come to earn the high respect and even, as Madison dared to hope, the veneration of the American people....The document sets forth, and rests upon, innovative principles original to the American experience, such as federalism; a proven balance in political mechanisms through separation of powers; specific guarantees for the accused in criminal cases; and broad provisions to secure individual freedom and preserve human dignity. These doctrines and guarantees are central to the American experience and remain essential to our present-day self-definition and national identity. Not the least of the reasons we honor the Constitution, then, is because we know it to be our own. It does not lessen our fidelity to the Constitution or our pride in its origins to acknowledge that the express affirmation of certain fundamental rights by other nations and peoples simply underscores the centrality of those same rights within our own heritage of freedom.

CHAPTER 21

The Right to Protection against Cruel and Unusual Punishments

In February 2006, an inmate in California was minutes away from execution when two doctors assigned to monitor his death suddenly refused to participate. They protested the use of a three-drug cocktail designed to put the condemned man to sleep before he received the heart-stopping dose. The method of death was inhumane, the physicians claimed, and because it was not foolproof, they could be required to revive the prisoner in the event of a botched execution. It violated both their Hippocratic oath to do no harm and the Eighth Amendment to the U.S. Constitution, which banned cruel and unusual punishments. Their withdrawal raised the possibility of a statewide moratorium on further executions because other physicians were likely to take the same position.

Even though many people considered lethal injection a humane method of capital punishment, the doctors' objections were not unusual. From the beginning of the republic, the death penalty has always been controversial. The United States uses it far more frequently than most Western nations—indeed, European states today uniformly outlaw death as a punishment—and each execution finds Americans divided over the practice. Advocates of the penalty point to brutal, senseless crimes and believe death is the only appropriate punishment for such wanton violence. Opponents are troubled by the possibility of executing an innocent man or woman. The death penalty is one of the most vexing moral and legal issues in modern American law.

The Eighth Amendment addresses the terms of punishment. It is the last in a series of four amendments dealing with rights of the accused. Its brief text addresses three separate items: "Excessive bail shall not be required, nor excessive fines imposed, nor cruel and unusual punishments inflicted." As was true with other guarantees in the Bill of Rights, the framers drew upon English history and their own experience in drafting this amendment. Various documents limited the king's ability to impose heavy fines, but royal judges often flouted this restriction. They also denied bail, keeping people in jail without trial, and exacted bloody punishments, especially when they wanted to remind the public of the government's power. After a series of harsh punishments was inflicted on participants in a failed uprising in 1685, the Parliament forced a new monarch to accept an English Bill of Rights (1689). One of the provisions contained the language later used in the Eighth Amendment.

The amendment promotes fairness in our system of criminal justice; the prohibition of excessive bails and fines, for example, especially protects poor defendants. But what the words mean in practice is not clear from the text of

"The death penalty cannot be useful, because of the example of barbarity it gives men. . . . It seems to be absurd that the laws, which are an expression of the public will, which detest and punish homicide, should themselves commit it, and that to deter citizens from murder, they order a public one."

—Cesare Beccaria, *On Crimes and Punishments* (1764)

> *"[T]he principles of republican governments... revive and establish the relations of fellow-citizens, friend, and brother. They appreciate human life, and increase public and private obligations to preserve it.... An execution in a republic is like a human sacrifice in religion. It is an offering to monarchy, and to that malignant being, who has been styled a murderer from the beginning, and who delights equally in murder, whether it be perpetuated by the cold, but vindictive arm of the law, or by the angry hand of private revenge."*
>
> —Benjamin Rush, "Considerations on the Injustice and Impolicy of Punishing Murder by Death" (1792)

the amendment. What is an excessive bail or fine? What makes a punishment cruel and unusual? For each guarantee, judges have leeway to consider the circumstances of each case, guided by laws that have developed over two centuries. The law of bails and fines generally has not attracted much attention; the same is not true for cruel and unusual punishments.

Criminal justice throughout history has resorted to physical punishments that we consider inhumane today. Loss of limbs, bodily mutilations, and whippings were common penalties for noncapital crimes, or crimes not punishable by execution, and few people considered death to be a cruel punishment. It certainly was not unusual. European history provided countless examples of what we would consider barbaric punishments, including beheading, burning at the stake, crucifixion, breaking on the rack, dismemberment. The American revolutionaries rejected these brutalities and considered punishment by death to be, in Thomas Jefferson's words, a "last melancholy resource." They accepted the argument of continental reformers that severe codes did little to diminish crime. Experience proved that juries hesitated to send defendants to the gallows, and many condemned prisoners received pardons, so how did the death penalty restrain wrongdoers? The aim of punishment, reformers argued, should be to redeem men and restore them to society. Execution should be reserved only for the most heinous crimes and for incorrigible, or unredeemable, criminals.

In 1786, Pennsylvania restricted capital punishment to cases of treason, murder, rape, and arson, and within two decades most states followed suit. A new institution, the penitentiary, emerged to hold prisoners convicted of serious offenses. The word itself, from the root *penitent* ("feeling sorrowful"), expressed the hopes of reformers. The belief that even evil people could be redeemed also led to campaigns to abolish the death penalty. In the 1840s, both Michigan and Wisconsin abolished the punishment; in most other states, executions held behind prison walls replaced the spectacle of public hangings. The arguments for and against capital punishment are the ones still heard today. Opponents protest the system's potential for prejudice and the possibility of killing an innocent person; supporters believe the death penalty acts as a deterrent to violent crime, and when it does not serve this purpose, it is a just and proportionate punishment for taking another life, especially for premeditated murder.

An increase in crime and violence, both real and perceived, slowed the movement to abolish the death penalty in the nineteenth century. Reformers instead worked to make its application more humane, which led, in part, to the inventions of the electric chair and gas chamber. Both methods were thought to produce speedier deaths than hanging, which could result in slow strangulation. Because criminal justice was considered a matter for the states, not the federal government, any attempts to abolish the death penalty had to proceed state by state. The twentieth century, however, introduced a new way to challenge the penalty. Gradually, the Supreme Court accepted the view that the due process clause of the Fourteenth Amendment included provisions of the Bill of Rights and therefore restricted what states could do.

Now, the nation's highest bench faced the question of how to interpret the phrase "cruel and unusual punishments." What made this task difficult was the horror of two world wars, and especially the barbarous punishment imposed by the Nazis on people whose only crime was their race, religion, ethnicity, or mental or physical disability. As Americans became more sensitive to the definition of cruelty—and the misuse of the death penalty—the justices faced agonizing choices between moral and democratic claims. Legislative majorities in state after state had enacted death penalty statutes, but experience both at home and abroad had revealed how discriminatory its use could be. Was execution cruel by definition and therefore unconstitutional? If not, when and how does society ensure due process to condemned persons?

Over the past several decades, these questions became central to bitter and divisive public debate. The Supreme Court especially, as the body that considers final appeals from the condemned, has struggled to determine the constitutionality of capital punishment. How difficult this task has been can be seen in a case involving a prisoner who faced the electric chair a second time after his first execution failed. The botched execution raised serious questions about the use of the death penalty and began a new debate over the meaning of the Eighth Amendment that still continues today.

Willie Francis was seventeen years old in 1946 when he was sentenced to die in Louisiana's electric chair. Two years earlier, the barely literate black youth had killed his boss, a druggist, and stolen his wallet containing four dollars. The discovery of the billfold on Francis ten months later provided the evidence that led to his confession. An all-white jury found him guilty of first-degree murder, which under state law carried a mandatory death sentence.

The day before the scheduled execution, prison officers set up the traveling chair in a makeshift death chamber inside the local courthouse. (The chair was portable and was often used in the parish, or county, where the crime had been committed.) Trusted inmates prepared Francis for electrocution by shaving his head and legs to ensure a good connection to the powerful electric current. Witnesses watched as guards strapped

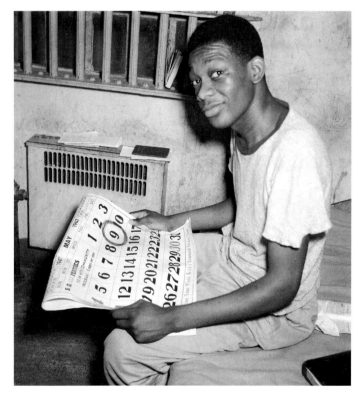

Willie Francis holds a calendar with his scheduled date of execution circled. On May 9, 1947, Francis sat in the electric chair for the second time—a year after the state's first attempt to execute him failed.

the dazed youth to the massive wooden chair and attached electrodes to his body. Francis's father was present, and he had brought a coffin with him.

When the captain in charge gave the signal, the boy's body jumped from the massive jolt of electricity. He groaned, his lips protruding from under the hood covering his face, and he strained so violently against the restraints that the chair came off the floor. Twice the executioner threw the switch, and witnesses heard Francis yell, "Take it off. . . . Let me breathe." The captain called for more juice, but to no avail. Finally, the parish sheriff halted the macabre proceeding, and Francis was returned to the holding cell. He showed no ill effects other than a rapid heartbeat. The execution was rescheduled.

Two new attorneys took the case and appealed to the state board of pardons, which concluded that electricity had never passed through Francis' body and thus he had not officially received his punishment. This reasoning made no sense to the inmate's lawyers: "He died mentally. . . . No man should have to go to the chair twice. The voice of humanity and justice cries out against such an outrage. . . . [I]s this an experiment in modern forms of torture. . . . Is the state of Louisiana trying to outdo the caesars, the Nazis?" The board denied the pardon, and Francis appealed to the U.S. Supreme Court. By now, his ordeal was national news.

The argument before the highest court was straightforward: the Fourteenth Amendment made the Eighth Amendment binding on the states, and making Francis face the chair again was cruel and unusual punishment. "How many times does the state get," his attorney asked, "before the due process clause of the Fourteenth Amendment can be used to protect the petitioner from torture?" Louisiana countered that Francis had never suffered the punishment his conviction required.

Two months later, the justices decided narrowly, 5 to 4, against Willie Francis. Four of the justices agreed that the Fourteenth Amendment incorporated, or included, the Eighth Amendment's ban on cruel and unusual punishments, but they did not believe sending the condemned man back to the chair was cruel. Four other justices believed that repeated attempts to execute were cruel by definition. It was a form of torture, one justice wrote, akin to burning at the stake. The fifth and deciding vote to deny Francis's appeal came from a justice who believed it was improper for federal judges to impose standards of fairness on the states unless the Constitution required it—and in this instance, he believed, it did not prohibit the state's action, even though he considered the punishment in this instance to be inhumane and lobbied the governor for a pardon.

The attorneys would not give up, however, and twice more filed appeals to the Supreme Court. Both times, the justices refused to hear their arguments but the last time the appeal was dismissed without prejudice, which meant the Court might reconsider in the light of new evidence that one of the executioners had been drunk and abusive toward Francis before bungling the job. But Willie Francis was tired of fighting. More than a year after his earlier date with death, he sat in the chair again. This time, his body went to an unmarked grave in the coffin his father had bought for his first execution.

From the time Willie Francis took his second walk to the chair until 1972, the Supreme Court heard many cases that challenged the constitutionality of executions. During this time, it overturned the death penalty in numerous individual cases, although the justices never declared capital punishment itself to be unconstitutional. It had only been misapplied in the particular cases before them.

During the 1970s, the Supreme Court set new standards for capital punishment. In *Furman* v. *Georgia* (1972), by a slim 5-to-4 majority, the justices decided that executions as practiced were unconstitutional because the judge and jury lacked specific guidelines to ensure fairness in sentencing. States responded by establishing a two-stage process for capital cases. One stage decided guilt or innocence, and the second stage allowed juries to consider aggravating or mitigating circumstances that would lead to a more informed decision about punishment. This change won Supreme Court approval in *Gregg* v. *Georgia* (1976), and most death-penalty states use this process today. Mandatory death sentences, that is, convictions that automatically require executions, are unconstitutional; the punishment should fit the crime.

The 1980s and 1990s brought further guidelines: states could not execute inmates who became, or remained, insane while on death row (although they could be executed if they regained their sanity); states could not mandate death for murders committed in prison; states could exclude opponents of the death penalty from serving in capital cases; and the list continued. Unwilling to declare the death penalty unconstitutional—after all, it

'No, That One Is Too Big And That One's Too Small . . . This One's Not Tied Properly And . . . '

In this cartoon published soon after the Supreme Court decided Gregg v. Georgia in 1976, the justices inspect various nooses and point out inconsistencies. The Court's decision in the Gregg case reaffirmed the constitutionality of the death penalty but also upheld guidelines that judges and juries must follow when deciding capital cases.

was mentioned in the Fifth Amendment, passed at the same time as the Eighth Amendment, so the framers clearly considered it an acceptable punishment—the justices sought ways to ensure its fair application, if not limit its use. One method was to look to what states permitted as punishment to learn whether a consensus of opinion existed as to which punishments were cruel and unusual. By this standard, the justices decided in 2002 that executing mentally retarded inmates was unconstitutional; in 2005, they reached the same conclusion for juveniles who committed a capital crime while younger than eighteen.

We as a society are still deciding whether capital punishment remains morally acceptable and, if so, under what circumstances. The United States is one of only four countries—the other three are China, Saudi Arabia, and Iran—that uses execution regularly, but we are no longer as convinced of its appropriateness as we once were. Currently, twelve states and the District of Columbia have abolished the death penalty. Five states account for the overwhelming majority of executions in the United States—slightly more than one thousand from 1976 through 2005. Texas tops the list, with more than 360 executions since 1976. Recently, the successful use of DNA evidence to challenge the accuracy of convictions has led some states—Illinois, Maryland, and Indiana, among others—to review capital sentences. The Illinois governor was so

In Austin, Texas, demonstrators march to the governor's mansion to protest the death penalty in 2003. The use of new evidence, especially DNA evidence, to overturn wrongful convictions has caused many Americans to reconsider the fairness of capital punishment. The number of executions in the United States has fallen since 1999, but every year Texas leads the nation in the number of people it executes.

disturbed by the number of errors—at least thirteen men wrongly convicted since 1976—and the potential for more mistakes that he pardoned four men and commuted all other capital sentences to life imprisonment before he left office in 2003. Since 1977, more than 110 inmates nationally have been released from death row after new evidence revealed they were convicted wrongly. Although support for capital punishment remains strong, recent surveys reveal that six in ten Americans now favor a moratorium on executions until questions about fairness are resolved.

The history of the Eighth Amendment makes clear that its meaning is continually evolving. The Constitution, with its Bill of Rights, is a living document. It did not fix our rights as they existed in times long past; it gave them room to grow. Oliver Wendell Holmes, Jr., appointed to the Supreme Court in 1902, wrote in 1884 that the "life of law is not logic but experience." Time brings changes, and the Constitution, like our other institutions, must adapt to new conditions. The framers of the Bill of Rights did not define excessive or cruel and unusual punishments because they knew these concepts would take their meaning from the changing conditions of society. They also trusted us, "We the People," to ensure that our society would be true to the words we pledged to live by. They expected us to judge in each election whether our government meets a high standard of morality and justice, as well as whether our laws express an acceptable balance between order and freedom. In this way, we continually give fresh meaning to the rights that guard our liberty.

Striking Down Capital Punishment

In Furman v. Georgia *(1972), by a 5-to-4 vote, the Supreme Court ruled for the first time that the death penalty violated the Eighth Amendment's ban on cruel and unusual punishment. All the justices for the majority and minority wrote opinions, making it difficult to know what standards states should use to judge whether or not capital punishment could ever be constitutional. Justice Thurgood Marshall, who concurred with the decision, concluded in a separate opinion that the death penalty, although acceptable earlier in the nation's history, no longer was consistent with public morality in the 1970s.*

Perhaps the most important principle in analyzing "cruel and unusual" punishment questions is one that is reiterated again and again in the prior opinions of the Court: i.e., the cruel and unusual language "must draw its meaning from the evolving standards of decency that mark the progress of a maturing society." Thus, a penalty that was permissible at one time in our Nation's history is not necessarily permissible today. . . .

In order to assess whether or not death is an excessive or unnecessary penalty, it is necessary to consider the reasons why a legislature might select it as punishment for one or more offenses, and examine whether less severe penalties would satisfy the legitimate legislative wants as well as capital punishment. If they would, then the death penalty is unnecessary cruelty, and, therefore, unconstitutional.

There are six purposes conceivably served by capital punishment: retribution, deterrence, prevention of repetitive criminal acts, encouragement of guilty pleas and confessions, eugenics, and economy. . . .

It is not improper at this point to take judicial notice of the fact that for more than 200 years men have labored to demonstrate that capital punishment serves no purpose that life imprisonment could not serve equally well. And they have done so with great success. Little, if any, evidence has been adduced to prove the contrary. The point has now been reached at which deference to the legislatures is tantamount to abdication of our judicial roles as factfinders, judges, and ultimate arbiters of the Constitution. We know that at some point the presumption of constitutionality accorded legislative acts gives way to a realistic assessment of those acts. This point comes when there is sufficient evidence available so that judges can determine, not whether the legislature acted wisely, but whether it had any rational basis whatsoever for acting. We have this evidence before us now. There is no rational basis for concluding that capital punishment is not excessive. It therefore violates the Eighth Amendment. . . .

At a time in our history when the streets of the Nation's cities inspire fear and despair, rather than pride and hope, it is difficult to maintain objectivity and concern for our fellow citizens. But, the measure of a country's greatness is its ability to retain compassion in time of crisis. No nation in the recorded history of man has a greater tradition of revering justice and fair treatment for all its citizens in times of turmoil, confusion, and tension than ours. This is a country which stands tallest in troubled times, a country that clings to fundamental principles, cherishes its constitutional heritage, and rejects simple solutions that compromise the values that lie at the roots of our democratic system.

In striking down capital punishment, this Court does not malign our system of government. On the contrary, it pays homage to it. Only in a free society could right triumph in difficult times, and could civilization record its magnificent advancement. In recognizing the humanity of our fellow beings, we pay ourselves the highest tribute. We achieve "a major milestone in the long road up from barbarism" and join the approximately 70 other jurisdictions in the world which celebrate their regard for civilization and humanity by shunning capital punishment.

Public Support for the Death Penalty

In his dissenting opinion in Furman v. Georgia *(1972), Chief Justice Warren Burger was joined by Harry Blackmun, Lewis Powell, and William Rehnquist. The four dissenting justices argued that support of the death penalty in state legislatures was proof of its support by the public.*

MR. CHIEF JUSTICE BURGER, with whom MR. JUSTICE BLACKMUN, MR. JUSTICE POWELL, and MR. JUSTICE REHNQUIST join, dissenting....

There are no obvious indications that capital punishment offends the conscience of society to such a degree that our traditional deference to the legislative judgment must be abandoned. It is not a punishment such as burning at the stake that everyone would ineffably find to be repugnant to all civilized standards. Nor is it a punishment so roundly condemned that only a few aberrant legislatures have retained it on the statute books. Capital punishment is authorized by statute in 40 States, the District of Columbia, and in the federal courts for the commission of certain crimes. On four occasions in the last 11 years Congress has added to the list of federal crimes punishable by death. In looking for reliable indicia of contemporary attitude, none more trustworthy has been advanced.

One conceivable source of evidence that legislatures have abdicated their essentially barometric role with respect to community values would be public opinion polls, of which there have been many in the past decade addressed to the question of capital punishment. Without assessing the reliability of such polls, or intimating that any judicial reliance could ever be placed on them, it need only be noted that the reported results have shown nothing approximating the universal condemnation of capital punishment that might lead us to suspect that the legislatures in general have lost touch with current social values.

The Death Penalty Is Not without Justification

Four years after its decision in Furman v. Georgia *(1972), the Supreme Court once again considered the constitutionality of the death penalty. In the earlier case, the justices, by a vote of 5 to 4, struck down capital punishment for the first time as "cruel and unusual punishment" prohibited by the Eighth Amendment. Their reasons differed, but the opinions left open the possibility that states could enact constitutional death penalty statutes if they developed standards to guide jury decisions to impose a capital sentence. In* Gregg v. Georgia *(1976), Justice Potter Stewart, for the 7-to-2 majority, upheld a Georgia death penalty law because it required jurors to consider the unique circumstances of each case before imposing a death sentence. The decision reflected the Court's recognition of public support for the death penalty, as expressed in new state laws, and effectively overruled the earlier* Furman *decision.*

The petitioners in the capital cases before the Court today renew the "standards of decency" argument, but developments during the four years since Furman have undercut substantially the assumptions upon which their argument rested. Despite the continuing debate, dating back to the 19th century, over the morality and utility of capital punishment, it is now evident that a large proportion of American society continues to regard it as an appropriate and necessary criminal sanction.

The most marked indication of society's endorsement of the death penalty for murder is the legislative response to Furman. The legislatures of at least 35 States have enacted new statutes that provide for the death penalty for at least some crimes that result in the death of another person. And the Congress of the United States, in 1974, enacted a statute providing the death penalty for aircraft piracy that results in death. These recently adopted statutes have attempted to address the concerns expressed by the Court in Furman primarily (i) by specifying the factors to be weighed and the procedures to be followed in deciding when to impose a capital sentence, or (ii) by making the death penalty mandatory for specified crimes. But all of the post-Furman statutes make clear that capital punishment itself has not been rejected by the elected representatives of the people. . . .

[T]he actions of juries in many States since Furman are fully compatible with the legislative judgments, reflected in the new statutes, as to the continued utility and necessity of capital punishment in appropriate cases. At the close of 1974 at least 254 persons had been sentenced to death since Furman, and by the end of March 1976, more than 460 persons were subject to death sentences. . . .

In sum, we cannot say that the judgment of the Georgia Legislature that capital punishment may be necessary in some cases is clearly wrong. Considerations of federalism, as well as respect for the ability of a legislature to evaluate, in terms of its particular State, the moral consensus concerning the death penalty and its social utility as a sanction, require us to conclude, in the absence of more convincing evidence, that the infliction of death as a punishment for murder is not without justification and thus is not unconstitutionally severe.

CHAPTER 22

The Right of Privacy

The right of privacy—the right to be left alone, as Justice Louis Brandeis once defined it—is fundamental to our understanding of freedom, but nowhere does the Constitution mention it. When Congress submitted the Bill of Rights to the people for ratification in 1789, privacy was not listed as a liberty that required protection from government. Yet today it is difficult to imagine American society without this right. How did privacy become an essential liberty?

For eighteenth-century men and women, privacy meant the right to be secure in one's home, safe from the powers of government. The common law phrase, "A man's home is his castle," expressed this understanding. All Englishmen, whether in the Old World or the New, believed that "the poorest man may in his cottage bid defiance to all the forces of the crown," as Sir William Pitt, former British prime minister, said in 1763. This definition of privacy made its way into the U.S. Bill of Rights, albeit indirectly, in two separate amendments. The Third Amendment restrained the government from housing soldiers in private homes; this amendment reaffirmed the English practice as expressed in the Petition of Right (1628). The Fourth Amendment protected homeowners from searches except for probable cause and only then with a properly approved warrant. These guarantees were important, but no one understood them to include the right to be left alone. What they meant instead was protection from arbitrary government.

Privacy in the sense of solitude and isolation—or an ability to have "my space," as we call it today—was a luxury enjoyed only by the wealthy until the industrial age of the nineteenth century. Most people before then lived on top of each other, literally as well as figuratively. Houses were small and bare. Entire families often slept in one room; toilets were neither separate nor private. The opportunities for intimacy we take for granted simply were not available to most people. The wealth created by industrialization began to change this condition. Houses grew in size, as did the number of people who could afford them, and with these developments came more physical separation and more opportunity to be left alone. The choices offered by a burgeoning marketplace and the vast scale of the American continent also encouraged individualism to a degree unknown in Europe. With these changes came a new meaning of privacy. Now it became a

Tenement housing was a fact of life for many urban Americans during the so-called Gilded Age. Several generations of a family often lived in a single, crowded apartment where children played and slept even as the adults took in work such as making and tailoring clothes. Privacy was almost nonexistent.

valued part of individual liberty; people assumed that what they did beyond public life, in their own homes, was no one's business but their own.

After the Civil War, both the rise of large cities and the emergence of new technologies reshaped the concept of privacy. Block upon block of tenement houses in New York City, Chicago, and other big cities re-created the crowded conditions of earlier times. Inventions such as the telephone and the camera made it possible to enter people's homes and their private lives without physical intrusion. Among the developments most threatening to the sense of privacy was the inexpensive daily newspaper, which regularly reported on the lives of the rich and famous for the amusement of ordinary folks. The stories carried by the new mass media had the ability to ruin reputations, and it was this threat that led to the first laws to protect privacy. These measures allowed harmed individuals to sue for damages by recognizing a general right to privacy, but not a fundamental or constitutional right. Future Supreme Court justice Louis Brandeis captured this new meaning in "The Right to Privacy," an important *Harvard Law Review* article in 1890 that outlined its common-law roots.

The Supreme Court began to consider a constitutional right to privacy in the 1920s. Cases involving the Fourth Amendment offered the first opportunity for the justices to consider privacy as a guaranteed right. In 1928, Justice Brandeis eloquently disagreed with the majority decision in *Olmstead* v. *United States* that wiretapping did not require a warrant because it involved no physical trespass. The framers of the Fourth and Fifth Amendments, he argued, "sought to protect Americans in their beliefs, their thoughts, their emotions, and their sensations. They conferred, as against the Government, the right to be let alone—the most comprehensive of rights and the one most valued by civilized men." His views on wiretapping ultimately prevailed, as did his belief that privacy was a constitutionally protected right.

But what about other areas of privacy? What rights did citizens have to make private decisions without governmental interference? Or stated another way, in what private decisions did government have a legitimate interest? Clearly, the right to privacy was not absolute: even in their own homes, citizens could not, for example, commit murder or molest a child. Where did the right to privacy end?

In the 1960s, the use of a new technology—the birth control pill—raised this question in a case that became the basis for our modern understanding of a right of privacy. This case was different from many the Supreme Court has used to interpret the Bill of Rights. It involved an act of civil disobedience for the specific purpose of testing a law. Also, the plaintiffs were well-educated and respected citizens, quite unlike the "not very nice people," as Justice Felix Frankfurter once labeled them, who were at the center of other rights controversies. The case did not lead to the cries of outrage that accompanied other expansions of rights in the 1960s, but it did set the Court on the path to its most divisive privacy decision, *Roe* v. *Wade,* which guaranteed a woman's right to choose an abortion.

Estelle Griswold was concerned about the problem of world overpopulation. A religious, well-educated woman and wife of an advertising executive, she had worked in Europe after World War II with the Church World Service, helping to relocate the continent's vast number of refugees. The experience shaped her views about the need to bring the world's resources and its people in better balance. "A look at the slums of the world, at the chaos of a war-scorched earth, and you realize that life at the point of survival, where food, water and shelter are unobtainable is close to reversion to an animal order," she wrote later. "Survival is first; civilization is second."

It was this concern that led her to become executive director of the Planned Parenthood League of Connecticut. She became a crusader for birth control in a campaign that would last the rest of her life, but as she admitted, she really knew little about the subject. She had never seen a diaphragm, then the leading means of birth control, at the time of her interview. What she knew was that women needed to be able to control this most intimate part of their lives.

Regulation of sex and birth control had a tortuous history in Connecticut, as it did in the nation. One of the state's best-known citizens in the nineteenth century was Anthony Comstock, a lobbyist for the Young Men's Christian Association's (YMCA) Committee for the Suppression of Vice. The son of Connecticut Calvinists and a lifelong advocate for religion, he rallied his fellow believers and persuaded Congress to pass the Comstock Act of 1873, which outlawed obscene and immoral materials from the U.S. mails. Among the banned items was anything "advertised or described in a manner calculated to lead another to use or apply it for contraception or abortion." Six years later, the Connecticut legislature went further and banned the use of any birth control device. State courts interpreted the law also to mean that doctors could not pre-scribe these devices.

Each year, supporters of Planned Parenthood lobbied the legislature to revise or repeal the ban on the use of birth control—among all the states, only Connecticut took this extreme position—but each year they failed. It was an unfair law, they argued, and its burden fell disproportionately on poor women who either had to refuse their husbands or risk their health and the family's pocketbook on an unwanted child. Planned Parenthood defied the law by opening clinics in Connecticut in 1935, but the police promptly shut them down. The legislature refused to repeal or modify the ban. Catholic presence was strong in the state, so the law persisted until the 1960s, even though by then it was largely ignored in practice.

It was this situation that Estelle Griswold was determined to remedy. With her allies, she identified two women whose health clearly would be endangered by a pregnancy and enlisted them to bring suit against the state for refusing to allow them to buy birth control devices. Their suit, *Poe* v. *Ullman,* made it to the U.S. Supreme Court in 1961, only to be rejected by the justices because of the state's long-standing refusal to prosecute anyone for violating the statute. There was no fear of enforcement, the Court said, so no harm was done. It would not "be umpire to debates concerning harmless, empty shadows." This rebuff spurred Griswold to turn the empty shadows into a real controversy. She opened a birth control clinic and set out to ensure that police had no choice but to arrest her for breaking the law. Acting on a complaint, police visited the clinic, where Griswold made certain they saw the banned activities and prod-ucts. Even though the prosecutor normally declined to bring cases like this to trial, Estelle Griswold's unwillingness to have the arrest dismissed led to her trial and conviction for violating the state law. She finally had the case that demonstrated harm.

When this case reached the Supreme Court in 1965, the justices sided with Griswold. Writing for the 7-to-2 majority, Justice William O. Douglas ruled that marital relations between a husband and wife were a basic "right of privacy older than the Bill of Rights." The Constitution protected this right even if it did not mention it specifically. It was an implied right, one that was part of the "penumbra," or shadow, of several amendments. The First Amendment, for example, contained a freedom to associate privately; the Third and Fourth Amendments protected the sanctity of private homes; the Fifth Amendment's guarantee against self-incrimination allowed an accused person to keep information private. The majority also found the right of privacy guaranteed in part by the Ninth Amendment, which reserved to the people any rights not named in the Bill of Rights. Rights are expansive, not restrictive, and whenever fundamental rights are at stake, Justice Arthur Goldberg noted in a concurring opinion, the state must have a compelling purpose for abridging these liberties. Invading the "sacred precincts of marital bedrooms" was not a legitimate reason, Goldberg wrote.

Estelle Griswold's efforts to legalize abortion were born of a desire to give women freedom in the most private of matters—the decision about whether to bear a child. Later, she accepted an award with Dr. Lee Buxton, with whom she opened her birth control clinic in New Haven in 1961, in recognition of their roles in the landmark Supreme Court case.

Griswold v. *Connecticut* was a landmark case in establishing constitutional protection for the right of privacy, and it received widespread approval. For Estelle Griswold, it was vindication for a cause she held dear. Three months after the decision, she reopened the birth control clinic in New Haven, and she remained active in women's causes until her death in 1981. By then, the right of privacy had come to include the right of women to choose whether or not to continue a pregnancy. Unlike the earlier decision, the right to an abortion unleashed a bitter debate that continues today and raises new questions about the limits of privacy in a free society.

In 1972, the Supreme Court extended the right of privacy by striking down a Massachusetts law barring the sale of contraceptives to unmarried couples. This decision was a prelude to *Roe* v. *Wade* (1973). The question in the *Roe* case was straightforward: did government have any compelling interest in a woman's pregnancy? In language rooted in *Griswold,* the answer was "no," at least not in the early stages of pregnancy. The right of privacy, the justices concluded, was "broad enough to encompass a woman's decision whether or not to terminate her pregnancy," although once the fetus became capable of living outside the womb, the state could intervene as long as the woman's health or life is protected.

Roe raised profound moral and religious questions for many Americans: When does life begin? At what point does the state's interest in protecting life outweigh the woman's right to privacy, personal autonomy, and equality? Opinion polls continue to reflect a lack of public agreement on these questions. Most Americans support the right to privacy, including a woman's control over

SPONSORED BY PEOPLE TO ABOLISH ABORTION LAWS 254-4488

This poster rallied New Yorkers for a 1970 New York City demonstration to protest the state's abortion laws. New York had made abortion a crime as early as 1828. In 1970, the state passed the first law in the country to allow abortion "on demand." It made elective abortions performed by a physician completely legal for the first twenty-four weeks of a pregnancy, but considered the procedure to be homicide thereafter.

her body, but they are uneasy with the idea that abortion might become a casual practice. The question raised by *Roe* is not whether abortion will continue to exist in the United States, but what is the extent of the constitutional protection?

Americans overwhelmingly want to keep government out of the bedroom, so the Court's recognition of a fundamental right to privacy in this area receives broad support, as seen by *Lawrence* v. *Texas,* a 2003 case striking down a law that prohibited consensual gay and lesbian sex. Is abortion different? During the three decades since *Roe,* the justices have reaffirmed the right to privacy in matters of abortion but also have accepted some legislative limits on its practice. In *Planned Parenthood of Southeastern Pennsylvania* v. *Casey* (1992), the Court retreated from its position in *Roe* v. *Wade.* It allowed some restrictions on the woman's right to choose, provided the government did not unduly burden or interfere with her ability to get an abortion. Among the limits the justices have found acceptable are laws mandating a twenty-four-hour waiting period, requiring doctors to provide information intended to discourage abortion, and restricting abortions for teenagers younger than a certain age, usually eighteen, if they do not have parental or judicial consent. Today, it is unclear if the justices will continue to trim the broad right it recognized in 1973. A reversal of the *Roe* decision would give states greater latitude to regulate or even outlaw abortion.

Controversies over privacy extend to more areas of modern life than the bedroom. New technologies are again pushing us to consider questions we have never faced before. Advances in medical technologies allow doctors to keep even critically ill patients alive for long periods of time, but can we keep people alive against their will? Do we have a right to die—or to have others make that decision for us, based on their understanding of our wishes, if we are incapable of making it for ourselves? In 1990, the Supreme Court faced this question for the first time and decided that the right of terminally ill patients to die was part of our right to privacy. Within a few years, all fifty states recognized this right, and a national law, the Patients' Bill of Rights, required federally funded hospitals to respect patients' decisions regarding their treatment. Oregon extended the meaning of personal autonomy to include a right to doctor-assisted suicide, and in 2006, the Court refused to allow the U.S. attorney general to prosecute assisting doctors under federal drug laws. Further advances in medical technology doubtless will continue to raise questions that require a balance between our right to privacy and society's interest in preserving life.

New communication technologies, including the Internet, also spur us to consider again our right to keep personal information private. Computers now capture reams of data about each of us, and this information helps to determine everything from our credit rating to the types of advertising we receive. Some

> *"How a person engages in sex should be irrelevant as a matter of state law. Sexual intimacy is a sensitive, key relationship of human existence and the development of human personality. In a diverse nation such as ours, we must preserve the individual freedom to choose, and not imply that there are any "right" ways of conducting relationships."*
>
> —Justice Harry Blackmun, dissenting opinion, *Bowers* v. *Hardwick* (1986)

of these data relate to things we expect to keep private, such as our medical records or our personal communications. What right do we have to this information, and what right do we have to keep it private? The questions have no simple answers. Knowledge of our purchasing habits allows marketers to provide us more of the goods we want, but it also may open us to sales pitches we prefer to avoid. Potentially far more serious in its consequence is the ability to capture new kinds of personal information, such as our DNA, as part of our medical care. Should insurance companies be allowed to use this information to set individual rates or to deny coverage to those who are genetically vulnerable to costly diseases? Should law enforcement or security agencies have routine access to our DNA, or do we have a expectation of privacy unless the government establishes probable cause to suspect us of a crime?

Increasingly, we as a society are trying to determine what privacy means in this brave new world of advanced technologies. The problem is not a new one. In his dissent in *Olmstead* v. *United States,* Justice Brandeis saw the threat to privacy that technical innovation posed to liberty: "Discovery and invention have made it possible for the government, by means far more effective than stretching upon the rack, to obtain disclosure in court of what is whispered in the closet." He warned that technology had the power not simply to make our lives more comfortable but also to threaten our liberty by invading our private lives.

The right to privacy is about defining the proper relationship between the individual and government. The founding generation aimed to permit individual citizens the widest latitude possible to live their lives and pursue their happiness without interference from government. It also vested sovereignty, or final authority, in the people at large, who in turn authorize elected representatives to act on their behalf. Our sense of democracy, as a result, rests firmly upon the idea of individual autonomy, or personal control over the decisions that affect us. The right of privacy supports our individuality, and it is our ability as individuals to make decisions, separately and collectively, about our present and our future that ultimately protects our liberty.

"The Right to Be Let Alone"

In 1890, overeager journalists attempted to crash an event hosted by a wealthy Boston lawyer-socialite, Samuel Warren, and his law partner, Louis D. Brandeis, who later became a justice on the U.S. Supreme Court. The two wrote an article, "The Right to Privacy," for the Harvard Law Review *that Dean Roscoe Pound of the Harvard Law School cited as "adding a chapter to our law." The authors argued for a right of privacy or, as Brandeis later defined it in the wiretapping case of* Olmstead v. United States *(1928), "the right to be let alone—the most comprehensive of rights and the right most valued by civilized men." Although the Constitution does not mention a right to privacy, the Supreme Court has inferred it from the language of the First, Third, Fourth, Fifth, and Ninth Amendments.*

That the individual shall have full protection in person and in property is a principle as old as the common law; but it has been found necessary from time to time to define anew the exact nature and extent of such protection. Political, social, and economic changes entail the recognition of new rights, and the common law, in its eternal youth, grows to meet the demands of society....

This development of the law was inevitable. The intense intellectual and emotional life, and the heightening of sensations which came with the advance of civilization, made it clear to man that only a part of the pain, pleasure, and profit of life lay in physical things. Thoughts, emotions, and sensations demanded legal recognition, and the beautiful capacity for growth which characterizes the common law enabled the judges to afford the requisite protection, without the interposition of the legislature.

Recent inventions and business methods call attention to the next step which must be taken for the protection of the person, and for securing to the individual what Judge Cooley calls the right "to be let alone."...

Of the desirability—indeed of the necessity—of some such protection, there can, it is believed, be no doubt.... The intensity and complexity of life, attendant upon advancing civilization, have rendered necessary some retreat from the world, and man, under the refining influence of culture, has become more sensitive to publicity, so that solitude and privacy have become more essential to the individual; but modern enterprise and invention have, through invasions upon his privacy, subjected him to mental pain and distress, far greater than could be inflicted by mere bodily injury. Nor is the harm wrought by such invasions confined to the suffering of those who may be made the subjects of journalistic or other enterprise. In this, as in other branches of commerce, the supply creates the demand. Each crop of unseemly gossip, thus harvested, becomes the seed of more, and, in direct proportion to its circulation, results in a lowering of social standards and of morality. Even gossip apparently harmless, when widely and persistently circulated, is potent for evil. It both belittles and perverts. It belittles by inverting the relative importance of things, thus dwarfing the thoughts and aspirations of a people. When personal gossip attains the dignity of print, and crowds the space available for matters of real interest to the community, what wonder that the ignorant and thoughtless mistake its relative importance....

[T]he protection afforded to thoughts, sentiments, and emotions, expressed through the medium of writing or of the arts, so far as it consists in preventing publication, is merely an instance of the enforcement of the more general right of the individual to be let alone. It is like the right not to be assaulted or beaten, the right not to be imprisoned, the right not to be maliciously prosecuted, the right not to be defamed. The principle which protects personal writings and all other personal productions...is in reality...the principle...of an inviolate personality.

Various Guarantees Create Zones of Privacy

Critics of the Supreme Court's decision in Griswold v. Connecticut *(1965), which recognized a right to privacy in marriage, chastised the majority justices because the Constitution does not mention a right to privacy specifically. Justice William O. Douglas, in the majority opinion, argued that the right can be inferred legitimately from the language of at least four amendments. He wrote about "penumbras, formed by emanations," metaphorical language that suggested that the right was as logically related to the amendments as were halos around the sun or other celestial objects.*

Specific guarantees in the Bill of Rights have penumbras, formed by emanations from those guarantees that help give them life and substance.... Various guarantees create zones of privacy. The right of association contained in the penumbra of the First Amendment is one.... The Third Amendment in its prohibition against the quartering of soldiers "in any house" in time of peace without the consent of the owner is another facet of that privacy. The Fourth Amendment explicitly affirms the "right of the people to be secure in their persons, houses, papers, and effects, against unreasonable searches and seizures." The Fifth Amendment in its Self-Incrimination Clause enables the citizen to create a zone of privacy which government may not force him to surrender to his detriment. The Ninth Amendment provides: "The enumeration in the Constitution, of certain rights, shall not be construed to deny or disparage others retained by the people."

Justice Arthur Goldberg, in his concurring opinion in Griswold v. Connecticut, *relied on the little-used Ninth Amendment, which reserved any rights not listed in the Constitution to the people in his argument in support of the right to privacy.*

The Ninth Amendment to the Constitution may be regarded by some as a recent discovery and may be forgotten by others, but since 1791 it has been a basic part of the Constitution which we are sworn to uphold. To hold that a right so basic and fundamental and so deep-rooted in our society as the right of privacy in marriage may be infringed because that right is not guaranteed in so many words by the first eight amendments to the Constitution is to ignore the Ninth Amendment and to give it no effect whatsoever. Moreover, a judicial construction that this fundamental right is not protected by the Constitution because it is not mentioned in explicit terms by one of the first eight amendments or elsewhere in the Constitution would violate the Ninth Amendment, which specifically states that "[t]he enumeration in the Constitution, of certain rights, shall not be construed to deny or disparage others retained by the people."...

Although the Constitution does not speak in so many words of the right of privacy in marriage, I cannot believe that it offers these fundamental rights no protection. The fact that no particular provision of the Constitution explicitly forbids the State from disrupting the traditional relation of the family—a relation as old and as fundamental as our entire civilization—surely does not show that the Government was meant to have the power to do so. Rather, as the Ninth Amendment expressly recognizes, there are fundamental personal rights such as this one, which are protected from abridgment by the Government though not specifically mentioned in the Constitution.

CHAPTER 23

The Right to Bear Arms

The Second Amendment is the only part of the Bill of Rights that contains a preamble: "A well-regulated militia, being necessary to the security of a free State, the right of the people to keep and bear Arms, shall not be infringed." These twenty-six words are bitterly contested in modern America. Does the amendment recognize an individual right to own guns for sport and self-defense or a collective right, exercised through a militia, or citizen guard, to possess firearms for defending the nation? The framers clearly believed the right was important, but what they meant by it has become a source of deep division. Is the preamble a restricting clause, one that restricts gun ownership to defense of the nation, or an amplifying clause, one that notes an important purpose for gun possession but does not limit other uses?

The English settlers in the New World were heirs to a five-century-old tradition governing both the right and the duty to bear arms. The idea of an armed citizenry responsible for the common defense existed in law alongside regulation of gun ownership. As far back as the twelfth century, English law imposed an obligation on citizens to participate in law enforcement. All able-bodied men between the ages of sixteen and sixty had to join the sheriff's *posse comitatus* (from the Latin, "force of the county") when the community was alerted to criminal danger. They were also part of the militia. Both of these legal duties required citizens to possess arms, but the law restricted the use of weapons according to social class. Common people had far more limited use of weapons than did noblemen. Laws also prohibited the carrying of arms in public places.

When the English monarchy attempted to disarm its political opponents in the late seventeenth century, what had been a duty came to be viewed as a fundamental right to defend liberty from political oppression. Conditions in colonial America strengthened this belief. Guns and militias were more common—and thought to be more necessary—in the harsher environment of the New World. At first, the goal was to provide food and to protect settlers against displaced natives, but the growth of slavery also spurred the arming of all white males. The conflict with Great Britain added another reason for an armed citizenry. Colonists began to view imperial regulations as an effort to strip them of their rights. Citizen militias were the ultimate defense against tyranny.

For the founding generation, the struggle with Great Britain reinforced the lessons their English ancestors had learned. It reminded Americans of the dangers of a standing, or permanent, army that could seize power or interfere in politics, and it transformed the idea of an armed population from a necessity to an important right. The Constitution gave Congress the power to organize, arm, and discipline the militia, which by custom included all white males from sixteen to sixty years of age, but opponents of ratification feared that this power could also be used to disarm the population at large. It was this concern that led to the Second Amendment. A universal militia and armed citizenry pro-

> *"AND WHEREAS it is of the utmost Importance to the Safety of every State, that it should always be in a Condition of Defence; and it is the Duty of every Man who enjoys the Protection of Society, to be prepared and willing to defend it; This Convention therefore, in the Name and by the Authority of the good People of this State, doth ORDAIN, DETERMINE, AND DECLARE, That the Militia of the State, at all Times hereafter, as well in Peace as in War, shall be armed and disciplined, and in Readiness for Service."*
>
> —New York Constitution (1777)

vided a check on governmental power, especially on what was then a distant central government.

The decades following the adoption of the amendment provided little opportunity for judicial interpretation of the right to bear arms. Gun ownership was widespread, and most laws restricting firearms regulated or prohibited their possession by native tribes, slaves, and free blacks. Commentators pointed to the connection between the right to bear arms and liberty. An early Supreme Court justice, Joseph Story, voiced the common interpretation when he wrote that "it offers a strong moral check against the usurpation and arbitrary power of rulers" because it would "enable the people to resist, and triumph over them." By the mid-nineteenth century, concern about increased crime led to laws prohibiting concealed weapons, but no one considered these measures a threat to the basic right to own a gun.

Post–Civil War Reconstruction brought the Second Amendment to the Supreme Court for the first time. The defeated southern states enacted the so-called Black Codes to keep ex-slaves in a subservient status; one law required blacks to have a license to carry firearms. Northern Republicans objected to this denial of a right considered essential to liberty. The attempt to disarm blacks, as well as to strip them of other rights, led to the Fourteenth Amendment,

A sheriff and his posse lead a band of criminals past the Mission of San Miguel toward San Luis Obispo, California, in 1864. The common law concept of posse comitatus *(Latin for "force of the county," a sort of militia) gave a sheriff the authority to conscript local men to help keep the peace and hunt for outlaws.*

through which lawmakers intended to apply the Bill of Rights to the states as well as the central government. The Supreme Court did not interpret the amendment in this manner at first, and in its only two cases involving the Second Amendment, the Court ruled that it limited the federal government only. This stance reaffirmed the power of states to regulate firearms.

The explosive growth of cities in the late nineteenth century, fueled by waves of immigration from southern and eastern Europe, led to new pressures for gun control. No one disputed the right to own guns, but increasingly people were concerned about their misuse. Many native-born Americans were especially fearful that new immigrants would bring crime and violence with them. In 1911, these fears led to the passage of New York's Sullivan Law, which went far beyond typical gun ordinances. It prohibited the unlicensed carrying of concealed weapons and required a permit for the purchase or ownership of a pistol. Violation of the act was a felony, punishable by a term in the state prison, and the first person convicted under the law was an Italian immigrant. The Sullivan Law was unusual, however. Most Americans enjoyed an unrestricted right to own and use guns.

World War I changed this situation. A new and fearsome weapon emerged from this bloody conflict, the Thomson submachine gun, or tommy-gun, which became the preferred gun of gangsters. During the 1920s and early 1930s, these automatic weapons, along with sawed-off shotguns and silencers, were associated with bootleggers and bank robbers, typified by John Dillinger, Pretty Boy Floyd, and Bonnie and Clyde. In response, Congress passed the first federal gun control law. The National Firearms Act of 1934 required registration, police permission, and a steep tax for so-called gangster weapons. This law, in turn, led to one of the few Supreme Court cases on the Second Amendment. In *United States* v. *Miller* (1939), the Court affirmed the right of citizens to own weapons suitable for use in the militia, but it ruled that the firearm in dispute, a sawed-off shotgun, was not a military weapon and could be controlled without violating the Second Amendment.

The 1960s put the question of gun control in a tragic new light. The assassinations of President John F. Kennedy, civil rights leader Martin Luther King, Jr., and Senator Robert F. Kennedy were only the most notable casualties in a decade of violence. Urban riots, civil rights repression, and political unrest prompted groups from the Ku Klux Klan to the Black Panthers to arm themselves or, in the Klan's case, to become more heavily armed. Homeowners followed suit; by decade's end, almost half of American households had at least one gun. Public concern led Congress to pass the Gun Control Act of 1968, the first federal law that seriously affected the right of Americans to buy and own firearms. The act limited the purchase of guns through the mails, restricted the importation of surplus military weapons, and prohibited convicted felons from owning guns.

The act also set off a continuing national debate about gun control, with the National Rifle Association and similar groups lobbying for no restrictions on gun ownership and gun control organizations and law enforcement agencies seeking even more limits. Finally in the 1980s, the often bitter conflict between the two positions came to a dramatic head when a small town in the Midwest sought to ban handguns for the first time in American history.

Bonnie Parker and Clyde Barrow gained national notoriety in the 1920s and 1930s for repeatedly committing armed robberies, killing numerous civilians and law enforcement officers in the process. They became two of the most sought-after fugitives in the country, and the massive publicity their exploits received fueled efforts to restrict gun ownership.

Morton Grove, Illinois, lies fourteen miles north of downtown Chicago. First settled in the 1830s, it was known at the turn of the twentieth century for its floral industry, with a local greenhouse producing the first-place rose at the 1904 St. Louis World's Fair. By the 1950s, the single-line railroad that had connected the village to Chicago had been replaced by a modern expressway, and Morton Grove grew rapidly into a suburban community of 15,000. Maintaining an orderly and peaceful town became paramount to residents, and in 1981, Morton Grove passed an ordinance restricting the private possession of handguns within the village. The ban on gun ownership was the first in the nation's history.

In October 1980, residents learned about an application to open a gun store inside the town limits. By the spring of the following year, with a local poll revealing overwhelming support for handgun legislation, opponents of the application pressed the village board not only to ban the sale of handguns but to prohibit their possession entirely. On a stormy night in June, hundreds of citizens packed the small council chambers, spilling over into the streets, to voice their opinions and witness the debate. At the end of the evening, the board passed the ordinance, which imposed a fine of up to $500 and six months in jail for violators. "I hope we saved a couple of lives," one of the supporting councilmen said. Significantly, the law did not seek to ban all guns, only handguns. The next day, a local attorney, Victor Quilici, filed suit in the county court, seeking to block the ordinance from taking effect. A few weeks later, four other residents sued in federal court, claiming it violated the Second Amendment.

By now the board's action was national news, and ABC TV planned a documentary on the handgun ban. Both the National Rifle Association and the

Second Amendment Foundation, pro-gun advocates, had joined the fight, alleging that the ordinance was unconstitutional. After reviewing the complaint, the federal district judge ruled that the ordinance did not violate the Second Amendment, which applied only to the federal government. Opponents quickly appealed to the U.S. Seventh Circuit Court. Regulation of handguns was not the issue—more than 22,000 measures already existed in cities and towns across the nation to control concealed weapons and ban them from such places as voting sites, public buildings, and schools—but Morton Grove's ordinance outlawed their possession, even in the privacy of one's home. The ordinance challenged traditional interpretations of an American right, but it also addressed a national concern over violence related to handguns. By 1980, 10,000 people were murdered annually in the United States with these small arms. A few months before the Morton Grove ordinance passed, an assailant used a handgun in an unsuccessful attempt to assassinate President Ronald Reagan; six weeks later, a would-be assassin shot Pope John Paul II in St. Peter's Square. In defense, gun advocates developed a slogan that soon became part of a national debate: "Guns don't kill people; people kill people." Kennesaw, Georgia, in protest of the Morton Grove ban, passed an ordinance requiring all homeowners to own a gun.

When the Morton Grove ordinance took effect on February 1, 1982, the legal campaign for reversal was well underway. Two cases were winding their way toward a decision—one in state courts, one in federal courts. Meanwhile, a survey revealed continued majority support for the ban among Morton Grove residents, although it also disclosed that handguns remained in 1,600 homes in the village. An attempt by local opponents to put the ordinance to a popular vote failed, but before other efforts could be made to repeal the measure, the federal appellate court upheld the district court ruling, 2 to 1. The majority accepted Morton Grove's argument that the framers had not intended handguns to be among the class of protected firearms. The words of the Second Amendment made it clear to them that the right to bear arms was "inextricably connected to the preservation of a militia." But the U.S. Supreme Court had not extended the amendment to the states, as it had done with other rights, so Morton Grove's action could not have been unconstitutional. The dissenting judge believed the ban on possession within the home abridged the right of privacy as well as a Second Amendment right of gun ownership.

Now, the case was headed to the U.S. Supreme Court, but in May 1983, the justices declined to hear the appeal. Their refusal meant that the appellate court's decision was final. When the state supreme court also rejected a challenge to the ordinance under the state constitution's guarantee of a right to bear arms—the right was subject to the power of the government to protect public safety, which the court ruled was the intent of the ordinance—the battle of Morton Grove was over. The village had the authority to ban the possession of handguns within its borders.

Quilici v. *Village of Morton Grove* remains the most important modern case on Second Amendment law, but the Supreme Court's refusal to hear the case meant the controversy would continue. As a result, the Second Amendment remains one of only four parts of the Bill of Rights that have not been applied as limits on the states under the Fourteenth Amendment. The Third Amendment, which says that soldiers, in times of peace, cannot be quartered in any house without the owner's consent; the Fifth Amendment's requirement of an indictment by a grand jury for capital crimes; and the Seventh Amendment's requirement for a jury trial in civil suits are the other provisions that restrain the federal government alone.

The lack of a definitive interpretation of the right to bear arms—Is it an individual right? Is it a collective right?—means that the issue finds its way into hundreds of local, state, and federal forums. Courts, legislatures, and city councils have acted in different ways to reconcile the meaning of this right, which appears in most state constitutions as well, with the threat posed by weapons in the hands of criminals. At the same time Morton Grove acted, for example, several neighboring towns adopted similar ordinances, while other towns in Illinois rejected attempts to ban small arms. Two decades later, another federal appeals court interpreted the Second Amendment differently from the appellate court that heard the Morton Grove case; the judges who heard *United States* v. *Everson* (2001) concluded that the Second Amendment guaranteed an individual right to own a handgun. The U.S. Supreme Court has not thus far resolved these conflicting interpretations.

The debate about gun control is among the most raucous in American history, and the opposing sides often take positions that are hard, if not impossible, to reconcile. An appeal to the original understanding does not solve the problem for us. The founding generation clearly thought the right to bear arms required protection, but the language they used was not entirely clear. Who were "the people?" Does this phrase refer to individuals or to the community? Do the words "to bear arms" refer to ownership of guns or to their use in the common defense? In fact, the words have both public and private meanings, which is why we have such difficulty settling on a single interpretation of the amendment.

The stakes of the debate are high. From the fiery conflict between federal officers and a religious sect, the Branch Davidians, at Waco, Texas, in 1993 to the deaths of high school students in a shooting spree at Columbine, Colorado, in 1999, we have witnessed too many recent instances of violence not to be concerned about the availability and use of guns in our society. But the contest about the meaning of the Second Amendment is not the first time in American history we have been divided over the extent of our rights. The fight for abolition of slavery, the struggle for woman suffrage, the campaign for personal privacy—these claims to liberty are only three of numerous battles fought throughout our history over the definition of our rights.

What is most striking about the public controversy over gun control is its democratic character. It is an open and participatory conversation about fundamental rights and the fundamental character of an orderly and just society. Among all the partisanship and intemperate rhetoric, what is most reassuring is the debate itself. It is this passionate, continuing, democratic debate that has given liberty and the expansion of our rights their historic energy. To deny debate in this instance would deprive us of the potential of growth in our understanding of freedom, rights, and social responsibility.

Gun Control

Disagreements about the meaning of the right to bear arms—and even disputes about the reason for the right itself—have existed since the earliest days of the republic. John Adams, a leader of the Revolution and second President of the United States, viewed the unregulated use of firearms by citizens to be dangerous to liberty, a position he put forth in A Defence of the Constitutions of Government of the United States *(1787–88).*

To suppose arms in the hands of citizens, to be used at individual discretion, except in private self-defense, or by partial orders of towns, countries or districts of a state, is to demolish every constitution, and lay the laws prostrate, so that liberty can be enjoyed by no man; it is a dissolution of the government. The fundamental law of the militia is, that it be created, directed and commanded by the laws, and ever for the support of the laws.

Joseph Story was a Supreme Court justice who served on the Court from 1811 until 1845. In his Commentaries on the Constitution *(1833), he ties an armed citizenry to the defense of liberty but only through a regulated militia, a body similar to the modern National Guard but one in which all able-bodied men had to serve.*

The importance of this article will scarcely be doubted by any persons, who have duly reflected upon the subject. The militia is the natural defence of a free country against sudden foreign invasions, domestic insurrections, and domestic usurpations of power by rules. It is against sound policy for a free people to keep up large military establishments and standing armies in time of peace, both from the enormous expenses, with which they are attended, and the facile means, which they afford to ambitious and unprincipled rulers, to subvert the government or trample upon the right of the people. The right of the citizens to keep and bear arms has justly been considered, as the palladium of the liberties of a republic: since it offers a strong moral check against the usurpation and arbitrary power of rulers; and will generally, even if these are successful in the first instance, enable the people to resist and triumph over them. And yet, though this truth would seem so undeniable, it cannot be disguised, that among the American people there is a growing indifference to any system of militia discipline, and a strong disposition, from a sense of its burthens, to be rid of all regulations. How it is practicable to keep the people duly armed without some organization, it is difficult to see. There is certainly no small danger, that indifference may lead to disgust, and disgust to contempt; and thus gradually undermine all the protection intended by this clause of our national bill of rights.

CHAPTER 24

The Right to Property

Few rights have been more prominent throughout American history than property rights. The drive to settle North America was above all an attempt to exploit the economic potential of a new world, especially its vast tracts of land. Even individuals who came to escape political or religious persecution hoped for financial reward. But the ownership of property was not an end in itself. It was a right that protected liberty, which is why it appears in the Fifth Amendment as a restraint on governmental power: "No person shall be...deprived of life, liberty, or property without due process of law; nor shall private property be taken for public use, without just compensation."

Colonists considered private ownership of property to be a birthright of Englishmen. They associated it with the time-honored guarantees of the Magna Carta (1215), which secured the rights of owners against seizure of their property without due process of law. As early as 1657, a Massachusetts court recognized as "a fundamental law" the principle that property could not be taken from another person or used "without his owne free consent." John Locke, the seventeenth-century English political philosopher, powerfully reinforced this colonial attachment to property in his *Second Treatise on Government.* He argued that government was based on a compact between the people and their rulers. Rulers agreed to protect the natural rights of the people in exchange for the authority to govern. One of these natural rights was the ability to own and control property. That right was not absolute, however. Government could regulate the use of private property, especially to prevent it from being used in a way that threatened public health and safety. It could also seize property without the owner's consent if the property was required for a legitimate public use. However, this power, known as eminent domain, required government to offer fair payment to the property owner.

The centrality of property rights to the American conception of liberty can scarcely be exaggerated: "The right of property," Arthur Lee of Virginia wrote in *An Appeal to the Justice and Interests of the People of Great Britain* (1775), "is the guardian of every other right, and to deprive a people of this, is in fact to deprive them of their liberty." For this reason, the framers of the Constitution provided numerous safeguards for property. They limited the ability of the federal government to tax land and granted Congress the authority to regulate interstate and foreign commerce, as well as to protect intellectual property, such as books and inventions. States were forbidden from enacting any law "impairing the obligations of contracts." But the document did not provide a general right to property, just as it did not list other rights Americans considered essential. The Bill of Rights remedied this problem. The Fifth Amendment contained two important clauses designed to guarantee property rights: no property could be taken without due process of law, and owners must be compensated if property was taken under the government's power of eminent domain. These rights provided a buffer protecting individuals from arbitrary government. Vice President John Adams in an essay, *Discourses on Davila* (1791), summed up the view of a new American creed: "Property must be secured or liberty cannot exist."

The strong connection between liberty and property caused early nineteenth-century lawmakers to place a premium on the protection of property rights. Some judges went so far as to declare them natural rights—the term they used was "vested rights"—that existed before constitutions and therefore limited all governments. This view justified striking down any limitation a legislature might place on the enjoyment of private property. No one disagreed that government could regulate the use of property to protect the public health and safety, but judges looked skeptically at any law or action that interfered unduly with property rights.

By the 1830s, however, the disadvantage of treating property rights as sacred was apparent to many observers. The issue came to its head when legislators attempted to spur competition in transportation, especially in the building of roads and bridges. During the first decades of nationhood, state and federal governments sought to avoid taxes as much as possible in an effort to limit the power of government. One consequence of this policy was a decision to grant private investors the right to collect tolls (fees) for long periods of time, sometimes for as much as a century, if they would build roads and bridges for public use. As the population grew and demands for new transportation routes increased, legislators offered charters, or grants of authority, to companies who would provide additional roads and bridges. Some of these new routes and structures competed directly with the older toll roads and bridges. The owners of the long-established transportation companies protested that this new competition was destroying the value of their property in violation of their contract.

In 1837, the U.S. Supreme Court ruled on this claim in one of the most important property rights cases of the nineteenth century. Five decades earlier, in 1785, Massachusetts had authorized the Charles River Bridge Company to build a toll bridge over the Charles River between Boston and Charlestown. Before this charter expired, the legislature empowered the Warren Bridge Company to build a second bridge, with the provision that it could collect tolls only until its construction costs were paid. Then, it would become free. Because a toll bridge cannot compete successfully with a free bridge, the Charles River Bridge Company claimed that the state had violated the charter, a legal contract, and destroyed the value of its property. The Supreme Court ruled in *Charles River Bridge* v. *Warren Bridge* (1837) that, although the Constitution prohibited states from violating contracts, nothing in the Charles River Bridge charter stated that the grant was exclusive. Writing for the Court, Chief Justice Roger B. Taney emphasized that the language of contracts must be interpreted strictly, or precisely. States could regulate property in the public interest unless the language of a charter explicitly prohibited it. Otherwise, he explained, no one would invest in new transportation or new technologies until the old charters ran their course. Economic progress at times required that existing property rights had to be destroyed to make room for innovation and improvement. Such was the price of progress.

VIEW OF THE NEW LAND IN 1828.

The late nineteenth century brought a dramatically different view of this issue. It was an age of industrial monopoly, and the Supreme Court interpreted the due process clause of the Fourteenth Amendment to sharply curtail the authority of states to regulate or control the use of property. In what came to be known as economic due process, the Court decided that legislatures could not pass unreasonable restrictions on property, such as regulating the prices a utility company or railroad could charge. Judges, not elected representatives, would determine what was reasonable. The justices also ruled that courts, not legislatures, would determine fair compensation for any property taken for public use under the state's power of eminent domain. The result was unprecedented protection of property rights—and a decrease in the ability of government to challenge monopolies or regulate businesses for the public good.

The Great Depression of the 1930s changed this approach to the rights of property. With as many as one-third of Americans out of work, the Supreme Court could not resist for long the demand that government had a duty to protect people from economic disaster. The New Deal was President Franklin Roosevelt's plan to stimulate the economy and provide economic support, such as jobs and welfare, to Americans hurt by the depression. It required much

The building of a second bridge over the Charles River, connecting Boston and Charlestown, Massachusetts, raised issues of property rights and contract interpretation. In Charles River Bridge v. Warren Bridge *(1837), the Supreme Court favored economic progress and innovation by interpreting contracts in favor of the public interest whenever their terms were unclear. This case removed legal obstacles to new forms of property, such as railroads, and encouraged the innovative practices that made the United States an economic power by the end of the nineteenth century.*

"In no other country in the world is the love of property keener or more alert than in the United States, and nowhere else does the majority display less inclination toward doctrines which in any way threaten the way property is owned."

—Alexis de Tocqueville, *Democracy in America* (1835)

Susette Kelo and her neighbors in New London, Connecticut, rally at City Hall in July 2005 in support of homeowners destined to lose their homes as a result of the Kelo *decision. In a compromise suggested by Kelo and accepted a year later by the city, her home would be saved and moved to another location. "I will be able to continue living in the home that means so much to me, with a real title to my property," she said.*

greater government involvement in the economy than was traditional. In the early 1930s, the Supreme Court ruled that these programs were unconstitutional; the justices struck down governmental efforts to control prices and set wages, for example, as violations of property rights, especially freedom of contract. By 1938, however, public support for the New Deal—and the retirement of some justices—persuaded the Court to change its stance. Instead of blocking federal laws to reform the economy, the justices adopted a position that Congress could act freely in economic matters under its authority to regulate interstate commerce if it believed good reasons existed to do so. Under this broad standard, property rights virtually disappeared from the Court's agenda. Once considered a right essential to liberty, property rights were now secondary to the desire to promote economic security and restrain too-powerful corporations. A wide array of laws and agencies sharply curtailed the unfettered private use of property in the name of a greater public good. The legal compass had swung almost 180 degrees from the Court's position in the late nineteenth and early twentieth centuries. It was a constitutional revolution of the first order.

In the 1980s and 1990s, the Supreme Court began to trim what had become vast congressional power to control the economy and the use of property. It especially gave more discretion to states to adopt their own standards in this area. It was not long, however, before the rights of property and the power of government came into conflict. The most volatile issues centered on the state's use of eminent domain to condemn property and turn it to private uses that claimed to have a public benefit. A case from Connecticut brought the conflict into stark focus—and resulted in a Supreme Court and a nation equally divided over where to draw the line between the power of government and the rights of property owners.

Susette Kelo, a registered nurse in New London, Connecticut, dreamed of owning an older house near water, so her 1997 purchase of a modest Victorian cottage on the Thames River, near its junction with Long Island Sound, seemed ideal. The ninety-year-old house was in reasonably good condition, and it had a small front yard for her flowers and a place to watch the ever-changing river from her front window. It was in the neighborhood known as Fort Trumbull, an area of older homes and families who had lived there for decades. Down the street from her was a house built in 1895, and a nearby family had been in the neighborhood for generations, dating to the time when William McKinley was President. A number of houses had been owned by the same families for several generations. Susette Kelo's next-door neighbor, for example, lived in the house once owned by his grandmother, who had started a garden the family still maintained. As Kelo and her husband restored their pink house, she realized how special her neighborhood was and how much potential it had for revitalization that would preserve its historic character.

Soon after she moved in, however, Kelo's world started to unravel. New London, Connecticut, once a prosperous city, had recently fallen on hard times. The federal government closed its 1,500-employee Naval Undersea Warfare Center in 1996, and by 1998, the city's unemployment rate was the highest in the state. It also was hemorrhaging population; New London's 24,000 residents was its lowest total since the 1920s. Then salvation arrived, or so it seemed, when a giant pharmaceutical company, Pfizer, began construction of a $300 million research facility on the outskirts of Fort Trumbull. Believing Pfizer's commitment offered an opportunity for a wider economic revival, New London asked its economic development corporation, a private nonprofit organization, to create a plan to revitalize the surrounding area, including the Fort Trumbull neighborhood.

The resulting plan was impressive: it envisioned a resort and conference center, a new state park, an upscale housing development, an office park, and high-end shopping centers. Enthusiastic city and state leaders approved the plan and set out to acquire land in Fort Trumbull. The development corporation offered to purchase the 115 houses in the neighborhood, and all but fifteen residents agreed to sell. For the holdouts, the issue was both personal and a matter of principle: "This is the second time someone from my family may have to move because the government wants to take their home for another private party," one resident said. "If that can happen to us twice, it can happen to anyone, anywhere, not just here in Connecticut. Basically, it's homeowner beware."

Finally, the city tired of negotiating. It assigned its power of eminent domain to the economic development corporation, which moved quickly to condemn the fifteen remaining properties. No one claimed the area was blighted or neglected, typical reasons for the use of eminent domain; the city wanted the land solely because it was in the redevelopment area. Kelo and the other homeowners sued the city, claiming that its use of eminent domain violated the Fifth and Fourteenth Amendments. The planned development, they argued, benefited private interests. In fact, while the case was pending, the redevelopment corporation offered a private company a ninety-nine-year lease on the property for an annual rent of one dollar a year. Where was the public purpose the amendments required?

Kelo v. *City of New London* was the first major eminent domain case to make it to the Supreme Court since the 1980s. The stakes were high because New London was not alone in its willingness to exercise eminent domain on behalf of private developers. It was an innovative use of government's power; eminent domain traditionally had allowed government to seize land for clearly public purposes, such as building a highway or a water treatment plant or ridding an area of blight. But many governments, eager to spur economic growth, were now pursuing similar strategies. If the justices sided with Susette Kelo and her fellow plaintiffs, their decision might threaten the economic revitalization of many distressed areas. But if they supported the city, would they not be requiring a few unfortunate property owners to sacrifice their rights for the benefit of wealthy private investors?

In 2005, the justices upheld the city's right to use eminent domain to support its economic development strategy, but the decision revealed a deeply divided court. Five justices agreed that government could not take property from one private party and transfer it to another private entity, even if it paid just compensation, but New London had used the seized property for a public purpose, they concluded. The new jobs and increased tax revenue promised by the developers met the constitutional requirements of public use; the primary benefit of the development would be to the community at large, they found,

HANDS OFF My Home

Citizens Fighting Eminent Domain Abuse
www.CastleCoalition.org

The Castle Coalition is a national grassroots property rights activism project organized by the Institute for Justice, the not-for-profit legal organization that represented Susette Kelo. It helps homeowners and small business owners protect themselves against governments and developers who seek to take their property through eminent domain.

even though the private investors in the project might profit from it as well. The concept of public welfare is broad and inclusive, the majority ruled, and it was not the Court's job to interfere with the judgment of public officials as to how best to serve public needs.

The four dissenting justices condemned the majority's conclusion. The majority's standard, Justice Sandra Day O'Connor warned, removed any meaningful distinction between public and private and effectively "delete[s] the words 'public use' from . . . the Fifth Amendment." It put all private property at risk: "Under the banner of economic development, all private property is now vulnerable to being taken and transferred to another private owner, so long as it might be upgraded." She dismissed the need to defer to elected officials. If they were the sole judge of what constituted public use, then the Fifth Amendment's restriction would be merely "hortatory fluff." The framers intended the amendment to protect individuals against arbitrary actions of government. Without this protection, "nothing is to prevent the state from replacing any Motel 6 with a Ritz-Carlton, any home with a shopping mall, or any farm with a factory." The result of the Court's decision would be to make government a reverse Robin Hood—taking from the poor to give to the rich. "The Founders," O'Connor concluded, "could not have intended such a perverse result."

Susette Kelo and her neighbors lost their battle, but perhaps not the war. Public outrage over the decision forced a moratorium on eviction notices while the Connecticut legislature and governor considered a remedy. "The abuse of eminent domain has become a national plague," wrote the *Boston Globe* in an editorial that reflected national sentiment. Within weeks, state legislatures across the country received pressure to strengthen laws protecting homeowners. By April 2006, twelve states had prohibited the use of eminent domain for private development, and similar proposals were being considered by twenty-seven other states. Only five states that took up the measure failed to pass a restriction. Clearly, *Kelo* v. *New London* had provoked a response in favor of stronger protections for property rights, a response that resulted from the involvement of citizens in democratic government.

This result, no doubt, would have pleased the founders, who universally accepted both the right to property and citizen participation in government as fundamental to liberty. But it left unanswered a wide array of questions related to the potential conflict between the right of individuals to enjoy their property and the public desire that government promote economic growth and protect jobs. This latter concern stems from one of the most devastating economic episodes in American history, the Great Depression. More recently, threats to financial security have come from the loss of jobs to lower-cost labor markets and the rise of Asia as an economic powerhouse. We want government to have enough power to act in the public's economic interests yet not enough power to threaten private property rights. Where is the balance point between individual property rights and economic security?

In this desire, we are not as far from the framers of the Constitution as we might imagine. We live in a remarkably different economic world in many ways, yet the fundamental issues are similar. We believe, as did the founding generation, that widespread property ownership encourages economic self-sufficiency and political independence. We affirm, as they did, that protection of private property is a hallmark of a good society. Yet we are also aware of the need to promote the general welfare, the pledge contained in the preamble to the Constitution, and we worry that unbridled economic power or unrestrained competition threatens our liberty as much as concentrated governmental power. The revolutionary generation was most concerned about the restraint of power in any form, although they saw it most gravely threatened by government. We, too, worry about how best to limit power, but we have come to view government as an effective counterbalance to corporate power.

Constitutional protection for the rights of property, we have learned, is necessary for both a healthy democracy and a healthy economy. The ability to buy, sell, and protect property not only constitutes the legal foundation of our free-market economy, but it also helps to secure the financial investments required for economic growth. The recognition of property rights also promotes individual liberty by increasing our economic independence, thus helping us resist interference in our lives from overbearing government or too powerful corporations. With economic independence and security, we are freer to participate fully in a democratic society. We may no longer treat property rights as the guardian of every other right, but we continue to value the economic freedom that enables us to fulfill our duty as citizens more effectively, including our obligation to protect liberty.

The Preservation of Property

John Locke was an English political philosopher whose writings greatly influenced the American revolutionaries. Locke believed that governments had an obligation to protect the individual's right to life, liberty, and property, all of which he viewed as natural rights, or rights that existed in a state of nature that predated societies or government. In his Second Treatise on Government *(1689), he also argued that people in this state of nature voluntarily entered a social compact, in which they agreed to give up some of their individual autonomy to government in exchange for its protection of their rights. In the Declaration of Independence, Thomas Jefferson changed Locke's formula of "life, liberty, and property" to "life, liberty, and the pursuit of happiness," but this modification did not diminish the strong American identification of the right to property as an essential liberty.*

The *Supream Power cannot take* from any Man any part of his *Property* without his consent. For the preservation of Property being the end of Government, and that for which Men enter into Society, it necessarily supposes and requires, that the People should *have Property*, without which they must be suppos'd to lose that by entring into Society, which was the end for which they entered into it, too gross an absurdity for any Man to own. . . .

'Tis true, Governments cannot be supported without great Charge, and 'tis fit every one who enjoys his share of the Protection, should pay out of his Estate his proportion for the maintenance of it. But still it must be with his own Consent, *i.e.* the Consent of the Majority, giving it either by themselves, or their Representatives chosen by them. For if any one shall claim a *Power to lay* and levy *Taxes* on the People, by his own Authority, and without such consent of the People, he thereby invades the *Fundamental Law of Property*, and subverts the end of Government. For what property have I in that which another may by right take, when he pleases to himself?

The Rights of the Community

Charles River Bridge v. Warren Bridge (1837) was one of the most important property rights cases in American history. In refusing to interpret a previous grant by the Massachusetts legislature as conferring a monopoly to the Charles River Bridge Company, the Court opened the way for competition in building bridges across the Charles River in Boston. Although Chief Justice Roger B. Taney, writing for the 4-to-3 majority, stated that although "the rights of private property must be sacredly guarded, . . . the object and end of all government is to promote the happiness and prosperity of the community." The Court's decision defined property rights as subordinate to the public interest and paved the way for faster incorporation of new technologies into American society.

But the object and end of all government is to promote the happiness and prosperity of the community by which it is established; and it can never be assumed, that the government intended to diminish its power of accomplishing the end for which it was created. And in a country like ours, free, active and enterprising, continually advancing in numbers and wealth, new channels of communication are daily found necessary, both for travel and trade, and are essential to the comfort, convenience and prosperity of the people. A state ought never to be presumed to surrender this power, because, like the taxing power, the whole community have an interest in preserving it undiminished. And when a corporation alleges, that a state has surrendered, for seventy years, its power of improvement and public accommodation, in a great and important line of travel, along which a vast number of its citizens must daily pass, the community have a right to insist, in the language of this court, above quoted, "that its abandonment ought not to be presumed, in a case, in which the deliberate purpose of the state to abandon it does not appear." The continued existence of a government would be of no great value, if, by implications and presumptions, it was disarmed of the powers necessary to accomplish the ends of its creation, and the functions it was designed to perform, transferred to the hands of privileged corporations. . . . No one will question, that the interests of the great body of the people of the state, would, in this instance, be affected by the surrender of this great line of travel to a single corporation, with the right to exact toll, and exclude competition, for seventy years. While the rights of private property are sacredly guarded, we must not forget, that the community also have rights, and that the happiness and well-being of every citizen depends on their faithful preservation. . . .

And what would be the fruits of this doctrine of implied contracts, on the part of the states, and of property in a line of travel, by a corporation, if it would now be sanctioned by this court? To what results would it lead us? If it is to be found in the charter to this bridge, the same process of reasoning must discover it, in the various acts which have been passed, within the last forty years, for turnpike companies. And what is to be the extent of the privileges of exclusion on the different sides of the road? . . . Let it once be understood, that such charters carry with them these implied contracts, and give this unknown and undefined property in a line of traveling; and you will soon find the old turnpike corporations awakening from their sleep, and calling upon this court to put down the improvements which have taken their place. The millions of property which have been invested in railroads and canals, upon lines of travel which had been before occupied by turnpike corporations, will be put in jeopardy. We shall be thrown back to the improvements of the last century, and obliged to stand still, until the claims of the old turnpike corporations shall be satisfied; and they shall consent to permit these states to avail themselves of the lights of modern science, and to partake of the benefit of those improvements which are now adding to the wealth and prosperity, and the convenience and comfort, of every other part of the civilized world.

"Common Reason and Legal Interpretation"

Justice Joseph Story, in his dissent in Charles River Bridge v. Warren Bridge *(1837), insisted that the grant to the Charles River Bridge Company was a public contract protected by the Constitution's contract clause in Article 1, Section 10: "No State...shall pass any Law impairing the Obligation of Contracts." He disagreed with the majority opinion that property rights were subordinate to the public interest.*

I maintain, that, upon the principles of common reason and legal interpretation, the present grant carries with it a necessary implication, that the legislature shall do no act to destroy or essentially to impair the franchise; that...there is an implied agreement that the state will not grant another bridge between Boston and Charlestown, so near as to draw away the custom from the old one; and... that there is an implied agreement of the state to grant the undisturbed use of the bridge and its tolls, so far as respects any acts of its own, or of any persons acting under its authority....Where the thing is given, the incidents, without which it cannot be enjoyed, are also given....I maintain, that a different doctrine is utterly repugnant to all the principles of the common law, applicable to all franchises of a like

nature; and that we must overturn some of the best securities of the rights of property, before it can be established. I maintain, that the common law is the birthright of every citizen of Massachusetts....I maintain, that under the principles of the common law, there exists no more right in the legislature of Massachusetts, to erect the Warren bridge, to the ruin of the franchise of the Charles River bridge, than exists to transfer the latter to the former, or to authorize the former to demolish the latter. If the legislature does not mean in its grant to give any exclusive rights, let it say so, expressly, directly, and in terms admitting of no misconstruction. The grantees will then take at their peril, and must abide the results of their overweening confidence, indiscretion and zeal.

CHAPTER 25

The Future of Our Rights

At a summit of world leaders in 2006, the chancellor of Austria noted that the United States historically had led the world in advancing "democracy, liberty, and individual rights." The remark was so widely accepted that it was a commonplace and quickly forgotten. In fact, the ordinary acceptance of the comment is what should draw our attention. It is remarkable because it identifies three key concepts of free societies—democracy, liberty, and individual rights—and takes their connections for granted. American history has convinced us that these three ideas are essential to freedom itself and that each depends upon the other for its fullest expression. The mention of individual rights especially testifies to their importance as both symbol and substance of our status as free people.

We often speak of the expansion of individual rights over time, and with good reason. History generally supports the view that we have greater individual freedom now than at any time in our past. This conclusion, however, obscures more than it reveals. Not only does it hide the long struggle to secure these individual liberties, but it also suggests more modern agreement on the meaning of these rights than exists in fact. The history of our rights is not a simple story, and the future of our rights no doubt will be equally complex.

Today, we tend to associate the development of rights with judicial decisions, especially rulings of the U.S. Supreme Court. We also view individual liberty primarily through the lens of the federal Bill of Rights. This perspective is more accurate now than it was earlier in our history, but it is incomplete. The rights revolution of the 1960s, especially decisions of the Supreme Court under Chief Justice Earl Warren, focused attention on the courts as guardians of our freedom. It identified much of the Bill of Rights, applied to states through the Fourteenth Amendment, as the primary source of our rights. Largely forgotten were two older traditions. The first looked to multiple sources—natural law, federalism, state constitutions, and legislative acts, among others—as equally important to the Bill of Rights in the growth of individual liberty. The other vested responsibility for individual liberty in all our political institutions, not courts alone.

The twenty-first century may witness a return to patterns established earlier in American history. Judges follow the election returns, an old saying goes, and over the past two decades, the American electorate generally has become more conservative politically and less willing to support judicial expansion of rights. In a democracy, unpopular laws usually cannot exist for long; the same is true for court decisions. Consider the right to abortion, which the Supreme Court concluded was part of the constitutionally protected right of privacy in *Roe* v. *Wade* (1973). Most opinion polls reveal support for a woman's right to choose an abortion, especially in cases of rape or incest or when necessary to protect a woman's life or health, but the polls also find support for some restrictions of this right. One result has been legislative regulation of the practice of abortion, such as laws that require parental notification for women under a

"Any citizen in this country is entitled to equality before the law; to equality of education; to equality at earning a living, as far as his abilities have made it possible for him to do; to equality of participation in government so that he or she may register their opinion in just the way that any other citizens do.

—Eleanor Roosevelt, "Civil Liberties—The Individual and the Community," address to Chicago Civil Liberties Committee, March 4, 1940 certain age. Although the Supreme Court has accepted many of these restrictions, it has repeatedly reaffirmed the right itself. More recently, some states have challenged *Roe* by passing laws to prohibit abortions completely. It remains unclear whether a different set of justices will reconsider the Supreme Court's earlier decision in the face of such repeated challenges. Or take the various anti-flag-burning laws passed after *Texas* v. *Johnson*, the 1989 case in which the justices ruled that burning the American flag was a protected form of free speech. Opponents are seeking to overturn the Court's decision by a constitutional amendment giving Congress the power to punish flag desecration. In 2006, Congress came within one vote in the Senate of sending the measure to the states for ratification.

These cases and countless others reveal that we are in a period of unusually intense public debate about what our rights are and who decides what they should be. The focus of the debate is shifting to some degree from the courts to the legislature. A reversal of *Roe* v. *Wade* would redefine the meaning of a federally protected right to privacy, but it would not end a woman's right to choose an abortion in states where the right is protected by state law or by the state constitution. Some observers believe a reversal would increase pressure on state lawmakers to wrestle with this issue, as they did in the days before *Roe*. Should a flag amendment be adopted, any law to protect the flag still must pass Congress and be signed by the President. In both examples, the question of rights would become a matter for majority decision. Defining liberty in these areas would be a political issue, not a judicial one.

Some commentators believe this result would be a good thing because it would place the question of rights at the center of our political life as a nation. We would have to debate and decide openly what rights we are willing to live by, thus lending popular support to whatever decision we reach about our catalog of individual liberties. Although this result certainly seems democratic, it also raises a question about which is most important, majority rule or minority rights. In our constitutional system, we believe some rights are fundamental; they are not subject to majority rule because they protect the ability of all people to participate in the political process, a basic requirement in a democracy in which the people at large are the ultimate authority. The rights of speech, religion, press, and assembly are central to the democratic process itself. Defining them according to the will of a majority limits the ability of a minority to seek a change in law or practice. In similar fashion, our experience has taught us the danger of making the rights of the accused or the rights of those with limited political power, such as youth or the poor, subject to majority rule. Here, the concern is not to protect citizen participation in decision making but to ensure fair and equal treatment.

Even with the recognition that certain rights are fundamental, how far these safeguards extend may be subject to legitimate debate and legislative action. Consider the right of a criminal defendant to have the advice of counsel. We now deem it vitally important to the guarantee of a fair trial, and as a matter of right we assign counsel at public expense to poor defendants who face a loss of liberty. But is the right to counsel unlimited? Should it apply to all appeals, no matter how many or how frivolous? Should a defendant have a

"Some might find it a bit disconcerting to consider that the responsibility for protecting our Constitution rests not just on judges but on a host of others as well. The responsibility is shared by state and federal legislators considering the constitutionality of proposed laws; by litigants who must marshal the time, money, and hope to take cases to court; by political officeholders (including the President himself) who must see that the Court's rulings are put into practice; and by citizens, who ultimately must determine the Nation's response to each major issue."

—Justice Sandra Day O'Connor, speech at the dedication
of the National Constitution Center, Philadelphia (2003)

right, at state expense, to as many lawyers as the prosecution has on its team? To whatever lawyer the defendant wants to represent him? What about the issue of effectiveness of the counsel? Few people would suggest that poor defendants be assigned incompetent attorneys, but does the right to counsel mean that the defendant's lawyer must be as well qualified as the state's attorney? The answers to these questions may impose additional expense on taxpayers, so it is not unreasonable to put them up to legislative debate—unless, of course, they are central to the meaning of the right to counsel itself.

The debate about majority rule and minority rights is perennial in American history. Democratic principles suggest that rights are best advanced and protected by majorities, but a constitution represents the permanent or fundamental will of all the people. The Bill of Rights especially represents the decision of the founding generation to protect the rights of the minority from a majority, which, in their experience, could be oppressive or tyrannical. Our history has proven their concerns to be well-founded. At one time in our past,

Neo-Nazis, members of the National Socialist Movement, give the Hitler salute at a rally outside the state capitol in Lansing, Michigan, in April 2006. They were protesting illegal immigration and exercising their free speech right protected by the First Amendment.

women and ethnic and racial minorities did not have equal protection of the laws, often because a democratic majority did not consider them worthy of this constitutional promise.

We accept in theory the need to protect individuals from oppressive majorities because we all understand that each of us may be in the minority on some issue or in some circumstance. The harder questions we face are about what our rights mean in practice, especially what the limits are on our individual liberty. We have confronted this issue most directly in debates over laws passed in response to the terrorist attacks of September 11, 2001. The USA PATRIOT Act of 2001, for example, brought needed change to our national intelligence agencies, especially improving coordination among intelligence agencies, but it also raised concerns about the future of constitutional safeguards, such as habeas corpus or the warrant requirements for search and seizure. Another response to 9/11 was a system of military courts operating solely within the executive branch, not subject to judicial review, to handle suspected terrorists. Many Americans saw nothing wrong with establishing commissions to try foreign suspects, but they were uncomfortable with abandoning all protections for the accused or denying judicial oversight. They were also wary of lessening legislative oversight of the executive branch. The problem is an old one: how do we balance our need for security with protection of our rights? The United States has faced the question in each national crisis, and Americans have, in retrospect, regretted some of the decisions, as in the case of internment for Japanese Americans during World War II. The larger issue is, in fact, the same one faced by the founding generation: how can we give government sufficient power to meet its responsibilities, including its obligation to keep us safe, and yet not give it power to threaten our liberty?

Most often, we have answered this question not by an appeal to the majority or to the legislature but rather by a reliance on courts to maintain our constitutional promises. Even when most concerned with our security, Americans have kept the courts open so that individual citizens can assert their claims that a right has been denied. Some people protest that such openness leads us to seek protection only in the courts rather than through the political process. An overreliance on courts to guard our liberties indeed may be one result, but as often an alert and independent judiciary has served as the best protector of our rights, much as James Madison predicted. It was in open courts with judges committed to the Constitution, he believed, that we could best balance our fundamental liberties, our need for security, and our commitment to the rule of democratic majorities.

These issues of liberty, security, and democracy will not fade in the next decade, but neither will they be our sole concern as we consider the future of our rights. New conditions and new expectations undoubtedly will lead to a demand for more or less individual liberty. We live in a world quite different from that of our parents, and we are far removed from the one inhabited by the founding generation. The Internet, still relatively new, already has transformed our society, as have other innovative technologies. We now participate in a global economy to an extent unknown in our past; never has the movement of people, goods, and ideas been so easy. We have embraced much of what has resulted, but already we are seeing how these changes challenge our traditional understanding of individual rights. For example, we have long resisted government interference with the freedom of press and speech, but now many people worry about the ready access children have to adult publications or to materials that promote violence or hatred. In an earlier day, we could easily remove these materials from the reach of minors—for example, we could keep them off library shelves—but it is all too easy to get past the parental controls offered by Internet providers. Other people are concerned about the threat new technologies pose to our privacy. Law enforcement officers can go on the Web and conduct searches previously imaginable only in futurist novels. Do their actions violate our constitutional protections under the Fourth Amendment? What about the harvesting of our private data for commercial purposes, to create, say, a targeted marketing campaign based on our online viewing habits? Does it undercut our expectations of privacy? In an increasingly wired world, how do we balance our commitment to an open exchange of information with protection of our privacy and other important values?

Advances in technology do not pose the only challenges to our understanding of individual rights; some people believe modern social and economic conditions require the creation of new rights or the recognition of rights implied by the Constitution. The world economy demands highly educated workforces— and without adequate education, the gap between rich and poor only grows wider—but we have never recognized education as a fundamental right of American citizenship. Education traditionally has been a state responsibility, and a number of states, but not all, have recognized this right as part of their constitutions. One result has been vastly unequal support of education among and even within states, with children in poorer districts receiving inferior educations because of lack of funding. Is it time to create a national right to education to guarantee equality, or is access to a quality education more an issue for state and national policies than a fundamental right? The same questions arise with health care. Do all citizens have a right to quality health care, or is this issue one that should be addressed instead through the political process or the marketplace? We can list countless other potential rights: rights to a clean environment or to a living wage or job security are only a few other rights claims that people have made over the past few decades. Today, there is no national consensus to support the creation of new rights to education, health

"The Constitution is not a document designed to solve the problems of a community at any level—local, state, or national. Rather it is a document that trusts people to solve those problems themselves. And it creates a framework for a government that will help them to do so. That framework foresees democratically determined solutions, protective of the individual's basic liberties."

—Justice Stephen Breyer, *Active Liberty: Interpreting Our Democratic Constitution* (2005)

At the start of the twenty-first century, many Americans, especially the elderly, struggle to pay for health care. As people live longer, and as costs for drugs and life-saving procedures increase, Americans will continue to debate whether a right to health care, among other potential rights, is an essential one that should be guaranteed by the government.

care, environmental cleanliness, or jobs, but the same conclusion was true in the 1830s about citizenship and equality for African Americans.

Even without the creation of new rights, courts and legislatures will continue to grapple with unanswered questions about constitutionally protected liberties. Governments at all levels often provide services through private agencies, including faith-based or religious organizations. Does government funding of faith-based social services, say a food bank or health clinic, violate the traditional understanding of a separation between church and state? If not, may faith-based organizations that receive government funding refuse to hire someone who does not share the organization's beliefs? May they offer favored treatment or more services to people who believe as they do? Or consider these questions: Do federal and state laws regulating how much political candidates can spend violate their freedom of speech? Does freedom of the press protect confidential sources of journalists? Congress can restrict indecent and obscene speech that is available to everyone in radio and television broadcasts, but should the same restrictions apply to paid services, such as cable channels, satellite radio, and broadband Internet? Can we outlaw hate crimes—can we ban the "n" word, for example without violating our commitment to free speech? These questions are not hypothetical. Even now, state and federal lawmakers are debating these issues, and cases are winding their way through courts across the nation.

If history is any guide, we always will confront questions and controversy about our individual rights. The language used by the Constitution and Bill of Rights is clear enough, but its meaning is often elusive. We know the words in the phrase "due process of law" but what the phrase means is not immediately apparent. It is not an empty vessel to be filled with whatever meaning we wish to assign—due process has a long history, after all, that helps us define it—but it is flexible and capable of change. Many observers have identified this characteristic as the genius of our fundamental law. We have repeatedly invested constitutional words with new substance. For example, due process at one time simply required government to follow its own laws in administering justice. People believed this practice would ensure fairness. What if government followed the law, but the result was unfair? This circumstance occurred in the 1930s in the Scottsboro case, when white officials in Alabama observed the forms required by law but denied any meaningful due process to the poor black defendants accused of rape. Today, we give due process a different and more powerful meaning. Procedure remains important, but now we have safeguards to ensure that procedures are actually fair in practice. The right to trial by jury, for instance, no longer means we can select jurors from only one racial or ethnic category, as was once the case.

We could list any number of unresolved rights and new claims of individual liberties—but so, too, could every preceding generation. When Americans celebrated the bicentennial of the Constitution in 1987, some commentators seized on the words in the preamble, "in order to form a more perfect union," and proclaimed, as Chief Justice Warren Burger did, that "the Declaration of Independence was the promise [of liberty]: the Constitution was the fulfillment." Others were uncomfortable with too much veneration of the nation's founding document. Burger's colleague on the bench, Justice Thurgood Marshall, the first African American to sit on the nation's highest bench, responded that "the government [the founders] devised was defective from the start, requiring several amendments, a civil war, and momentous social transformation to attain the system of constitutional government, and respect for individual freedoms and human rights, that we hold as fundamental today."

Change has been a constant theme of our constitutional experience. We have sought to fulfill the founding generation's promise to form a more prefect union, but who is responsible for these changes? Here, the preamble again is our guide. It begins, "We the people." We, not they. Rights are claims of liberty made by any of us, regardless of age or circumstance. When twelve-year-old Lillian Gobitas refused to salute the American flag because of her religion, she was claiming a right essential to her freedom—and ours. When an Iowa eighth grader, Mary Beth Tinker, wore an armband to protest the Vietnam War, she was claiming her right to speak—and ours. When the Chinese immigrant Yick Wo refused to accept the consequences of a discriminatory law, he was demanding his right to equal treatment—and ours. When Gerald Gault insisted on confronting his accuser in juvenile court, he was claiming his constitutional protections—and ours. In a democracy, we all are responsible for advancing and defending liberty and the individual rights that safeguard it.

It is inevitable that our rights will acquire new interpretation in future years and that we will identify new rights essential to our liberty. Rights gain meaning from experience, and undoubtedly they will continue to do so. We can expect disagreement on the proper balance between order and liberty, on the role of courts and legislatures in defining rights, on questions of majority rule versus minority rights, and on the interpretation of constitutional phrases such as "due process" and "equal protection." What should be reassuring, however, is the debate itself, which makes real the idea of popular democracy and revitalizes the American commitment to a society governed by law. We cannot seek to restore the original expression of our rights, even if it were possible to do so. The founders did not leave us a dead legacy, one incapable of growth, but rather with a living framework that we can make our own. Each time we claim our rights, we act on this inheritance and in the process reaffirm the success of America's great experiment in liberty.

The Four Freedoms

In 1941, the nation was emerging from the Great Depression and World War II was already underway in Europe, a war the United States would join less than a year later. In his address to Congress, Roosevelt spoke about the threat to democracy posed by Nazi Germany, and he proposed that the nation commit itself to securing four essential freedoms throughout the world. The first two freedoms—speech and religion—were well known to Americans. But the other two freedoms—the freedom from want (economic security) and the freedom from fear—were to be new rights. In this speech, Roosevelt reminded Americans that the work of freedom—and the rights that sustain it—is never done. The Four Freedoms are engraved on the Franklin Delano Roosevelt Memorial in Washington, D.C.

In the future days, which we seek to make secure, we look forward to a world founded upon four essential human freedoms.

The first is freedom of speech and expression—everywhere in the world.

The second is freedom of every person to worship God in his own way—everywhere in the world.

The third is freedom from want—which, translated into world terms, means economic understandings which will secure to every nation a healthy peacetime life for its inhabitants—everywhere in the world.

The fourth is freedom from fear—which, translated into world terms, means a world-wide reduction of armaments to such a point and in such a thorough fashion that no nation will be in a position to commit an act of physical aggression against any neighbor—anywhere in the world.

That is no vision of a distant millennium. It is a definite basis for a kind of world attainable in our own time and generation. That kind of world is the very antithesis of the so-called new order of tyranny which the dictators seek to create with the crash of a bomb.

To that new order we oppose the greater conception—the moral order. A good society is able to face schemes of world domination and foreign revolutions alike without fear.

Since the beginning of our American history, we have been engaged in change—in a perpetual peaceful revolution—a revolution which goes on steadily, quietly adjusting itself to changing conditions—without the concentration camp or the quick-lime in the ditch. The world order which we seek is the cooperation of free countries, working together in a friendly, civilized society.

This nation has placed its destiny in the hands and heads and hearts of its millions of free men and women; and its faith in freedom under the guidance of God. Freedom means the supremacy of human rights everywhere. Our support goes to those who struggle to gain those rights or keep them. Our strength is our unity of purpose. To that high concept there can be no end save victory.

The Bill of Rights

During the debates on the adoption of the Constitution, opponents (Anti-Federalists) charged that the proposed document gave too much power to the central government and not enough protection to individual rights. They demanded a "bill of rights," and several state ratifying conventions asked for amendments to the Constitution. Other states voted to ratify with the understanding that the amendments would be offered.

On September 25, 1789, the First Congress of the United States proposed to the state legislatures twelve amendments to the Constitution. States did not ratify the first two proposed amendments, which concerned the number of constituents for each representative and the compensation of congressmen. Articles 3 to 12, however, were ratified by three-fourths of the state legislatures. They constitute the first ten amendments of the Constitution, known as the Bill of Rights.

The Conventions of a number of the States having, at the time of adopting the Constitution, expressed a desire, in order to prevent misconstruction or abuse of its powers, that further declaratory and restrictive clauses should be added, and as extending the ground of public confidence in the Government will best insure the beneficent ends of its institution;

Resolved, by the Senate and House of Representatives of the United States of America, in Congress assembled, two-thirds of both Houses concurring, that the following articles be proposed to the Legislatures of the several States, as amendments to the Constitution of the United States; all or any of which articles, when ratified by three-fourths of the said Legislatures, to be valid to all intents and purposes as part of the said Constitution, namely:

Amendment I

Congress shall make no law respecting an establishment of religion, or prohibiting the free exercise thereof; or abridging the freedom of speech, or of the press; or the right of the people peaceably to assemble, and to petition the government for a redress of grievances.

Amendment II

A well regulated militia, being necessary to the security of a free state, the right of the people to keep and bear arms, shall not be infringed.

Amendment III

No soldier shall, in time of peace be quartered in any house, without the consent of the owner, nor in time of war, but in a manner to be prescribed by law.

Amendment IV

The right of the people to be secure in their persons, houses, papers, and effects, against unreasonable searches and seizures, shall not be violated, and no warrants shall issue, but upon probable cause, supported by oath or affirmation, and particularly describing the place to be searched, and the persons or things to be seized.

Amendment V

No person shall be held to answer for a capital, or otherwise infamous crime, unless on a presentment or indictment of a grand jury, except in cases arising in the land or naval forces, or in the militia, when in actual service in time of war or public danger; nor shall any person be subject for the same offense to be twice put in jeopardy of life or limb; nor shall be compelled in any criminal case to be a witness against himself, nor be deprived of life, liberty, or property, without due process of law; nor shall private property be taken for public use, without just compensation.

Amendment VI

In all criminal prosecutions, the accused shall enjoy the right to a speedy and public trial, by an impartial jury of the state and district wherein the crime shall have been committed, which district shall have been previously ascertained by law, and to be informed of the nature and cause of the accusation; to be confronted with the witnesses against him; to have compulsory process for obtaining witnesses in his favor, and to have the assistance of counsel for his defense.

Amendment VII

In suits at common law, where the value in controversy shall exceed twenty dollars, the right of trial by jury shall be preserved, and no fact tried by a jury, shall be otherwise reexamined in any court of the United States, than according to the rules of the common law.

Amendment VIII

Excessive bail shall not be required, nor excessive fines imposed, nor cruel and unusual punishments inflicted.

Amendment IX

The enumeration in the Constitution, of certain rights, shall not be construed to deny or disparage others retained by the people.

Amendment X

The powers not delegated to the United States by the Constitution, nor prohibited by it to the states, are reserved to the states respectively, or to the people.

Timeline

1215

English barons force King John to sign the Magna Carta (Great Charter) to guarantee their rights and privileges and to acknowledge that the monarch's power is not absolute.

1636

Banished from Massachusetts Bay Colony, Roger Williams founds Rhode Island, the only colony to embrace complete religious freedom as a matter of law.

1641

The Massachusetts General Court drafts the Massachusetts Body of Liberties, the first bill of rights in American history. It includes the promise of a speedy trial and equal justice, protection against double jeopardy, and a prohibition against torture, among other rights.

1679

In England, the Habeas Corpus Act reinforces the power of courts to issue a writ of habeas corpus, which protects individuals against arbitrary detention by the state.

1682

The Pennsylvania Charter of Liberties and Frame of Government protect the rights of colonists from government interference. Other colonies also adopt this practice of committing customary rights and privileges into written protections.

1688–89

In England, during the Glorious Revolution, Parliament forces the Catholic James II to abdicate his throne in favor of the Protestant William and Mary. The new king and queen agree to the provisions in a written bill of rights, which shifts power from the monarch to the Parliament and extends rights—such as the right of petition, a limited form of free speech, and a prohibition against excessive fines—to the English population as a whole, including the colonists.

1776

On July 4, the Continental Congress adopts the final draft of the Declaration of Independence.

The Virginia Convention of Delegates adopts the Virginia Declaration of Rights, the first written listing of rights of citizens in the United States. It serves as the model for other state declarations of rights as well as the federal Bill of Rights.

1786

The Virginia Statute for Religious Freedom guarantees that "all men shall be free to profess, and by argument to maintain, their opinion in matters of religion" and ensures that the state will not support any religion. It becomes a model for the religion clause of the First Amendment.

1787

The Constitutional Convention meets in Philadelphia, signs the new U.S. Constitution into law, and sends it to the states for final approval.

1789

The U.S. Congress approves the Bill of Rights, the first ten amendments to the Constitution.

The Judiciary Act empowers all federal courts "to grant writs of habeas corpus for the purpose of an inquiry into the cause of commitment."

1798

The Sedition Act makes it a crime to criticize the government.

1833

In *Barron* v. *Baltimore,* the Supreme Court rules that the Bill of Rights restrains only the federal government and not the individual states.

1837

In *Charles River Bridge* v. *Warren Bridge,* a case concerning competing bridge companies and their contract rights, the Supreme Court rules that states can regulate property in the public interest. The Court refuses to interpret a previous grant by the Massachusetts legislature as conferring a monopoly to the Charles River Bridge Company, thereby spurring free enterprise.

1848

At the Seneca Falls Convention in New York, women's rights advocates issue the Declaration of Sentiments, Grievances, and Resolutions, which calls for voting rights and property rights for women.

1857

The Supreme Court rules in *Scott* v. *Sandford* that no black person, slave or free, can be a citizen of the United States and upholds the slaveholder's right to own another person.

1863

President Abraham Lincoln issues the Emancipation Proclamation, which outlaws slavery in regions not under Union control.

1865

The Thirteenth Amendment, abolishing slavery, is ratified.

1866

In *Ex Parte Milligan,* the Supreme Court upholds the right of citizens to due process of law, even in times of war.

1868

The Fourteenth Amendment, granting blacks citizenship and guaranteeing their equality, is ratified. It provides for all citizens the "equal protection of the laws" and "due process of law."

1870

The Fifteenth Amendment, granting black males the right to vote, is ratified.

1873

The Comstock Act outlaws obscene and immoral materials from the U.S. mails.

1875

Congress passes the Civil Rights Act, prohibiting discrimination in public accommodations and enforcing the "equal protection of the laws" clause of the Fourteenth Amendment.

1883

The Supreme Court rules in the *Civil Rights Cases* that the Fourteenth Amendment bans the violation of individual rights only by government, not privately owned facilities. It rules that the Civil Rights Act of 1875 is unconstitutional because it tries to regulate the private behavior of individuals in regard to racial discrimination.

1886

In *Yick Wo* v. *Hopkins,* the Supreme Court overturns a discriminatory San Francisco law that had tried to restrict Chinese laundries in violation of the Fourteenth Amendment's guarantee of equal protection of the laws.

1896

In *Plessy* v. *Ferguson,* the Supreme Court rules that state-mandated racial segregation of railroad cars does not violate the equal protection clause of the Fourteenth Amendment. The "separate but equal" doctrine established with this case justifies segregation for the coming decades.

1908

In *Twining* v. *New Jersey,* the Supreme Court rules that the Fifth Amendment's right against self-incrimination cannot be applied to state governments under the due process clause of the Fourteenth Amendment. Even so, this case opens the way for selective incorporation of the Bill of the Rights, on a case-by-case basis, under the Fourteenth Amendment.

1914

In *Weeks* v. *United States,* the Supreme Court rules that evidence obtained in violation of a person's constitutional rights must be excluded from federal trials.

1919

The Supreme Court puts limits on free speech with its decision in *Schenck* v. *United States* and establishes the "clear and present danger test": when speech or written words create an immediate threat, government can constrain such speech.

1920

The American Civil Liberties Union is founded to protect constitutional rights.

The Nineteenth Amendment grants women the right to vote.

1925

The Supreme Court rules, for the first time, in *Gitlow* v. *New York* that the freedoms of speech and press "are among the fundamental personal rights protected by the due process clause of the Fourteenth Amendment from impairment by the states." This case is a foundation for the Supreme Court's incorporation doctrine.

1929

The Great Depression begins and lasts through most of the 1930s.

1931

In *Near* v. *Minnesota,* the Supreme Court invalidates a permanent injunction against a newspaper publisher and concludes that the First Amendment prohibits prior restraints of the press.

1932

In *Powell* v. *Alabama,* the Supreme Court rules that the right to counsel is an essential part of due process for poor defendants whenever lack of counsel would result in an unfair trial. This decision overturns the convictions of nine black youths who had been accused of raping two white women because the defendants, too poor to hire a lawyer, had not received adequate legal assistance.

1934

The National Firearms Act, the first federal gun control law, requires registration, police permission, and taxes on certain weapons.

1937

In *DeJonge* v. *Oregon,* the Supreme Court reverses the conviction of an individual for participating in a Communist party meeting and upholds the First Amendment's right to assemble peacefully.

1939

In *United States* v. *Miller,* the Supreme Court affirms the right of citizens to own weapons suitable for use in a militia, but it rules that the firearm in dispute in this case, a sawed-off shotgun, is not a military weapon and can be controlled without violating the Second Amendment's guarantee of the right to bear arms.

1940

In *Cantwell* v. *Connecticut,* the Supreme Court holds for the first time that the due process clause of the Fourteenth Amendment makes the free exercise clause of the First Amendment applicable to the states.

The Supreme Court rules in *Minersville School District* v. *Gobitis* that a school board can require a student to salute the U.S. flag even if it violates that student's religious beliefs.

1941

The United States enters World War II after the Japanese bomb Pearl Harbor in Hawaii.

1943

The Supreme Court overturns its *Minersville* decision in *West Virginia State Board of Education* v. *Barnette.* The Court rules that the First Amendment protects freedom of religion from state interference.

1947

In *Everson* v. *Board of Education,* the Supreme Court holds that the due process clause of the Fourteenth Amendment makes the First Amendment's principle of separation of church and state applicable to the states.

In *Francis* v. *Resweber,* the Supreme Court rules that a convicted murderer whose execution by electric chair failed to kill him could be electrocuted again. The Court decides that repeated attempts at execution do not violate the Eighth Amendment's ban on cruel and unusual punishments.

1954

In *Brown* v. *Board of Education,* the Supreme Court rejects racial segregation in schools and rules that the doctrine of "separate but equal" is unconstitutional.

1961

In *Mapp* v. *Ohio,* the Supreme Court overturns the conviction of a woman because police had searched her house without a warrant and found evidence they later used against her. The Court rules, for the first time, that the Fourth Amendment's guarantee against unreasonable searches applies to the state governments as well as the federal.

1962

In *Engel* v. *Vitale,* the Supreme Court rules against school prayer and upholds a strict separation of church and state, as established in the First Amendment.

1963

In *Gideon* v. *Wainwright,* the Supreme Court rules that in all criminal cases, defendants who are too poor to afford a lawyer must be provided with an attorney as part of their due process rights.

1964

In *Escobedo* v. *Illinois,* the Supreme Court extends the Sixth Amendment's right to counsel to include police interrogations as well as trials.

In *New York Times Co.* v. *Sullivan,* the Supreme Court overturns a libel judgment against the *Times* and rules that public officials may not recover damages unless a false statement was made with actual malice.

Congress passes the Civil Rights Act, banning discrimination on the basis of race, color, or national origin.

1965

Congress passes the Voting Rights Act, prohibiting discrimination in voting on the basis of race, color, or national origin.

In *Griswold* v. *Connecticut,* the Supreme Court strikes down a Connecticut law banning the use of drugs, materials, or instruments to prevent contraception. The Court rules that this law is an unconstitutional invasion of an individual's right to privacy, which is not mentioned specifically in the Constitution but is an implied right.

1966

In *Miranda* v. *Arizona,* the Supreme Court rules that police officers are required to inform suspects of their rights, such as the right to remain silent and the right to consult a lawyer, as part of the Fifth Amendment's guarantee that no person shall be compelled to be a witness against himself.

In *Sheppard* v. *Maxwell,* the Supreme Court reverses a murder conviction because hostile news coverage and publicity surrounding the trial prejudiced the jury and made a fair trial impossible. The Court rules that this trial failed to meet the constitutional standard of a trial by an impartial jury.

1967

In *In re Gault,* the Supreme Court establishes that juvenile defendants have certain rights, such as the right to legal counsel, that cannot be taken away because of age.

In *Loving* v. *Virginia,* the Supreme Court strikes down a state law that prohibits interracial marriage as a violation of the Fourteenth Amendment's guarantee of equality.

1968

The Gun Control Act is the first federal law to seriously affect the right of Americans to buy and own firearms. The act limits the purchase of guns through the mails, restricts the importation of surplus military weapons, and prohibits convicted felons from owning guns.

1969

In *Tinker* v. *Des Moines Independent School District*, the Supreme Court rules that the suspension of students for wearing black armbands to protest the Vietnam War violates the students' First Amendment rights to freedom of speech.

In *Brandenburg* v. *Ohio*, the Supreme Court expands the scope of political free speech and strikes down an Ohio law prohibiting speech that advocates violence as a means of political reform. The Court rules that political speech can be limited only if it can be proved that such speech is likely to incite immediate lawless action.

In *Benton* v. *Maryland*, the Supreme Court rules that the Fifth Amendment's protection against double jeopardy is applicable to state governments through the due process clause of the Fourteenth Amendment.

1971

In *New York Times Co.* v. *United States*, the Supreme Court rules that newspapers are free from prepublication restraints (prior restraint), even during wartime, and allows the *Times* to continue publishing the Pentagon Papers, which included classified information about policies in the Vietnam War.

In *Lemon* v. *Kurtzman*, the Supreme Court uses a three-part test to determine whether a governmental action violates the First Amendment's prohibition against an establishment of religion. To pass the test, the action must have a secular purpose, its primary effect must neither advance nor inhibit religion, and there must be no excessive government entanglement with religion.

1972

In *Furman* v. *Georgia*, the Supreme Court decides that executions as practiced are unconstitutional because the judge and jury lack specific guidelines to ensure fairness in sentencing.

1973

In *Roe* v. *Wade*, the Supreme Court guarantees a woman's right to have an abortion as part of her right to privacy.

1976

In *Gregg* v. *Georgia*, the Supreme Court upholds statutes that guide the judge and jury when imposing the death penalty, which the Court does not find to be unconstitutional.

1978

In *Regents of the University of California* v. *Bakke*, the Supreme Court rules in favor of a white student who had been denied admission to medical school so that a quota of black students could be admitted as part of an affirmative action program. The decision, while outlawing racial quotas, did allow that race could be considered in making admissions decisions.

1989

In *Texas* v. *Johnson*, the Supreme Court upholds flag burning as protected speech under the First Amendment.

1990

The American with Disabilities Act establishes legal rights for physically and mentally handicapped citizens.

1991

The Civil Rights Act is passed in response to several Supreme Court decisions that had limited employees' rights to sue in cases of discrimination and allows individuals to collect damages from those who deny their rights.

1992

In *Planned Parenthood of Southeastern Pennsylvania* v. *Casey*, the Supreme Court retreats from its position in *Roe* v. *Wade* and allows some restrictions on a woman's right to choose an abortion, provided the government does not unduly burden or interfere with her ability to get an abortion.

1993

In *Church of the Lukumi Babalu Aye* v. *City of Hialeah*, the Supreme Court upholds the right of believers in a folk religion to practice animal sacrifice, as part of their First Amendment right to free exercise of religion, in defiance of public health laws.

1995

In *Rosenberger* v. *University of Virginia*, the Supreme Court rules that the First Amendment's establishment clause does not prohibit a school from supporting religious publications, as long as the distribution of funds is evenhanded.

2001

In response to the terrorist attacks of September 11, 2001, Congress passes the USA PATRIOT Act. The legislation expands government's authority to monitor phone calls, search homes and offices, and obtain business records, among other things, in an attempt to prevent future terrorist attacks.

2005

In *Kelo* v. *City of New London*, the Supreme Court upholds the Connecticut city's right to use eminent domain to support its economic development strategy. The decision to allow private developers, working for the government, to take personal property causes a backlash and state legislatures pass new laws to protect homeowners.

2006

The Senate fails by one vote to pass the Flag Protection Amendment.

Further Reading

General Works on the Constitution and Bill of Rights

Alderman, Ellen, and Caroline Kennedy. *In Our Defense: The Bill of Rights in Action.* New York: William Morrow, 1991.

Amar, Akhil Reed. *America's Constitution: A Biography.* New York: Random House, 2005.

Amar, Akhil Reed, and Alan Hirsch. *For the People: What the Constitution Really Says about Your Rights.* New York: Free Press, 1998.

Bernstein, Richard B., with Jerome Agel. *Amending America: If We Love the Constitution So Much, Why Do We Keep Trying to Change It?* New York: Times Books, 1993.

Biskupic, Joan, and Elder Witt. *The Supreme Court and Individual Rights.* Washington, D.C.: Congressional Quarterly Press, 1997.

Blanchard, Margaret. *Revolutionary Sparks: Freedom of Expression in Modern America.* New York: Oxford University Press, 1992.

Bodenhamer, David J., and James W. Ely, Jr., eds. *The Bill of Rights in Modern America after 200 Years.* Bloomington: Indiana University Press, 1993.

Bollinger, Lee C. *The Tolerant Society.* New York: Oxford University Press, 1986.

Burns, James McGregor, and Stewart Burns. *A People's Charter: The Pursuit of Rights in America.* New York: Knopf, 1991.

Carnes, Jim. *Us and Them: A History of Intolerance in America.* New York: Oxford University Press, 1996.

Dinan, John J. *Keeping the People's Liberties: Legislators, Citizens, and Judges as Guardians of Rights.* Lawrence: University Press of Kansas, 1998.

Ellis, Joseph J. *What Did the Declaration Declare?* Boston: Bedford, 1999.

Farber, Daniel A. *The First Amendment.* 2nd ed. New York: Foundation Press, 2003.

Friendly, Fred W., and Martha Elliot. *The Constitution: That Delicate Balance.* New York: Random House, 1984.

Glasser, Ira. *Visions of Liberty: The Bill of Rights for All Americans.* New York: Arcade, 1991.

Hall, Kermit L., ed. *By and For the People: Constitutional Rights in American History.* Arlington Heights, Ill.: Davidson, 1991.

Hall, Kermit L., ed. *The Oxford Companion to the Supreme Court of the United States.* 2nd ed. New York: Oxford University Press, 2005.

Haynes, Charles, Sam Chaltain, and Susan Glisson. *First Freedoms: A Documentary History of First Amendment Rights in America.* New York: Oxford University Press, 2006.

Hentoff, Nat. *Living the Bill of Rights.* Berkeley: University of California Press, 1999.

Irons, Peter. *The Courage of Their Convictions: Sixteen Americans Who Fought Their Way to the Supreme Court.* New York: Free Press, 1988.

Kyvig, David E. *Explicit and Authentic Acts: Amending the U.S. Constitution.* Lawrence: University Press of Kansas, 1996.

Meltzer, Milton. *The Bill of Rights: How We Got It and What It Means.* New York: Crowell, 1990.

Monk, Linda R. *The Bill of Rights: A User's Guide.* Alexandria, Va.: Close Up Publishing, 1995.

Patrick, John J. *The Bill of Rights: A History in Documents.* New York: Oxford University Press, 2003.

Patrick, John J. *The Supreme Court of the United States: A Student Companion.* 3rd ed. New York: Oxford University Press, 2006.

Rakove, Jack N. *Declaring Rights: A Brief History with Documents.* Boston: Bedford, 1998.

Raskin, Jamin B. *We the Students: Supreme Court Cases for and about Students.* Washington, D.C.: Congressional Quarterly Press, 2000.

Schudson, Michael. *The Good Citizen: A History of American Civic Life.* Cambridge, Mass.: Harvard University Press, 1998.

Schwartz, Bernard. *The Great Rights of Mankind: A History of the American Bill of Rights.* Madison, Wis.: Madison House, 1992.

Shiffrin, Steven. *The First Amendment, Democracy, and Romance.* Cambridge, Mass.: Harvard University Press, 1990.

Stephens, Otis H., John M. Scheb, and Kara E. Stooksbury, eds. *Encyclopedia of American Civil Liberties and Rights.* Westport, Conn.: Greenwood, 2006.

Urofsky, Melvin I. *100 Americans Making Constitutional History: A Biographical History.* Washington, D.C.: Congressional Quarterly Press, 2004.

Wagman, Robert J. *The First Amendment Book.* New York: Pharos, 1991.

Chapter 1
Our Rights in American History

Amar, Akhil Reed. *The Bill of Rights: Creation and Reconstruction.* New Haven, Conn.: Yale University Press, 1998.

Cogan, Neil, ed. *The Complete Bill of Rights: The Drafts, Debates, Sources, and Origins.* New York: Oxford University Press, 1997.

Conley, Patrick T., and John P. Kaminski, eds. *The Bill of Rights and the States: The Colonial and Revolutionary Origins of American Liberties.* Madison, Wis.: Madison House, 1992.

Estep, William. *Revolution within the Revolution: The First Amendment in Historical Context, 1612–1789.* Grand Rapids, Mich.: William B. Eerdmans, 1990.

Howard, A. E. Dick. *The Road from Runnymede: Magna Carta and Constitutionalism in America.* Charlottesville: University Press of Virginia, 1998.

Levy, Leonard. *Origins of the Bill of Rights.* New Haven, Conn.: Yale University Press, 1999.

Miller, William Lee. *The Business of May Next: James Madison and the Founding.* Charlottesville: University Press of Virginia, 1992.

Chapter 2
The Right to Freedom

Abraham, Henry J., and Barbara A. Perry. *Freedom and the Court: Civil Rights and Liberties in the United States.* New York: Oxford University Press, 1998.

Richards, David A. J. *Conscience and the Constitution: History, Theory, and Law of the Reconstruction Amendments.* Princeton, N.J.: Princeton University Press, 1993.

Ten Broek, Jacobus. *Equal under Law.* Enlarged ed. New York: Collier Books, 1965.

Vorenberg, Michael. *Final Freedom: The Civil War, the Abolition of Slavery, and the Thirteenth Amendment.* New York: Cambridge University Press, 2001.

Chapter 3
The Right to Equal Protection of the Laws

Branch, Taylor. *Parting the Waters: America in the King Years, 1954–1963.* New York: Simon & Schuster, 1988.

Hyman, Harold W., and William M. Wiecek. *Equal Justice under Law: Constitutional Development, 1835–1875.* New York: Harper & Row, 1982.

Leonard, Ira M., and Robert D. Parmet. *American Nativism, 1830–1860.* New York: Van Nostrand Reinhold, 1971.

McMillen, Neil. *Dark Journey: Black Mississippians in the Age of Jim Crow.* Chicago: University of Illinois Press, 1990.

Morris, Aldon D. *The Origins of the Civil Rights Movement: Black Communities Organizing for Change.* New York: Free Press, 1984.

Nieman, Donald G. *Promises to Keep: African-Americans and the Constitutional Order.* New York: Oxford University Press, 1991.

Sitkoff, Harvard. *The Struggle for Black Equality, 1954–1992.* New York: Hill and Wang, 1993.

Wertheimer, Barbara Mayer. *We Were There: The Story of Working Women in America.* New York: Pantheon, 1977.

Chapters 4 and 5
The Right to Free Exercise of Religion and Separation of Church and State

Alley, Robert S., ed. *James Madison on Religious Liberty.* Buffalo, N.Y.: Prometheus, 1985.

Belth, Nathan C. *A Promise to Keep: A Narrative of the American Encounter with Anti-Semitism.* New York: Schocken, 1981.

Butler, Jon, Grant Wacker, and Randall Balmer. *Religion in American Life: A Short History.* New York: Oxford University Press, 2000.

Curry, Thomas J. *The First Freedoms: Church and State in America to the Passage of the First Amendment.* New York: Oxford University Press, 1986.

Gaustad, Edwin S. *Church and State in America.* 2nd ed. New York: Oxford University Press, 2003.

Gaustad, Edwin S. *Roger Williams: Prophet of Liberty.* New York: Oxford University Press, 2001.

Lambert, Frank. *The Founding Fathers and the Place of Religion in America.* Princeton, N.J.: Princeton University Press, 2003.

Levy, Leonard W. *The Establishment Clause: Religion and the First Amendment.* New York: Macmillan, 1986.

Long, Carolyn N. *Religious Freedom and Indian Rights: The Case of Oregon v. Smith.* Lawrence: University Press of Kansas, 2000.

Miller, William Lee. *The First Liberty: Religion and the American Republic.* Washington, D.C.: Georgetown University Press, 2003.

Patrick, John J., and Gerald P. Long. *Constitutional Debates on Freedom of Religion.* Westport, Conn.: Greenwood, 1999.

Urofsky, Melvin I. *Religious Freedom: Rights and Liberties under the Law.* Santa Barbara, Calif.: ABC-CLIO, 2002.

Williams, Peter. *American Religions from their Origins to the Twenty-first Century.* Urbana: University of Illinois Press, 2002.

Wilson, John F., and Donald L. Drakeman. *Church and State in American History.* Boulder, Colo.: Westview, 2003.

Witte, John, Jr. *Religion and the American Constitutional Experiment.* Boulder, Colo.: Westview Press, 2000.

Wuthnow, Robert. *America and the Challenges of Religious Diversity.* Princeton, N.J.: Princeton University Press, 2005.

Chapter 6
The Right to Freedom of Speech

Baker, C. Edwin. *Human Liberty and Freedom of Speech.* New York: Oxford University Press, 1989.

Chafee, Zechariah. *Free Speech in the United States.* Cambridge, Mass.: Harvard University Press, 1967.

Curtis, Michael Kent. *Free Speech: The People's Darling Privilege.* Durham, N.C.: Duke University Press, 2000.

Eastland, Terry. *Freedom of Expression in the Supreme Court.* New York: Rowman & Littlefield, 2000.

Farish, Leah. *Tinker v. Des Moines: Student Protest.* Springfield, N.J.: Enslow, 1997.

Fraleigh, Douglas M., and Joseph S. Tuman. *Freedom of Speech in the Marketplace of Ideas.* New York: St. Martin's, 1997.

Goldstein, Robert Justin. *Flag Burning and Free Speech.* Lawrence: University Press of Kansas, 2000.

Johnson, John W. *The Struggle for Student Rights.* Lawrence: University Press of Kansas, 1997.

Kalven, Harry, Jr., ed. *A Worthy Tradition: Freedom of Speech in America.* New York: Harper & Row, 1988.

Levy, Leonard. *Freedom of Speech and Press in Early American History: Legacy of Suppression.* New York: Harper Torchbooks, 1963.

Polenberg, Richard. *Fighting Faiths: The Abrams Case, the Supreme Court, and Free Speech.* Ithaca, N.Y.: Cornell University Press, 1987.

Russomanno, Joseph. *Speaking Our Minds: Conversations with the People behind Landmark First Amendment Cases.* Mahwah, N.J.: Lawrence Erlbaum, 2002.

Smith, James Morton. *Freedom's Fetters: The Alien and Sedition Laws and American Civil Liberties.* Ithaca, N.Y.: Cornell University Press, 1956.

Stone, Geoffrey. *Perilous Times: Free Speech in Wartime.* New York: W. W. Norton, 2004.

Chapter 7
The Right to Freedom of the Press

Friendly, Fred W. *Minnesota Rag: The Dramatic Story of the Landmark Case that Gave New Meaning to Freedom of the Press.* New York: Random House, 1981.

Levy, Leonard W. *Emergence of a Free Press.* New York: Oxford University Press, 1985.

Lewis, Anthony. *Make No Law: The Sullivan Case and the First Amendment.* New York: Vintage, 1992.

Rudenstine, David. *The Day the Presses Stopped: A History of the Pentagon Papers Case.* Berkeley: University of California Press, 1996.

Chapter 8
The Right to Freedom of Assembly

Lisio, Donald. *The President and Protest: Hoover, MacArthur, and the Bonus Riot.* New York: Fordham University Press, 1994.

O'Reilly, Kenneth. *Hoover and the Un-Americans: The FBI, HUAC, and the Red Menace.* Philadelphia: Temple University Press, 1983.

Strum, Philippa. *When the Nazis Came to Skokie: Freedom for Speech We Hate.* Lawrence: University Press of Kansas, 1999.

Chapter 9
The Right to Petition

Barber, Lucy G. *Marching on Washington: The Forging of an American Political Tradition.* Berkeley: University of California Press, 2002.

Miller, William Lee. *Arguing about Slavery: John Quincy Adams and the Great Battle in the United States Congress.* New York: Knopf, 1996.

Walker, Samuel. *The Rights Revolution: Rights and Community in Modern America.* New York: Oxford University Press, 1998.

Chapter 10
The Right to Freedom from Racial Discrimination

Fehrenbacher, Don E. *The Dred Scott Case: Its Significance in American History.* New ed. New York: Oxford University Press, 2001.

McClain, Charles J. *In Search of Equality: The Chinese Struggle against Discrimination in Nineteenth-Century America.* Berkeley: University of California Press, 1996.

Nelson, William E. *The Fourteenth Amendment: From Political Principle to Judicial Doctrine.* Cambridge, Mass.: Harvard University Press, 1988.

Salyer, Lucy E. *Laws Harsh as Tigers: Chinese Immigrants and the Shaping of Modern Immigration Law.* Chapel Hill: University of North Carolina Press, 1995.

Chapter 11
The Right to Vote

Barry, Kathleen. *Susan B. Anthony: A Biography of a Singular Feminist.* New York: Ballantine Books, 1990.

Deutsch, Sarah Jane. *From Ballots to Breadlines: American Women, 1920–1940.* New York: Oxford University Press, 1994.

DuBois, Ellen Carol. *Harriot Stanton Blatch and the Winning of Woman Suffrage.* New Haven, Conn.: Yale University Press, 1997.

Gillette, William. *The Right to Vote: Politics and the Passage of the Fifteenth Amendment.* Baltimore: John Hopkins University Press, 1965.

Griffith, Elisabeth. *In Her Own Right: The Life of Elizabeth Cady Stanton.* New York: Oxford University Press, 1985.

Kousser, J. Morgan. *Colorblind Injustice: Minority Voting Rights and the Undoing of the Second Reconstruction.* Chapel Hill: University of North Carolina Press, 1999.

Wheeler, Marjorie Spruill, ed. *One Woman, One Vote: Rediscovering the Woman Suffrage Movement.* Troutdale, Oreg.: New Sage, 1995.

Chapter 12
The Right to a Fair Trial

Bodenhamer, David. *Fair Trial: Rights of the Accused in American History.* New York: Oxford University Press, 1992.

Friedman, Lawrence M. *Crime and Punishment in American History.* New York: Basic Books, 1993.

Phillips, Steven J. *No Heroes, No Villains: The Story of a Murder Trial.* New York: Random House, 1978.

Walker, Samuel. *Popular Justice: A History of American Criminal Justice.* New York: Oxford University Press, 1980.

Chapter 13
The Right to Due Process

Bodenhamer, David J. *The Pursuit of Justice: Crime and Law in Antebellum Indiana.* New York: Garland, 1986.

Carter, Dan T. *Scottsboro: A Tragedy of the American South.* Rev. ed. Baton Rouge: Louisiana State University Press, 1979.

Chapin, Bradley. *Criminal Justice in Colonial America, 1606–1660.* Athens: University of Georgia Press, 1983.

Chapter 14
The Right to Habeas Corpus

Duker, William F. *A Constitutional History of Habeas Corpus.* Westport, Conn.: Greenwood Press, 1980.

Irons, Peter. *Justice at War: The Story of the Japanese American Internment Cases.* Berkeley: University of California Press, 1993.

Robinson, Greg. *By Order of the President: FDR and the Internment of Japanese Americans.* Cambridge, Mass.: Harvard University Press, 2001.

Chapter 15
The Right to Protection against Illegal Search and Seizure

Leone, Richard C., and Greg Anrig, Jr., eds. *The War on Our Freedoms: Civil Liberties in an Age of Terrorism.* New York: BBS Public Affairs, 2003.

Long, Carolyn Nestor. *Mapp v. Ohio: Guarding against Unreasonable Searches and Seizures.* Lawrence: University Press of Kansas, 2006.

Stevens, Otis, and Richard A Glenn. *Unreasonable Searches and Seizures : Rights and Liberties under the Law.* Santa Barbara, Calif.: ABC-CLIO, 2006.

Chapter 16
The Right to Protection against Double Jeopardy

Garcia, Alfred. *The Fifth Amendment: A Comprehensive Approach.* Westport, Conn.: Greenwood Press, 2002.

Sigler, Jay. *Double Jeopardy: The Development of a Legal and Social Policy.* Ithaca, N.Y.: Cornell University Press, 1968.

Thomas, George C. *Double Jeopardy: The History, the Law.* New York: New York University Press, 1998.

Chapter 17
The Privilege against Self-Incrimination

Baker, Liva. *Miranda: Crime, Law, and Politics.* New York: Atheneum, 1983.

Levy, Leonard W. *Origins of the Fifth Amendment: The Right against Self-Incrimination.* New York: Oxford University Press, 1968.

Stuart, Gary L. *Miranda: The Story of America's Right to Remain Silent.* Tucson: University of Arizona Press, 2004.

Chapter 18
The Right to Trial by Jury

Kalven, Harry, and Hans Zeisal. *The American Jury.* Chicago: University of Chicago Press, 1966.

Jonakait, Randolph N. *The American Jury System.* New Haven, Conn.: Yale University Press, 2003.

Levy, Leonard W. *The Palladium of Justice: Origins of Trial by Jury.* Chicago: Ivan R. Dee, 1999.

Chapter 19
The Right to Counsel

Cortner, Richard C. *A "Scottsboro" Case in Mississippi: The Supreme Court and Brown v. Mississippi.* Jackson: University Press of Mississippi, 1986.

Lewis, Anthony. *Gideon's Trumpet.* New York: Random House, 1964.

Taylor, John B. *The Right to Counsel and Privilege against Self-Incrimination: Rights and Liberties under the Law.* Santa Barbara, Calif.: ABC-CLIO, 2004.

Chapter 20
The Rights of Juvenile Defendants

Martin, Gus. *Juvenile Justice: Process and Systems.* Thousand Oaks, Calif.: Sage, 2005.

Platt, Anthony M. *The Child-Savers: The Invention of Delinquency.* Chicago: University of Chicago Press, 1972.

Rosenheim, Margaret K. *A Century of Juvenile Justice.* Chicago: University of Chicago Press, 2002.

Chapter 21
The Right to Protection against Cruel and Unusual Punishments

Banner, Stuart. *The Death Penalty: An American History.* Cambridge, Mass.: Harvard University Press, 2002.

Masur, Louis. *Rites of Execution: Capital Punishment and the Transformation of American Culture, 1776–1865.* New York: Oxford University Press, 1989.

Miller, Arthur S., and Jeffrey H. Bowman. *Death by Installments: The Ordeal of Willie Francis.* New York: Greenwood, 1988.

Chapter 22
The Right of Privacy

Alderman, Ellen, and Caroline Kennedy. *The Right to Privacy.* New York: Knopf, 1995.

Barnett, Randy E., ed. *The Rights Retained by the People: The History and Meaning of the Ninth Amendment.* Fairfax, Va.: George Mason University Press, 1989.

Johnson, John W. *Griswold v. Connecticut: Birth Control and the Constitutional Right of Privacy.* Lawrence: University Press of Kansas, 2005.

Rosen, Jeffrey. *Unwanted Gaze: The Destruction of Privacy in America.* New York: Random House, 2000.

Chapter 23
The Right to Bear Arms

Bogus, Carl T., and Michael A Bellesiles. *The Second Amendment in Law and History: Historians and Constitutional Scholars on the Right to Bear Arms.* New York: New Press, 2000.

Cornell, Saul. *A Well-Regulated Militia: The Founding Fathers and the Origins of Gun Control in America.* New York: Oxford University Press, 2006.

Halbrook, Stephen P. *A Right to Bear Arms: State and Federal Bills of Rights and Constitutional Guarantees.* New York: Greenwood, 1989.

Chapter 24
The Right to Property

Ely, James W., Jr. *The Guardian of Every Other Right: A Constitutional History of Property Rights.* 2nd ed. New York: Oxford University Press, 1998.

Epstein, Richard A. *Takings: Private Property and the Power of Eminent Domain.* Cambridge, Mass: Harvard University Press, 1985.

Siegan, Bernard. *Economic Liberties and the Constitution.* Chicago: University of Chicago Press, 1980.

Websites

American Bar Association (ABA), Division for Public Education
www.abanet.org/publiced

The mission of the ABA Division for Public Education is to promote public understanding of law and its role in society. The Student Central section of the site offers information on careers in law, identifies ways for students to engage in civic involvement, and invites students to take part in online discussions with students across the nation.

American Society of Newspaper Editors (ASNE) High School Journalism Project
www.highschooljournalism.org

This project is geared toward teen journalists, their teachers and guidance counselors, and the editors and staffs of professional daily newspapers. Its goal is to encourage a diverse group of young people to make newspaper journalism their career. The project works to foster a deeper appreciation of the First Amendment and the role newspapers play in a free, informed society. This site provides resources and information on scholarships and workshops for teachers, journalism advisers, and student editors.

Bill of Rights Institute
www.billofrightsinstitute.org

Founded in 1999, the Bill of Rights Institute's mission is to educate high school students about the Bill of Rights through classroom material and programs that teach what the Bill of Rights protects, both explicitly and implicitly; how the Bill of Rights affects our daily lives; and how the Bill of Rights shapes our society. The site includes classroom lessons and other materials for teachers, landmark Supreme Court cases, and historical documents.

Center for Civic Education
www.civiced.org

The center specializes in civic and citizenship education, law-related education, and international educational exchange programs for developing democracies. Programs focus on the U.S. Constitution and Bill of Rights; American political traditions and institutions at the federal, state, and local levels; constitutionalism; civic participation; and the rights and responsibilities of citizens. This site provides civic education curricular materials, research, and articles as well as a catalogue of the center's publications.

Close Up Foundation
www.closeup.org

Each year, more than 20,000 students and teachers travel to Washington, D.C., with the Close Up Foundation for a "close-up" experience in government. The foundation's website offers curricular materials for civic education, as well as information about Close Up's state and local programs.

Constitutional Rights Foundation
www.crf-usa.org

The Constitutional Rights Foundation (CRF) is a nonprofit, nonpartisan, community-based organization dedicated to educating America's young people about the importance of civic participation in a democratic society. CRF develops, produces, and distributes programs and materials to teachers, students, and public-minded citizens all across the nation in the areas of law, government, and civic participation. The website offers information on the foundation's many programs for high school students: Summer Law Institute, Mock Trial, Youth Internships, Youth for Justice, and Youth Leadership for Action.

Cornell Legal Information Institute
www.law.cornell.edu

This site of the Cornell University Law School contains all U.S. Supreme Court opinions since May 1990 and six hundred opinions on major cases throughout the Court's history. It also includes information on current events and issues involving the courts, judges, and law.

Federal Judicial Center
www.fjc.gov

This site provides general information about the federal judiciary, including a history of federal courts, a biographical database of federal judges since 1789, and information on key legislation about the federal judiciary throughout U.S. history.

Federal Judiciary
www.uscourts.gov

The site provides news about current events and basic information about the federal judicial system, and it includes information about the structure and functions of the federal courts with links to the U.S. Supreme Court, U.S. Courts of Appeals, and the U.S. district courts.

FindLaw

www.findlaw.com

FindLaw includes information about the U.S. federal judiciary and the judiciaries of the fifty states. It provides opinions from the Supreme Court, all federal circuits, and the appellate courts of the fifty states, and it presents information about current legal events and issues.

First Amendment Center

www.firstamendmentcenter.org

An independent affiliate of the Freedom Forum, the center works to preserve and protect First Amendment freedoms through information and education, in part by tracking court rulings, legislation, and other events that are related to the First Amendment freedoms. The First Amendment Center Online offers daily news, analysis, commentary, overviews, trends, and case law about a wide range of First Amendment topics.

First Amendment Schools Project

www.firstamendmentschools.org

This project is a national reform initiative sponsored by the First Amendment Center and the Association for Supervision and Curriculum Development (ASCD) designed to transform how schools teach and practice the rights and responsibilities of citizenship that frame civic life in our democracy. This website offers information on the project as well as lesson plans, sample policies, reports and research, and news articles on the First Amendment and education.

H-LAW

www.h-net.org/~law

This online discussion list stresses legal and constitutional history and contemporary issues in the law. It includes book reviews and links to the American Society of Legal History, which sponsors this site.

Journalism Education Association (JEA)

www.jea.org

The JEA is the only independent national scholastic journalism organization for teachers and advisers. Founded in 1924, JEA is a volunteer organization that supports free and responsible scholastic journalism by providing resources and education opportunities, by promoting professionalism, by encouraging and rewarding student excellence and teacher achievement, and by fostering an atmosphere that encompasses diversity yet builds unity. The website offers information on JEA workshops, awards, and conferences.

Jurist: Legal News and Research

http://jurist.law.pitt.edu

This site of the University of Pittsburgh School of Law includes a broad range of current legal news and information about federal and state courts with emphasis on the U.S.

Supreme Court. Research and expert commentary about current legal events and issues are provided. Decisions of the Supreme Court are available.

Justice Learning

www.justicelearning.org

This site, a collaboration of National Public Radio's *Justice Talking* and the New York Times Learning Network, offers resources for teachers and students on law and justice issues. The site includes an annotated Constitution with historical timelines for each article and amendment.

Landmark Supreme Court Cases

www.landmarkcases.org

This site, provided through collaboration by Street Law and the Supreme Court Historical Society, includes instructional resources for teachers and students. The site offers basic information about key decisions of the Supreme Court along with teaching strategies and lesson plans.

Lexis-Nexis

www.lexisnexis.com

This legal research service offers a broad range of data on historical and current topics. Opinions, briefs, and secondary sources on U.S. Supreme Court cases are available through this site, as are materials pertaining to all federal district courts, U.S. courts of appeals, specialized federal courts, and state courts. Through its daily opinion service, immediate access to decisions of all federal and state courts is provided. In addition, primary and secondary sources on current events and legislation are available.

Library of Congress

www.loc.gov

The Library of Congress is the nation's oldest federal cultural institution and serves as the research arm of Congress. It is also the largest library in the world, with more than 130 million items on approximately 530 miles of bookshelves. Students can access millions of documents, recordings, photographs, maps, and manuscripts online.

Library of Congress: U.S. Judiciary

www.loc.gov/law/guide/usjudic.html

Links are provided here to many sites related to the federal judicial branch of government, including those with information about legal history, federal laws, judicial opinions, court rules, law journals, and legal news.

National Archives and Records Administration (NARA)

www.archives.gov

The National Archives and Records Administration is an independent federal agency that preserves our nation's history and oversees the management of all federal records. Students can access America's historical documents and interact with exhibits to meet the Founding Fathers, for example, or sign the Declaration of Independence. Teachers can access teaching lessons and tools and sign up for training and remote workshops.

National Scholastic Press Association (NSPA)

www.studentpress.org/nspa

In 1921, NSPA began helping students and teachers to improve their school newspapers and journals. Today, the NSPA continues to help students to become better reporters, writers, editors, photographers, designers, and desktop publishers, as well as advertising and business staffers. This site provides forums for student discussion of press issues, reports trends in high school media, and promotes the organization's contests and conventions.

Our Documents: 100 Milestone Documents

www.ourdocuments.gov

Our Documents is a national initiative on American history, civics, and service that invites all Americans to participate in a series of events and programs to get us thinking, talking, and teaching about the rights and responsibilities of citizens in our democracy. At the heart of this initiative are one hundred milestone documents of American history, which students can explore on the website. Through classroom activities and competitions, Our Documents encourages students, teachers, parents, and the general public to discuss the meanings of these documents and decide which are the most significant and why.

Oyez: U.S. Supreme Court Multimedia Database

www.oyez.org

This site is a project of Northwestern University and includes information about Supreme Court cases, biographies of Supreme Court justices, and instructional materials for teachers and students.

Student Press Law Center (SPLC)

http://splc.org

SPLC is an advocate for students' free press rights. The center provides information, advice, and legal assistance at no charge to students and the educators who work with them. Three times a year, SPLC also publishes a magazine that summarizes current cases, controversies, and legislation and analyzes trends involving student media law. This site provides information for student journalists who have a specific question and need legal help or research.

Street Law

www.streetlaw.org

Street Law is a practical, participatory educational organization focusing on law, democracy, and human rights. A unique blend of content and methodology, Street Law uses techniques that promote cooperative learning, critical thinking, and the ability to participate in a democratic society. For thirty years, Street Law's programs and curricula have promoted knowledge of legal rights and responsibilities, engagement in the democratic process, and belief in the rule of law, among both youth and adults. At this site, students and teachers may access landmark Supreme Court case summaries and teaching lessons and learn about building stronger communities through two of Street Law's programs: Community Works and Youth Act!

Supreme Court Historical Society

www.supremecourthistory.org

This site provides access to opinions of notable Supreme Court cases and information on the historical society's programs and publications.

Supreme Court of the United States

www.supremecourtus.gov

This official site of the Court includes information about the history, structure, functions, and rules of the federal judiciary. It presents opinions on all cases that have gone before the Court, oral arguments, the Court's docket, and a guide to visiting the Court.

U.S. Department of Justice

www.usdoj.gov

This site provides information about the institutional structure and work of the federal Department of Justice. The duties, activities, and reports of the attorney general are highlighted.

Westlaw

www.westlaw.com

Westlaw provides access to opinions, briefs, oral arguments, and secondary materials related to cases of the U.S. Supreme Court.

Index

Text Credits

p. 6: Charles Fried, testimony before the House Judiciary Committee, July 19, 1989, as quoted in Robert Justin Goldstein, *Flag Burning and Free Speech* (Lawrence: University of Kansas Press, 2000), 132.

p. 8: Hugo L. Black, concurring opinion, *New York Times Co.* v. *United States,* 403 U.S. 713 (June 30, 1971).

p. 11: Abraham Lincoln, c. January 1861, "Fragment on the Constitution and the Union," in *Collected Works of Abraham Lincoln, 1809–1865,* vol. 4, ed. Roy T. Basler (New Brunswick, N.J.: Rutgers University Press, 1953), 168–69.

p. 22: Benjamin Cardozo, *Palko* v. *Connecticut,* 302 U.S. 319, 327 (December 6, 1937).

p. 28: Stephen Breyer, New School University Commencement Address, New York City, May 20, 2005, found at *http://www.supremecourtus.gov/publicinfo/speeches/sp_05-20-05.html.*

pp. 29–30: Virginia Declaration of Rights, 1776, found at *http://www.yale.edu/lawweb/avalon/virginia.htm.*

p. 30: John Marshall, *Barron* v. *Baltimore,* 7 Pet. 243 (February 16, 1835).

p. 32: William J. Brennan, Jr., "My Life on the Court," in *Reason and Passion: Justice Brennan's Enduring Influence,* ed. E. Joshua Rosenkranz and Bernard Schwartz (New York: Norton, 1997), 18–21.

p. 35: Anthony M. Kennedy, American Bar Association Annual Meeting, August 9, 2003, found at *http://www.supremecourtus.gov/publicinfo/speeches/sp_08-09-03.html.*

p. 36: Joseph P. Bradley, majority opinion, *Civil Rights Cases,* 109 U.S. 3 (October 15, 1883); John Marshall Harlan, disssenting opinion, *Civil Rights Cases,* 109 U.S. 3 (October 15, 1883).

p. 37: Abraham Lincoln, Gettysburg Address, November 19, 1863, in *Our Documents: 100 Milestone Documents from the National Archives* (New York: Oxford University Press, 2003), 94.

p. 38: Thomas Jefferson, First Inaugural Address, March 4, 1801, in *The Founders' Constitution,* vol. 5, ed. Philip B. Kurland and Ralph Lerner (Chicago: University of Chicago Press, 1987), 151.

p. 39: Alexis de Tocqueville, *Democracy in America,* trans. Arthur Goldhammer. (New York: Library Classics of the United States, 2004), 584. [Originally published in 1835.]

p. 40: John Marshall Harlan, dissenting opinion, *Plessy* v. *Ferguson,* 163 U.S. 559 (1896).

p. 44: Margaret Fuller, *Woman in the Nineteenth Century* (New York: Norton, 1971), 24, 37–38, 119–20.

p. 45: Memo from Byron White to Earl Warren, May 31, 1967. Papers of Earl Warren, Library of Congress, Box 620, *Loving v. Virginia.*

p. 46: Thomas Jefferson, letter to Danbury Baptist Association, January 1, 1802, in *The Founders' Constitution,* vol. 5, ed. Philip B. Kurland and Ralph Lerner (Chicago: University of Chicago Press, 1987), 96.

p. 53: Roger Williams, *The Bloody Tenent, Of Persecution for Cause of Conscience,* 1644, in *The Founders' Constitution,* vol. 5, ed. Philip B. Kurland and Ralph Lerner (Chicago: University of Chicago Press, 1987), 48; Pennsylvania Charter of Liberty, Laws Agreed Upon in England, Etc., 1682, in *The Founders' Constitution,* vol. 5, ed. Philip B. Kurland and Ralph Lerner (Chicago: University of Chicago Press, 1987), 52; Thomas Paine, *Common Sense,* January 10, 1776, in *The Founders' Constitution,* vol. 5, ed. Philip B. Kurland and Ralph Lerner (Chicago: University of Chicago Press, 1987), 69.

p. 54: Warren E. Burger, *Wisconsin* v. *Yoder,* 406 U.S. 205 (May 15, 1972).

p. 56: Roger Williams, *The Bloody Tenent, Of Persecution for Cause of Conscience,* 1644, in *The Founders' Constitution,* vol. 5, ed. Philip B. Kurland and Ralph Lerner (Chicago: University of Chicago Press, 1987), 48.

p. 60: John F. Kennedy, address to the Greater Houston Ministerial Association (September 12, 1960).

p. 61: Warren E. Burger, *Lemon* v. *Kurtzman,* 403 U.S. 602 (June 28, 1971).

pp. 63–64: James Madison, "Memorial and Remonstrance against Religious Assessments," 1785, in *James Madison: Writings* (New York: Library Classics of the United States, 1999), 29–36.

p. 64: Hugo Black, *Everson* v. *Board of Education,* 330 U.S. 1 (February 10, 1947).

p. 65: Pennsylvania Constitution, 1790, in *The Complete Bill of Rights: The Drafts, Debates, Sources, and Origins,* ed. Neil H. Cogan (New York: Oxford University Press, 1997), 95.

p. 66: Oliver Wendell Holmes, Jr., *Schenck* v. *United States,* 249 U.S. 47 (March 3, 1919).

p. 69: William O. Douglas, "The One Un-American Act," *Nieman Reports,* vol. 7, no. 1 (January 1953): 20.

p. 70: Oliver Wendell Holmes, Jr., dissenting opinion, *Abrams* v. *United States,* 250 U.S. 616 (November 10, 1919).

pp. 71–72: The Sedition Act of 1798, in *Liberty and Justice: A Historical Record of American Constitutional Development,* ed. James Morton Smith and Paul L. Murphy (New York: Knopf, 1958), 99–100; Virginia Resolutions against the Alien and Sedition Acts in *James Madison: Writings* (New York, Library Classics of the United States, 1999), 589–92; Kentucky Resolutions, November 16, 1798, in N. S. Shaler, *Kentucky: A Pioneer Commonwealth* (Boston: Houghton Mifflin, 1885), 410.

p. 73: Virginia Declaration of Rights, Sec. 12, June 12, 1776, in *The Founders' Constitution,* vol. 5, ed. Philip B. Kurland and Ralph Lerner (Chicago: University of Chicago Press, 1987), 121.

p. 77: Charles Evans Hughes, *Near* v. *Minnesota,* 283 U.S. 697 (June 1, 1931).

p. 78: George Sutherland, *Grosjean* v. *American Press Co.* 297 U.S. 233 (February 10, 1936).

p. 79: J. P. Tumulty to Woodrow Wilson, May 8, 1917, in *The Papers of Woodrow Wilson*, vol. 42, ed. Arthur S. Link (Princeton, N.J.: Princeton University Press, 1982, 1985), 246.

p. 80: William J. Brennan, concurring opinion, *New York Times Co. v. United States; United States v. Washington Post Co.*, 403 U.S. 713 (June 30, 1971).

p. 85: John Marshall Harlan II, *NAACP v. Alabama*, 357 U.S. 449 (June 30, 1958).

p. 87: Alexis de Tocqueville, *Democracy in America*, vol. 1, ed. Phillips Bradley (New York: Vintage, 1945), 199, 203. [Originally published in 1835.]

p. 88: Charles Evans Hughes, *DeJonge v. Oregon*, 299 U.S. 353 (January 4, 1937).

p. 89: Pierce Butler, *Hague v. Committee for Industrial Organization*, 307 U.S. 496 (June 5, 1939).

p. 91: Massachusetts Body of Liberties, 1641, in *The Complete Bill of Rights: The Drafts, Debates, Sources, and Origins*, ed. Neil H. Cogan (New York: Oxford University Press, 1997), 94.

p. 95: Editorial from the *New York Tribune*, December 5, 1844, quoted in William Lee Miller, *Arguing about Slavery: The Great Battle in the United States Congress* (New York: Knopf, 1996), 477.

p. 96: Reception of the Abolition Petition in the U.S. Senate, 1836, in *The Founders' Constitution*, vol. 5, ed. Philip B. Kurland and Ralph Lerner (Chicago: University of Chicago Press, 1987), 207–8.

p. 99: Robert G. Ingersoll, "Should the Chinese Be Excluded?" *North American Review* 157 (July 1893): 52–58.

p. 102: Earl Warren, *Brown v. Board of Education*, 347 U.S. 483 (1954).

p. 104: *New York Tribune*, July 19, 1854, in *Witness for Freedom: African American Voices on Race, Slavery, and Emancipation*, ed. C. Peter Ripley et al. (Chapel Hill: University of North Carolina Press, 1993), 60–61.

p. 105: Administration Instruction No. 22 issued by the War Relocation Authority, 1942.

p. 108: *The Selected Papers of Elizabeth Cady Stanton and Susan B. Anthony*, vol. 1, ed. Ann D. Gordon (New Brunswick, N.J.: Rutgers University Press, 1997), 105.

p. 111: Lyndon Johnson's remarks in the Capitol Rotunda, upon signing the Voting Rights Act, August 6, 1965, found at *http://www.lbjlib.utexas.edu/Johnson/archives.hom/speeches.hom/65080 6.asp.*

p. 112: Morrison R. Waite, writing for a unanimous court in *Minor v. Happersett*, 88 U.S. 162 (March 9, 1875).

p. 113: Lyndon B. Johnson, March 15, 1965, speech to a Joint Session of Congress in support of the Voting Rights Act, found at *http://www.hpol.org/lbj/voting/.*

p. 114: Virginia Declaration of Rights, 1776, in *The Complete Bill of Rights: The Drafts, Debates, Sources, and Origins*, ed. Neil H. Cogan (New York: Oxford University Press, 1997), 330.

p. 116: Felix Frankfurter, *Malinski v. New York*, 324 U.S. 401, 414 (March 26, 1945).

p. 122: Massachusetts Body of Liberties, 1641, in *The Complete Bill of Rights: The Drafts, Debates, Sources, and Origins*, ed. Neil H. Cogan (New York: Oxford University Press, 1997), 641–42.

pp. 122–23: Lewis Powell, *Barker v. Wingo*, 407 U.S. 514 (June 22, 1972).

p. 124: Magna Carta (1215), found at *http://www.bl.uk/treasures/magnacarta/translation.html.*

p. 125: Mahlon Pitney, *Grannis v. Ordean*, 234 U.S. 385 (June 8, 1914).

p. 128: Felix Frankfurter, *Malinski v. New York*, 324 U.S. 401, 414 (March 26, 1945).

p. 130: Charles Evans Hughes, *Brown v. State of Mississippi*, 297 U.S. 278 (February 17, 1936).

p. 131: Hugo Black, dissenting opinion, *Shaughnessy v. Mezei* 345 U.S. 206, 216 (March 16, 1953).

p. 133: William Rawle, *A View of the Constitution of the United States*, 1829, in *The Founders' Constitution*, vol. 3, ed. Philip B. Kurland and Ralph Lerner (Chicago: University of Chicago Press, 1987), 341.

p. 137: Sandra Day O'Connor, *Hamdi v. Rumsfeld*, 542 U.S. 507 (June 28, 2004).

p. 138: Debate in Massachusetts Ratifying Convention, January 26, 1788, in *The Founders' Constitution*, vol. 3, ed. Philip B. Kurland and Ralph Lerner (Chicago: University of Chicago Press, 1987), 328; Massachusetts Ratifying Convention, February 1, 1788, in *The Debate on the Constitution*, vol. 1 (New York: The Library of America, 1993), 929.

p. 139: William J. Brennan, *Fay v. Noia*, 372 U.S. 391 (March 18, 1963).

p. 141: Joseph P. Bradley, *Boyd v. United States*, 116 U.S. 616 (February 1, 1886).

p. 142: Virginia Declaration of Rights, June 12, 1776, in *The Founders' Constitution*, vol. 5, ed. Philip B. Kurland and Ralph Lerner (Chicago: University of Chicago Press, 1987), 237.

p. 145: Antonin Scalia, *Kyllo v. United States*, 533 U.S. 27 (June 11, 2001).

p. 146: William R. Day, *Weeks v. United States*, 232 U.S. 383 (February 24, 1914).

p. 147: Louis D. Brandeis, dissenting opinion, *Olmstead v. United States*, 277 U.S. 438 (June 4, 1928).

p. 148: Massachusetts Body of Liberties, 1641, in *The Complete Bill of Rights: The Drafts, Debates, Sources, and Origins*, ed. Neil H. Cogan (New York: Oxford University Press, 1997), 309.

p. 152: Potter Stewart, *North Carolina v. Pearce*, 395 U.S. 711 (June 23, 1969).

pp. 153–54: Hugo L. Black, *Green v. United States*, 355 U.S. 184 (December 16, 1957).

p. 154: Thurgood Marshall, *Benton v. Maryland*, 395 U.S. 784 (June 23, 1969).

p. 157: Massachusetts Body of Liberties, 1641, in *The Complete Bill of Rights: The Drafts, Debates, Sources, and Origins*, ed. Neil H. Cogan (New York: Oxford University Press, 1997), 328.

p. 158: Mississippi Supreme Court, *Fisher v. State*, 145 Miss. 116, 134 (1926).

p. 162: Papers of Earl Warren, Library of Congress, Box 616, *Miranda v. Arizona*; Earl Warren, *Miranda v. Arizona*, 384 U.S. 436 (June 13, 1966).

p. 163: Senator Wayne Morse, *Congressional Record* (June 15, 1966): 12644.

p. 171: John Adams, "Instructions of the Town of Braintree on the Stamp Act," October 10, 1765, in *The Founders' Constitution*, vol. 5, ed. Philip B. Kurland and Ralph Lerner (Chicago: University of Chicago Press, 1987), 251; Continental Congress, Declaration and Resolves, October 14, 1774, in *The Founders' Constitution*, vol. 5, ed. Philip B. Kurland and Ralph Lerner (Chicago: University of Chicago Press, 1987), 258.

p. 172: Tom Clark, *Sheppard* v. *Maxwell*, 384 U.S. 333 (June 6, 1966).

p. 173: Massachusetts Body of Liberties, 1641, in *Sources of Our Liberties,* ed. Richard L. Perry (Chicago: American Bar Foundation, 1959), 151.

p. 177: Lewis Powell, *Argersinger* v. *Hamlin,* 407 U.S. 25 (June 12, 1972).

p. 178: George Sutherland, *Powell* v. *Alabama,* 287 U.S. 45 (November 7, 1932).

p. 179: Abe Fortas, counsel for petitioner, oral argument in *Gideon* v. *Wainwright,* 372 U.S. 335 (1963) in *May It Please the Court,* ed. Peter Irons and Stephanie Guitton (New York: New Press, 1993), 187.

p. 186: *Commonwealth* v. *Fisher,* 213 Pa. 48 (1905); Julian Mack, "The Juvenile Court," *Harvard Law Review* (1909): 120.

pp. 187–88: Anthony M. Kennedy, *Roper* v. *Simmons,* No. 03–633 (March 1, 2005).

p. 189: Cesare Beccaria, *On Crimes and Punishments,* trans. Henry Paolucci (Indianapolis: Bobbs-Merrill, 1963), 50. [Originally published in 1764.]

p. 190: Benjamin Rush, "On Punishing Murder by Death," 1792, in *The Founders' Constitution*, vol. 5, ed. Philip B. Kurland and Ralph Lerner (Chicago, University of Chicago Press, 1987), 378–79.

p. 192: Indiana Constitution of 1851, in *Constitution Making in Indiana: A Source Book of Constitutional Documents with Historical Introduction and Critical Notes,* vol. 1, ed. Charles Kettleborough (1916, reprint; Indianapolis: Indiana Historical Bureau, 1971).

p. 195: Thurgood Marshall, concurring opinion, *Furman* v. *Georgia,* 408 U.S. 238 (June 29, 1972).

p. 196: Warren Burger, dissenting opinion, *Furman* v. *Georgia,* 408 U.S. 238 (June 29, 1972).

p. 197: Potter Stewart, *Gregg* v. *Georgia,* 428 U.S. 153 (July 2, 1976).

p. 203: Harry Blackmun, dissenting opinion, *Bowers* v. *Hardwick,* 478 U.S. 186 (June 30, 1986).

p. 204: Samuel Warren and Louis D. Brandeis, "The Right to Privacy," Harvard Law Review 193 (1890).

p. 205: William O. Douglas, majority opinion, *Griswold* v. *Connecticut,* 381 U.S. 479 (June 7, 1965); Arthur Goldberg, concurring opinion, *Griswold* v. *Connecticut,* 381 U.S. 479 (June 7, 1965).

p. 207: New York Constitution, 1777, in *The Complete Bill of Rights: The Drafts, Debates, Sources, and Origins,* ed. Neil H. Cogan (New York: Oxford University Press, 1997), 183.

p. 208: Black Codes of Mississippi, *Laws of the State of Mississippi,* 1865, in *For the Record: A Documentary History of America,* vol. 2, ed. David E. Shi and Holly A. Mayer (New York: Norton, 1999), 10.

p. 212: John Adams, *A Defence of the Constitutions of Government of the United States* (1787–88), found at *www.gmu.edu/departments/ economic/wew/quotes/arms.html*; Joseph Story, *Commentaries on the Constitution,* in *The Founders' Constitution,* vol. 5, ed. Philip B. Kurland and Ralph Lerner (Chicago: University of Chicago Press, 1987), 214.

p. 214: James Madison, "Property," *National Gazette* (March 29, 1792).

p. 215: Alexis de Tocqueville, *Democracy in America,* 13th ed., ed. J. Mayer (New York: Harper & Row, 1966), 638–39. [Originally published in 1835.]

p. 216: Felix Frankfurter, *Of Law and Men* (New York: Harcourt Brace, 1956), 19.

p. 220: John Locke, *Second Treatise on Government,* 1689, in *The Founders' Constitution,* vol. 5, ed. Philip B. Kurland and Ralph Lerner (Chicago: University of Chicago Press, 1987), 310.

p. 221: Roger Taney, *Charles River Bridge* v. *Warren Bridge,* 36 U.S. 420 (February 12, 1837).

p. 222: Joseph Storey, dissenting opinion, *Charles River Bridge* v. *Warren Bridge,* 36 U.S. 420 (February 12, 1837).

p. 223: Eleanor Roosevelt, "Civil Liberties—The Individual and the Community," *The Reference Shelf* 14 (1939–40): 177–82.

p. 225: Sandra Day O'Connor, speech at the dedication of the National Constitution Center, Philadelphia, July 4, 2003.

p. 227: Stephen Breyer, *Active Liberty: Interpreting Our Democratic Constitution* (New York: Knopf, 2005), 134.

p. 230: Franklin D. Roosevelt, Annual Message to Congress, January 6, 1941, in *Our Documents: 100 Milestone Documents from the National Archives* (New York: Oxford University Press, 2003), 170–71.

Picture Credits

American Civil Liberties Union Archives, Public Policy Division, Department of Rare Books and Special Collections, Princeton University Library: 84, 176; John Anderson/*Austin Chronicle:* 194; AP Photos: 7 (Greg Gibson), 228 (Pat Little), 41, 110, 126, 127, 158, 191, 103 (Goodrich), 225 (Carlos Osorio); Arizona State Library, Archives and Public Records, History and Archives Division, Phoenix: 48 (97-7385), 159 (00-0517); courtesy of the Bancroft Library, University of California, Berkeley: 100, 137, 207; Copyright © Bettmann/CORBIS: 201; Boston Athenaeum: 93, 215; courtesy of the Bostonian Society/Old State House: 141; California Historical Society, FN-21559: 99; Chattanooga Regional History Museum, Chattanooga, Tennessee: 107; Chicago History Museum: 66; Special Collections, Cleveland State University Library: 167; Fan, c. 1944, Harry Buffalohead, Ponca (feathers, silver, beads, hair), Denver Art Museum Collection, Native American acquisition funds, 1951.110: 51; courtesy of the Department of the Public Defender, County of San Diego: 177; Copyright © 1976 Engelhardt in the *St. Louis Post-Dispatch,* reprinted with permission: 193; the Gilder Lehrman Collection, on deposit at the New York Historical Society, NY, GLC 2107: 14; Hancock Historical Museum: 81; courtesy of the Harry S. Truman Library: 134; courtesy of the Institute for Justice: cover (far right, inset), 218; Library of Congress: cover (far left, inset), 9 (LC-USW3-013603-E), 20 (LC-U9-183B-20), 31 (LC-USZCN4-285), 33 (LC-USZ62-127599), 40 (LC-USZ62-116815), 42 (LC-U9-9956-30), 59 (LC-USF34-036592-), 68, 75 (LC-USZ62-116943), 86 (LC-USZ62-111433), 94 (LC-USZC4-12521), 101 (LC-U9-1033-16), 128 (LC-USZ62-110591), 133 (LC-USZC4-12565), 135 (LC-USZ62-75189), 150 (LC-USZ62-134492), 160 (LC-USZ62-114911), 169 (LC-USZ62-126273), 174 (LC-USZ62-121435), 183 (LC-USZ62-82764), 198 (LC-USZ62-75197), 202 (LC-USZC4-6100); the Library of Virginia: 57; collections of the Maine Historical Society: 95; the Metropolitan Museum of Art, Gift of I. N. Phelps Stokes, Edward S. Hawes, Alice Mary Hawes, and Marion Augusta Hawes, 1937 (37.14.34), image © the Metropolitan Museum of Art: 92; Minnesota Historical Society: 76; National Archives and Records Administration, Washington, D.C.: cover background (record group 360), 2 (NAF 1a-b), 39 [NWDNS-208-NP-6QQQ(1)], 67 (NWDNS-179-WP-1533), 74, 118 (NWDNS-412-DA-14211), 120 (306-PS-176-S-51-141), 129 (NWDNS-119-CAL-10); courtesy National Archives and Records Administration (San Francisco): 136; courtesy of the Newberry Library, Chicago: 34; Picture Collection, the Branch Libraries, the New York Public Library, Astor, Lenox and Tilden Foundations: 181 (805081), 182 (809430); courtesy of the North Carolina Office of Archives and History, Raleigh, North Carolina: 164, 165; [A67.137.57138.1] The Jury and Attorney, copyright © the Dorothea Lange Collection, the Oakland Museum of California, City of Oakland, Gift of Paul S. Taylor: 24; with permission from the Office of Juvenile Justice and Delinquency Prevention: 185; The *Plain Dealer,* Cleveland, Ohio, copyright © September 1993: 143; San Diego Historical Society: 19, 82; San Joaquin Valley Library System: 18; Shutterstock: cover (center right, inset); courtesy of the Department of Special Collections, Spencer Research Library, University of Kansas Libraries: 156; collection of the Supreme Court of the United States: 175 (1996.68.1); courtesy *Tampa Tribune*: 144; courtesy of the Tennessee State Library and Archives: 108, 109; Nora Wertz: cover (center left, inset); reprinted with permission of Watch Tower, 25 Columbia Heights, Brooklyn, New York 11201, USA: 49; courtesy of Ted Whittenkraus, www.WellsMaine.com: 216.

Acknowledgments

Our Rights is intended to introduce students and general readers to the individual rights we enjoy as Americans. Its list of rights is not comprehensive, nor is its treatment of them definitive. What I have sought to do is make readers aware of the long history of these guarantees of our freedom, as well as their importance to us today. None of our liberties was earned easily; each of them has life today only because we as citizens continue to support and defend them. I have also wanted to call attention to the controversies that often surround our efforts to extend our rights or apply them to new circumstances. We cannot shy away from these debates, no matter how strident or shrill the voices become, because how we define our rights ultimately is how we define our society. Rights are our protections against abuse of governmental and private power. As such, they are our claims to liberty, the freedom to act on our personal choices and follow our individual beliefs. We all have an investment in these rights, which we entrust our constitutional system of government to protect.

I have looked forward to the day I could thank the people who made this book possible. The Annenberg Foundation, which supported this work, deserves credit for its recognition that education in individual rights is an important civic enterprise. Karen Fein, Tara Deal, and Nancy Toff, editors at Oxford University Press, were patient and wise guides who saved me much embarrassment. Chris Compston did a masterful job of identifying and securing copies of the materials used in the sidebars. The anonymous reviewers read the draft manuscript carefully and offered insightful comments, caught mistakes, and made the book much better than it would have been otherwise. I am saddened that Kermit Hall, who recommended me for this project and who co-authored a companion work, did not live to see its completion. The world is much richer because of his accomplishments, just as we individually are much poorer by his absence.

My greatest intellectual debt is to those individuals who have written on individual rights. Any misinterpretation of their work is my fault alone, but without them *Our Rights* would be an impoverished and uninspired book. Regrettably, I can blame errors on no one but myself.

I owe thanks especially to my colleagues at the Polis Center, Indiana University–Purdue University Indianapolis, who tolerated my working at home for two or more days each week while I was laboring to produce the manuscript. I fear they may have enjoyed my absence from the office so much that they will want me to make it a habit.

The support of friends and colleagues is important in writing a book, but the encouragement of family makes it worthwhile. Karen, Jeff, and Jace, our children, and Raven and Joey, our grandchildren—and Pippi and Zorro, they informed me—had nothing to do with this work except to remind me how precious the world is outside my study. My wife, Penny, persuaded me to write this book. My best friend and greatest supporter, she also was my most important reader. I cannot repay her enough, although it will be my pleasure to spend a lifetime trying.

About the Author

David J. Bodenhamer is professor of history and (founding) executive director of the Polis Center, a multidisciplinary research unit of Indiana University–Purdue University Indianapolis. He is the author or editor of eight books, including *Fair Trial: Rights of the Accused in American History*, *The Bill of Rights in Modern America*, and *The History of Indiana Law*. He has written more than twenty-five journal articles and book chapters and has made more than one hundred presentations to audiences on four continents. Born in Georgia, he earned his Ph.D. from Indiana University in 1977 and was a university administrator in Mississippi before returning to Indiana in 1989. He has three children and two grandchildren. He and his wife, Penny, live in Carmel, Indiana.

About the Annenberg Foundation Trust at Sunnylands

The Annenberg Foundation Trust at Sunnylands was established in 2001 by the Annenberg Foundation to advance public understanding of and appreciation for democracy and to address serious issues facing the country and the world. The Trust convenes:

- leaders of the United States to focus on ways to improve the functioning of the three branches of government, the press, and the public schools;
- educators to determine how to better teach about the Constitution and the fundamental principles of democracy;
- leaders of major social institutions including learned societies to determine how these institutions can better serve the public and the public good;
- scholars addressing ways to improve the well-being of the nation in such areas as media, education, and philanthropy.

The Annenberg Classroom (*www.annenbergclassroom.org*), *www.justicelearning.org*, and a collection of books on the U.S. Constitution, democracy, and related topics are all projects of the Annenberg Foundation Trust at Sunnylands.

About Justice Learning

Justice Learning, a joint effort with the *New York Times* Learning Network, is a comprehensive on-line resource on civics education. The website offers balanced radio debates from National Public Radio's *Justice Talking*, topical and age-appropriate articles from the *New York Times*, and a host of primary source materials, timelines, and lesson plans on a wide range of justice issues. Visit on-line at *www.justicelearning.org*.